TRAVELLER'S GUIDE TO
THE
MIDDLE
EAST

NSL

Swansea University
WITHDRAWN FROM STOCK
Information Services & Systems

D1433777

an IC publication

PUBLISHER

Afif Ben Yedder

EDITOR

Richard Synge

ASSISTANT EDITORS

Musa Budeiri
Rosalind Mazzawi

PRODUCTION

Elaine Wigg (Editor)
Kevin Pearce (Managing)
Celia Stothard (Art Director)
Ann Deed (Advertising)
Ernie Godden Scorpion Graphics
(Maps)

PUBLISHED

by **IC Magazines Limited**
63 Long Acre, London WC2E 9JH
Telephone 01-836 8731
Cables Machrak London WC2. Telex 8811757
© 1978 IC Magazines Limited

TYPESETTING AND ORGANISATION
by Camden Typesetters
31-39 Camden Road,
London NW1 9DR

COVER PHOTOGRAPH
Martyr's Mosque, Bagdad
Middle East Archive, Alistaire Duncan

ISSN 0140-1319
ISBN 0 905268 05 9

Swansea University
WITHDRAWN FROM STOCK
Information Services & Systems
LIBRARY
SWANSEA

CONTENTS

Page No.

4   Regional Map

5   Introduction

6   1978 Calendar of Holidays and Islamic Festivals in the Middle East

9   Embassies in London

10   Communications Map

11   Airlines Serving Principal Middle Eastern Airports

14   Temperature Maps

16   Some Leading Hotels in the Middle East

18   Rainfall Map

19   Middle East Currency Table

21   The Arab World, its society and culture, *by Rosalind Mazzawi*

48   A Short Booklist on the Middle East

THE MIDDLE EAST COUNTRY BY COUNTRY

52	Afghanistan	212	Malta
64	Algeria	222	Morocco
84	Bahrain	242	Oman
92	Cyprus	250	Qatar
100	Egypt	256	Saudi Arabia
118	Greece	268	Sudan
138	Iran	280	Syria
156	Iraq	292	Tunisia
166	Jordan	310	Turkey
176	Kuwait	324	United Arab Emirates
184	Lebanon	338	Yemen Arab Republic
200	Libya	348	Yemen, Peoples Democratic Republic

355   Can You Help Us?

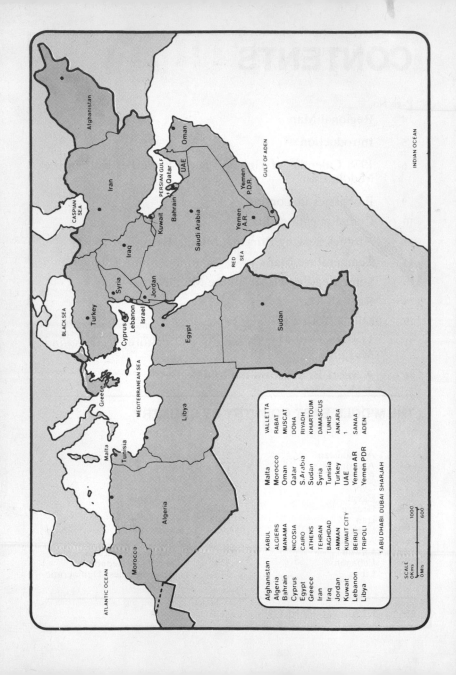

INTRODUCTION

The *Traveller's Guide to the Middle East* is the first book of its kind covering a region that is opening up to many kinds of travel. The reasons people go to the Middle East nowadays are varied; business, contract work, family visits, package tours, overland travel, cultural interest or academic study.

Whatever the purpose of the trip, the *Traveller's Guide to the Middle East* is designed to serve a wide variety of needs, but it is a service that requires continuous feedback. As we go into revised editions in the years to come we hope to cover in more detail the specific needs of travellers with particular interests, and to expand the coverage of each country. Please refer to the questionnaire at the back of the book.

At present there are three major regions of tourism in the Middle East countries covered in this book, namely Egypt, the Maghreb and the 'Eastern Mediterranean and beyond'. Of these three, Egypt stands on its own as a destination in itself, the Maghreb covers the well-known and much visited North African nations of Morocco, Algeria and Tunisia, and the 'Eastern Mediterranean and beyond'—a far less easily definable region, stretching from Greece through Turkey, to the vast lands of Iran and Afghanistan; it takes in Syria, Lebanon and Jordan, as well as the island of Cyprus.

Between these three regions lie countries that have yet to develop their tourist industries, the Gulf states of Kuwait, Bahrain, Qatar, the UAE and the large Arabian peninsula countries of Saudi Arabia and Oman. But even here the passenger traffic to and from these countries is growing daily.

There are also the countries which could be termed marginal tourist regions, where there are a growing number of travellers and tourists, but where the 'package tour' facilities have yet to spring up. In this context one might list Iraq, North Yemen, Sudan and Libya.

As road and air communications develop, the travel trade will inevitably expand throughout the Middle East and adjacent regions, and we intend to cover the new developments in future editions.

The editor wishes to thank all those who have contributed to the compilation of this volume, particularly the writers named on the chapters and others who have contributed sections, including Musa Budeiri, Erica Flegg, Julietta Harvey, Veronica Kemp, Rosalind Mazzawi, Terence Mirabelli, Metin Munir, Christine Osborne, Judith Perera, Naomi Sakr, John Seekings, Barbara Wace, John Wallace and Elaine Wigg. The national tourist offices of the countries covered in this book also supplied important information.

1978 CALENDAR OF HOLIDAYS AND ISLAMIC FESTIVALS

in the Middle East

1 January	New Year's Day (Algeria, Bahrain, Cyprus, Iraq, Jordan, Kuwait, Lebanon, Syria, Turkey, UAE, Yemen-Aden)
	Independence Day (Sudan)
6 January	Epiphany (Cyprus)
	Army Day (Iraq)
15 January	Tree Day (Jordan)
18 January	Revolution Day (Tunisia)
19 January	President Makarios' Name Day (Cyprus)
7 February	Death of the Prophet and Imam Hasan (Iraq)
8 February	Ramadan Revolution Day (Iraq)
9 February	Feast of St Maroun (Lebanon)
15 February	Anniversary of the Swearing in of the First President (Afghanistan)
20 February	Mawlid al-Nabi—Birthday of the Prophet
22 February	Accession of the Amir (Qatar)
	Arab Unity Day (Egypt, Syria)
25 February	Birthday of the Prophet and Imam Jaafar Sadegh (Iran)
	National Day (Kuwait)
1-3 March	National Day (Morocco)
3 March	Unity Day (Sudan)
8 March	Syrian Revolution Day (Egypt, Libya, Syria)
20 March	Independence Day (Tunisia)
21 March	Now Ruz Festival—Iranian New Year (Afghanistan, Iran, Iraq)
22 March	Now Ruz Festival (Iran)
	Arab League Day (Lebanon)
24 March	Good Friday (Lebanon, Syria)
25 March	Greek Independence Day (Cyprus)
27 March	Easter Monday (Syria)
28 March	UK Evacuation Day (Libya)
1 April	Eoka Day (Cyprus)
2 April	Thirteenth of the New Year (Iran)
9 April	Martyr's Day (Tunisia)
17 April	National Day (Syria)

23 April	National Sovereignty Day and Children's Day (Turkey)
26 April	Sham al-Nessim (Egypt, Sudan)
28 April	Good Friday (Cyprus, Lebanon)
29 April	Holy Saturday (Cyprus)
30 April	Easter Day (Cyprus, Lebanon)
1 May	Labour Day (Algeria, Cyprus, Iraq, Jordan, Lebanon, Morocco, Syria, Tunisia, Yemen-Aden, Yemen-Sanaa)
	Spring Holiday (Turkey)
6 May	Martyr's Day (Lebanon, Syria)
18-19 May	Youth & Sports Day (Turkey)
25 May	Independence Day (Jordan)
	Sudan Revolution Day (Libya, Sudan)
26-27 May	Freedom & Constitution Day (Turkey)
27 May	Independence Day (Afghanistan)
1-2 June	Victory Days (Tunisia)
11 June	US Evacuation Day (Libya)
13 June	Anniversary of Corrective Movement (Yemen-Sanaa)
18 June	Evacuation Day—1956 (Egypt)
19 June	National Day—Sursaut Revolutionnaire (Algeria)
3 July	Isra al-Maaraj—The Prophet's Night Journey to Heaven
	The Prophet's Mission (Iran)
5 July	Independence Day (Algeria)
9 July	King Hasan's Birthday (Morocco)
14 July	Revolution Day—Declaration of the Republic (Iraq)
17 July	Baath Revolution Day (Iraq)
17-19 July	Republican Anniversary (Afghanistan)
21 July	Birthday of the 12th Imam (Iran)
23 July	Egypt Revolution Day (Egypt, Libya, Syria)
25 July	Republic Day (Tunisia)
3 August	President's Birthday (Tunisia)
5 August	Constitution Day (Iran)
	Start of Ramadan
6 August	Accession of the Ruler of Abu Dhabi (Abu Dhabi)
11 August	Accession of King Hussain (Jordan)
13 August	Women's Day (Tunisia)
15 August	Assumption (Lebanon)
	Virgin Mary's Day (Cyprus)
27 August	Martyrdom of Imam Ali (Iran)
30 August	Victory Day (Turkey)
31 August	Pashtunistan Day (Afghanistan)
1 September	Libya National Day (Egypt, Libya, Syria)
3-6 September	Eid al-Fitr—end of Ramadan
4 September	Commemoration Day (Tunisia)
	National Day (Qatar)

RAMADAN

9 September	National Assembly Day (Afghanistan)
26 September	Yemen-Sanaa Revolution Day (Yemen-Aden, Yemen-Sanaa)
28 September	Death of Imam Jaafar Sadegh (Iran)
6 October	Armed Forces Day (Egypt)
7 October	Italian Evacuation Day (Libya)
14 October	Birthday of Imam Reza (Iran)
	Yemen-Aden National Day (Yemen-Aden, Yemen-Sanaa)
15 October	Evacuation Day (Tunisia)
	Nejat Day (Afghanistan)
24 October	Suez Day (Egypt)
	United Nations Day (Afghanistan)
26 October	Birthday of the Shah (Iran)
28 October	Ohi Day (Cyprus)
28-30 October	Republic Days (Turkey)
1 November	Revolution Day (Algeria)
6 November	Anniversary of the Green March (Morocco)
10-13 November	Eid al-Adhur—Feast of the Sacrifice
14 November	Birthday of King Hussain (Jordan)
16 November	Corrective Movement Day (Syria)
18 November	National Day (Oman)
	Independence Day (Morocco)
	Ghadir Festival (Iran)
19 November	Birthday of Sultan Qabous Bin-Said (Oman)
22 November	Independence Day (Lebanon)
30 November	Independence Day (Yemen-Aden)
2 December	National Day (UAE)
	Muslim New Year
11 December	Al-Ashoura
16 December	Ruler's Accession Day (Bahrain)
24 December	Christmas Eve (Cyprus)
25 December	Christmas Day (Cyprus, Kuwait, Lebanon, Sudan, Syria, UAE)
26 December	Boxing Day (Cyprus, UAE)
31 December	Evacuation Day (Lebanon)

The Islamic year consists of 12 lunar months, about 355 days. For this reason all religious festivals move forward about 11 days per year in terms of the Western calendar. The Islamic day begins at sundown (instead of midnight) and the festival may continue through the day following that listed above. Travellers would be well advised to check with Embassies before departure.

Fasting in Ramadan lasts from first light to darkness, and an observing Muslim will refuse both food and water. For this reason, business both public and private is restricted to the minimum possible. If you must do business in Ramadan, the earlier in the day the better, as far as dealing with those who observe the restrictions.

EMBASSIES IN LONDON

Some Middle Eastern countries no longer require visas for tourists from the UK, the USA and Western Europe, but it is important to check beforehand with the visa regulations spelt out under the country chapters in this book, and, in the cases where visas are necessary, to allow several weeks for obtaining visas before departure. It is important to remember the widespread prohibition in Arab countries on prospective visitors who have been to Israel—or more accurately those who have evidence of having been to Israel stamped in their passport. Some of the more austere regimes, like Iraq and Saudi Arabia, also require information on parentage and religion.

Afghanistan: 31 Prince's Gate, London SW7 1QQ. tel: 01-589 8891

Algeria: 6 Hyde Park Gate, London SW7 5EW. tel: 01-584 9502

Bahrain: 98 Gloucester Road, London SW7 4AU. tel: 01-370 5123

Cyprus: 93 Park Gate, London W1Y 4ET. tel: 01-499 8272

Egypt: 26 South Street, London W1Y 6DD. tel: 01-499 2401

Greece: 1A Holland Park, London W11 3TP. tel: 01-727 8040

Iran: 16 Prince's Gate, London SW7 1PX. tel: 01-584 8101

Iraq: 21-22 Queen's Gate, London SW7 5JG. tel: 01-584 7141

Jordan: 6 Upper Phillimore Gardens, London W8 7HE. tel: 01-937 3685

Kuwait: 40 Devonshire Street, London W1N 2AX. tel: 01-580 8471

Lebanon: 21 Kensington Palace Gardens, London W8 4QM. tel: 01-229 7265

Libya: 58 Prince's Gate, London SW7 2PW. tel: 01-589 5235

Malta: 24 Haymarket, London SW1Y 4DJ. tel: 01-930 9851

Morocco: 49 Queen's Gate Gardens, London SW7 5NE. tel: 01-584 8827

Oman: 64 Ennismore Gardens, London SW7 5DN. tel: 01-584 6782

Qatar: 10 Reeves Mews, London W1Y 3PB. tel: 01-499 8831

Saudi Arabia: 30 Belgrave Square, London SW1X 8QB. tel: 01-235 0831

Sudan: 3 Cleveland Row, St. James's, London SW1A 1DD. tel: 01-839 8080

Syria: 5 Eaton Terrace, London SW1W 8EX. tel: 01-730 0384

Tunisia: 29 Prince's Gate, London SW7 1QG. tel: 01-584 8117

Turkey: 43 Belgrave Square, London SW1X 8PA. tel: 01-235 5252

United Arab Emirates: 30 Prince's Gate, London SW7 1PT. tel: 01-581 1281

Yemen Arab Republic: 41 South Street, London W1Y 5PD. tel: 01-499 5246

Yemen, People's Democratic Republic: 57 Cromwell Road, London SW7 2ED. tel: 01-584 6607

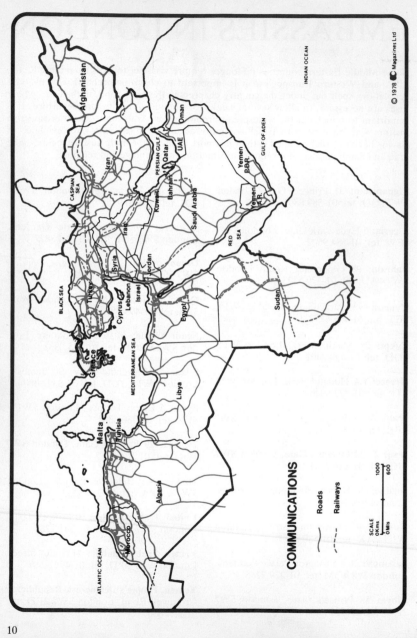

© 1978 Magazines Ltd

COMMUNICATIONS

Roads

Railways

SCALE
0 Kms   1000
0 Mls   600

AIRLINES SERVING PRINCIPAL MIDDLE EASTERN AIRPORTS

Listed below are the main airlines serving the countries contained in this book. For further information of air transport in any of these countries, see the individual chapters under the sub-headings of 'How to Get There' and 'Transport'.

AFGHANISTAN

Kabul (KBL)
Ariana Afghan Airlines, Aeroflot, Indian Airlines, Iran Air and Pakistan International Airlines (PIA). Internal services by Bakhtar Afgan Airlines.

ALGERIA

Algiers—Dar el Beida (ALG)
Aeroflot, Air Algérie, Air France, Alitalia, Aviaco, Balkan Bulgarian, British Airways, CSA, EgyptAir, Iberia, Interflug Iraqi Airways, Libyan Arab, LOT, Lufthansa, Sabena, Saudia, Swissair, Syrianair, Tarom and Tunis Air.

BAHRAIN

Bahrain—Muharraq (BAH)
Alia, British Airways, Cathay Pacific, Cyprus Airways, EgyptAir, Ethiopian Airlines, Gulf Air, Iran Air, Iraqi Airways, KLM, Kuwait Airways, MEA, PanAm, PIA, Qantas, Saudia, Singapore Airlines, Sudan Airways, TWA and UTA.

CYPRUS

Larnaca (LCA)
Aeroflot, Alia, Balkan, British Airways, Cyprus Airways, Interflug, Middle East Airlines, Olympic Airways and Syrianair.

EGYPT

Cairo International (CAI)
Aeroflot, Alia, Air Algérie, Air France, Air India, Air Malta, Alitalia, Alyemda, Austrian Airlines, Balkan Bulgarian, British Airways, CSA, Cyprus Airways, Ethiopian Airlines, EgyptAir, Gulf Air, Interflug, Iran Air, Iraqi Airways, JAL, JAT, Kenya Airways, KLM, Kuwait Airways, LOT, Lufthansa, Libyan Airways, Malev, MEA, Olympic Airways, PIA, Royal Air Maroc, Sabena, SAS, Saudia, Somali Airlines, Sudan Airways, Swissair, Syrianair, Tarom, Tunis Air, TWA and Yemen Airways.

IRAN

Tehran—Mehrabad (THR)
Aeroflot, Air France, Air India, Alia, Alitalia, Ariana, British Airways, CAAC, CSA, El Al, Iran Air, Iraqi Airways, JAL, KLM, Kuwait Airways, Lufthansa, PIA, PanAm, Sabena, Singapore Airlines, Swissair and Syrianair.

IRAQ

Baghdad International (BGW)
Aeroflot, Air France, Air India, Alia,

11

Alitalia, Balkan Bulgarian, British Airways, CSA, EgyptAir, Gulf Air, Interflug, Iran Air, Iraqi Airways, JAT, KLM, Kuwait Airways, LOT, Lufthansa, MEA, PIA, Sabena, SAS, Saudia, Swissair, Syrianair and Thai Airways.

JORDAN

Amman (AMM)
Aeroflot, Air France, Alia, Alitalia, British Airways, EgyptAir, Gulf Air, Iraqi Airways, KLM, Kuwait Airways, Lufthansa, MEA, Saudia and Tarom.

KUWAIT

Kuwait International Airport (KWI)
Aeroflot, Air France, Air India, Alia, Alitalia, Alyemda, British Airways, CSA, Cyprus Airways, EgyptAir, Gulf Air, Iran Air, Iraqi Airways, JAT, KLM, Kuwait Airways, Lufthansa, Malaysian Airlines System, MEA, Olympic Airways, PIA, Royal Air Maroc, SAS, Saudia, Swissair, Syrianair, Tarom, Tunis Air and Yemen Airways.

LEBANON

Beirut International (BEY)
Aeroflot, Air France, Alia, Austrian Airlines, Balkan Bulgarian, British Airways, CSA, Cyprus Airways, EgyptAir, Iberia, Interflug, KLM, Kuwait Airways, LOT, Lufthansa, Malev, MEA, Royal Air Maroc, Sabena, Swissair, Tarom and TWA.

LIBYA

Tripoli International (TIP)
Aeroflot, Air Afrique, Air Algérie, Air Malta, Alitalia, Alyemda, Balkan Bulgarian, British Airways, CSA, EgyptAir, Iraqi Airways, JAT, KLM, Kuwait Air

ways, Libyan Arab, Lufthansa, PIA, Royal Air Maroc, Saudia, Sudan Airways, Swissair, Syrianair, Tarom, Tunis Air and UTA.

MALTA

Malta (MLA)
Air France, Air Malta, Alitalia, British Airways, JAL and Libyan Arab Airlines.

MOROCCO

Casablanca—Nouasser (CMN)
Air Afrique, Air France, Air Mali, Alia, Balkan Bulgarian, British Caledonian, Iberia, Iraqi Airways, KLM, Kuwait Airways, Lufthansa, Libyan Arab, Royal Air Maroc, Royal Air International, Sabena, Saudia, Sierra Leone Airways, Swissair, Syrianair, Tunis Air and TWA.

OMAN

Seeb International—Muscat (MCT)
Alia, Air India, British Airways, Cyprus Airways, Gulf Air, Iran Air, Kuwait Airways, MEA, PIA, Saudia, Somali Airlines and UTA.

QATAR

Doha (DOH)
Air France, Air India, Alia, British Airways, EgyptAir, Gulf Air, Iran Air, Iraqi Airways, Kuwait Airways, MEA, PIA, Saudia, Syrianair and Yemen Airways.

SAUDI ARABIA

Dhahran (DHA)
Air France, Air India, Alia, Alitalia, British Airways, Gulf Air, Iran Air, Iraqi Airways, KLM, Kuwait Airways, Libyan Arab, Lufthansa, MEA, Olympic Air-

ways, PIA, Sabena, Saudia, Swissair and Syrianair.

Jeddah—Kandara (JED)
Air Djibouti, Air Algérie, Air France, Air India, Alia, Alitalia, Alyemda, British Airways, EgyptAir, Ethiopian Airlines, Garuda, Iran Air, Iraqi Airways, KLM, Korean Air Lines, Lufthansa, MEA, PIA, Royal Air Maroc, Saudia, Somali Airlines, Sudan Airways, Syrianair, Tunis Air and Yemen Airways.

SUDAN

Khartoum (KRT)
Aeroflot, Alitalia, British Airways, EgyptAir, Ethiopian Airlines, Interflug, Lufthansa, MEA, SAS, Saudia and TWA.

SYRIA

Damascus International (DAM)
Aeroflot, Air France, Alia, Alitalia, Ariana, Austrian Airlines, Balkan Bulgarian, British Airways, CSA, Cyprus Airways, EgyptAir, Interflug, Iraqi Airways, JAT, KLM, Kuwait Airways, LOT, Lufthansa, Libyan Arab, Syrianair, Tarom, Tunis Air and Yemen Airways.

TUNISIA

Tunis—Carthage (TUN)
Aeroflot, Air Algerie, Air France, Alitalia, Balkan Bulgarian, British Airways, CSA, EgyptAir, Iraqi Airways, JAT, KLM, Kuwait Airways, Libyan Arab, LOT, Lufthansa, Royal Air Maroc, Sabena, Saudia, Syrianair and Tunis Air.

TURKEY

Istanbul (IST)
Alitalia, Austrian Airlines, Balkan, British Airways, El Al, JAT, KLM, LOT, Lufthansa, Malev, Middle East Airlines, Olympic Airways, PanAm, PIA, SAS, Swissair, Thai International, Turkish Airlines.

UNITED ARAB EMIRATES

Abu Dhabi International (AUH)
Air France, Air India, Alia, Bangladesh Biman, British Airways, EgyptAir, Ethiopian Airlines, Gulf Air, Iran Air, Iraqi Airways, KLM, Kuwait Airways, Lufthansa, MEA, PIA, Sabena, Saudia, Somali Airlines, Sudan Airways, Swissair, Syrianair, Tunis Air and Yemen Airways.

Dubai International (DXB)
Air France, Air India, Alia, Alitalia, Bangladesh Biman, British Airways, Cathay Pacific, Cyprus Airways, EgyptAir, Gulf Air, Iran Air, Iraqi Airways, KLM, Kuwait Airways, Libyan Arab, LOT, Lufthansa, MEA, Olympic Airways, PIA, Sabena, Saudia, Singapore Airlines, Swissair and Syrianair.

Sharjah (SHJ)
Air Ceylon, EgyptAir, Gulf Air, Iran Air, Syrianair and Yemen Airways.

YEMEN ARAB REPUBLIC

Sana'a el-Rahaba (SAH)
Aeroflot, Alyemda, Egypt Air, Ethiopian Airlines, Kuwait Airways, Saudia, Somalia Airlines, Sudan Airways, Syrianair and Yemen Airways.

YEMEN PEOPLE'S DEMO-CRATIC REPUBLIC

Aden—Khormaksar (ADE)
Aeroflot, Air Djibouti, Air India, Alyemda, EgyptAir, Ethiopian Airlines, Kuwait Airways, MEA, Somali Airlines and Yemen Airways.

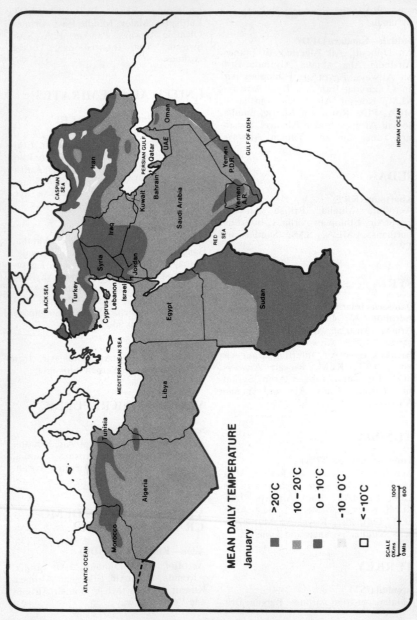

MEAN DAILY TEMPERATURE
January

>20°C

10 – 20°C

0 – 10°C

-10 – 0°C

< -10°C

SCALE
0 Kms   1000
0 Mls   600

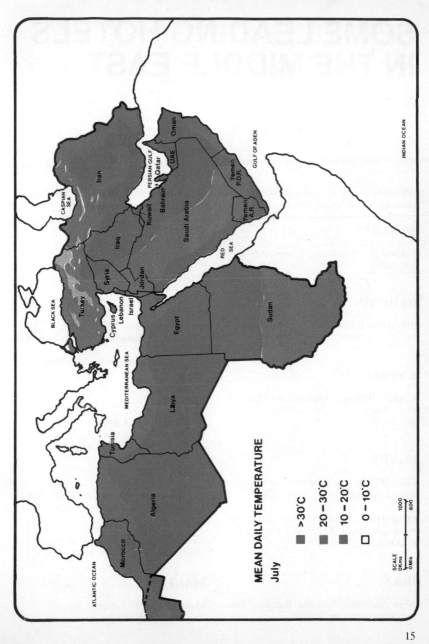

MEAN DAILY TEMPERATURE
July

■ >30°C
■ 20–30°C
■ 10–20°C
□ 0–10°C

SCALE
0Kms
0Mls
1000
600

15

SOME LEADING HOTELS IN THE MIDDLE EAST

Listed below is a small selection of leading hotels in the Middle East. For further information on hotels, please see the individual chapter on each country.

ALGERIA

Aurassi, Avenue Frantz Fanon, Algiers. 500 rooms, tel: 648252, telex: 52475

BAHRAIN

Hilton Hotel, PO Box 1090, Manama. 188 rooms, tel: 50000, telex: 8288.

CYPRUS

Cyprus Hilton, Archbishop Makarios Ave, Nicosia. tel: 64040, telex: 2388.

EGYPT

Cairo Hilton, Tahrir Square, Cairo. 400 rooms, tel: 811811, telex: 2222.

Mena House Oberoi, Sharia el Haram, Pyramids Road, Giza. 310 rooms, tel: 85544.

IRAN

Arya Sheraton, Khiaban Pahlavi, Tehran. 204 rooms, tel: 260107.

JORDAN

Jordan Intercontinental, Queen Zein Street, Jebel, Amman. 250 rooms, tel: 41361, telex: AMN 1207.

KUWAIT

Sheraton, Fahad al-Salem Street, Kuwait. 261 rooms, tel: 422055, telex: 2106.

LIBYA

Al Shati, Hai al Andalus, Tripoli. tel: 71641.

LEBANON

Le Vendôme, Minet el Hosn Street, Beirut. 125 rooms, tel: 369280, telex: 20859 Vendome.

Le Bristol, Madame Curie Street, Beirut. 162 rooms, tel: 351400, telex: 20710.

MALTA

Malta Hilton, St. Julians. 204 rooms, tel: 64040.

MOROCCO

Europamaroc, Place Muhammad V, Casablanca.
300 rooms, tel: 222. 57, telex: 22905M.

Les Merinides, Fez.
113 rooms, tel: 34556.

Hotel Mamounia, Marrakesh.
220 rooms, tel: 32381, telex: 72018.

Hilton, Souissi, Rabat.
259 rooms, tel: 72151, telex: 31913.

OMAN

Intercontinental, PO Box 1398, Muttrah.
308 rooms, tel: 36201.

SAUDI ARABIA

Al Gosaibi Hotel, Khobar, Dhahran.
171 rooms, 18 suites, tel: 42160, telex: 67008.

Al Yammamah, Airport Road, Riyadh.
200 rooms, tel: 28200, telex: 20056.

Kandara Palace, PO Box 473, Jeddah.
148 rooms, tel: 23155.

SYRIA

Meridien Hotel, Choukry Kouatly Avenue, Damascus.
372 rooms, tel: 222856, telex: 11379.

Baron Hotel, Baron Street, Aleppo.
46 rooms, tel: 10880.

TUNISIA

Meridien Africa, 50 Avenue Habib, Bourguiba, Tunis.
200 rooms, tel: 247477, telex: 12536.

TURKEY

Hilton Oteli, Cumhuriyet Cad, Harbiye, Istanbul.
417 rooms, tel: 467050, telex: 22379 ISHI TR.

Intercontinental Oteli, Taksim, Istanbul.
420 rooms, tel: 448850, telex: INHO TR.

Pera Palas, Mesrutiyet Cad, 98/100 Tepebasi, Istanbul.
194 rooms, tel: 452230, telex: 22029 PERA TR.

UNITED ARAB EMIRATES

Hilton, PO Box 877, Abu Dhabi.
174 rooms, 16 suites, tel: 61900, telex: AH 2122.

Intercontinental, PO Box 476, Dubai.
331 rooms, tel: 27171, telex: DB 5779.

Carlton, PO Box 1198, Sharjah.
170 rooms, tel: 23711, telex: Carlton SH 5459.

Prices are not given as they change so rapidly. It may be assumed that they are high, between $30 and $120 per night for a double room, depending on the country.

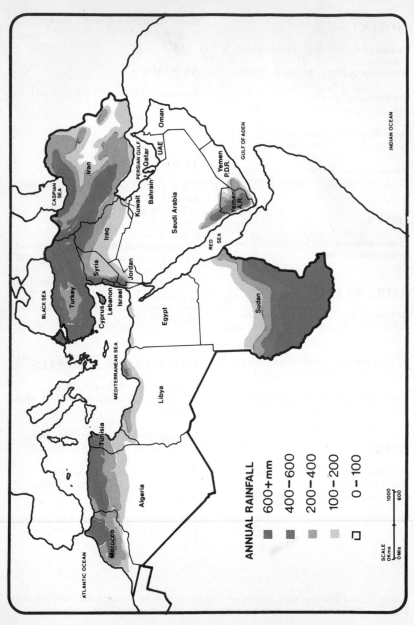

ANNUAL RAINFALL

- 600+mm
- 400–600
- 200–400
- 100–200
- 0–100

SCALE
0 Kms   1000
0 Mls   600

MIDDLE EAST CURRENCY TABLE

COUNTRY	CURRENCY	VALUE TO £1.00	VALUE TO $1.00
Afghanistan	Afghani	83.00	45.00
Algeria	Dinar	7.834	4.141
Bahrain	Dinar	0.750	0.395
Cyprus	Cyprus Pound	0.744	0.383
Egypt	Egypt Pound	0.736	0.389
Greece	Drachma	70.262	36.05
Iran	Rial	135.00	70.55
Iraq	Iraq Dinar	0.571	0.289
Jordan	Jdn. Dinar	0.600	0.312
Kuwait	Kuwait Dinar	0.544	0.280
Lebanon	Leb. Pound	5.829	2.998
Libya	Libyan Dinar	0.574	0.289
Malta	Maltese Pound	0.762	0.396
Morocco	Dirham	8.35	4.351
Oman	Omani Rial	0.671	0.345
Qatar	Qatar Rial	7.52	3.950
Saudi Arabia	Ryal	6.73	3.47
Sudan	Sudan Pound	0.876	0.348
Syria	Syria Pound	7.614	3.925
Tunisia	Tunisian Dinar	0.772	0.413
Turkey	Turkish Lira	34.70	19.25
UAE	UAE Dirham	7.52	3.90
Yemen Arab Rep.	Yemen Ryal	8.73	4.547
Yemen People's Dem. Rep.	Yemen Dinar	0.662	0.341

Exchange rates as of January 1978

Facts, figures, and tourist information at your fingertips

MIDDLE EAST YEARBOOK 1978

The Middle East's statistics, geography politics, economics, history, population

Essential dates facts and figures

AVAILABLE NOW
ONLY $25
INCLUDES FREE COLOUR
WALL-MAP OF
THE MIDDLE EAST

INTERNATIONAL COMMUNICATIONS

63 Long Acre, London WC2E 9JH, England.
Tel: 01-836 8731   Telex: 8811757
Cables: Machrak London WC2

THE ARAB WORLD

its society and culture

Rosalind Mazzawi

This outline introduction to the Arab world seems necessary because so many people who arrive there for the first time, or who meet Arabs, know little or nothing of what to expect. They are confronted with a completely new way of life, with its own religion, customs, and arts, with which they must come to terms.

The Arab countries have changed enormously during the past 20 years, and will go on doing so, particularly while vast quantities of oil, needed by the rest of the world, are found in Arab countries. The sale of this oil has generated vast wealth, as everyone knows. A little money is spent frivolously, a good deal on providing health, education, communications and technological comforts, but most on building an infrastructure to develop other natural resources, and industry, against the time when there will be no more oil. And if there is no more oil in Arabia, then in a very short time there will be no more oil anywhere, and alternative sources of energy will have to be developed. There will be many countries in the race, and the Arabs will certainly not be last.

Many Arabs have had a Western-style education, in English, American or French systems, so that they adjust more easily to a Western life style than do Westerners to the Arab one. It is much commoner to find Arabs who speak good English or French, sometimes both, than it is to find people whose native language is English or French speaking good Arabic.

An immense variety of both scholarly and partisan works have been written on various aspects of Arab history, politics, economics, language and culture, but few deal with the present, and even fewer are easy to read or to carry about for quick reference. There are some excellent guides to individual countries, and a few sensational and inaccurate books better forgotten. This study, however, could not have been written had not *Caravan* by Dr Carleton Coon been published in 1951. It is far more extensive than this outline claims to be, and deals also with non-Arab peoples in the Middle Eastern region. Inevitably, some of the information is now out of date, but I owe Dr Coon an enormous debt. Anyone who wishes to know more of the matters touched upon here may turn to *Caravan*, which will both divert and instruct them.

Topography

The Arab world stretches from the Atlantic to the Gulf, as shown on the map. It includes every conceivable kind of geographical feature, and vast differences in rainfall, population and altitude.

Beginning in the far West, the Atlantic, a coastal plain rises to the steep mountains and high plateaux of the Atlas. Here the rainfall is high and all kinds of crops can be cultivated. Farther south there is a steppe region, with moderate rainfall, providing enough pasture to make it possible for camels, goats, sheep, donkeys and a few horses to be raised. This shades off into the almost rainless Sahara region, where the only water is found at scattered oases and a few wells. The Sahara desert runs right across North Africa, so that the southern parts of Morocco, Algeria, Tunisia, Libya, most of Egypt and the north of the Sudan are desert areas.

Libya is perhaps the least fertile North African country; only a narrow coastal strip, the Jebel Akhdar behind Benghazi in the east and parts of the Fezzan in the south have natural vegetation. Egypt has almost no rain but the Nile irrigates a narrow and densely populated strip of land from the Sudanese frontier to the sea, about 2,400 km. long. Sudan is divided between the desert of the north, much like Egypt, and the swamps of the White Nile in the south, known as the Sudd. Crossing eastwards into Asia, we traverse the barren mountainous Sinai Peninsula, and come to Jordan, which is balanced between desert and fertility. Here mountainous gorges of Petra and the Wadi Rum slope down to the port of Aqaba on the Red Sea in the south.

Syria has its capital, Damascus, situated in the Ghouta, the biggest oasis in the world, and some of the most barren mountains, the Anti-Lebanon, which slope down to the fertile plain now known as the Bekaka (formerly Coelo-Syria.) This plain is now within the boundaries of the Republic of Lebanon—and another range of mountains—Jebel Lubnan (the Mountain of Lebanon) must be crossed to reach the narrow fertile coastal plain and the sea. Since the Lebanon range usually receives a heavy winter rainfall all kinds of temperate fruits and vegetables can be cultivated there: apples and soft fruit as well as olives. The coastal plains of both Lebanon and Syria produce excellent citrus fruits.

The northern part of Syria, where Aleppo is the chief city, is again steppe country; with the increase of irrigation a good deal of cotton is grown along the

Wadi Rum

ROYAL JORDANIAN EMBASSY

Euphrates valley. The Euphrates flows down into Iraq, which is well watered by this river and the Tigris, which like the Euphrates rises in the rain-fed mountains of Turkey. Only the eastern hills of Iraq and the northern mountain valleys receive any appreciable rainfall. Vast date gardens are found at Basra, the port on the Arabian Gulf.

Kuwait, Bahrain, Qatar and the United Arab Emirates are the small, sandy oil-rich principalities along the Gulf. They have very hot humid summers, very little rain, and agreeably mild winters. Until the advent of large-scale desalinisation the water supply was a great problem, except in Bahrain where fresh water springs come up under the sea. The pearl divers used to fill jars from them before the water was piped ashore.

The Sultanate of Oman, at the southern end of the Gulf, is fearfully hot on the coast, but has high mountains in the south-east corner where there is more rain, some captured from the tail-end of the East African monsoon. Indeed, all the southern coast of Arabia is subject to the monsoon, and is therefore comparatively fertile. The valley of the Hadramaut, now part of the People's Democratic Republic of Yemen, has long-standing links with Indonesia and Malaya. Many of the men migrated there to make money in these Muslim countries, the winds being favourable for ships at certain times of the year, and returned 20 or 30 years later. The south-west corner of the peninsula, the ancient Arabia Felix, is now the Yemen Arab Republic (capital Sanaa). It is mountainous, wooded, fertile, picturesque, and has undergone very little development as yet.

Finally there is Saudi Arabia with much of its interior desert, including the Rub al-Khali or Empty Quarter in the south. The Eastern Province on the Gulf is the greatest oil-producing area in the world. The capital, Riyadh is near the centre of the country in the Hejaz. It is a desert city, though much underground water exists. The province of Nejd, which extends to the Red Sea, contains Jeddah, the great commercial port, and the Holy Cities of Mecca and Medina. Here too the climate is hot and humid. But the summer resort of Taif is in the mountains that descend from Yemen, and is much cooler.

The Mediterranean climate of those countries bordering upon it has developed a typical scenery and typical agriculture. This traditional cultivation is now undergoing change, and modern development is responding to the increased demand for products. Thus in Lebanon fruit and vegetables are despatched to the Gulf by a freight plane every night.

With the Libyan rise in population since the development of the oil industry the Jebel Akhdar is now being seriously cultivated. Parts of Algeria were uncultivated for some time after the French withdrew, especially near Oran. However, the land has benefited from its period of rest and having been redistributed, is now producing bountiful crops. The rapid industrial development of Algeria has benefited the farmer too.

Religion

Islam is the religion of most Arabs and is divided into two principal sects, Sunni and Shi'a. The Sunni are the more orthodox and are found in Syria, parts of Lebanon, Egypt, all North Africa, and in the original homeland, Saudi Arabia and the Gulf States. The Shi'a are in some ways less puritan, and lean more to mystical beliefs; they are found in Iraq and southern Lebanon. Turks are Sunni, Iranians mostly Shi'a. There are also Arab Christians of at least 12 sects chiefly in Lebanon, though minorities exist in Jordan, Syria, Iraq and Egypt. Breakaway sects from Islam have strong links with Zoroastrianism and the ancient mystery religions. These include the Druse in Lebanon, Syria and Palestine, the

Alawi in the Syrian mountains and the Yezidi in Northern Iraq.

The five Pillars of Islam, or basic beliefs, common to both Sunni and Shi'a are:

1) The Profession of Faith, by which a person declares himself a Muslim: 'There is no God but God, and Muhammad is the Messenger of God.'

2) The Pilgrimage to Mecca, or Hajj, which all believers should go on, if at all possible, at least once during their lifetimes.

3) Giving 10% of one's income to charity, and for the benefit of widows and orphans.

4) Praying five times a day: dawn, mid-morning, noon, sunset, and before sleeping.

5) Fasting during the month of Ramadan, which means abstaining totally from food, drink, and tobacco from dawn until sunset. Ramadan is a lunar month of four weeks, which falls 11 days earlier each year; in summer the fast is obviously more of an endurance test than in winter.

Most Muslims observe these at least partially, and the proportion of those who practise all the tenets of the Faith is probably higher than in most other faiths. For Islam is a complete way of life; the social and hygienic habits described in other sections all stem from Koranic precepts. The position of women is often brought up as a fault in Islam by others; but in Islamic society women have at least always been able to possess and use their own property in their own names. Restrictions upon the role of women in public life have been enforced by the older women, but now that education is becoming universal they are gradually becoming eroded. Polygamy does still exist, and is not discouraged in Saudi Arabia where there are still far too few people to develop the enormous resources of the country. Polygamy is one method of assisting rapid increase in the Saudi population, and indeed it developed as a social institution at a time when men were frequently killed in battle and left their wives with no protection. The Koran says categorically: 'If you fear that you cannot be equal, then marry only one . . . do not love one to distraction to the prejudice of another whom you keep in suspense,' and elsewhere: 'You may marry two, or three, or four, provided you treat them equally.' But Western society has for a long time accepted serial polygamy, and liaisons which give the woman no protection.

Complete veiling and seclusion grew out of necessity in a society almost continually at war, and often ruling as a minority in hostile lands, to keep women and young children protected. It was also vital for a man to be sure that his children were his own; as circumstances have changed and economic prosperity has reached the Arab countries, these reasons are no longer valid, and will gradually wither away.

Bedouin woman

CHRISTINE OSBORNE

It has been confirmed by recent public debate in Britain that death is there regarded as embarrassing; the Victorian protocols of mourning have fallen into disuse and nothing has replaced them. The Irish wake is the only survival in the British Isles, and its manifestations are different. *The Times* of 14 December 1976 said: 'Our society is still tongue-tied and embarrassed by death . . . yet there are no good reasons for this deceit or for the loneliness of the western way of death. It is a sterile convention that has grown out of reticence and fear . . . The change that is needed is in attitudes to death. More honesty and more openness backed by more expertise.' Such embarrassment and reticence are unknown to the Arabs. Violent death has perhaps in the past been a more familiar companion to them than it has in the West, although that is changing too. But there are certain conventions which are so accepted and familiar when someone dies, that the shock is faced and absorbed after a period of open mourning. Normally burial takes place within 24 hours of death, a custom arising from necessity in hot climates and even today strictly observed. A Muslim goes to his grave in a coffin carried by close relatives and friends, but is interred simply in a shroud. Traditionally only men walk in funeral processions.

Close male and female relatives receive visitors who offer their condolences, usually separated by sex, either in different houses or at different times, on the day of the funeral, on the third day and the seventh day after the death, and then, finally, on the 40th day. These 40 days are the period of mourning, when close relatives stay at home, dress in sober (though not necessarily black) clothes, and have no flowers or luxury foods in the house. Women wear long white silk scarves, either around the neck or over the head. On the 41st day mourning is ended and ordinary life begins again.

It is customary to weep loudly at funerals, and to recite the Koranic prayers for the dead, also often extempore verses extolling the dead person's merits. This is a catharsis; the ceremony is extremely exhausting for all present, but the bereaved are comforted by many who obviously share in their grief, and by the necessity of receiving visitors. The visitors are offered unsweetened coffee and cigarettes, and may converse in low voices upon general topics after offering formal condolences. Absence from work on account of a funeral, or mourning for a close relative, is perfectly understood, and even long-stay prisoners are let out for a few hours to attend their parents' or spouses' funerals.

It is the custom to visit friends, business colleagues and prominent citizens when there is a death in the family, even if the dead person was not actually known to the visitor. The visitors sit in a large circle in the reception room on chairs often rented for the purpose, and remain for between 30 to 50 minutes. There are several firms in each Arab country who make substantial livings from hiring out chairs for weddings and funerals. A common subject for idle conversation when stuck in a traffic jam, behind a small pickup truck loaded down with chairs, is who is being married or buried, and where.

Illnesses are also more public than in Europe; neither at home nor in hospital are the sick ever left alone. In cases of extreme fatigue the patient will be surrounded by silent sympathisers, and if he or she is in pain there is no convention of attempting to suppress groans and moans. This is particularly true of childbirth, where cries are expected. It is considered a compliment to close friends to ask them to be present when waking up from the anaesthetic after a surgical operation; apart from the obligatory presence of a member of the family the awakening is greatly cheered by seeing a friend as one emerges into consciousness. But the importance of family closeness cannot be too greatly emphasised; it is the strength of the Arabs.

Domestic customs and personal behaviour

The advantages of another, sometimes alien, culture being imposed upon an existing one are obvious; it broadens the horizons, introduces interesting and often improved habits, and is frequently an economic advantage. The British spread their culture through India and parts of the Far East, and brought back in return a fondness for tea and curry, and a taste for Indian bric-a-brac and chinoiserie. But the new culture may be difficult to understand, and minor differences may cause major misunderstandings because the simple explanations that would solve them are not provided.

Arab manners and social customs are in some ways much more formal and stylised than those found in the West. Hospitality is the chief virtue of the Arab world; respect for others' privacy seems to be more important in the West. There are many phrases for greeting guests, with set replies, also at least six different ways of saying 'Please' and 'Thank you'. If anyone appears at meal times it is customary to invite him to share the meal, whether he be a friend, a person delivering goods, a gas meter reader, or a carpenter who has come to do household repairs. In more traditional households women may appear veiled before a male who is no relation, but this is gradually dying out, especially among Arabs in Europe. It does not prevent those same ladies from ruling the household very firmly: on the whole families are run by mothers rather than wives.

When outside their own countries—where the rules vary, Libya, Saudi Arabia and Kuwait being 'dry' but other Arab countries permitting the sale and consumption of alcohol within certain limits—most Arabs will drink beer, wine, or spirits and offer them to their guests. In Saudi Arabia, however, any form of alcoholic drink is regarded much as are hard drugs in England, available at an exorbitant price but not consumed by the vast majority of law-abiding citizens. Drunkenness is rare anywhere, and considered quite disgraceful, so a guest should not accept more than he can gracefully manage.

Most households will have a television set in the living-room; it is usual to have it on all the time, and especially when guests are present. This is because they should be provided with whatever facilities are available in the household, and TV is obviously one of them. If the sound is so loud as to drown conversation it is permissible to lower it a little, but no one would dream of turning it off, any more than they would sit in the dark when they can turn on the light.

Privacy is not greatly esteemed by Arabs, because it means being alone, and originally being alone in a primitive desert environment meant death. The extended rather than the nuclear family is the custom, and this means that there are very few lonely or neglected old people. Indeed, there is much respect for age, and the old grandfather or grandmother is head of the family until death. Young couples with Western education may have some difficulties in finding time and opportunities to develop a personal relationship, but this is also true in the 'rat-race' environment of Western society. However prosperous a family may be, all unmarried children will share bedrooms, usually one for the boys and one for the girls. Nor is it considered unseemly for grown brothers and sisters to share a bedroom, especially for a brief period, such as in a hotel, or on a journey.

Guest bedrooms are almost unknown, although guests are far more common than in Western society; a guest is provided with everything except privacy. If he wanted that, why would he come and visit his friends? On the other hand, nakedness, except of small children, or of married couples between themselves, is totally unacceptable, and indeed shocking. Most Arabs sleep in underwear, vest and underpants, or bra and pants according to the sex, changed daily, with pyjamas or nightdress on top. It is quite in order to receive guests in unrevealing pyjamas or housegowns at home, especially in the morning. However many servants she may have for menial tasks, the lady of the house always attends to its supervision, and often does a good deal of cooking before getting dressed to go out, or to receive guests for lunch. No Arab lady would ever be seen with her hair in curlers, except by female relatives in her bedroom, or at the hairdresser. A great deal of time and money and effort is spent by both sexes on clothes and beauty products, and the results are often spectacular, though at times they can be overpowering. The 'natural look' is not yet fashionable in Arabia.

Western-style furniture, often of the more ornate variety, is now common in Arab houses, though the traditional reception room, or *Dar*, with hard oblong cushions placed around three sides of a large room with a fountain or brazier in the middle, according to the season, still exists in the Arab countries, and is indeed admired for its picturesque qualities and adherence to tradition. In the same way, some banquets are still offered with the food placed on cloths on the floor, or on low round copper tables, with the guests seated around on cushions. Oriental carpets are usually hung on the walls; of course in a chillier climate fitted plain carpets are appreciated. But it has always been the custom for both kitchens and bathrooms to have stone, tile, or marble floors with a drain in one corner, so that any liquid spilt can be swept away with an ordinary straw brush, or dirt rinsed off with buckets of water. European houses do not generally have this convenience, which causes difficulties for Arab servants.

Hygiene is very thorough and elaborate, both because of the hot climate, and Koranic precepts. It is enjoined that persons should wash their mouth and

Reception room or *Dar*

hands both before and after meals, and their private parts before and after sexual intercourse. Special bowls and towels are normally provided in bathrooms for this purpose, and all ablutions should be carried out in running water. Bidets are common, and there are far more showers than bath-tubs, though a combination is now usually found. Soaking in one's own dirt in the tub is always followed by a shower to rinse it off. Toilet paper is another Western invention; the usual method of cleansing is with water in a long-spouted brass or plastic water can. In the desert this is replaced by stones or sand.

Laundry is traditionally done at home, and no aesthetic objections have ever been raised about hanging it to dry on roofs or balconies. However, Arabs have taken to washing machines and automatic driers as enthusiastically as everyone else, and use them, indeed, rather more.

IRAN INFORMATION AND TOURIST CENTRE

Public baths in Iran

It is the custom to change underwear and socks daily, towels and sheets at least once a week. The Arab equivalent of the duvet is a stitched and padded cotton quilt called *lhaf*, with a washable cover. Elaborately embroidered coloured sheets may also be used.

The noise level is higher, as is natural in a society where outdoor living is possible for much of the year, and where there is competition with other people and the television. Arabs do not object to transistor radios in public, car horns, or loud conversation. They do, on the other hand, regard as highly offensive and ill mannered any sitting posture which places the soles of the feet towards anyone present. It is considered a deliberate insult, as is the American custom of placing the feet upon the desk and then leaning back to consider a matter, in the presence of others. Shoes and slippers are never left lying with their soles upwards; on the same basis this is an insult to the Lord. It is quite acceptable to sit crosslegged, on a cushion or on the sofa or a chair, though preferable to remove the shoes first. Females should, obviously, wear trousers or long skirts in order to do this decently; indeed any clothes that reveal too much of the female form are to be avoided. It is far more comfortable and cooler to wear long sleeved loose hiplength shirts over trousers, long skirts, or loose caftan-type dresses. European women in low-necked, sleeveless, short dresses are both uncomfortable in great heat, and laughed at for their ridiculous attire.

It may be relevant here to say something about the Arab attitude to drugs, and to informal relationships between the sexes. It is generally believed that the countries of the Levant, i.e. Turkey, Syria, Lebanon and Egypt, are ideal places for obtaining and consuming both hashish or marijuana and opium. It is true that the opium poppy is cultivated in Turkey, under strict government supervision, and that occasionally some opium has been known to be diverted to the illegal market, mostly for conversion to heroin in French or Italian underground laboratories, and subsequent smuggling into the USA. It is also true that hashish grows in Morocco, Lebanon and Syria, wild, and that in some remote areas the peasants cultivate it as a cash crop, and sell it to middlemen who then export it. But it is far easier to obtain the hard drugs in London or New York than in Beirut or Cairo, and it is not culturally acceptable to use them. Hashish is obtainable with less difficulty, and young people are sometimes tempted to smoke the odd cigarette. It is, however, strictly illegal in all the Arab countries to use, possess, or trade in any kind of narcotic, and many Americans and Europeans have ended up in prison because they ignored this rule. Some deserve no sympathy because they came specifically to buy hashish at a lower price than at home, smuggle it back and sell it at a profit. Others are very much the victims of circumstances.

Another Western illusion is that the Arab world is a paradise for homosexuals: if those Westerners in search of handsome and available young men could hear what the Arabs say out of their hearing, or at least their understanding, they would soon abandon their quest. Homosexuality is regarded in the Arab world as an inferior substitute for heterosexual relations, as well as being, as elsewhere, a stage of adolescence through which many boys pass. Arab male homosexuality exists where large numbers of men are assembled without the company of women, and as sex outside marriage is culturally unacceptable for Arab women, many men have been obliged to resort to this substitute before they could marry. The arrival of wealthy foreigners, willing to pay for male company, when at home they could freely consort with all the females the heart could desire, was a matter for mirth and amazement. But in less prosperous times, these foreigners provided a welcome windfall—this was especially true of North Africa in the days of the French occupation—and many young men saved enough money from their protectors to get married and furnish a house.

Certain places in the Arab world still have a somewhat equivocal reputation in this respect: Qatar used to be one. Here it is worth noting that until very recently the women of Qatar have been the most shut away, shrouded, veiled, and uninstructed. Nevertheless, any foreigner who attempts to make advances may be aggressively rebuffed. If he has gone to work in an oil state to make money, he may find himself declared *persona non grata*. If he is good at his job and wishes to keep it, he would do better to consort with a compatriot, or make discreet arrangements with other foreigners, preferably through third parties so that no one is offended.

Female homosexuality, however, is not condemned in the same way; it is regarded as amusing, and a suitable occupation for women deprived of men. This is probably derived from long separation in time of war, and the Turkish custom of keeping large harems which could hardly receive adequate attention from one Pasha. Moreover, women do not use up as much energy in homosexual diversion in the same way as men do. But few females, and then only those with unhappy marriages, would prefer the sexual company of women to men. Close friendship and understanding is another matter.

Relations between the sexes are also more strictly controlled by custom, and 'dating' in the American sense does not exist. As university education becomes more widespread students may meet on the campus, study together, and discuss philosophy and politics. But an invitation to a girl from a boy which would involve the two being alone together even briefly is interpreted either as a proposal of marriage or a deadly insult. An Arab proverb says: 'Do not trust a man and a woman alone together for any longer than it takes for water to run out of a jar'. Arab students at Western universities get their worst cultural shock when they observe dating customs. The boys immediately assume that any girl who accepts an invitation from them is willing to leap into bed straight away; the girls are insulted by an invitation to a concert from the President of the Student Council. In fact both are wrong.

It is still mandatory for a girl to be a virgin when she marries, and doctors who will do a 'repair job' for a fee are known to exist. Among the less educated section of the population a girl's virginity is deemed her most precious possession, and if she is even suspected of losing it she may well have her throat cut by her father or brothers, who believe that they can only avenge 'family honour' in this way. The present writer saw this happen some years ago in Beirut, when a bus stopped at traffic lights and a girl was hauled out and summarily despatched. No one dared to interfere once the word 'sharaf' (honour) was uttered, and when the police appeared shortly afterwards—long enough, nevertheless, for the girl to bleed to death—the two men responsible gave themselves up quite willingly. They would receive a sentence of at most two years in prison; no judge would dare impose more because public opinion was then in favour of family honour being thus protected. If a man marries a girl supposing her to be a virgin, and discovers on the first night that she is not intact, he has the right to send her back to her family, reclaim the dowry paid, and receive damages as well.

Once married it is up to the husband to keep his wife faithful to him, and while Koranic tradition reports that the Prophet said that adulterous women should be stoned to death, he added that in order to merit this punishment they must be found *in flagrante delicto* by four adult male muslim witnesses. Few adulterous wives would be so careless. In the more traditional societies girls are married as soon as they reach puberty, between 12 and 15. Of course they are emotionally and intellectually immature, but most husbands who value education encourage their wives to pursue it, and temptation is avoided both for the girls themselves and the men who may covet them.

Divorce and re-marriage are quite easy, and carry little social stigma. In Islam marriage is a civil contract, governed by the Shari'a, and the contract may be drawn up with various stipulations which the two parties have agreed upon, including the wife's right (as well as the husband's) to ask for divorce. Children of divorced parents usually go to their father, after the age of five for a boy and eight for a girl. This tends to keep marriages going that might otherwise founder, for often a woman's loyalty is to her children rather than to her husband. Also, in the past, the majority of divorces took place because the wife could not have children, or the husband could not beget them. If a couple do split up the woman can remarry far more easily if she is not burdened with children. The tradition of children belonging to the father is so strong that when a young widow

wishes to remarry after a decent interval (one to three years) her deceased husband's parents may want to keep the children, and will insist at least on frequent visits. Property distribution is governed by the Shari'a.

It should be obvious that a foreigner visiting the Arab world should not attempt to enter into sexual relationships unless a very definite invitation is issued, and the visitor is ready to accept the dangers involved. When the traditional hospitality is so much greater than that shown in the West this may seem something of a paradox. In some ways Arabs are more demonstrative in public; men embrace each other, and walk along hand-in-hand, as do women. But there is no public display of heterosexual affection, and Western women who acquire Arab suitors may well find them affectionate and generous, but will be unrespected and swiftly discarded if they manifest emotion in public. There is a somewhat ambivalent attitude to such females, in that they are known to be sexually much freer than Arabs, and therefore available, but because of this they are a bad example and a bad influence. Unfortunately, in both dress and manners they often do little credit to their countries of origin.

The reasons for the almost total exclusion of sexual relations from the otherwise generous Arab hospitality are the ancient necessity for ensuring the legitimacy of children, and the closeness of family life, which must be protected at all costs. Women are the guardians of the home, the 'precious gardens', and should not need to stray outside them. Men, being weak and fickle, can go off and return without upsetting the reflection of cosmic harmony that a well-run home presents.

Gambling, especially card playing, is a popular diversion, particularly around the New Year holidays. It is quite common to spend the whole of New Year's Eve, until the morning, at poker, even

BENTE FASSLER

Camel racing in Abu Dhabi

when the players would do so at no other time. And casinos which provide games of chance flourish where permitted to do so. Most countries have national lotteries, and horse-racing is also popular. But there are no football pools, bookmakers or official betting agents or shops, neither is greyhound racing known. In the cities with racecourses there are one or two tote agencies in the centre of the town, for that week's racing, but any other kind of betting is unofficial and illegal. Horse and camel racing flourish in Bahrain, Kuwait and the UAE, because the sheikhs are interested in the animals and the sport, but no official gambling is attached to this.

A great many people smoke cigarettes, cigars, and pipes. Tobacco is cheap by European standards as it has not been considered the universal revenue producer, and medical warnings concerning its

dangers have not been given much publicity yet. Also, there is a much greater range of cigarette prices than in the West; the local tobacco of Latakia and Lebanon is of excellent quality, but its lower grades are made into cheap cigarettes smoked by soldiers and the poorest labourers. The more prosperous citizens will smoke American or French cigarettes, probably because of the cachet, existing all over the world, that attaches to imported products, rather than the better quality they possess. It has become the custom to offer cigarettes to guests, and in the reception rooms of most houses there will be a large dish on which are placed several packets of different varieties, in readiness. It is a particular compliment for the host to take a cigarette from a pack and offer it to a specially favoured guest, and it is necessary to be a total non-smoker to refuse.

31

The occasional smoker may find the occasions more frequent among Arabs.

Another way of smoking is the water pipe, known in Arabic as the *narghileh*, in India as the hookah, and in the West, colloquially, or, rather, onomatopoeically, as the hubble-bubble. The tobacco is kept glowing by small pieces of charcoal placed on top of it, and the art of keeping it alight while not burning the tobacco too quickly, is considerable. Smoking a *narghileh* is a fairly lengthy operation, and various rituals are connected with it; hardened smokers have their own *narghileh*, but more often it is a social affair among friends in a house, or café, with the mouthpiece being passed from hand to hand. The fastidious may use their own silver mouthpieces, which are fitted into the communal one. It is difficult to smoke a *narghileh* and do much else at the same time, except converse with one's friends, and it is probably for this reason that the habit has never become popular in the West; it is the product of a more leisured society, and as such may well die out as the pace of Arab life quickens.

In Egypt, and all the Arab countries to the east, parents, from the time that their first son is born, are always known by his name, with the prefix Abu (Father of) or Umm (Mother of) added. This custom seems to have died out, or never existed, in the North African countries; it is an extremely practical one because it does away with the awkwardness of not knowing how to address people for whom a first-name basis would be too familiar and surname too formal. The equilvalent of 'Mister' is Sayyid for Muslim, and Khawaja for a Christian; ladies are Sayida, or Sitt, and girls Anissa (for Miss). After a certain age all ladies are Sitt, the Arabic equivalent of Ms. Indeed, with murmurings of Women's Lib. and the general education and gradual equality of women, it is sometimes observed that parents, instead of being addressed invariably as Umm Fahid or Abu Hassan (both boys' names), may sometimes be Umm Leila or Abu Nala, if their first-born is a girl, or they have only daughters. Other titles have died out; in Egypt there used to be beys and pashas, but both the words and the ranks were Turkish imports. The Arab and Islamic custom holds that no man is better than another (though some may be richer), and the words Amir (Prince) and Malik (King) are purely functional. The Arab kings keep none of the rigid court protocol that may be seen in Iran today, and any of their subjects have the right of audience, and of addressing them by their names directly.

On the whole, there is a somewhat ambivalent attitude to older customs; people want the new technological toys and comforts of the West, yet they value the past too, particularly family and religious traditions. Very recently there has arisen an interest in old buildings and artifacts, as witness the new museum in Qatar and the one planned for Saudi Arabia.

Food

Several large volumes have been written on Middle Eastern food. Claudia Roden's *Middle Eastern Cooking* (Penguin) is probably the most accessible. Arab food is spicier and more strongly flavoured than that of Europe. Most Arabs who can afford it eat basically Arab food, with European 'extras'. Flat unleavened bread flaps (made and sold in Europe by Greek bakeries as 'pitta' bread) are consumed in large quantities, chiefly for wrapping around pieces of other foods and eating without implements. Rice is the staple cereal, served with stews, or grilled meat on skewers; also used are lentils, cracked wheat (burghul) and chick peas (hummos). Lamb is the principal meat, beef being scarce, expensive, and tough, and pork forbiden by Koranic injunction. Chickens, turkeys, and ducks are popular, so is fish (mostly grilled on charcoal) and game. Any animals or birds must be killed in the Islamic fashion, by cutting the throat, so that all the blood drains out, and reciting the invocation 'Bismillah al-rahman al-rahim' (In the name of God, the Merciful, the Compassionate). This is usually done to birds that have been shot, on the understanding that they are not dead until their throats have been slit.

Pork is forbidden in the Islamic, as in the Mosaic, law, because pigs are unclean feeders, and in a hot country it is very easy to get trichinosis from eating it. Few Muslims will eat pork, even in Europe, but they are not quite so strict always about ham and bacon, which taste delicious and are subject to rigid quality control which is assumed to have killed any bacteria. In London now there are many shops, mostly run by Pakistanis, which advertise 'Halal' meat; this means meat killed according to Islamic ritual. This is normally lamb or chicken, slightly more expensive, and a great deal fresher and better tasting than supermarket fare.

Butter is very little used in Arab cooking; its place is taken by olive oil or samni, which is clarified sheep or goat butter, much like Indian ghee. But this has become less common; vegetable oils such as maize, sunflower, or peanut are now considered healthier. Indeed, some modern ideas have now taken over; fatness is no longer an obligatory sign of prosperity, and fewer middle-class men have large paunches to indicate their wealth.

The usual eating pattern is a substantial breakfast which would consist of tea or sometimes coffee, bread flaps, black olives, goat cheese, cream or cottage cheese called *labneh* which is solidified from *laban* (yoghurt), eggs fried in oil, and fruit juice or fruit. Lunch, served at any time between 1.30 and 3 p.m., remembering that in many Arab countries offices close at 2 p.m. for the day (having begun work at 7.30 a.m.), is the principal meal, with soup, rice with a meat and vegetable stew, another meat dish such as grilled chicken, *kufta* (minced meat on skewers or baked in a round tray in the oven), or kebab. There will be certainly one or two salads, some pickles and sauces, then cheeses and fruits. Depending on the formality of the meal, there might be Arabic cakes (*baklawa, halwa* etc) or an elaborate European-style creamy dessert. Much esteemed, and usually eaten as an afternoon snack, is rice pudding, known as *riz ma haleeb* (rice with milk). It is eaten cold, quite solid, and flavoured with vanilla or orange flower essence. Coffee is always served at the end of a meal; Arabic coffee in tiny cups, un-sweetened, very strong, flavoured with cardamon. In traditional families servants pass around a basin, ewer, and towels, then eau de cologne, and sometimes incense in a brazier to restore agreeable odours that have nothing to do with food. In more modern households people simply make for the nearest bathroom, where a large bottle of eau de cologne will always be provided. All Arabs use some form of scent.

Making Arabic coffee

IRAN INFORMATION AND TOURISM CENTRE

A tea room in Iran

Tea, whether Indian, Chinese, or mint (in North Africa especially), is normally drunk for breakfast in cups, and throughout the day in small handleless tulip-shaped glasses, as an alternative to Arabic coffee in china cups. It is always drunk very sweet, and tea without sugar is something of an aberration. Milk is not relevant to tea, though some people drink it hot and sweet by itself, in the morning.

Fresh vegetables and fruit are important, and no meal is complete without salad. Arabs are not by tradition great meat-eaters, originally for economic reasons, and the commonest types of main dish are peppers or aubergines or tomatoes, baked with a stuffing of rice, minced meat, raisins and pine-nuts: or *yakhni*, a stew with a rich gravy, small pieces of meat, and okra, beans, or peas. On special occasions lambs or kids might be roasted whole out of doors over a char-

coal fire: these are known as *ouzi* or *mechoui*. Much cheese and yoghurt is eaten also.

The Arabic equivalents of hors d'oeuvres are known as *mezzeh*, and consist of up to 40 small dishes placed on the table at the beginning of a meal, either in a house or restaurant. There will be all kinds of pickled vegetables, and *tabbuleh*, the famous Lebanese salad now eaten everywhere. This is a mixture of parsley, mint, green onions, burghul and tomatoes, dressed with oil, lemon juice, pepper and salt.

Then there is *hummos*, a dip made of chick peas and *tahineh*, and *mtabbal*, a dip of roasted and pounded aubergines also mixed with *tahineh*. *Tahineh* is thick, creamy sesame oil with a very distinctive smoky flavour. Also included in a *mezzeh* are small pieces of meat, fish, liver and bone marrow; sometimes raw lamb's liver, which is recommended to those who like steak tartare. All these morsels usually have sharp or spicy sauces. Then there are slices of various smoked meats, cheese, fried bread, various kinds of nuts, and whole tomatoes, hard-boiled eggs, green peppers, lettuce and apples. It is customary for the host or hostess to cut up these whole items and distribute the pieces to the guests: in a restaurant the person who invites, or who wishes to establish his right of paying the bill, does so. He then has a legitimate claim to be the host.

Mezzeh may be served at lunch or dinner, as part of a leisurely meal which may go on for hours. *Arak* (grape spirit flavoured with aniseed, which turns white when water is added), or beer is usually drunk with *mezzeh:* indeed arak is never drunk without some *mezzeh* dishes to accompany it. The Arabs believe that no-one should consume alcohol without eating at the same time. However, at everyday meals people drink water when they have finished eating, usually from an *ibriq*, a glass or pottery jug with a narrow spout from which the drinker swallows a stream of water without allowing his lips to touch the spout. Some can swallow the water without spilling a drop, from a distance of two feet; it is a trick that has to be learnt.

Tabbuleh, the salad described earlier, may also be served as a meal, usually in spring or early summer, when vegetables are at their freshest, and sitting out of doors is pleasant. People invite their friends for 'a tabbuleh', or say 'We're making tabbuleh on Wednedsay; do you care to join us?'. This takes place at tea time, between five and seven in the afternoon, and also served are plates of lettuce leaves, the lettuce being used to convey the tabbuleh to the mouth, as a kind of scoop, open sandwiches with cold meat and cheese, a sweet dish such as *mhalibieh* (much resembling very sugary junket), and fruit. Freshly made lemonade, beer, and sometimes tea, are appropriate drinks

Particularly in Lebanon, where there is an abundance of fruit, people make their own syrups from fruit juice and sugar, which when diluted make excellent cold drinks. Tut, or mulberry, is the most frequently found because there are still many mulberry trees planted at the time when the breeding of silkworms was common in both Syria and Lebanon. Other syrups are lemon, orange, rose, pomegranate and quince. A guest arriving in summer is always offered a cold drink, or Arabic coffee with a glass of cold water.

Various jams and jellies are made, quince jelly being the most popular. Strawberries grow in Lebanon, Egypt, and parts of North Africa: they are not indigenous and are regarded as a great luxury, as is their jam. Peaches are common and there are many varieties of citrus fruit; the usual oranges, lemons, grapefruit, tangerines (known commonly as *Yusuf Effendi*, or Mr Joseph), blood oranges, moghrabeh (sweet oranges), *uglis* (a cross between orange and grapefruit, bigger than either), sweet lemons,

big navel oranges, and bitter Seville oranges for marmalade. Dates grow in Iraq, Saudi Arabia, and North Africa; the harvest is in September and October. Fresh dates are quite different from the preserved kind, and there are many varieties.

Large irregular shaped tomatoes are common everywhere; and most Arabs prepare their own tomato paste, boiling the fresh tomatoes slowly for hours out of doors over wood fires. They are gradually rendered down; the paste is then spread out to dry on wood or metal trays and finally bottled.

Nearly all the common European vegetables are known, though some undergo considerable change in the kitchen. Spinach is used as a stuffing, with minced meat, pine-nuts, and onions, for tiny short-crust pasties pinched shut on one side and then fried (*fatayeh*). Pieces of cauliflower are often fried, and then eaten cold with a tahineh sauce. Okra and molokiyeh are two unfamiliar vegetables, both being slightly glutinous: molokiyeh look rather like nettles, green with serrated and pointed leaves, though they do not sting. Instead they serve as the base of a celebrated Egyptian dish, stewed in chicken or lamb stock, with the pieces of meat added, and rice, chopped raw onion, and garlic and coriander sauce served on the side.

Onions, cabbage, and cauliflower are all very popular, but considered to be bad for nursing mothers, because they can give the baby indigestion. Cabbage is normally shredded raw for salad, or the whole leaves are used to wrap a mixture of rice and minced meat which is then steamed. This stuffed cabbage is a favourite winter dish, as is *cous-cous*, a semolina dish which is the national food in North Africa, and is known as *mograbieh* in Syria and Lebanon. The North African kind has much smaller grains and is prepared in a special steamer over a sauce of various vegetables (carrots, tomatoes, onions, turnips, leeks, peppers) and lamb, with a fiery chili sauce served alongside. The larger grains of *mograbieh* can be bought in Aleppo and Beirut; they are stewed in meat stock to which small button onions, a few whole chick peas, and lamb or chicken, or sometimes both, are added.

The long leaved crisp cos lettuces are the usual variety found in the Arab countries, though other kinds do exist. Radishes are small, round, and red, or long and white, with a strong flavour. There are several salad plants such as rocca and bacli, almost unknown in Europe. Carrots can be black as well as orange. Turnips are mostly made into pickles.

Spices most used are thyme, rosemary, cumin, cardamon, cinnamon, nutmeg, and sumac. A common accompaniment to breakfast is powdered thyme moistened with olive oil into which bread is dipped. *Mana'ish* is also eaten at breakfast; it consists of a pizza-like dough on which a thyme, mint and oil mixture is spread, and the whole put into a baker's oven, then eaten hot. Rosemary flavours lamb, cumin any lentil or pulse dish and cardamon coffee. Cinnamon is powdered on top of rice, and nutmeg put in to salads or sweet dishes. Sumac is sprinkled on fried eggs, as are pomegranate molasses (dibis roumane). Orange flower essence and rosewater are used to flavour cakes and desserts.

Business

Laws concerning buying and selling are quite precise; for example giving short weight or a false rate of exchange are both heavily condemned. Arabs regard their word as their bond, and expect the same behaviour from others. They may take a good deal of time and persuasion to make up their minds to buy an object or a property, or employ a person, and will enjoy bargaining fiercely over the price. But once they have agreed, they carry the deal through unless the purchaser is simply unable to find the money, and the practice known as 'gazumping' in England would result in business ostracism in any Arab country. Not that Arabs object to bargains, but the business community is small enough for most large merchants to know each other, at least by reputation. Of course tourists can be fleeced by small shopkeepers and unscrupulous hoteliers, but usually they have only themselves to blame.

Questions are often asked about methods of doing business in the Arab world, now that there is so much business to be done. The normal social courtesies must of course be observed, but it is even more important to note that business must be done on a personal introduction basis. An example might be the British sales manager of a firm selling aluminium window frames, who could not go directly to a local contractor putting up buildings requiring these, unless he had been asked to do so, or had a personal introduction from a friend or business colleague. As a total stranger, he may be politely received, but he is 'of no known origin', and thus cannot be regarded seriously.

Very often, when a large contract is being negotiated, it is obvious that the Arab negotiator will expect some recompense for his services. No awkwardness need be felt about this; it is quite in order to enquire what percentage of the contract (depending on its size this should be between 1% and 2%) he expects for himself, and when he states a figure, which will probably be higher than that given above, it can be bargained over in the normal fashion. If this question is not asked, the negotiator will, doubtless correctly, assume that the people with whom he is dealing have no knowledge of the Arab world, and the deal will almost certainly fall through.

Most Arabs will live up to, and beyond, their incomes. They will run up debts, and pay them eventually; too great a loss of respect is involved in not doing so.

Arab Cultural Preoccupations

There is a marked difference in Arab civilisation between the static and the lively arts. The static arts are concerned with architecture and decoration, and may be described as the arts of Being. A beautiful building, or city or artifact is created for a purpose; in the Arab Weltanschaung function and beauty are necessary partners. A beautiful object will have a use; an object designed to fulfil its function perfectly will be beautiful. Obvious examples are carpets, woven materials, pottery dishes and jugs and glass lamps. These objects are considered to reflect cosmic harmony, and thus in a minor degree the Divine Essence, for they exist as independent creations, and are not expected to change. They represent 'being'; they are not 'becoming' anything.

The Arabic language is the bridge between the static and the lively arts, for it manifests the nature of both. Muslims regard the Koran as a visible manifestation of the uncreated Word of God—on the same level as the committed Christian regards the sacraments—and the sacred Word is enshrined in the purest form of the language. Any change automatically means debasement, so that here the aspect of 'being' is obvious. But language is also used to express thought, to write poetry and prose and songs, to move men's minds to love or war, and here we have the aspect of 'becoming', of change; in fact, of the lively arts, which are described in the second part of this section. Very little seems to be known outside the Arab world about the modern lively arts, although a great many learned volumes have been written about the Islamic arts from the Eighth to the 19th centuries.

Architecture is the first of the static arts, and has been principally concerned with the mosque and the madrassah (religious school) since the time of the Prophet Muhammad. Fortresses and fortifications show this in a lesser degree, and the Islamic styles flowered in Iran, where the mosques of Shiraz and Isfahan are 'fairer than tongue can tell'. Whole cities were planned to facilitate the Arab and Islamic way of life, centred upon the mosque.

One of the best examples of such a city is Fez, in Morocco, where the focal points are the mosques upon which the streets converge, but the material necessities of market places, defending walls, water

Al-Ahzar Mosque, Cairo, Egypt

CHRISTINE OSBORNE

supplies, inns, baths and dwelling houses are also considered. The static quality of the architecture ('being') is balanced by the life running so strongly in the streets, of the buyers and sellers, travellers and soldiers.

The hallmarks of Arab architecture are the domes, elaborate geometric or arabesque decorative patterns, and the frozen music of the pendentives and squinches in contrast to the dull rectangular corners familiar in modern concrete buildings. This is a style that cannot be mistaken for any other, though it is difficult to date, for it does not evolve as European architectural styles have done. The bulbous Byzantine domes of Eastern Europe have some Arab echoes; they too are in an unchanging style.

The other arts within the periphery of architecture, partaking of both its static and religious nature, or devoted to religious purposes, are textiles and embroidery, jewellery, especially the art of the musabah, ivory and wood carving, glass, metalwork, ceramics, leatherwork, calligraphy and book illumination, marble, stucco, mosaic decoration and painting. All these arts, up to the 18th century, are elaborately described and beautifully illustrated in at least 50 books on Islamic art, many published in London in 1976 on the occasion of the Islamic Festival and the various exhibitions held there.

But even the modern static arts have been neglected. Perhaps the purists consider that they have been debased through the centuries, and scholars prefer to study them at one remove, in a museum. Nevertheless, they exist today, and their creators know that they must be both functional and decorative, because the divorce between 'art' and 'craftsmanship' is a recent European phenomenon.

Art involves technique and science, but is contemplative in its essence, implying the integration of parts to a whole, and forming a mirror of unseen unity. To quote Titus Burckhardt in *The Art of Islam, Language and Meaning:* 'Use and beauty go hand in hand in traditional art: they are two inseparable aspects of perfection, for in the words of the Koran "God has prescribed perfection for all things". Every manual skill carries an intrinsic value, in so far as it may be performed with more or less perfection. The craftsman's greatest achievement is the mastery he gains over himself: the affinity between art and contemplation is strong enough in many Islamic cities for the craft corporations to be linked with particular Sufi orders. Sufism is the inward, mystical dimension of Islam, bearing witness to the Divine Unity; easy to read about, difficult to attain'.

It should be indicated here that the flood of material comforts which have recently become available in the Arab world, nearly all imported from other parts of the globe, have tended to obscure this original creative philosophy. But artifacts are still created, and may be both observed and acquired. Sometimes the decoration is over-elaborate for non-Arab tastes; sometimes the function, essential to an Arab, does not exist in another culture.

However, with increased prosperity there is more demand, and more trade in the static arts described in some detail on the following pages. People use the objects; other people buy and sell them, so that in 1978 they are alive and flourishing.

Textiles

The best known Middle Eastern textiles are, of course, carpets. The traditions of carpet-making date from remotest antiquity and are still alive. The complex designs of 'Persian' carpets are made by knotting pieces of woollen or silk thread on to the weft according to a design drawn above the loom, with the number of knots of each colour indicated. The knots are so fine that they must be done by children between the ages of nine and

Prayer rug, circa 1900

SOTHEBY PARKE BERNET & CO.

15—after that their eyesight is no longer sufficiently acute—who may be seen at work today in some parts of Iran.

In the Arab countries today there are both loom-woven carpets in stripes or patterns, known as *kelims*, and carpets knotted in much coarser wool. This is done in the North African countries and in the remoter regions of Syria. Finer carpets are traditionally used as wall hangings, for both warmth and decoration, and on mosque floors, and the smaller ones have a *kibla* or niche woven into them and are used as prayer rugs.

Both hand and machine embroidery are renowned, and may still be bought in the bazaars of Aleppo, Damascus and Cairo. Long embroidered shirts and tunics, and caftan-styled dresses in velvet, cotton, silk and satin are extremely elegant, as are the hand-sewn dresses made in Syria and by Palestinian refugees.

Traditional Arab headdress

Much admired also are the cotton or organdie machine-embroidered tablecloths in various sizes and shapes, including circular ones, with matching napkins.

Then there are various kinds of headgear, including the *keffiyah* or headcloth, bound with the *agal*, a black or golden cord, to keep it in place. The *keffiyah* differs in different regions; in Saudi Arabia and the Gulf it is of fine white cotton and in Jordan or Palestine of check red and white or black and white. The mountain Christians of Syria and Lebanon wear a black *keffiyah*.

Older men can still be seen in the red felt *tarboosh* (a flower pot shaped brimless hat, known in Europe as the fez) in the Levant; in North Africa a *cheche*, or turban, is draped about the head. It can be black, white, khaki or purple. The Moroccans wear long cloaks with intergral hoods in grey, brown, beige or white, or striped in these colours. The women often wear similar velvet garments in jewel colours, as witness a Moroccan female customs official, carrying out her duties clad in a garnet velvet *djelabiyeh*, and undisturbed by the temperature of 32°C.

Those who have made the pilgrimage to Mecca, the Hajj, wear a green turban wrapped around a *tarboosh*, or a cap; in Iraq the Shi'a mullahs cover their heads with round black turbans elaborately folded. The clergy of Christian sects, to be observed principally in Lebanon and Egypt, wear distinctive headgear, the octagonal black velvet of the Armenians being perhaps the most elegant.

Each community, religious or secular, wore in the past an easily identified costume, for clothes place people according to their function and community; the gradual adoption of Western attire permits greater anonymity, and makes for greater discomfort, but it also deprives the wearer of easy identification and assistance. In England, people are 'placed' by the way they speak; in the Arab world, as in the US, accents and use of language indicate a geographical rather than a cultural identity. Further confusion can be added by non-Arabs, wearing Arab clothes. These garments are both practical and picturesque, but it should be remembered that the wearers assume an Arab identity, and so are also expected to assume Arab behaviour.

Jewellery

Fascination with jewellery is common throughout the world. Arabs delight in adorning themselves with as much jewellery as possible, and the gold *souks* in Marrakesh, Cairo and Damascus are ablaze with bracelets, necklaces, brooches and swords. A sword encrusted with gold and jewels is a favourite present given by one ruler or president when visiting another. Pearls are found in oysters in the warm, shallow Gulf waters.

Making jewellery

Gold and diamonds are bought as investments, but to be worn, not locked away in a bank. A girl from a prosperous family will often wear her dowry in the form of gold bracelets or coins. It is the custom for the bridegroom to offer the bride what jewellery he can afford: obviously the two exchange gold rings, but he should also 'lay on the contract' a gold necklace, brooch and earrings, set with diamonds if his means permit. She should then wear the jewellery whenever she pays or receives visits during the first year of married life. Jewellery is all handmade, and therefore it is possible to order a piece designed from a drawing or photograph, for little more than the cost of the gold or stones.

The special Arab contribution to the jeweller's art is the *musbaha (musabah)* or Arabic rosary, often known as 'worry beads'. They consist of 33 or 99 beads, with a divider after every 11, and represent the 99 names of Allah. Devout Muslims will count them, reciting a name for each bead—the Merciful, the Generous, the Law Giver, the Excellent and so

on. Less devout citizens will run them through their fingers, in a nervous, excited, or joyful fashion: one can tell much about people's characters from the way they handle their *musbahas*, and often enough they replace both cigarettes and tranquillisers. They can be made of plastic, bone, glass or the most exquisitely carved amber, ivory, jade, coral or precious stones. A 33-bead *musbaha* made of matched pearls, and a whole cluster of pink pearls at the finish knot, is worth many thousands of pounds. Several wealthy Arabs have fine collections. But they must be used (as pearls must be worn), and they take on the qualities of the owners, so that a close friend may share in the owners' feelings, or an enemy drop the beads and run screaming from the house (as attested by an eyewitness).

Ivory, wood carving and glass

These are ancient arts which are still found today, both as small decorative

41

caskets for jewels and unguents, chess sets (chess is a very ancient game, originating in Iran), doors and ship decorations mostly of African hardwoods. Ivory has always been imported from East Africa. The Arabic name is Sin el-Fil (Tooth of the Elephant) and Cairo is the most ancient Arab centre of ivory carving. Nowadays most carved ivory is imported from China and Hong Kong; also well known are miniature paintings (usually Persian, but available throughout the Arab world) on ivory or bone.

Wood has always been scarce, and valuable, in the Arab world. The mountains of Lebanon are covered with scrub and maquis which were used as fodder for goats, or burned for charcoal. A very few of the famous cedars have survived the depredations of centuries, and fairly well advanced afforestation is now taking place. But wooden furniture has always been costly: the furniture and carved wooden ceilings of Damascus were reserved for the rich. This furniture is thickly inlaid with mother-of-pearl, sometimes with ivory trim, and needs a large, cool, well-proportioned room to contain it. In all the cities elaborately carved teak doors closed off the houses from the streets, and carpentry was one of the most skilled of trades. An Arab regards the European fashion of wooden floors as an unbelievable luxury, as well as something of a fire hazard.

Glass was known to the Greeks and Romans, and there has always been a glass industry in the Middle East. The Crusaders brought the use of glass as a relatively cheap window material to Europe, because they were able to discover the easy process of glass-making. Before that it was an expensive imported luxury used for valuable vases and bowls. Nowadays, in Lebanon, Syria and Iraq small glass-blowing furnaces are found, turning out drinking ware and decorative dishes in deep rich blues, greens, browns and purples. Glass costume jewellery is made too. Tea is traditionally drunk in small

tulip shaped glasses, which may be of local manufacture, often decorated with-gilt motifs. In Bahrain small heat-proof glasses with handles are used: those most used are manufactured in France.

Antique glass can still be bought in the *souks*, particularly mosque lamps with inscriptions, drinking flagons and glasses, which bear witness to the creative abilities of craftsmen over the centuries of Islam.

Metalwork, ceramics and leatherwork

Weapons, especially swords, are the finest examples of traditional metalwork; armour, horse harnesses, baskets, inlaid bowls and trays may all be seen in Western museums. Swords are still exchanged as gifts of honour, and it is possible today to buy all the items listed above in the *souks* of the principal cities. Food is served on large round brass or metal inlaid trays, with inscriptions from the Koran and arabesque or geometric designs. Sometimes they are used as table tops supported on wooden legs or carved and mother-of-pearl inlaid stools, and the guests sit around them on cushions. Metal ewers and bowls are used for ceremonial hand-washing before and after meals, and where there are no showers special metal bowls, known as *tusht*, are used for rinsing the body. The metalworkers can still be seen hammering out their products in traditional fashion.

Ceramics, or pottery, are among the oldest of Middle Eastern artifacts, and are found in Stone Age remains. Elegant and decorative plates can be bought in any *souk*: many are of Turkish origin or design; others were made by the Palestine Pottery in Arab Jerusalem until 1967, and in most towns plain earthenware water jars and cooking vessels are made and sold. they are cheap and break easily, but they are perfectly adapted to their function, and are easily replaced.

Tiled shrine in Iran

They keep the flavour of the food cooked in them, not spoiling it with a metallic taste. Rashaya, in the south of Lebanon, still decorates its brown earthenware with distinctive elegant black and dark red spiral patterns. The clay for making these vessels must be of a special kind, able to withstand the heat of oven firing, and of course the water jars allow slow evaporation, keeping the water cool. The same is true of goat or sheepskin water bags, which may be seen slung on the outsides of trucks in Afghanistan and Iran. Trucks from Syria and Lebanon have, preferably, a niche near the tool-box, into which the pottery ibriq or water-jar fits.

Tiles are more decorative in the Arab world than elsewhere. This is because the traditional designs follow certain fundamental geometric patterns which are repetitive to the horizons of infinity, without tiring the eyes or the imagination. The colours are varied but rarely harsh: blues, greens, a burnt sienna red, purples and occasionally yellow. In Turkey from 1500 onwards tiles with tree or tulip designs were made and can still be seen in the Istanbul mosques.

The shrines of Isfahan, in Iran, combine the art of the calligrapher with that of the tile-maker in the most harmonious fashion ever achieved. Some examples of the traditional tile can occasionally be found in the *souks* of Arab cities, but less formal modern designs are more common.

However, most of the finer porcelain seen today comes from either Czechoslovakia or the Far East, especially Japan and China. The small cups for serving Arabic coffee, with or without handles, are mostly Japanese. Expensive European imports can be found too, but these hardly fall within the category of Arabic art. Although craft revivals are taking place in various places, pottery, not porcelain, is the modern Arab version of ceramic art.

Leatherwork is a typically nomad art, for nomads need saddles, whips, boots and scabbards for their animals and themselves, and produce skins from which these objects may be made. On the other hand, the preparation of skins is a long and often noisome process, which requires fixed installations and skilled craftsmen. These may be found in the city of Fez, in Morocco, which has a very long established tanning industry, and produces a great deal of beautiful leather, both in pieces and as finished articles. North Africa in general is famous for its bags, slippers, and stuffed cushions used as stools for sitting around low tables. The same articles may be found in Cairo and Aleppo, with slightly different designs. Nowadays leather and suéde coats and jackets are made, more in Turkey and Afghanistan than in the Arab world itself.

Calligraphy and book illumination

Calligraphy is an art which reached its highest perfection among the Arabs, for the language lends itself to the swirls and designs of the calamus, and the calligrapher, transcribing the Word of God, is an artist worthy of the highest esteem.

Because it gives visible form to the revealed word of the Koran, calligraphy is considered the most noble of the arts. The progression of the writing, right to left, indicates the journey from the outward form to the inner meaning; the symbolism of writing is allied to that of weaving. Both refer to the crossing of the cosmic axes; the vertical lines signify the eternal, being, the tree of life; the horizontal ones signify the temporal, becoming, the river of life.

There are two principal forms of script, the Kufic and the Naskhi. Kufic characters are square almost static (being) whereas the Naskhi is cursive and elegant (becoming). Syntheses of the two styles exist, and the most magnificent handwriting is found in Korans. The art is still practised today; the writer of an elegant script is considered fortunate and greatly talented. Many people hang sacred inscriptions on the walls of their houses, rather than pictures, and others encourage their children to use their artistic bent in calligraphy.

Because reproducing the sacred words of the Koran is the chief aim of the calligrapher, Muslim manuscripts are not illuminated in the Western sense, by capital letters becoming pictures, nor by any representation of living beings in the text. There is, however, a certain parallel between Islamic and Celtic art, in their flowing 'arabesque' forms 'whose elements, abstract rather than descriptive, are linked to a universal and primordial symbolism. The symbolic character is suddenly discussed by the flowering of ornamental possibilities inherent in them. This metamorphosis is directly perceptible in the Christian art of Ireland, where it is calligraphy that lays hold of, and transforms most naturally, the ancient heritage of forms. . . geometrical enlacement represents the most intellectually satisfying form, for it is an extremely direct expression of the idea of Divine Unity underlying the inexhaustible variety of the world'.[1] So, the illumination of the Koran and other precious documents is one of geometrical form, and of colours elegantly applied.

Painting

Painting is a static art, but today often

[1] Titus Burckhardt, *The Art of Islam*, Ch. IV Section 3 *'The Arabesque'*

represents lively actions. For painting in Islam is, or should be, non-representational, and only the Iranians disobeyed this injunction in the early days. But now Arab artists feel free to produce both representational and abstract paintings, and indeed the tradition of abstract art is so ancient that it is today old-fashioned, in contrast to its position in the West.

The Islamic injunction was made to prevent the representation of God, or of any divine entity, which might then be worshipped idolatrously, the image being mistaken for the essence, the created for the Creator. The present, more sophisticated, view has altered this, instead artists reflect the political and cultural matters that preoccupy their minds and those of the societies in which they live. There are Palestinian artists whose paintings reflect the agony of there people; barbed wire, weapons, agonised expressions depicted with more or less talent, but immense feeling. Joumana Husseini paints birds as a symbol of freedom in clear enamelled colours; sharply outlined buildings, and woodcarvings with gilded highlights; all echoes of Jerusalem, her birthplace.

Fateh Mudarres is a Syrian with considerable talent, who depicts children's faces against mysterious backgrounds, often ornamented with Arabic calligraphy. He studied in Italy for a time, and many of his paintings seem poised in Mediterranean space. A painter of the naive tradition is the Lebanese Khalil Zgheib, who began life as a barber and found that he had a talent for decorating his shop, depicting local events, festivals and marriages as well as landscapes—particularly flowering trees and rivers.

There are also several Iraqi painters who show the subtle colours of the desert and the Two Rivers in their work, and in Egypt there are Muhammad Sabri, Salah Tahe and Abdul-Hamid Hamdi who do both figurative and abstract work. In all these paintings people or places are busily 'becoming' something, or going some-

STUART H. STOOSHNOFF

Children by Fateh Mudarres (1962)

where, the people and the objects can be 'dated'. The 'being' of earlier Arab art, expressed principally in arabesque stone or stucco decorations on buildings, the 'frozen music' of the pendentives, the elaborate tile decorations of the Hara-mal-Sharif in Jerusalem are all timeless and therefore difficult to date. Persian miniature painting is both idealised and stylised: and has a somewhat different ancestry.

In the 18th and 19th centuries the rich merchants of Syria had made for their houses elaborate carved and painted wooden ceilings. The painted panels represented principally small bright flowers in formally arranged designs, and piercing colours: some still exist today and may be seen in the Museum and the Azem Palace in Damascus, or the house of M. Henri Pharaon in Lebanon. But today interior decoration in carried out on a scale that has little to do with authentic Arab art.

The Lively Arts

The lively arts are poetry, both classical and colloquial (*diwan* and *zajal*), music, the theatre and the film. All are widely practised in the Arab world today.

Poetry may be divided into two categories, according to the use of the classical or colloquial tongues. In the British Isles the difference would correspond to the use of regular verse forms in BBC English, and regional dialects producing free-verse forms with many puns and local references.

Poetry is divorced from everyday life in the Arab world; it is one of the liveliest of the arts, and nearly everyone knows a great deal of classical poetry by heart. Poets are not people devoted solely to their art and obliged only by material necessity to earn their livings as best they can; rather they belong to different occupations, manual or intellectual, and compose and recite poetry as a recreation, adding an extra dimension to their lives.

Classical poems are known as *qasidah*, or odes, and are usually collected in an anthology by one or several writers, known as a diwan. This poetry is meant to be recited and it is a common diversion to compose a poem ex tempore on a particular subject and declaim it to friends, or to recite an appropriate one that already exists. Here the superior memory and sense of rhythm of those who have little or no book learning comes into play: The word 'illiterate' carries to a Westerner connotations of 'stupid and ignorant', whereas often those who cannot read or write are highly intelligent and have better memories. If you have to remember a fact, a direction, or a poem, and are unable to write it down, your memory becomes far more highly developed. Zajal flourishes in different forms in most Arab countries: the local dialect is used to compose a series of rhythmic lines on a particular subject, very often a political or personal event.

Competitions are held: in Lebanon and Syria they are televised, and two teams take part. They may continue for several hours until one leader signifies defeat, being unable to compose any more. The referee sets the subjects: the leader of one side recites four lines, the last two being repeated by the four or five members of his chorus. The rhythm is beaten on tambourines, and the programmes are enormously popular. It is traditional for the two sides to be seated on either side of a large table covered with little dishes of food (mezzeh), and for arak to be drunk in delicate quantities. Sometimes television programmes are shot live in a restaurant and the audience is composed of other diners, who enter fully into the spirit of the contest. The nearest Western equivalents are the French and German satirical cabarets, but there the competitive element is absent.

Modern prose literature is less important than poetry, in the Arab world, although there is a good deal. Novels and biographies are written, and read, but reading for pleasure is not so popular in the Arab world as in the West; it comes part way between the static and the lively arts, and of 10 people who will assemble to declaim and discuss poetry, either written by themselves or others, only one will go home and read a novel.

Reading is not a pastime so much as a means of acquiring information and of learning technical subjects. Newspapers and magazines are widely read; Arabs who know English, French or German may read in these languages for diversion, when they would never think of doing so in Arabic. This has partly to do with Islam, the Koran is the Word of God revealed, and since it is written down, all written material, especially in Arabic, the language of the angels, should show high seriousness rather than simple pleasure— and partly to do with the fact that education has only recently become universal in the Arab world. The literate man was respected by his fellow-citizens as having a special, almost esoteric, knowledge not vouchsafed to them. It may well be argued that universal education tends to debase literary taste, but only the fanatic would wish to restrict it because it could be misused.

Many of the most talented modern Arabic writers produce film and TV scripts, which are lucrative, and otherwise concentrate on scholarly or instructive works, or poetry. There is an obvious market for sex and violence, especially in Egypt: most of these productions are translations, or hack adaptations (often with no acknowledgment) from books first written in English, French, or German. And of course there are comics for children, which feature such characters as Superman and Batman.

Pornography is found in magazines, of the same standard as those on any European railway bookstall, but there is a much older tradition of literary frankness that is erotic, not pornographic. Examples of this are in the unexpurgated edition of the *Arabian Nights*.or the *Perfumed Garden* of the Shaikh Nefzawe; both are available in translation in Europe, but the foreign reader should not expect to be at once, if indeed ever, admitted to the gardens of earthly delight that they portray, once he reaches Arabian shores.

Television has become enormously popular, and shows a good many American and European series programmes: 'Kojak', 'Hawaii 50' and 'Bionic Woman' for example. 'The Forsyte Saga' was much enjoyed in Lebanon, and also 'Upstairs, Downstairs'. Some of the shows are dubbed, but most are subtitled, as are the films: after a time the foreigner living in the Arab world feels that there is something missing when a non-subtitled movie or TV programme appears. Arabs have little shyness before the camera; directors sometimes have difficulty in persuading their actors to accept their direction, but they rarely have to cope with either professionals or amateurs feeling ill at ease, or suffering from 'nerves'.

Each country makes its own programmes, including domestic shows (the equivalent of 'Coronation Street'), documentaries, religious and educational programmes (especially in Saudi Arabia) and news and current affairs. Some of the funniest situation shows come from Egypt. The Egyptian sense of humour is well known.

It is obvious that where people live largely within their family circles, TV enlarges their horizons considerably. This is particularly true in Saudi Arabia, where video-tape machines have been imported, and people returning from abroad bring back films, and foreign TV programmes taped onto cassettes. They are soon circulated, and the behaviour of Westerners in certain situations is as strange and indecent to Arabs as is the behaviour of gorillas in their forest homes to most Westerners. It takes practice, much travel and a good deal of sophistication to accept totally different life styles in their own setting without suffering from cultural shock.

The film industry has developed considerably along commercial lines in Egypt and Lebanon and in a somewhat more intellectual fashion in Syria and Iraq. Algeria and Tunisia also have several good directors and some studios. But in these countries the cinema is subject to strict political and cultural control. Algerian directors sometimes shoot on location in Algeria with local actors, and then transfer actors and non-edited film to France for the studio shooting and technical work. Co-production Algero-Français is often seen on the credits: in some ways this is useful, but it means that if French facilities were not available it would be necessary to find them elsewhere.

Egypt turns out vast quantities of popular films, some of which give genuine insight into Egyptian life, and others which are very funny. But most are of the 'soap opera' type, well known on British and American TV.

A SHORT BOOKLIST ON THE MIDDLE EAST

HISTORY

Carleton Coon, *Caravan* (Jonathan Cape)

Philip K. Hitti, *History of the Arabs* (Macmillan)

A.H. Hourani, *Minorities in the Arab World* (Royal Institute of International Affairs)

George Antonius, *The Arab Awakening*

GEOGRAPHY

W.B. Fisher, *The Middle East* (Methuen)

A.K. Hatem, *Land of the Arabs* (Longman)

S.H. Longrigg and J. Jankowski, *The Middle East—A Social Geography* (Duckworth)

K.E.M. Melville, *Stay Alive in the Desert* (Jerboa Press)

RELIGION

A.J. Arberry, *Religion in the Middle East*, in two volumes (Cambridge University Press)

Kenneth Cragg, *The Call of the Minaret* (Galaxy)

Gibb and Kramers, *The Shorter Encyclopaedia of Islam* (Brill)

Alfred Guillaume, *Islam* (Penguin)

P.M. Holt, *The Cambridge History of Islam*, In two volumes (Cambridge University Press)

Bernard Lewis, *Islam*, in two volumes (Torchbooks—Harper and Row)

Seyyid Hossein Nasr, *The Holy Koran* (Allahabad University)

M.M. Pickthall, *The Meaning of the Glorious Koran* (Mentor Books, New American Library)

F. Schuon, *Islam and the Perennial Philosophy* (World of Islam Publishing Co.)

ART AND CULTURE

A.J. Arberry, *Aspects of Islamic Civilization*

A.J. Arberry, *Modern Arabic Poetry* (Cambridge University Press)

Sir T.W. Arnold, *Painting in Islam* (Dover Publications)

L. Binyon, J.U.S. Wilkinson & Basil Gray, *Persian Miniature Painting* (Oxford 1933)

Titus Burckhardt, *The Art of Islam: Language and Meaning* (World of Islam Festival Press)

K.A.C. Creswell, *Early Muslim architecture*, in three volumes (Oxford University Press)

Ernst Kuhnel, *Islamic Arts* (G. Bell)

Issam el Said and Ayse Parman, *Geometric Concepts in Islamic Art* (World of Islam Festival Press)

Claudia Roden, *Middle Eastern Cooking* (Penguin)

Charles Doughty, *Arabia Deserta*

T.E. Lawrence, *The Seven Pillars of Wisdom*

Ronald Storrs, *Orientations*

THE GULF STATES—GENERAL

A.M. Abu Hakimia, *History of Eastern Arabia 1750-1800: The rise and Development of Bahrain and Kuwait* (Khayat—Beirut)

H.R.P. Dickson, *The Arab of the Desert* (Allen and Unwin)

Fred Halliday, *Arabia without Sultans* (Pelican)

Sir Rupert Hay, *The Persian Gulf States* (Middle East Institute, Washington)

David Holden, *Farewell to Arabia*

D. Hopwood, *The Arabian Peninsula: Society and Politics* (Allen and Unwin)

J.B. Kelly, *Eastern Arabian Frontiers* (Faber and Faber)

P. Kilner, J. Wallace, and S. Milmo, *The Gulf Handbook 1978* (Travel and Trade Publications with MEED)

S.H. Longrigg, *Oil in the Middle East*

Wilfred Thesiger, *Arabian Sands* (Penguin)

Sir A.T. Wilson, *The Persian Gulf* (Oxford University Press)

CYPRUS

Alastos Zeno, *Cyprus in History: A Survey of 5,000 Years*

Lawrence Durrell, *Bitter Lemons* (Faber)

Sir Harry Luke, *Cyprus under the Turks 1571-1878* (C. Hurst)

Meyer and Vassilliou, *The Economy of Cyprus* (Harvard University Press)

Nagel Guide

EGYPT

I.E.S. Edwards, *The Pyramids of Egypt* (Penguin)

Sir Alan Gardiner, *Egypt of the Pharaohs* (Oxford University Press)

Alan Moorehead, *The White Nile* (Penguin)

J.C.B. Richmond, *Egypt 1798-1952: Her Advance Towards a Modern Identity* (Methuen)

Fodor Guide

IRAN

W.B. Fisher, *The Cambridge History of Iran* (Cambridge University Press)

R. Ghirshman, *Iran from the Earliest Times to the Islamic Conquests* (Penguin)

Jean Hureau, *Iran Today* (Jeune Afrique)

James Morris and Denis Wright, *Persia*

Antony Smith, *Blind White Fish in Persia* (Allen and Unwin)

Guy le Strange and R.A. Nicholson, *The Lands of the Eastern Caliphate: Mesopotamia, Persia and Central Asia* (F. Cass)

IRAQ

S.H. Longrigg, *Four Centuries of Modern Iraq*

Georges Roux, *Ancient Iraq*

F.H. Seton Lloyd, *Twin Rivers: A Brief History of Iraq from the Earliest Times to the Present Day* (Oxford)

Wilfred Thesiger, *The Marsh Arabs* (Penguin)

JORDAN

Sir Alexander Kennedy, *Petra: Its History and Monuments*

Leon de Laborde, *Journey through Arabia Petraea*

G.Lankester Harding, *The Antiquities of Jordan*

F.G. Peake, *History of Jordan and its Tribes*

Bahaeddine Toukan, *A Short History of Jordan*

LEBANON

Bruce Condé, *See Lebanon* (Beirut 1960)

Dar al Machreq, *Byblos Through the Ages* (Beirut)

Dar al Machreq, *Roman Temples of Lebanon* (Beirut)

Dar al Machreq, *Sidon* (Beirut)

Dar al Machreq, *Tyre* (Beirut)

P.K. Hitti, *Lebanon in History* (Macmillan)

Raymond Morineau, *Lebanon Today* (Jeune Afrique)

Georges Rayess, *Art of Lebanese Cooking*

LIBYA

Ruth First, *Libya: The Elusive Revolution* (Penguin)

S.A. Hajjaji, *The New Libya*

R. Owen, *Libya: A Brief Political and Economic Survey*

Philip Ward, *Touring Libya*

MOROCCO

Samir Amin, *The Maghreb in the Modern World* (Penguin)

E.W. Bovill, *The Golden Trade of the Moors*

Jean Hureau, *Le Maroc Aujourd'hui* (Jeune Afrique)

C. Kininmonth, *Traveller's Guide to Morocco* (Jonathan Cape)

Rom Landau, *The Moroccan Drama 1900-55* (Hale)

Gavin Maxwell, *Lords of the Atlas* (Longmans)

SAUDI ARABIA

G.C. Armstrong, *Lord of Arabia*

S. Benoist Méchin, *Ibn Séoud ou la Naissance d'un Royaume* (Albin Michel, Paris)

D. Van der Meulen, *The Wells of Ibn Saud*

Karl S. Twitchell and Edward J. Jurji, *Saudi Arabia* (Princeton)

R.Bayly, *Saudi Arabia in the 19th Century* (R. Bayly Winder)

SYRIA

Gertrude Bell, *The Desert and the Sown* (Aris & Phillips)

Robin Fedden, *Syria and Lebanon* (John Murray)

Jean Hureau, *Syria Today* (Jeune Afrique)

Patrick Seale, *The Struggle for Syria*

A.L. Tibawi, *A Modern History of Syria*

TURKEY

H. Frankfort, *Art and Architecture of the Ancient Orient* (Pelican)

Lord Kinross, *Europa Minor* (John Murray)

C. Mair, *A Time in Turkey* (John Murray)

James Mellaart, *Catal Huyuk* (Thames and Hudson)

Dux Schneider, *Traveller's Guide to Turkey* (Cape 1975)

YEMEN ARAB REPUBLIC

H. Ingrams, *The Yemen: Imams, Rulers and Revolutions*

Edgar O'Ballance, *The War in the Yemen* (Faber)

H. Scott, *In the High Yemen* (John Murray)

M.W. Wenner, *Modern Yemen 1918-66* (John Hopkins Press Baltimore)

YEMEN PEOPLE'S DEMOCRATIC REPUBLIC

Doreen Ingrams, *A Survey of the Social and Economic Conditions of the Aden Protectorate*

Harold Ingrams, *Arabia and the Isles* (John Murray)

G. Lankester Harding, *Archaeology in the Aden Protectorate* (Her Majesty's Stationery Office)

Tom Little, *South Arabia* (Pall Mall Press)

D. Van der Meulen, *Hadramaut, Some of its Mysteries Unveiled*

We'll show you around Africa

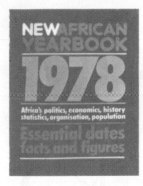

NEW AFRICAN YEARBOOK (1st Edition)

($25 Includes free colour wall map of Africa)

An indispensable reference work containing:—
- Up to date statistics
- Articles on Africa's Geography, History, Politics & Economy
- African Organizations
- Africa & the World
- Country by Country Section

This hardback volume of over 250 pages is packed with information about one of the most important areas of the World.

TRAVELLERS GUIDE TO AFRICA
(2nd Edition)
(available in English or French)

($15 Includes free colour wall map of Africa)

The comprehensive pocket guide for the traveller & tourist containing:—
- Tourist information
- Places to visit & how to get there
- Charts, Maps, Photographs
- Culture, Climate, Holidays
- Main cities, Transport, Banks, Accommodation etc.

This 'limp-cloth cover' guide has over 420 pages of essential travel information about Africa.

Available From:—

INTERNATIONAL COMMUNICATIONS

63 Long Acre, London WC2E 9JH
Tel: 01 836 8731 Telex: 8811757
Cables: Machrak London WC2

51

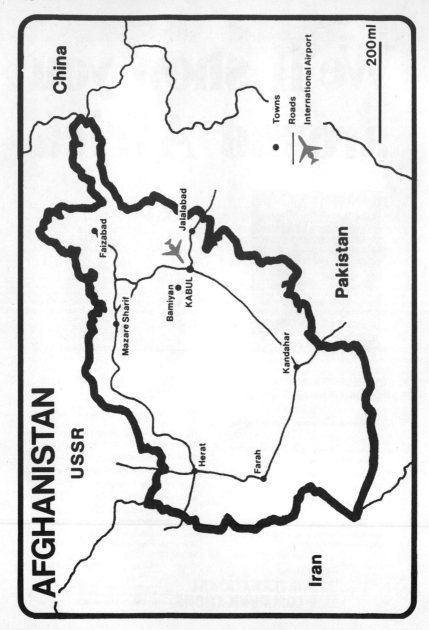

AFGHANISTAN

Considered one of the most stimulating and friendly countries on the Asian Highway, Afghanistan is now attracting thousands of visitors every year, not just those passing through on their way elsewhere but those wanting to study and explore an ancient and beautiful country.

On the trans-Asia journey Kabul is an excellent place to rest and eat well, although it is inevitably becoming increasingly commercialised. However, commerce has been thriving in Kabul for over 3,000 years, as a result of its position as 'gateway' between East and West. Its bustling bazaars have not changed in character; they merely have more merchandise than ever before, from all over the world and still at bargain prices.

There are other towns that retain their traditional character more completely than Kabul. Those most popular with visitors are Jalalabad, Kandahar, Mazare Sharif and Herat. The remote but astonishing historical sites of Bamiyan and the 'Minaret of Jam' make a difficult drive, being well off the Asian Highway, but they are worth the trouble of getting there. There are of course air services to most tourist sites.

Situated between the Iranian mountains and plains to the west and the Himalayan mountain system to the east, Afghanistan consists of a complex of mountain ranges that grow higher and steeper towards the east. Furthest east are the mountains known collectively as the Hindu Kush, with an average altitude of 4,000 metres.

Scattered throughout Afghanistan are areas of thriving agriculture and comparatively high population. These include the lush mountain valleys, the river basins, the stream-fed plains and the fertile 'lowlands' around Jalalabad. There are also deserts and semi-deserts, particularly in Bactria in the north and Registan in the west, both the traditional haunts of nomads.

The Afghani population contains great ethnic variety, illustrating the country's position throughout history as a 'crossroads of Asia'. In the centre of the country the Pashtuns predominate; other groups are the Ghilzais, the Uzbeks, the Tadzhiks, the Hazara, the Chahar Aimak and the Nuristanis. Some of these peoples are related to the Persians, others to the Turks and still others to the Mongols. Perhaps the longest-established indigenous group is the Nuristani.

People have made their living in Afghanistan over the centuries either as settled subsistence farmers or as pastoral nomads. In every case the identity of the different peoples has remained strong to this day and the way of life has not changed greatly. Agriculture is still the mainstay of the economy, although there is much commerce and a growing industrial sector. Natural gas is being produced and other mining activity may follow.

HISTORICAL SUMMARY

BC1500-600	Home of nomadic and pastoral peoples. Afghanistan already known as the 'Crossroads of Asia'.
600-330	Afghanistan is the easternmost province of the Achaemenid Empire of Darius I.
327-300	Alexander enters Afghanistan, subduing the Empire of Darius III.
300-AD 48	Afghanistan under the influence of Hellenism through the Seleucid Empire.
AD 48-241	The Kushan Empire centered at Kapisa. Establishment of the 'Silk Route' through Afghanistan. Greco-Buddhism flourishes.
241-962	A period of confusion, followed by the advance of Islam into Afghanistan.
962-1186	The Ghaznavid Empire. Its summer capital at Ghazni and winter capital at Bost (Lashkargah) become great centres of fine arts and poetry.
1186-1220	The Ghorid dynasty displaces the Ghaznavid Empire and destroys Ghazni.
1220-1332	Genghis Khan rides across Afghanistan.
1364-1506	Tamerlane conquers Afghanistan; a period of refinement and construction of its capital, Herat.
1506-1709	Babur establishes the Moghul dynasty from Kabul.
circa 1747	Ahmad Shah Durrani initiates the modern State of Afghanistan at Kandahar.

1826-1863	Amir Dost Mohammed. First Anglo-Afghan War (1839-1842).
1863-1878	Era of Amir Sher Ali.
1878-1879	Second Anglo-Afghan War (Amir Mohammad Yakub).
1880-1901	Amir Abdur Rahman works to centralise the Government at Kabul.
1901-1919	Amir Habibullah, a period of relative calm. Start of modern development.
1919-1929	King Amanullah. Third Anglo-Afghan War, full recognition of Afghanistan's independence and striving for modernisation.
1929	Amanullah abdicates because of a revolt led by Bacha Saqao.
1929-1933	King Nadir Shah rescues the country from anarchy.
1933-1973	Reign of Mohammed Zahir Shah, son of Nadir Shah.
1973	17 July, Monarchy overthrown, Proclamation of Republic under the leadership of Mohammad Daoud.
1977	First Loya Girgah (Grand National Assembly) of the Republic and election of Mohammad Daoud as the first president.

GENERAL INFORMATION

Area: 720,000 sq. km.
Population: 18 million.
Capital: Kabul.
Head of State: President Mohammed Daoud.
Government: Republican.
Languages: Pashtu (national language), Dari (a form of Persian). Many people have some knowledge of English.
Religion: Islam.
Currency: Afghan, divided into 100 puls. £1 sterling=Af.80. $1=Af.45.
Time: GMT + 4½.

HOW TO GET THERE

By air: Ariana Afghan Airlines is Afghanistan's international airline, with flights from London, Amsterdam, Paris, Frankfurt, Rome, Istanbul, Moscow, Damascus, Teheran and New Delhi. Other airlines serving Kabul are Aeroflot, Air India, Iran Air and PIA.

By road: The Asian Highway runs 1,400 km. through Afghanistan from West to East, curving through the southern part of the country from Islam Qala and Herat, through Kandahar, where it turns north-east towards Ghazni and Kabul. After Kabul the Highway climbs to Jalalabad, Torkham and the Khyber Pass into Pakistan. There is a southern alternative route into Pakistan, which may be preferable in mid-winter. The only other main roads entering the country are from the Soviet Union. All vehicles entering Afghanistan require third party insurance coverage; policies can be obtained at border posts.

Visas and health regulations

All visitors to Afghanistan require a tourist visa, which is valid for one month and may be obtained from Afghan embassies or consulates abroad or on arrival at Kabul Airport. A visa costs about US$5. It may be renewed in Kabul only twice, each time for one month. Tourists arriving by land may obtain visas at the Afghan embassies in Teheran or Islamabad. Tourists are required to fill in registration forms at each hotel they stay in, or to register with police if staying in private homes.

Tourists must have a valid smallpox vaccination certificate.

Currency and customs regulations

All foreign currency carried into Afghanistan must be declared. The declaration must be shown when currencies are changed at banks, and the remaining amounts have to be declared on departure.

Duty-free items for tourists entering Afghanistan include most personal goods, but cars, cameras, radios, tape recorders, etc., have to be registered. Visitors may take out without paying duty 30 sq. metres of carpet, 10 skins, precious stones, handicrafts and some antiques, as long as the antiques have export approval from Kabul Museum.

CLIMATE

There are extreme variations of temperature throughout the year and in different regions. The summers are generally hot and dry, while winters are cold and wet. Kabul has a pleasant climate, being not excessively hot in summer.

ACCOMMODATION AND FOOD

Most towns of any size have some form of comfortable accommodation. In some isolated areas hotels are run by the provincial government.

In Kabul there is varied accommodation, from the luxury Intercontinental to reasonably-priced second-class hotels and some rudimentary but cheap lodgings.

Most of the modern restaurants in Kabul offer both international dishes and a wide variety of Afghan specialities, including pilaws, kebabs, bolani and ashak. Throughout the country are *chaikhanas*, which serve traditional food and tea at reasonable prices.

SHOPPING, HANDICRAFTS AND ENTERTAINMENTS

Among Afghanistan's best-known products are lamb fur and suede leather jackets and coats, Turkman hats, Kandahar embroidery, Istalif pottery, rustic glassware from Herat, nomad jewellery, handwoven carpets and rugs, Nuristani woodcarving, silkware, brass, copper and silver work and antique weapons.

Traditional Afghan music and dances and sporting events always appeal to visitors, but perhaps the most spectacular is the Buzkashi horse sport, which is unique to Afghanistan. Buzkashi reflects a fierce equestrian tradition and dates back to the time of Alexander the Great. In Kabul Buzkashi is played in late October when some of the finest teams from the north compete in the Ghazi stadium. At the Afghan New Year a 10-day Buzkashi festival is held in Kunduz.

TRANSPORT

By air: The local airline is Bakhtar Afghan Airlines, which flies regularly from Kabul to Bamiyan, Herat, Kandahar, Mazare Sharif, Kunduz and other centres. It also provides charter services. The sales office of the airline is at Hotel Kabul, tel: 24451.

By road: The only paved roads in Afghanistan are the Asian Highway and roads north from Kabul to Kunduz and Mazare Sharif. The condition of the other roads varies according to the season, spring and early summer being the most difficult times to travel. Tourist offices usually have information on the condition of these roads.

There are regular bus services to most towns, run by a variety of companies. There are also minibuses, and it is possible to hitch-hike.

Taxi fares are reasonable in the main towns.

BANKING HOURS

Summer: 08.00-12.00, 13.00-16.30, closed Thursday afternoon and Friday.

Winter: 09.00-12.00, 13.00-15.30, closed Thursday afternoon and Friday.

EMBASSIES IN KABUL

Austria, Bangladesh, Bulgaria, China (P.R.), Czechoslovakia, Egypt, France, West Germany, India, Indonesia, Iran, Iraq, Italy, Japan, North Korea, South Korea, Libya, Pakistan, Poland, Saudi Arabia, Turkey, UK, USA, USSR, Yugoslavia.

TOURIST OFFICES

Afghantour, branches at Hotel Intercontinental and Hotel Kabul and head office at Kabul Salang Watt. Handles reservations, travel arrangements, package tours, scenic tours and special activities, including mountaineering, trekking and fishing. Sales: tel: 24464. Reservations: tel: 20380.

KABUL

Kabul, capital of Afghanistan since 1776, is a fast-growing city where tall modern buildings nuzzle against bustling bazaars, wide avenues are filled with colourful flowing turbans, gaily striped chapans and a multitude of handsome faces. The city is ringed with mountains gleaming emerald green in spring and glistening white in winter. In summer they have an ever-changing beauty turning from deep purple to brilliant pink under the rising and setting sun. Two craggy ranges crowned with ancient bastions divide the city, and the Kabul river flows through a narrow pass between them to meander through the heart of the city.

Places of interest
Rising above the plain, the Bala Hissar citadel served for centuries as the seat of the rulers of Afghanistan until 1880,

ALFRED GREGORY, CAMERA PRESS

A street bazaar in Kabul

when it was destroyed during the Second Anglo-Afghan War. Amir Abdur Rahman (1880-1901) built the Arg (palace) to replace the Bala Hissar palaces. Within the Arg are the Salam Khana (Hall of Salutation) and the Dilkosha Palace (Heart's Delight). It now houses the Presidential Offices. The ancient walls of Kabul begin at Bala Hissar. They are seven metres high and three metres thick and date from the Hephthalite period (fifth century).

A charming landmark of the city is the mausoleum of Amir Abdur Rahman, one of Afghanistan's most dynamic rulers. It stands in Zarengar Park, in the centre of the city as a fine example of 19th century architecture. The imposing white-marbled, blue-domed mausoleum of Nadir Shah stands on the hill known as Tapa Maranjan overlooking Kabul. A graceful, many-domed palace, known as Baghe Bala, glimmers on a hill to the north of the city. it was built as a summer residence and now houses a distinguished restaurant specialising in traditional Afghan food.

Babhur's Gardens, laid out by the founder of the Moghul Dynasty, in the middle of the 16th century, include a summer pavilion added by Amir Abdur Rahman, a commemorative mosque built by the Emperor Shah Jahan and the tomb of Babhur himself.

The National Museum at Darulaman contains an impressive collection of artifacts, illustrating Afghanistan's past from prehistory to modern times.

Kabul has many interesting mosques. The most famous in the centre of the city are: Masjide Pule Khesti, Masjide Shahe Du Shamshira, Masjide Sherpur (Blue Mosque), Masjide Id Gah and Masjide Sayed Majnun Shah.

Hotels

Hotel Inter-Continental, Baghe Bala Road, Kabul, tel: 31851, cable: Inhotelcor, 200 rooms, restaurants, swimming pool, etc.

Hotel Kabul, central, tel: 24750.
Hotel Spinzar, central, tel: 22961.
Park Hotel, central, tel: 25202.
Hotel Metropol, tel: 26061.
Yama Hotel, central, tel: 26509.
Hotel Ariana, camping and parking.
There are many cheaper hotels, such as the **Mustafa, Sina, Noor,** etc.

AROUND KABUL

ISTALIF: Istalif lies north of Kabul in the Koh Daman, a valley ringed by barren hills dotted with villages nestling in green orchards. It is one of the biggest, most ancient and loveliest valleys of all. Istalif is famous for its green and blue pottery and its picturesque bazaar. A visit to this place combines a view of beautiful scenery with an introduction to Afghan village life.

KABUL GORGE: Afghanistan is a country of impressive gorges and the Kabul Gorge (Tange Gharu) is the most spectacular. Three km. of switchback roads lead down to the foot, giving a full experience of the gorge's ruggedness.

GULDARA STUPA: An interesting historic site of the fourth century standing on a platform having a square base with Corinthian columns; statues once occupied the niches. The walls present a fine example of Kushan workmanship known as diaper masonry.

PAGHMAN: Paghman is the most favoured summer resort of Kabul. The imposing victory arch, standing in the central square, was built by King Amanullah in commemoration of the War of Independence in 1919. The road passes by the Baghe Umumi (Public Garden). Returning to Kabul, one passes Kargha Lake with the Spozhmay (Moonlight) restaurant and the Kabul Golf Course.

GHAZNI

An important market town, particularly famous for embroidered sheepskin coats, Ghazni was from 994-1160 the capital of the Ghaznavid Empire, encompassing much of northern India, Persia and Central Asia. Many campaigns into India were launched from here, resulting in the spread of Islam to the East. This glorious city was razed to the ground by Arab invaders in 869, by the Ghorid Sultan Alauddin in 1151 and by Genghis Khan in 1221. The city did not recover its former grandeur, but it enjoys a strategic position in the country's economy.

The citadel was one of the most imposing fortresses in Afghanistan, until destroyed during the First Anglo-Afghan War. It was rebuilt, but never to its previous splendour. The Palace of Sultan Masoud III was the very centre of the Ghaznavid court, a vast complex including a throne room, government offices, soldiers' quarters, a mosque with its minarets and pockets of gardens in addition to the royal apartments.

The two remaining minarets, built by Sultan Masoud III (1099-1114) and Bahram Shah (1118-1152) and now only a fraction of their original height, served as models for the spectacular tower of Jam, which in turn inspired the Qutob Minar at Delhi. The intricate decoration is in raised brick and includes epigraphic friezes in square Kufic and Noshki script, in addition to panels of floral and geometric designs. That of Sultan Masoud is more elaborate.

Hotel Ghazni

KANDAHAR

Kandahar, the birthplace and first capital of modern Afghanistan, founded by Amad Shah Durrani in 1747, is today the second-biggest city of Afghanistan, located on the Asian Highway halfway between Kabul and Herat. The area is rich in ancient history. Here, Alexander the Great founded Alexandria of Arachosia and the region was repeatedly fought over by the Saffavids and Moghuls. It was the independent-minded Afghans of Kandahar, first under the leadership of Mir Wais and then of Ahmad Shah Durrani, who hastened the decline of both empires and annexed much of their territories to the young Afghan Kingdom in the 18th century.

To the south-west of Kandahar are Lashkargah and Bost. From the 11th until mid-12th century Bost prospered as the winter capital of the Ghaznavids, but it was burned and looted in 1151 by the Ghorids and then demolished by Genghis Khan in 1220. Today the remains of the great palace of Masoud still give the visitor an idea of the splendour of the court of what was then the greatest empire of the East. The most remarkable monument is the magnificently decorated arch.

Hotels
Hotel Kandahar, Kandahar.

Hotel Ahmad Shah Baba, Kandahar, tel: 2839.
Hotel Bost, Lashkargah.

HERAT

The history of Herat has been one of repeated destruction and reconstruction. Conqueror after conqueror, from the time of Alexander the Great, has taken it, destroyed it and then rebuilt it. In the 4th century B.C. Alexander the Great built the fort which still stands in the centre of the city. From 1040 to 1175 the city was ruled by the Seljuks, who defeated the Ghaznavids and destroyed the fortress. Herat was then captured by the Ghorids and held until it fell under the control of the Khwarazm Empire. In 1221 Herat was taken by the Mongols, and Tuli, son of Genghis Khan, ruled it for a time, but the citizens revolted and killed the Mongol garrison. In revenge Genghis Khan rode upon the city with 80,000 troops and besieged it for six months,

leaving only 40 people living. In 1245 Herat was given to the Kart Maliks. Tamerlane destroyed Herat in 1381 but his son, Shah Rukh, rebuilt it and started the cultural renaissance which made it a centre of learning and culture. During the Timurid rule, the famous poet of Herat, Jami, and the miniaturist Behzad were born, Queen Gawhar Shad's Musalla was built and Gazergah restored. For the second time the city flourished. In 1718 the Afghan clan Hotaki struggled for Herat's independence, which continued until 1880, when finally the city became an integral part of Afghanistan.

Places of interest
The citadel, originally built by Alexander the Great, suffered repeated attacks but still dominates the landscape of Herat. The great mosque, Masjide Jami, in the centre of the city has been a place of worship since the time of Zoroaster. It has been rebuilt several times, and now stands in splendour since its most recent restoration.

Part of the Hindu Kush mountain range

Today only six of the original 12 minarets remain of Queen Gawhar Shad's great Musalla complex, built in the late 1400s. It was the Queen's contribution to the Timurid Empire during a period of cultural accomplishments. It consisted of a madrassa, or place of learning, and a musalla, or place of worship. These magnificent buildings flanked by the minarets were described at one time as the most imposing and eloquent structures to be seen in all Asia.

Herat's bazaars are full of fascination and colour and were once an important trading centre on the caravan route from Europe to China. Today, items of interest to visitors include the famous handwoven Herati carpets and the beautiful and rustic blue glass produced by the traditional glass blowers of the city.

Hotels
Hotel Herat.
Mowafaq Hotel.
Cheap hotels include **Pardees, Jami** and **Kair.**

THE ROAD TO BALKH

The road to Balkh crosses the Hindu Kush by the Salang Pass through the highest tunnel in the world (3,363 m.). A drive over this pass offers, besides scenic beauty, a thrilling experience of high altitude.

En route about 240 km. from Kabul (12 km. from Pule Khumri) lies Surkh Kotal, site of a famous temple, founded in 130 AD by Kanishka the Great, King of the Kushans, and burned by the Hephthalites, nomadic rivals and the ultimate successors to the Kushans. 70 km. farther north lies Aibak, the capital of the Samangan province. 2 km. away is an important Buddhist site, dating from the 4th century, and locally known as Takhte Rustam (Rustam's Throne).

60 km. north lies Tashkurghan (Kulm) with one of the last traditional Central

Asian covered bazaars left in Afghanistan. The large domed Tim Bazaar is of special interest. So are the Bala Hissar, the charming palace of Amir Abdur Rhman (Baghe Jahan Numa) and the tomb of Qilich Ali Beg, the most notable ruler of Khulm (1786-1817).

ALFRED GREGORY, CAMERA PRESS

Shrine of Hazarate Ali, at Mazare Sharif

MAZARE SHARIF

Mazare Sharif, the capital of Balkh province, is a major trading centre famous for karakul, a great variety of traditional Turkman carpets and high quality, long-staple cotton. The city is named after the magnificent shrine of Hazarate Ali, cousin and son-in-law of the Prophet Muhammad and the Fourth Caliph of Islam. Hazarate Ali was assassinated in 661 and buried at Kufa, near Baghdad.

Mazare Sharif is visited by countless pilgrims throughout the year, and particularly on Nawroz when the great Janda (religious banner) is raised to announce the beginning of spring and the coming of the New Year, which is the most elaborately celebrated festival in Afghanistan.

Hotels
Hotel Mazar.
Hotel Caravan Saray, for reservations contact Caravan Travels, P.O. Box 3043, Kabul, tel: 31113.

BALKH

Balkh, today only a small town, is famous for its glorious past. Zoroaster preached here sometime between 1000 and 600 BC. Rites celebrated at the shrine to Anahita, Goddess of the Oxus, attracted thousands during the fifth century, and Alexander the Great chose it for his base in the fourth century BC. Under the Kushans, when Buddhism was practised throughout Afghanistan, many temples flourished in Balkh. The Arabs called Balkh the mother of cities. By the ninth century AD, during the rule of the Samanid Dynasty, about 40 Friday Mosques stood within the city.

Balkh was the home of Rabia Balkhi, the first woman poet of the Islamic period, and of Mauwlana Jalaluddin Balkhi (Rumi), perhaps the most distinguished Sufi poet. His Masnawi is considered the greatest poem ever written in the Persian language. Balkh's glorious history closed in 1220 when the men of Genghis Khan rode through and left it devastated. The city, nevertheless, lying on an important trade route, recovered under the rule of Shah Rukh and his Queen Gawhar Shad, of Herat.

JALALABAD

Jalalabad lies 150 km. east of Kabul, the road passing Kabul Gorge, and Naghlu, Sarobi and Darunta Lakes. The capital of

Masjede Sabz Mausoleum at Balkh

Ningrahar province is an oasis ringed by mountains. Palaces, large gardens and tree-lined avenues speak of its long history as a favoured winter capital. Today hundreds of small villas indicate its popularity as a resort. Among many festivities taking place in this city, the most famous are the Mushaira or Poet's festival, dedicated to Jalalabad's orange blossoms, and Waisak, a Hindu religious festival.

Eleven kilometres south of the city lies Hadda, one of the most sacred places of the Buddhist world, dating from the second to the seventh century AD, and built on a site visited by Buddha.

Countless pilgrims came from every corner of the earth to worship at its many holy temples, maintained by thousands of monks and priests living in large monastery complexes. This important archaeological site is still under excavation. Much of it has been turned into an open air museum.

NURISTAN

Nuristan refers to the area of Laghman

61

and Ningrahar inhabited by approximately 600,000 Nuristanis. The area covers five main and numerous side valleys, inhabited by separate tribes speaking their own languages, which in many cases are mutually unintelligible and are grouped under the name Dardic, within the Indo-European language family.

There are many physical and cultural differences between the people of Nuristan and those living around them. Language is one. The fact that they prefer stools and chairs to a rug on the floor is another obvious difference. Nuristani music is quite distinct, as are their instruments, among which the harp is the most noticeable. Alexander the Great invited the young men to join his army for the Indian campaign, and they proved their fighting quality with distinction. Many so-called Greek motifs and customs found in the Nuristani culture may well date from this experience.

Throughout the centuries that followed, the people of these mountains defied conquest and conversion even as Buddhism and Hinduism were replaced by Islam on the plains below. The Muslims labelled them 'Kafirs' because they worshipped a wide pantheon of nature spirits and practised other customs incompatible with the Muslim religion. In 1895 the army of Amir Abdur Rahman finally succeeded in subduing the Kafirs and converting them to Islam. When his victorious army arrived in Kabul, the Amir announced that henceforth Kafiristan (Land of the Infidels) was to be known as Nuristan (Land of Light).

A large part of Nuristan is inaccessible to all but foot travellers, for the trails are difficult and precipitous and the narrow bridges, 10 m. and more above angry frothing waters cannot be negotiated by horses.

Almost all Nuristani villages are built on high peaks. The houses spill over the mountainside, the roof of one serving as the front porch and playground of the house above. Children play vigorous games on these roofs, hanging precariously over precipices.

BAMIYAN

Bamiyan, with its archaeological remains, is the most conspicuous tourist site of Afghanistan. The village lies about 2,500 m. above sea level, 240 km. west of Kabul, and attracts thousands of visitors annually. The exquisite beauty of this valley is embraced by the snow-capped Kohe Baba mountains in the south and in the north by steep cliffs in which massive images of Buddha are carved.

The area of Bamiyan developed under Kanishka the Great to become a major commercial and religious centre and the smaller statue of Buddha (38 m. high) was built during his reign. Two centuries later the colossal Buddha statue (55 m. high) was carved. Thousands of ornamented caves, inhabited by yellow-robed monks, extended into Folladi and Kakrak valley, where a smaller statue of Buddha (6.5 m.) stands. Pilgrims from all over the Buddhist world poured into Bamiyan. Bamiyan fell to the Islamic conquerors in the ninth century, but the Islamic city of Bamiyan was destroyed by Genghis Khan in 1221 in revenge for the death of his grandson Mutugen. The ruins of the citadel, called the city of noise, still give evidence of its magnitude before the Mongol devastation.

The beautiful and lush Ajar valley edged by picturesque mountains of fascinating formations and ever-changing colours, has a sparkling clear stream, full of trout, leading into a breathtaking chasm.

Hotel
Bamiyan Hotel, contact Afghantour, Kabul, tel: 20380.

BANDE AMIR

Of all the natural wonders of Afghani-

Afghani women collecting water

stan, the blue lakes of Bande Amir are perhaps the most outstanding. They are situated in the mountainous Hazarajat at an altitude of approximately 3,000 m. and are 75 km. from Bamiyan.

MINARET OF JAM

The central route from Kabul to Herat is a fascinating experience but should be undertaken only by adventurous travellers. Passing the first highlights, Bamiyan and Bande Amir, this route leads via Panjaw to Chaghcharan, the capital of the Ghor province. The road continues via Sharak towards the north, where in a lonely, remote valley, closely surrounded by barren mountains stands the 65m high Minaret of Jam, on the southern bank of the Hari Rod River. This is the only well preserved architectural monument from the Ghorid period. En route to Herat, the Ghorid tombs of Cheste Sharif and

the hot mineral springs of Obe are favoured stops.

TREKKING

For the tourist who has grown weary of the usual package tours and wishes to see more of a country than the standard 'tourist attractions', Afghanistan has almost unlimited appeal. Much of the country's life and travel occurs off the main highways and along the numerous trails and paths which serve even the remotest rural areas. This is the domain of the horse, the donkey or the camel—and the trekker.

Recommended itineraries are: Bamiyan—Sayghan—Bande Amir; Bamiyan—Ajar Valley—Bande Amir; Panjsher—Mirsamir—Panjsher; Panjsher—Anjoman—Jurm; Panjsher—Anjoman—Zebak.

Advice is obtainable from the Afghan Tourist Organisation.

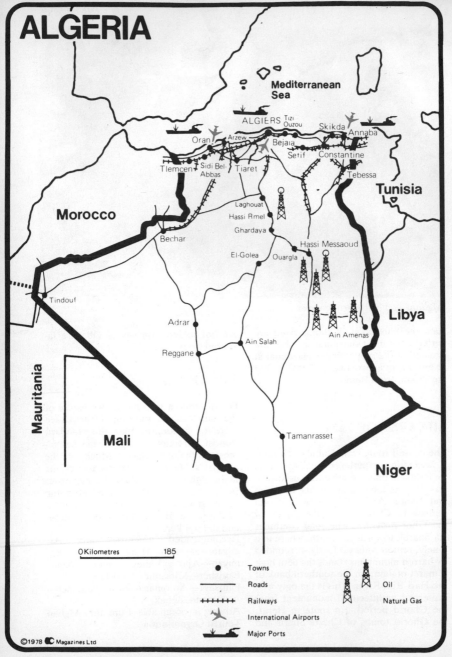

ALGERIA

Mediterranean Sea

ALGIERS
Tizi Ouzou
Skikda
Annaba
Oran
Arzew
Bejaia
Setif
Constantine
Tlemcen
Sidi Bel-Abbas
Tiaret
Tebessa

Tunisia

Morocco

Laghouat
Hassi Rmel
Ghardaya
Hassi Messaoud
Bechar
El-Golea
Ouargla

Libya

Tindouf

Adrar

Ain Salah
Ain Amenas

Reggane

Mauritania

Mali

Tamanrasset

Niger

0 Kilometres 185

●	Towns
—	Roads
++++++	Railways
✈	International Airports
⬇	Major Ports
♀	Oil
🗼	Natural Gas

©1978 C Magazines Ltd

64

ALGERIA

Perhaps because of its commitment to socialism, Algeria has the reputation of not encouraging tourism. It has certainly not rushed into the mass package-tour market, or permitted the mushrooming beach resorts and lack of proper planning that have afflicted so many Mediterranean tourist centres, but it does have a flourishing tourist industry and can boast at least as many attractions for the visitor as its better-known neighbours Morocco and Tunisia.

Hundreds of thousands of foreign visitors enter Algeria each year and the figure is steadily rising as the country's reputation grows and facilities expand. The Algerian National Tourist Office advertises the country on the strength of its 'sun, sea and Sahara' but there is much more to it than that. Geography and history have modelled Algeria into a country that is at one and the same time African, Oriental and Mediterranean. Its vast expanse of two million square kilometres embraces an astonishing variety of peoples, cultures and landscapes.

The 1,000 km. of Mediterranean coast shelter beaches, villages and towns with names of Berber, Phoenician, Latin and Arabic origin. Behind these tower the mountains of Kabylia, Aures and Ouarsenis, covered with cedars, pines and cypresses. The plateaux and highlands are separated by broad plains and rich farmlands.

Beyond the Atlas mountain ranges lies the Sahara, with its endless expanses of dunes, pebble wastelands and barren rocky mountains. The Sahara was populated by a succession of peoples who have left fascinating relics of their civilisations and their means of livelihood; there is evidence that huge herds of game once roamed the plains.

A cornerstone of national policy is that the Sahara should be opened up, for the exploitation of both oil and tourism. A tarred road being pushed southwards towards Tamanrasset will enable large numbers of tourists to experience one of the world's most terrifying terrains in safety and comfort. At present Saharan travel is an undeniably hazardous undertaking, even with the most painstaking precautions.

Those who can afford air travel, however, are already assured quick and easy service into the deepest Sahara. For example from the beautiful oasis of Djanet tourists can explore the eerie Tassili plateau—known as 'the largest open-air museum in the world' for its innumerable rock paintings and engravings.

The northern Sahara has been easily reached for many years, by good roads and in some places by rail. An excellent circuit can be made by way of the oases of Laghouat, Ghardaia, Ouargla, Touggourt and Biskra. This takes one through the fascinating M'Zab region, famed for its cubist architecture which has inspired Le Corbusier and other modern architects.

All over Algeria there are architectural wonders, from the Berber tombs and Roman ruins of Tipasa and Cherchell to the Islamic architecture of the towns and cities. Unfortunately most of the ancient city of Algiers itself has been displaced by 20th century buildings, but the two museums in the city are among the best in Africa.

THE LAND AND THE PEOPLE

Algeria is huge, but since most of it is uninhabitable desert or arid mountains, nine-tenths of the population are concentrated in the northern coastal strip, known as the Tell, or hill, in Arabic. This 1,200 km. strip of coast, some 100 to 200 km. wide, is fertile but hard to farm. After the departure of thousands of *colons* or European settler-farmers, the land was distributed to the people under a Government-supervised 'self-management' scheme. Every attempt was made to use the land to the utmost, to produce food for the country and to provide a decent living for the farmers. In this fertile part of Algeria, there is also a concentration of people in the cities as a result of rural exodus. The four biggest cities already have a population running into millions and an increasingly difficult housing problem.

South of the Tell is an area of high plateaux and mountains rising from 1,000 to over 2,000 m. high and centred in the Kabylian and Aures ranges. Although the area is rather dry, there is enough grass and forest for the million inhabitants to live off cattle or sheep grazing and various handicrafts. Further south, the few streams are rarely filled with water, and life is even more precarious except in the oases scattered through the vast Saharan region.

Covering fully 85% of the territory, the high plateau sustains only about 500,000 people; these include nomadic tribes moving with their camels and goats, and the permanent inhabitants of the oases, where cereals and dates are grown. All around are seemingly endless, rolling sand dunes, although the altitude continues rising to reach its peak in the Hoggar. In recent years, however, the silence of the desert has been broken by the booming oil towns in the far south, and iron or other mining operations.

Since independence, there has been a radical change in the composition of Algeria's population. The nearly one million Europeans of French, Spanish, Italian and other descent who had immigrated during French rule began to leave, and so did some 150,000 Algerian Jews. With this exodus the population became considerably more homogeneous, the two basic strains being Berber and Arab. After the centuries of Arab conquest and migration there had been considerable intermarriage and much of the population was mixed, although in certain more remote areas there were relatively pure Arabs and many Berbers, living in the Kabylian and Aures mountains. The primary, and official, national language was Arabic, although perhaps a quarter of the population spoke Berber dialects, and many French-educated people, especially in the cities, used French, sometimes as their first language. But the great unifier was Islam, some 99% of the population being adherents of the Sunni or the Malekite rites.

HISTORY

The original inhabitants (and still a major part of the population) were the Berbers, who periodically withdrew to the high plateaux and mountains when invaders arrived. The first to come were the Phoenicians, followed by the Carthaginians, who controlled the eastern coast around 1100 BC. A thousand years later, the region was drawn into the Roman Empire. The Romans built fortresses and towns further along the coast and inland, and co-existed with Berber monarchies. The Vandals drove the Romans out in the fifth century. They were defeated, in turn, by Byzantine Emperor Justinian I in the sixth century; and in the seventh century the Arab invasions began. These invasions continued for five centuries and entailed vast migrations of people and the colonisation of the whole coast of Algeria, Morocco and even Spain. During this process many of the Berbers were converted to Islam.

Algeria, seen not as a separate entity but merely as part of the Maghreb, was ruled intermittently by the Almoravids, Almohads and various local dynasties whose realms expanded and contracted over the centuries. Later, the Spaniards, having recovered their national territory, pushed on and occupied several coastal towns and threatened Algiers. The Barbarossa brothers, Turkish pirates, came to its rescue and soon ruled the country themselves as part of the Ottoman Empire. After 1518, Turkish beys under the

Bey of Algiers introduced a broader, if somewhat unstable, administration. Meanwhile Algiers became a haven for the Barbary pirates who preyed on shipping throughout the Mediterranean. After three centuries of this harassment, on the pretext of an insult to its consul-general, France launched a major military campaign in 1830. It dragged on far longer than expected, and it was not until 1847 that the able and courageous Emir Abd-el-Kader, leader of the Algerian resistance, was finally captured. For several decades more the Berbers held out in their mountain fastness. By 1902, French control was expanded to cover present-day Algeria.

Unlike its neighbours, Algeria was not looked upon as a potential nation but merely an extension of France, and was brought into the latter's national administration. Over the years integration was wrought far more by settling of the French (and other Europeans) in the new departments, and the creation of a modern superstructure, than by education and assimilation of the native Algerians. The masses remained largely outside, and

Algerian architecture

hostile or passive towards this French Algeria.

After the Second World War, various political movements were founded by local intellectuals to increase rights within the existing framework. Later they were transcended and then destroyed by the National Liberation Front (FLN) which launched a war for independence in November 1954. Its first leader, Ferhat Abbas, soon constituted a Provisional Government of the Algerian Republic (GPRA) which obtained some support abroad. For several years the French army ruthlessly put down the guerrilla units and expanded its army to half a million men. With President de Gaulle's return to power in 1958, there was an increased willingness for accommodation; this was approved by most Frenchmen in France but rejected by the military and settlers in Algeria. By 1961, however, serious negotiations had begun and despite a last-ditch struggle by OAS (Secret Army Organisation) terrorists, Algeria became independent on 5 July 1962.

The victory was due to FLN tenacity and unity; but the common front collapsed soon after and Ahmed Ben Bella, who had been in prison much of this time, emerged as the first Prime Minister. He began to purge the FLN of more conservative elements and to turn it into a political party to support his policies. These included nationalisation of French and other land and property and the introduction of an ill-defined local version of socialism, with strong support of non-alignment and Afro-Asian solidarity abroad.

In June 1965, the more conservative Colonel Houari Boumedienne took power, and introduced austere social and economic policies. Algeria maintained its international role by actively promoting the "New World Economic Order". However, the country entered into a severe conflict with its neighbour Morocco over the future of the Western Sahara.

CULTURE

Algeria, unlike its neighbours, was never the major centre of the many civilisations that have held sway in the region; but it was an important outlying province of so many cultures that the historical remains are most impressive. Going back to 6000 BC, before the Sahara was a desert, there are the paintings in the Tassili caves.

Far easier to visit are the Phoenician and Punic ruins, the Roman temples, aqueducts and amphitheatres at Tipaza and Caesaria near Algiers, at Timgad, and other sites near Constantine. The present major cities are often built upon or around settlements of the early Arab conquerors. The best preserved is Tlemcen. But in every modern city constructed by the French over the past century there remains a kasbah, an older town where the native Algerians held on to their way of life. Similarly, in the Kabylian and Aures mountains, the Berbers and Arabo-Berbers have maintained many of their traditions and speak their own dialects.

Algerian art has its own originality expressed in pottery, ceramics, brasswork, lace, embroidery, leatherwork and weaving. Well-stitched carpets can be obtained in many centres. Wool and

Algerian pottery

goat-hair *Telli* carpets, boldly and colourfully decorated, come from the Aures. Woven *Dragga* carpets fuse Berber and Oriental motifs.

Basketwork from the western Sahara Touat region, the Hoggar and from Kabylia is worked in delicate shades of green and yellow. There is white basketwork from Dellys. The pottery is a living reminder of the past. Its shape, technique and decoration are identical with those of pottery discovered in prehistoric dolmens.

The jewellery from Kabylia, the Aures, Ghardaia and Tamanrasset is often exquisitely worked from silver, with filigree, coral or enamel.

ECONOMY

The Algerian economy has shown great advances since the discovery of oil and gas. The majority of the population, however, depends on agriculture for its livelihood. The coastal region of plains and valleys produces wheat, wine, olives and fruit. In the mountains grazing and forestry are the main activities. The Sahara region supports scattered herds of sheep, goats, cattle and camels. Algeria is also the third-largest date producer in the world.

The large estates owned by Europeans before independence have been taken over by the Government as part of a general policy of socialisation of land, the expropriated land being managed by workers' committees. The socialist agricultural sector employs 100,000 workers (out of a total peasant population of seven million) but accounts for 75% of the country's agricultural production.

The rich mineral resources are the mainstay of Algeria's foreign trade. Production of oil began in 1958. The main producing region is the eastern Sahara, around Hassi-Messaoud. Oil exports each year contribute over 30% of total exports. The Government company, Son-

atrach, has a virtual monopoly of all oil and natural gas operations in the country, most foreign firms having been nationalised in the years after independence. The country's trade is still dominated by France, though the influence is gradually diminishing.

The industrial sector is expanding rapidly. Food processing, building materials, chemicals and textiles are important, but the biggest industrial complexes are linked to mineral production—eg, a steel complex at Annaba, gas liquefaction plants at Arzew and Skikda and several oil refineries.

GENERAL INFORMATION

Area: 2,380,000 sq. km.
Population: 16 million.
Capital: Algiers.
Head of State: President Houari Boumedienne.
Government: Revolutionary Council in charge of single political party, the National Liberation Front (FLN).
Date of Independence: 5 July 1962.
Languages: Arabic (official), French (commercial) and Berber.
Religion: Islam. There are Christian and Jewish minorities.
Currency: Algerian dinar, divided into 100 centimes. 7.94 dinars = £1 sterling, 4.141 = $1.
Time: GMT + 1 (winter); GMT + 2 (summer).

HOW TO GET THERE

By air: There are direct regular flights to Algiers by international airlines from Paris, Rome, Madrid, Geneva, Frankfurt, Marseilles, Lyons, Nice, Strasbourg, Toulouse, Alicante, Palma, Belgrade, Moscow, Benghazi, Cairo, Casablanca, Tripoli and Tunis. There are two direct flights each way each week between London and Algiers by Air Algerie and British Caledonian.

There are also flights to Annaba, Constantine and Oran from French cities, and from Casablanca and Tunis.

The main airlines serving Algeria, apart from Air Algerie, are: Air France, Aeroflot, Alitalia, Egyptair, Royal Air Maroc, Swissair, TWA, Interflug, CSA Tunis Air and British Caledonian.

The airport for Algiers is about 20 km. from the city at Dar el-Beida.

By sea: There are regular shipping services to Algiers, Oran, Annaba and Skikda from Marseilles, Palma and Alicante. The main companies serving Algeria are Compagnie Generale Transatlantique, Paris, and Compagnie de Navigation Mixte, Marseilles.

By road: Main points of entry: from Morocco at Maghnia; from Tunisia at El Kala, Souk Ahras and Tebessa; from Libya at Fort Thiriet; from Niger at In Guezzam; from Mali at Bordj Mokhtar (see section on Crossing the Sahara).

Cars are allowed into Algeria for three months without payment of duty. An extension of three months is possible. The log-book and driving licence should be presented to the authorities. Insurance must be purchased at the border. Green card is not valid.

By rail: There is a daily service in both directions between Algeria (Oran) and Morocco (Casablanca). The frontier post is at Zoudj Beghal (Maghnia). There is also a daily service in both directions between Algeria (Annaba and Constantine) and Tunisia (Tunis). The frontier post is at Souk Ahras.

Visas and health regulations

A visa is not necessary for visitors in possession of a passport from Andorra, Denmark, Egypt, Finland, France, Guinea, Iceland, Iraq, Italy, Jordan, Kuwait, Lebanon, Liechtenstein, Mali, Monaco, Morocco, Norway, San Marino, Spain, Sudan, Sweden, Switzerland, Syria, Tunisia, UK or Yugoslavia.

For visitors from other countries a passport and visa are required. Visas are issued by Algerian diplomatic missions and consulates abroad or (for a maximum of three months) on arrival at frontiers or airports. The fee is 15 dinars for initial visas and 25 dinars for an extension. Visitors in transit do not need a visa. A landing or transit permit can be obtained, valid for two to five days.

Certificates of vaccination against smallpox are required for visitors from all countries. Certificates of inoculation against yellow fever and cholera are required for visitors coming from infected areas.

Customs and currency regulations

The following are admitted free of duty: personal baggage and articles for personal use, including 200 cigarettes, 50 cigars or 400 grammes of tobacco, and a bottle of spirits and two bottles of wine.

Prohibited goods include arms and ammunition, drugs, pornographic literature and contraceptives.

With the exception of gold coins, any amount of foreign currency may be taken into the country. On leaving Algeria visitors must present the currency declaration form completed on arrival, in order to take out any unused foreign currency. The amount of foreign currency must tally with what has been delared and changed.

Not all hotels are allowed to change travellers' cheques. It is advisable to change cheques at airports or at the Central Bank or National Bank offices in Algiers, Annaba, Constantine or Oran.

CLIMATE

Along the coast the climate is temperate, ranging from 13°C to 24°C. The summer months from June to September are hot and humid with the day temperature between 27°C and 32°C. There is variable rain between October and May, though it is most likely to fall between November and February. In the desert it is hot and dry in the day but cold at night. The daytime summer temperature can reach 43°C.

What to wear

Light or tropical clothes are required in summer. For the rest of the year clothes as worn in Europe are suitable. In the Sahara take sun-glasses, a wide-brimmed hat to give cover against the sun and warm clothing for protection against the cold nights (both in summer and winter). A *cheche* (Saharan veil) will protect the head against the wind and sand.

Health precautions

In the towns the water supply is reliable. When travelling take bottled mineral water. In the Sahara take a moisturising face cream and pastilles against the dryness and dust (but not chewing gum, which dries the mouth).

BANKS

The only banks authorised to change travellers' cheques are the Banque Centrale d'Algerie (head office: blvd Zirout Youcef, Algiers) and the Banque Nationale d'Algerie (head office: blvd Che Guevara, Algiers). Other banks authorised for foreign business are the Banque Exterieure d'Algerie and the Credit Populaire d'Algerie.

Business hours

Banks: 0800-1500 Saturday to Wednesday.
Offices: Winter 0800-1200, 1430-1800 Wednesday to Saturday; 0800-1200 Thursday. Summer 0800-1200, 1500-1830 Saturday to Wednesday; 0800-1200 Thursday.

PUBLIC HOLIDAYS

The fixed holidays are: 1 January, 1 May, 19 June, 5 July (Independence Day), 1 November. The variable Muslim holidays are Eid el-Adha, New Year, Achoura, Mouloud and Eid el-Fitr.

There are numerous local festivals throughout Algeria, with brilliant displays of Arab and Berber culture: music, drama, dancing, traditional rituals, costumes and handicrafts. The Djebel Amour Festival, held in Aflou in June, is noted for its horse racing and 'fantasia' displays. The Spring Festival, held in Biskra over the Easter period, highlights folk dances, mime and music. The Orange Festival at Boufarik in April or May symbolises the fruit harvest. Bou Saada has two festivals, at the end of the Christian year and during Easter, with the famous Ouled Nail dancers. Djelfa has its Sheep Festival in June, with horse racing 'fantasias' and folk dances.

Tindouf's festival is one of the most colourful, attracting people from all over Algeria to watch the spellbinding dances of the 'blue people' of the desert. Touggourt has a Date Festival in March or April to celebrate the fertilisation of the date-palm. There are camel races and displays of local Saharan culture.

ACCOMMODATION

In the summer months it is advisable to arrange hotel bookings before leaving for Algeria. Algerian hotels have been categorised as follows: de luxe (5 and 4 stars); second class (3 stars); tourist class (2 stars and 1 star).

Hotels

Bookings for hotels belonging to Sonatour should be addressed to Sonatour, Direction Commerciale, 5, Bd Ben Boulaid, Algiers. Tel: 64 15 51, telex: Etour 52214.

ALGERIAN HOTELS

(☆☆☆☆ = star rating)

Town	Address	Telephone	Telex
ALGIERS			
Aurassi☆☆☆☆	Avenue Frantz Fanon	64 82 52	52475
Aletti☆☆☆☆	Rue Asselah Hocine	63 50 40	52142
St George☆☆☆☆	24 Avenue Souidani Boudjemaa	66 53 00	52484
Albert 1er☆☆☆	5 Avenue Pasteur	63 00 20	
Angleterre☆☆☆	11 rue Ben Boulaid	63 65 40	
Suisse☆☆☆	6 rue Drouillet	63 49 52	
Geneve☆☆☆	30 rue Abane Ramdane	63 24 41	
Oasis☆☆☆	2 rue Kerrar Smain	62 52 04	
AIN SEFRA			
El Mekter☆☆☆	Ain Sefra	1.40	
ANNABA			
Plaza☆☆☆☆	Rue Sainte Monique	82 35 77	
Nice	11 rue Lamara	82 22 09	
Orient	3 Cours de la Revolution	82 20 51	
BATNA			
Orient☆☆	9 Avenue de la Republique	0.40	
BECHAR			
Transat☆☆☆	Avenue du Sahara	2 18	
BEJAIA			
Les Hammadites☆☆☆	Tichy	17	
Orient☆☆	7 rue Si Lahouas	92 11 31	
BENI ABBES			
Rym☆☆☆	Beni Abbes		
Grand Erg☆☆	Beni Abbes		
BENI YENNI			
Auberge le Bracelet d'Argent	Beni Yenni	59	
BERRIANE			
Balloull	Berriane	0 72	

Algerian Hotels continued

BISKRA
Okba☆☆☆	Biskra	0.67
Transatlantique	2 rue Ben Badis	4.94

BOUIRA
Nedjma	9 rue Abane Ramdane	0.2

BOU SAADA
Le Caid☆☆☆	Bou Saada	1.56
Transatlantique	Bou Saada	0 11

CHEHOUA
Grand Hotel	Chehoua	0.1

CHERCHELL
Cesaree	Cherchell	51

CHREA
Les Cedres	Chrea	13

CONSTANTINE
Cirta☆☆☆	1 Avenue Rahmani Cherif	93 31 43
Panoramique	59 Avenue Aouati Mostefa	93 24 52

DJANET
Zeribas	Djanet	

EL ASNAM
Le Cheliff☆☆	El Asnam	6 16

EL GOLEA
El Boustan☆☆☆	El Golea	40
Grand Erg	El Golea	61

EL KALA (ANNABA)
El Morjan☆☆☆		78

EL OUED
Le Souf☆☆☆	El Oued	2 95
Transatlantique	El Oued	0 9

GHARDAIA
Les Rostemides☆☆☆☆	Ghardaia	89 12 49
Transatlantique	Ghardaia	89 10 01

Algerian Hotels continued

Atlantide	Ghardaia	89 11 02
LAGHOUAT		
Marhaba☆☆☆	5 Bd des Martyrs	4 32
IN SALAH		
Bajoudas	In Salah	0 19
MAGHNIA		
La Tafna☆☆	Maghnia	0 29
MORETTI (ALGIERS)		
El Minzah☆☆☆	Station balneaire de Moretti	81 44 35
MOSTAGANEM		
Albert 1er	1 rue Belhamri	29 23
ORAN		
Les Andalouses		
(Bungalows)☆☆☆	Oran, les Andalouses	0 4
Residence Timgad	22 Bd Emir Abdelkader	33 63 36
Royal	3 Bd de la Soumman	33 38 52
Windsor	1 rue Ben M'hidi	33 31 75
OUARGLA		
El Mehri☆☆☆	Ouargla	5 80
Transatlantique	Ouargla	1 54
SAIDA		
Hotel d'Orient	4 Avenue de l'Independence	1 86
SERAIDA (ANNABA)		
El Mountazah☆☆☆☆	Seraida	0 4
SETIF		
Grand Hotel	13 Avenue du 8 mai 1945	20 43
SIDI BEL ABBES		
Versailles	31 rue larbi Tebessi	38 89
SIDI FREDJ (ALGIERS)		
El Riadh☆☆☆☆	Sidi Fredj	81 44 02
Du Port☆☆☆☆	Sidi Fredj	80 13 15
El Manar☆☆☆	Sidi Fredj	78 38 16

Algerian Hotels continued

SKIKDA

Es Salem	Skikda	
Orient	2 Place du 1er novembre	95 58 51
Excelsior	Place du 1er novembre	95 65 61

TAMANRASSET

Tinhinan	Tamanrasset	09

TEBESSA

Theveste	20 rue Abane Ramdane	0 35

TIARET

Orient	Place des Martyrs	5 58

TIGZIRT-SUR-MER

Mizrana	Tigzirt	0 46

TIMGAD

Djemila	Timgad	0 01

TIMIMOUN

Gourara☆☆☆	Timimoun	50
Oasis Rouge	Timimoun	17

TINDOUF

El Mouggar☆☆☆	Tindouf	

TIPASA (ALGIERS)

De la Baie☆☆☆☆	Tipasa-Matares	0 73

TIZI OUZOU

Lala Khedidja	Tizi Ouzou	40 29 01
Beloua	Tizi Ouzou	40 19 90

TLEMCEN

Les Ziannides☆☆☆☆	Rue Khedim Ali	20 43 63
Moghreb☆☆☆	Avenue Cdt Faradj	20 32 03
Villa Rivaud☆☆☆	El Kalaa superieure	20 20 22

TOUGGOURT

Oasis☆☆☆	Touggourt	4 69
Transatlantique	Touggourt	0 17

ZERALDA (ALGIERS)

Les Sables d'Or☆☆☆☆	Zeralda	81 20 34

Camping is free on common land or on the beaches, with permission from the local authorities or the police. The Touring Club of Algeria has camping sites at Larhat, Ain el-Turk and Annaba, complete with all mod cons.

RESTAURANTS

There are good restaurants in all the main towns, serving both European and Arab dishes. There are restaurants, night clubs, discotheques, entertainment, sports (swimming, sailing, water skiing, tennis, riding etc.) in the holiday villages.

Algerian wine is justly famous. Good red wines are: Mascara, Lismara and Medea. Rosés include Mascara, Mansourah and Medea.

Tipping is normal, but is not obligatory.

TRANSPORT

By air: Air Algerie operates frequent internal services from Algiers to Annaba, Constantine, El Golea, Oran, Ouargla, Tamanrasset, Touggourt and several other smaller centres, and between these towns.

By rail: The rail network covers 4,000 km. and links the main coastal towns with those inland. The main west-east service links Morocco to Tunisia through Maghnia, Tlemcen, Oran, Algiers, Constantine and Souk Ahras.

By road: The road system covers 65,000 km. comprising good trunk and secondary roads in the north, and Saharan tracks, some of which have recently been surfaced. The best guide to road conditions is Michelin.

Travelling in one's own car or a hired vehicle (see below) is obviously the best way to see the country, but there are extensive bus services to all parts of Algeria, operating principally from Algiers, Constantine and Oran. Ask for details from your hotel. The city bus services in Algiers, Constantine and Oran are also very efficient.

Taxis are plentiful in all main towns.

Car hire: ATA (Agence touristique algerienne), Head office: 2 Place Cheikh Ben, Badis, Algiers. Tel: 62 26 00.

CROSSING THE SAHARA

A fascinating glimpse of the Sahara's many faces is obtained by crossing the desert by the central route (to In Salah) or the western route (to Adrar). Here is some practical advice.

From Algiers, the central road (RN1) goes to Djelfa, Laghouat, Ghardaia, El-Golea and In Salah. The hard-surface road ends 260 km. south of In Salah, but tracks lead from there to Tamanrasset and Agades in the Niger Republic. Also from Algiers, RN8 through Bou-Saada joins the main road at Djelfa.

The trans-Saharan highway under construction will be the continuation of this central southern route.

From Morocco, the western route (RN6) coming from Saidia, Berkane, Oujda or Figuig passes through Saida, Ain-Sefra on the way to Bechar, Abadia, Beni-Abbes and Adrar. The hard-surface road ends in Adrar and continues by track to Reggane, Tanezrouft and Gao in Mali.

Connection can be made with the central route 60 km. south of El-Golea on the tarred road which passes through Timimoun (RN51). The main route can also be joined at Reggane from the Aoulef track which continues to In Salah. The Bechar-Abadia-Tindouf road (RN50) has now been completed.

From Tunisia, coming via Tabarka or Ghardimaou, the eastern route passes through Batna, Biskra, Touggourt, Ouargla, Hassi-Messaoud, Hassi-Bel

Guebbour (RN3) where it branches off into two roads. The first branch: Hard-surfaced road through Mazoula, Tin Fouye, In-Amenas. From In-Amenas a track goes to Djanet through El Adeb Larache, Illizi and Zaouatanlaz.

The second branch: A track connects Hassi-Bel Guebbour and Amguid and then divides into two forks, one leading to Djanet and the other to Tamanrasset. The Tozeur (Tunisia)-El Oued road has also been completed. It is the fastest road to the Algerian south from Tunisia. The In-Amenas-Ghadames road offers a modern connection between neighbouring countries across southern Algeria.

Roads and Tracks
To assist motorists on the southern roads (northern Sahara) and on the tracks of the deep South (the Grand Sahara) the roads are classified according to their practicability.

Class A roads: presenting no risks for motorists: Laghouat-El Golea-In-Salah (RN1); Ghardaia-Ouargla (RN49); Ouargla-Touggourt (RN2); Touggourt-El-Oued (RN16) to Tozeur (Tunisia); Ouargla-Hassi-Messaoud (RN49); Hassi-Messaoud-Bel Guebbour, Mazoula, Tin Fouye, In-Amenas (RN3); El-Oued-Stile (RN48); Bechar-Abadia-Adrar (RN6); Adrar-Timimoun-El-Golea (RN6, RN51, RN1); Bechar-Abadia-Tindouf (tarred) (RN50); Bechar-Taghit-Igli.

Class B roads: These requiring special safety precautions, can be divided into two categories: B1, well travelled and regularly maintained tracks, and B2, seldom-used tracks with little or no maintenance. **B1:** Tadjmout-Arak-In-Ekker-In Amguel-Tamanrasset (RN1); In-Salah-Aoulef-Reggane (RN52); Adrar-Reggane (RN6); Hassi Bel Guebbour-Bordj Omar Driss (RN54); El Abed Larache-Illizi-Djanet (RN3). **B2:** Reggane-Bordj Mokhtar to Gao (Mali) (RN6); Tamanrasset-In Amguel (RN1); Ideles-Zaouataniaz (RN55); Illizi-In Amenas (RN3); Fort Thiriet-Ghadames (Libya) (RN53); Bordj Omar Driss-Amguid-in Ekker (RN54); Zaouataniaz-Ideles-in-Amguel (RN55); Zaouataniaz-Djanet (RN3); In-Ekker-In Amguel-Ta-

Ouargla Oasis

manrasset-In-Guezzam (RN1) to Agades (Niger).

Class C roads: Traffic is prohibited on the following tracks: Touggourt-Ghardaia through Guerrara; Guerrara-Berriane; Laghouat-Stile; Djanet to the Chad border; Tamanrasset-Tin-Zaouaten; Tamanrasset-Bordj Mokhtar and all those not listed under class A and class B roads. Driving on class C roads can only be authorised by decision of the Wali who will determine those special safety measures to be taken in addition to those applicable for class B roads.

The track from Reggane to Tessalit (Mali) contains three danger points (heavy sand drifts) at the 140, 350 and 600 markers.

Motorists must contact local authorities (wilayate, police, gendarmeries, dairate, Department of Road and Bridges) for information on road conditions at each leg of their crossing on a class B road and must make application for a travel permit from the administration authorities at the point of departure (wilayate or dairate). This permit is granted upon receipt of the following information: type and make of vehicle; number of passengers and their identity; time and date of departure; final destination and stopovers; estimated arrival time and date of next stopover (on the basis of the type of vehicle and road conditions); purpose of trip. The administration authorities, after verification of the motor vehicle and its equipment, may grant or refuse the travel permit. The travel permit must be presented to highway police along the route.

Private cars may travel unaccompanied on class B1 tracks, but they must travel in convoys of a minimum of two cars on class B2 tracks. Motorists should not stray from the tracks. Night driving is prohibited on class B2 tracks. Motorists travel on class B tracks at their own risk. The travel permit guarantees that safety conditions have been met but does not imply responsibility of the State. All costs for search and repair must be borne by the travellers.

The tracks of the deep South require sturdy vehicles in perfect working order and mounted with special track tyres as well as an oil filter to keep sand out of the motor. Car springs should also be reinforced. So as to limit the risk of punctures, sand traps or axle problems, a maximum of four passengers is recommended on the Saharan tracks for cars. In addition to sand equipment (perforated metal sheets, short-handled shovels, powerful jacks), all vehicles must be equipped with: spare parts, oil cans, fan belts, sparking plugs, leaf springs, spare tyres and a complete tool kit for repairs, reserve water supplies and lubricants.

Take food for at least an extra two days, salt tablets, 10 litres of drinking water per person and a first-aid kit, as well as a mirror or white sheet for signalling aircraft, two smoke bombs (one black and one red) and a compass.

In the event of a breakdown or straying from the track, passengers should in no case move out of sight of their vehicle. In the event of a violent sandstorm, the vehicle should be parked with the motor facing in the opposite direction to the wind so as to avoid sanding. To avoid getting caught in the sand, tyres should be partly deflated (the car should carry an air pump).

Crossings of the Sahara are not recommended from 1 June to 15 September because of the intense heat and frequency of sandstorms.

Water points

In the deep South, water points are very far apart, located essentially in the population centres. On the Adrar-Bordj Mokhtar track (on the Mali border), drinking water is available only at Reggane and Bordj Mokhtar. The first water hole on the Malian side is at Tessalit. On the Tamanrasset-In Guezzam track (Niger border), there is no water before

In Guezzam. The first watering point in Niger is at In Abbangarit.

Fuel

Refuelling stations are found along the main roads in the following localities: Central route: El Golea, In Salah, Tadjmout, Tamanrasset. Eastern route: Ain Sefra, Bechar, Beni Abbes, Kerzaz, Adrar, Reggane. Junction beween the central and western route: at Timimoun (RN51). Eastern route: Hassi Messaoud, Hassi Bel Ghobbour, In Amenas, Djanet. Junction between the eastern and central road: at Amguid (RN54).

Formalities

Customs and police formalities on leaving Algeria for the Adrar-Gao track are handled at the Adrar Wilaya; the In-Salah-Agades track at the Tamanrasset Wilaya or In-Salah Daira.

Travellers requiring a visa for Algeria who intend to return to Algeria after a tour in the neighbouring Saharan countries, should make certain that their visa covers a long enough period.

Visas for Mali or Niger should be obtained in the visitor's country of origin or at the embassies of Mali in Paris and Niger in Algiers. Any further information and advice can be obtained from: ONAT (Algerian National Tourist Office), 25-27 Rue Khelifa Boukhalfa. tel: 64-68-64. Telex: 52947.

EMBASSIES IN ALGIERS

EUROPE

Austria: Cite Dar el Kef, rue Shakespeare, El Mouradia. **Belgium:** 1 rue el Khet Tabi. **Denmark:** 23 blvd Zirout Youcef. **Finland:** 2 blvd Mohammed V. **France:** Rue Larbi Alik, Hydra. **Sweden:** 4 blvd Mohammed V. **UK:** 7 chemin des Glycines.

MIDDLE EAST

Egypt: Chemin de la Madeleine, Hydra.

Iran: 60 rue Didouche Mourad. **Iraq:** 4 rue Areski, Abri, Hydra. **Jordan:** 6 rue Chanoua. **Kuwait:** 1 rue Didouche Mourad. **Lebanon:** 9 rue Kaid Ahmed el Biar. **Libya:** 15 chemin Bachir Brahimi. **Saudi Arabia:** 7 chemin des Glycines. **Sudan:** 27 rue de Carthage, Hydra. **Syria:** Chemin de la Madeleine, El Biar. **Tunisia:** 11 rue du Bois de Boulogne, Hydra. **Yemen AR:** 74 rue Bouraba. **PDR Yemen:** 105 ave Mustapha Ali Khodja, El Biar.

NORTH AMERICA

Canada: 27 bis rue d'Anjoy, Hydra. **USA:** 4 chemin Bachir Brahimi.

TOURIST OFFICES

Algiers: 2 rue Hassiba Ben Bouali. **Constantine:** 35 ave Aouati Mustapha. **Oran:** 6 blvd Emir Abdelkader. **Annaba:** 24 rue Larbi Tebessi. **Batna:** 12 allee Ben Boulaid. **Bou Saada (south):** 2 rue Larbi Ben M'Hidi. **Mostaganem:** 2 ave Khemisti. **Setif:** 7 ave du 1er Novembre. **Tizi Ouzou:** Prefecture de Tizi Ouzou. **Tlemcen:** 15 rue de l'Independance.

TOURIST OFFICES ABROAD

France: 28 ave de l'Opera, Paris 75002. **Sweden:** Sturegatan 20, Box 5016, Stockholm 10241. **West Germany:** Tanusstrasse 20, Frankfurt/M. **UK:** 35 St. James's Street, London SW1.

ALGIERS

The capital city, located in the middle of Algeria's northern coastline, gave its name to the whole country. Even under the Romans there was a port here, which changed hands over the centuries under the Arabs and Turks. Algiers was feared during the age of the Barbary pirates but it became just another modern commercial port under the French. From several thousand inhabitants in 1830, at the time of the French conquest, it grew to a city of over one million by 1970. It is the principal centre of trade, commerce and administration, the seat of the main university, and the focus of artistic and intellectual life. It is also the seat of government.

The Kasbah is a maze of twisting streets. A young guide could be helpful. A good place to start in the Kasbah is the old fortress; from there one can zig-zag down, passing the old patriarchal houses and stopping at the Cemetery of the Princesses, the Sidi-Abderahmane Mosque and the Grand Mosque. At the foot of the Kasbah is a museum of popular arts.

Coming out of this mass of houses and people, one reaches the calmer and more modern area around the Admiralty; it was from here that the Barbary pirates once launched their raids. To the east is the fishing port and the market (with numerous restaurants) at the Pecherie.

Considerably higher up, in the neighbourhood called Mustapha Superieur, dominating the city and with a splendid view of the bay, is the former Summer Palace of the Governor with its magnificent gardens. Nearby are two museums. The Bardo Museum has an excellent ethnographic collection such as clothing and jewellery, musical instruments, and weapons. The museum is an 18th Century villa typical of those lived in by wealthier Turkish officials or Barbary pirates. The Stephane Gsell Museum has a collection of Roman antiques as well as of Islamic art and archaeology.

Set in the shady part of Mount Riant is an interesting children's museum. The National Museum of Fine Arts has one of the most important collections of paintings and sculptures in Africa. The former Serkadj prison is now the Museum of the

Fishing port in Algiers

Revolution.

Spread around the Bay of Algiers is a string of beautiful beaches, fishing villages and fashionable resorts with aquatic sports, restaurants, fine hotels and casinos. There are also delightful drives through the distinctive Kabylian region. Tizi Ouzou, well up in the hill country, is 140 km. from Algiers.

Restaurants

There are excellent restaurants at the **Aletti** and **Saint Georges** hotels and good ones in the other hotels, where the food is largely international style. The fish restaurants at the Pecherie are excellent. For Algerian cooking, one can ask at the hotels or try some of the following restaurants in Algiers: **Alhambra**, 29 rue Ben M'Hidi Larbi; **Bacour**, rue Ali Boumendjel; **Bardo**, 128 ruc Didouche Mourad; **Marhaba**, rue Hamani.

Entertainments

There is a **National Theatre** at place Port-Said and other smaller theatres where one can find visiting troupes. Often these are from Eastern Europe, China, Cuba, or African countries, or groups of French actors. These productions alternate with evenings of Algerian music and folk dancing. Cinemas are plentiful and it is possible to find French and sometimes Engish films. **Hotel Aletti** has a night club. Dinner at **Dar El Alia** is followed by oriental dancing. Other night spots in and around Algiers are: **El-Djezair** (Aletti), rue Hicine Asselah, Algiers; **Blue Note**, 97 rue Didouche Mourad, Algiers; **Dar El Alia**, la Bouzareah, just outside town; **Casino Yasmina**, Moretti; **El Djamila**, Djamila; **Diplomate**, Wydra.

Shopping and markets

Algerian handicrafts are available from souvenir shops near the major hotels and along the former rue Michelet, now with different names along each segment, but especially on Didouche Mourad. There are also two large, State-run handicraft centres: one at 2 blvd Khemisti and the other at the airport. The Government prices can serve as a guide-line for prices to be paid in small shops, where some shrewd bargaining may be necessary.

ORAN

Algeria's second biggest city, Oran is primarily an outlet for the western part of the country. Like Algiers, it was built along the coastal plateau and up the hills. The old town, founded in the 8th century, was embellished by the Andalusian Arabs and then expanded by the Spaniards who ruled the region from the 16th century. After its return to Islam and Turkish rule, the town came under France in 1831.

There is a particularly interesting kasbah and many mosques through the Moorish Gate or the Spanish Gate. At the top of the hill and dominating the port is the 16th century Santa Cruz Fortress, looking down over the modern city and, only 8 km. away, the former French naval base of Mers el Kebir.

Restaurants

Apart from the hotel restaurants the following are worth trying: **Le Belvedere, Le Biarritz, La Comette, El Gallo**. For Algerian specialities try: **Nahawand, El Djazair, Nuits du Liban**.

CONSTANTINE

Both the oldest and the most indigenous of the major cities, Constantine is the third largest with a population of 260,000. Established by the Roman emperor of that name, it later fell under the Vandals, Arabs and Turks. Being further east and in the mountains, it resisted French attempts to capture it, and they did not succeed in doing so until 1837. Even then it maintained its personality, with the Algerian element dominating in the city as a whole. Among the monuments are the Ahmed Bey Palace and the graceful Djema el-Kebir Mosque.

Restaurants
Apart from the hotel restaurants the following are worth trying: **Casino Municipal, Bagatelle, Saint George, Rally.** For Algerian specialities: **Bandjelloul, Victoire, Dounyazad**.

ANNABA

Throughout history this has been a major port. Now, however, its value and size are explained by the proximity of iron mines and the site of a huge steel complex. Only 2 km. from the present city are the remains of Hippo Regius, the ancient Phoenician and then Roman port, with an interesting archaeological museum.

TLEMCEN

Tlemcen is located in the Tellien Atlas mountains in the westerly part of the country. It was the capital of major Moroccan dynasties from the 12th to the 16th centuries, and has the best preserved remains of Arab culture. Tlemcen is graced by the famous Grand Mosque and the mosque and museum of Bel Hassane. In the still lively old town one can visit the shops of the weavers, the coppersmiths and ironmongers, and the many rug factories.

BEJAIA

The former Bougie, another ancient Mediterranean port, has gained modern significance as the end of the pipeline from Hassi Messaoud. But the tourist is drawn by some of the loveliest scenery and 30 km. of fine beaches along its gulf, running from Cap Carbon to Cap Aokas.

THE SAHARA

By far the largest part of Algeria is the relatively uninhabited Sahara, which is steadily becoming a paradise for tourists in winter, when the dry air of the oases is most bracing. With the discovery of oil and other mineral wealth, the Sahara has also become more accessible. The roads are being improved, and Air Algerie has many flights to the oases and oil towns. Air-conditioned buses also connect the main oases. Three major routes lead into the Sahara (see the section on Crossing the Sahara).

Greater than the adventure of reaching the oases is the excitement of living there, even for a few days. It is worth while choosing one or two oases, rather than trying to visit many—and then taking full advantage of the stay. This means visiting the town, the shops and mosques, the palm groves and date plantations, as well as the many historical monuments. One can observe the lives of the oasis dwellers and the nomads who come to the markets with their caravans. The population is extremely mixed—Arab, Berber and black.

The western route starts in Oran and runs through the excellent farmland and vineyards around Mascara, through Saida and into Ain Sefra, an old French garrison town. Then one continues to Bechar. Over the years this has become a major administrative centre, of interest to the tourist for its picturesque fort. But Bechar is primarily the gateway to other oases, like Tindouf far off to the south-west where Algeria, Morocco and Mauritania meet. More directly south are the oases of Tarhit, a small kasbah village, and Beni Abbes, lost in its palm groves amid beautiful sand-dunes. Like the others, Adrar and Timimoun are made of red clay in the typical Sudanese style of architecture. Finally come the groups of oases around Reggane.

The central route, leaving from Algiers, is considerably more interesting for the tourist. It runs due south through the Atlas mountains, past Ksar el-Boukhari to Djelfa, long an important market town for the nomads. Then come the famous oases. Laghouat, founded in the 11th century, is renowned for its beautiful gardens. One should also visit the Chetett quarter, El Atlik Mosque and the tomb of Si el Hadj Aissa. The five towns of M'Zab, the most impressive being Ghardaia, are a favourite spot for a longer stay. Perched on the surrounding hills, the white houses and mosques reach upward, and the bustling market places have a special charm. Here many caravans congregate, and one gets a real feeling of desert life. Further south, the lovely oasis of El Golea is dominated by its citadel or ksar.

In Salah, reputedly the hottest place in the Sahara, is a growing oil town and an important staging post but holds little interest. Its surroundings are stark, sandy and barren. The visitor pressing south towards Tamanrasset is rewarded with the sight of the moon-like Hoggar mountains, which reach a height of 3,000 m. The hermit priest at Assekrem loves to receive visitors. Tamanrasset, which can be reached by air, is increasingly popular as a romantic holiday destination where blue-robed nomads throng the streets. Its hotel facilities are rather meagre.

The eastern route leaves from Constantine and passes through the Aures mountains to Biskra. Another road comes down from Algiers and passes through the much-frequented pre-Saharan oasis of Bou Saada. Biskra, on the northern fringe of the desert, has been known since Roman times for its exceptionally healthy climate and is known today for its vast palm groves and the fine Deglet en Nour dates.

In the far south-east lies the Tassili plateau—scene of the world's largest open-air museum, full of rock paintings, engravings and scattered remains of an ancient civilisation that flourished when herds of animals roamed these parts. The

Rock paintings at Tassili

beautiful oasis of Djanet can be reached by air and is the centre of mule and donkey expeditions into the region.

WHAT TO BUY

The centre of oasis life is the market where purchases can include local products or those brought in from afar by caravans. There are leather goods and pouffes, pottery and copper-ware, and some jewellery. Two of the most interesting markets are in M'Zab—at the caravan centre at Ghardaia and the auction market in the neighbouring town of Beni-Izquen. A special carpet festival is held in the spring. Some of the oases specialise in rug-making. Laghouat has its own rather attractive style of knotted carpets, and El Oued produces brown and beige wool and camelhair rugs.

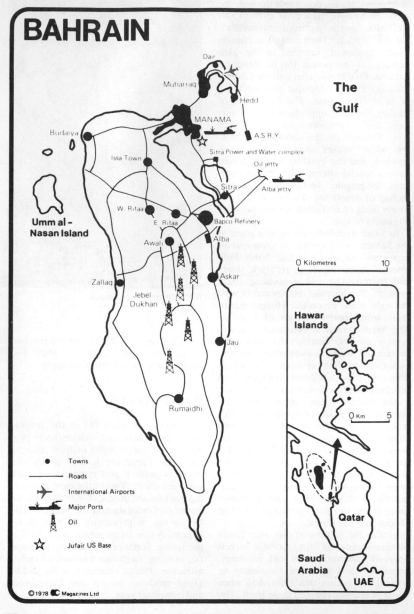

BAHRAIN

Dair

Muharraq

Hedd

The Gulf

MANAMA

A.S.R.Y.

Budaiya

Sitra Power and Water complex

Issa Town

Oil jetty

Sitra

Alba jetty

Umm al-Nasan Island

W. Rifaa

E. Rifaa

Bapco Refinery

Awali

Alba

0 Kilometres 10

Zallaq

Jebel Dukhan

Askar

Jau

Rumaidhi

● Towns

— Roads

✈ International Airports

⚓ Major Ports

🛢 Oil

☆ Jufair US Base

Hawar Islands

0 Km 5

Qatar

Saudi Arabia

UAE

© 1978 Magazines Ltd

BAHRAIN

Rosalind Mazzawi

Many people know that Bahrain is an island, or, rather, a group of 33 islands, but few realise that its physical detachment from the coast has resulted in an equal detachment of its people from the more radical and puritan attitude of those on the mainland. The main island, Bahrain itself, has one ancient and valuable geographical asset, all too rare in the Gulf; an adequate supply of fresh water from sources both on and offshore. There are artesian wells on the island, and fresh water sources in the shallow seas; formerly, divers swam down, held goatskin containers over these springs, and brought the precious fresh water triumphantly to the surface. There were, and still are, extensive date gardens in the northern part of Bahrain island, as well as irrigated fruit and vegetable gardens. These, together with the pearls gathered from the sea floor, brought prosperity to the archipelago from the earliest recorded time.

Bahrain was an important transit port in the third millenium BC, and has been identified as the legendary island of Dilmun mentioned in Babylonian and Sumerian records. The merchants of Dilmun exercised a powerful influence over the sea trade of the Indus Valley civilisations.

Through the centuries Bahrain suffered the fluctuations of fate as ambitious neighbouring dynasties rose and fell. Although the rulers of Bahrain generally sought peaceful co-existence with their neighbours, powerful nations, attracted by Bahrain's strategic geographical position and her wealthy pearling industry, continually vied for control of the islands.

Bahrain was invaded at the end of the eighth century BC, by the Assyrians and was later visited by the expeditions of Alexander. Islam came to Bahrain in AD 628, and for the next 350 years Bahrain was ruled by Governors on behalf of the Caliphs. Amongst those who fought for control of Bahrain were the Carmathians, the Omanis, the Portuguese and the Persians. Political stability came to Bahrain only with the conquest and consolidation of the islands under the Al Khalifa family, who entered Bahrain in 1782.

Britain first began her association with Bahrain in the 19th century, and British influence remained paramount until the Declaration of Independence on 15 August 1971.

Oil was first found in 1932: Bahrain is the first Gulf country to develop its oil and will probably be the first to run out of it. New discoveries of gas have, however, enhanced the State's future economic prospects, and it has also become an important trading, banking, and industrial centre. Goods are transshipped between Europe and Asia, and to other Arab countries. There is one of the world's largest oil refineries, an aluminium smelter, and a dry dock for super tankers. The fishing industry is also important; apart from oil the two chief exports are aluminium and shrimps.

At Mina Sulman there is a deep water harbour, and at Mina Sitra the Bahrain Petroleum Company (BAPCO) oil terminal. Muharraq airport is one of the largest and best equipped in the Gulf; in 1976 it handled about 1.3 million passengers and 10,000 tonnes of air cargo. The terminal can handle 760 arriving and 630 departing passengers per hour, and is still being enlarged. The airport is situated on the island of Muharraq, joined by a causeway to Manama, the capital, on the main island. Plans to build a causeway 26 km. long, joining Saudi Arabia to Bahrain, are well advanced; it will cost about $800 million and be financed by Saudi Arabia.

Bahrain is the headquarters of Gulf Air and of Gulf Helicopters. The Bahrain Airport Services Company was formed in 1977 to provide services and catering for these companies and the various other airlines that serve Bahrain. This includes British Airways' Concorde, which since January 1976 has been operating regular services to Bahrain. Recently the Concorde service was extended to Singapore, under the aegis of Singapore Airways.

About 80% of the 266,000 population are Bahraini nationals, a high proportion for the Gulf. The remainder are Arabs from Saudi Arabia, Oman, and North Yemen—about 10%, and the other 10% are made up of Palestinians, Iranians, Indians, Pakistanis and British. About 55% of the population live in the towns.

The original inhabitants are thought to descend from Arabs taken into Iraq by Nebuchadnezzar, who later fled to the island. There are about equal numbers of Sunni and Shi'a Muslims; the Sunnis arrived in the 18th century with the ruling Al Khalifa family; the Shi'a are the original inhabitants and live mostly in the villages. A number of the descendants of freed African slaves also live on the islands, they too are Sunni.

GENERAL INFORMATION

Area: 622 sq. km.—on 33 islands.
Population: 266,000.
Capital: Manama.
Head of State: The Amir or Ruler: Sheikh Isa bin Salman Al Khalifa.
Government: Bahrain was a British protectorate until August 1971, when it became independent under the Amir. A constitution was promulgated in December 1973, when a National Assembly, was elected by adult male suffrage. However, it was suspended in August 1975.
Languages: Arabic is the language of the country. English is widely spoken and understood.
Religion: Islam is the State religion: Christian, Bahai, Hindu and Parsee minorities exist and have their own places of worship.
Currency: Bahraini dinar=BD divided into 1000 fils. £1=0.758BD. $1=0.395BD.
Time: GMT+3.

HOW TO GET THERE

By air: British Airways from London—Concorde 4¼ hours; Gulf Air from London—Tri Star; UTA from Paris; and Middle East Airlines from Beirut.

Also Air Ceylon, Air India, Cathay Pacific, Cyprus Airways, Egypt Air, Ethiopian Airways, Iran Air, Iraqi Airways, Korean Airlines, Kuwait Airways, Pakistan International Airlines, Pan Am, Qantas, Alia, KLM, Saudia, Singapore Airlines, Sudan Airways, Syrian Airways, TMA, TWA, Yemen Airlines, fly to Muharraq Airport.

By sea: No scheduled passenger lines call at Bahrain, but many general cargo ships, and oil tankers, have some passenger

Choose **MEA** to Bahrain or any of the other important business centres on the Gulf.

You'll appreciate the special kind of service you get from an airline with 32 years experience.

MEA
the natural
choice airline

accommodation. Journeys can be long and tedious with no fixed time-table, but the cabins are usually comfortable, food good, and the arrangement is suitable for someone either needing a sea cruise for their health, or writing a book. The same applies to any of the Gulf ports, Kuwait, Dhahran, Doha, Abu Dhabi, Dubai, Sharjah, Muscat, Bandar Abbas, Abadan, and Basra.

By road: Overland to Kuwait, then down the coast to the Saudi Arabian town of Dhahran, whence there are shuttle air services to Bahrain. Launches or dhows may be rented by private agreement.

By rail: As far as Basra, Iraq (see section on Iraq), then independent arrangements by land or sea. These are rarely made, but are feasible at a price.

Visas and health regulations
Citizens of the UK, Saudi Arabia, Kuwait, Qatar, Oman and the UAE require only valid passports, not entry visas. Other nationals must obtain business or tourist visas from their nearest Bahraini Embassy. Transit visas for 72 hours are obtainable at the Bahrain Airport Immigration Office.

Vaccination against smallpox is required, and visitors arriving from infected areas should have yellow fever inoculations.

TAB is recommended but not required.

Currency and customs regulations
There are no currency restrictions, any amount of any currency may be freely imported and exported. A duty-free allowance of 400 cigarettes, 50 cigars, half a pound of tobacco and eight ounces of perfume is permitted, plus, for non-Muslims, a reasonable quantity of spirits. Personal effects and trade samples are also duty-free. It is forbidden to import pearls produced outside The Gulf, arms and ammunition, and black-listed goods

on the Arab League boycott list.

CLIMATE

October, November, April and May are pleasant months in Bahrain. In the height of summer, June to September, the weather is very hot and humid. Most hotels, offices and restaurants are equipped with air-conditioning. From December to March the weather is much cooler particularly in the evenings. Rainfall is slight.

What to wear
Medium-weight clothing is adequate from the end of November to the end of March. Light-weight clothing is necessary for the remainder of the year. Bahrain is more liberal in its attitude to women than most other Gulf states. Sports clothes may be worn in the streets, and short dresses are acceptable. But in the summer, protection from, rather than exposure to the sun is advisable.

ACCOMMODATION AND FOOD

Hotel accommodation is readily available and prices vary between 50BD and 15BD per day per double room. Reservations should be made well in advance and reconfirmed. There are new hotels under construction inluding Le Vendome, Holiday Inn, and Sheraton. Hilton and Gulf are building new wings.

There is a total of 33 restaurants which serve all kinds of food: Arabic, European, Indian, Chinese, Russian and American.

TRANSPORT

Private car, taxi, service taxi, and bus network covering all the islands. Taxis have orange sidewings and black-on-yellow number plates. Minimum charge in Manama is 500 fils ($\frac{1}{2}$ BD). After midnight all fares are subject to a 50% increase. Taxi fares outside Manama should be agreed upon with the driver before beginning a journey.

Car hire: International Driving Licences are accepted; cars may be rented from the Hilton Garage, Lolo Road, PO Box 5033, Manama, tel: 55026, at daily rates of 6BD, weekly 42BD, monthly 120BD. Petrol costs 30 fils per litre and traffic keeps to the right.

BANKS

American Express International Banking Group, tel: 53660.
Arab Bank, tel: 55988.
Barclays Bank, tel: 54046
British Bank of the Middle East, tel: 55933.
Chartered Bank, tel: 55946.
Chase Manhattan Bank, tel: 51401.
Credit Suisse, tel: 50677.
First National City Bank, tel: 54755.
Grindlays Bank, tel: 54707.
National Bank of Bahrain, tel: 55973.

Business hours
Friday is the weekly holiday when all businesses are closed although some shops in the bazaar are open for a few hours in the morning. The Bahrain Petroleum Co. and Aluminium Bahrain are closed on Thursdays and Fridays.
Government offices: 0700 to 1300 Saturday to Thursday;
Commercial establishments: 0700 to 1200 and 1430 to 1700 Saturday to Thursday;
Bazaars: 0800 to 1200 and 1530 to 1830 Saturday to Thursday;
Banks: 0730 to 1200 Saturday to Wednesday, and 0730 to 1100 Thursday.

PUBLIC HOLIDAYS

Prophet's Birthday, 20 February

Eid al Fitr, 3-6 September
Eid al Adha, 10-13 November
Muslim New Year, 2 December
National Day, 16 December
Al Ashura, 10 December

EMBASSIES IN MANAMA

Egypt: 3105/7 Adliya
France: Mahooz 1785/7
India: Sh. Isa Road 2299/7
Iran: Sh. Isa Road 1018/7
Iraq: Almutanabi Road 911/8
Jordan: Sh. Issa Road
Kuwait: Bani Atba Road 2105/7
Pakistan: Sh. Isa Road
Saudi Arabia: Sulmaniyya Road
UK: Al Mathaf Square
USA: Sh. Isa Road

TOURIST INFORMATION

Tourist information office: Maharraq Airport, tel: 21648.
Ministry of information: PO Box 2053 Jufair/Manama, tel: 8711.

MANAMA

The capital city is at the north end of the Island. It is growing so rapidly that a description written one year will be outdated the next. However, it has the government buildings, banks, chief hotels, and the *souk* or covered market. The Rulers Palace is at Quadabiya, and in the evenings many people walk there beside the sea where it is cooler, look at the illuminations, and patronise the café in the park.

Much land has been reclaimed from the sea here, and work is continuing. Manama has been a town since the 15th century, when contemporary Portuguese writers mention it, but the ancient capital of Bahrain, **Bilad al Qadim**, is just outside the modern city. It dates from AD

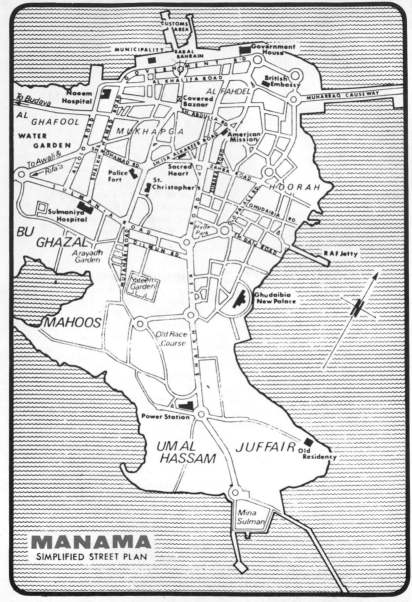

MANAMA
SIMPLIFIED STREET PLAN

Crown Copyright
Reproduced with the permission of the controller of Her Majesty's Stationery Office

900, and is now mostly in ruins, though some interesting archaeological remains have been found.

The Ruler is responsible for a large residential development called **Isa Town**, 8km. from Manama, which at present provides housing for 15,000 Bahrainis, and will eventually have 35,000 residents. The centre is forbidden to car traffic, and is decorated with fountains and climbing plants. There are two elegant mosques with tall minarets and blue domes, also a sports stadium, swimming pool, cinema, library, children's playground, and clinic.

Although almost everything is provided to make the inhabitants comfortable, the town-planners who designed it have made two great errors, in not having provided pavements or drains, and in laying out the streets as long wide thoroughfares, rather than as narrow shady alleys which protect pedestrians from the sun.

Hotels
Hilton Hotel, tel: 50000
Ramada Inn, tel: 58100
Delmon Hotel, tel: 54761
Moon Plaza Hotel, tel: 8263
Tylos Hotel, tel: 52600
Gulf Hotel, tel: 712881
Middle East Hotel, tel: 54733
Sahara Hotel, tel: 50850
Omar Khayyam Hotel, tel: 713841
Capital Hotel, tel: 55955
Bristol Hotel, tel: 58989

Restaurants
Pearl Restaurant, tel: 52852
Keith's Bistro, tel: 713163
Airport Restaurant, tel: 21418
Paradise Restaurant, tel: 51271
Chinese Restaurant, tel: 713603

OTHER TOWNS

The village of **A'ali** is just south of the date gardens, on the edge of the ancient Dilmun tumuli. It is famous for its pottery, and the kilns can be seen smoking from afar: some are actually inside the burial mounds. Red clay is shaped into traditional pots, bowls, water-jars and dishes, and the only full-time potter left, Abdul Hussain, says that his family have been potters for centuries, but that today he is the only one left. Bahrainis find that jobs at BAPCO, or the associated industries, are far more profitable, if less intrinsically satisfying. On the other hand, the cost of living rises almost daily, and people have to keep up with it somehow.

The oil company town, **Awali**, justifies the somewhat unkind description of 'Surbiton-in-the-sand' sometimes given to it. It could be any English or American suburb, in a somewhat fiercer climate. It was built by BAPCO to provide housing, shops, and leisure facilities for its expatriate staff.

The Ruler's country residence is in a modern small town, **Rifaa al Gharbi**, situated beween Isa Town and Awali. Just south of it is the *Saafra* race-course where horse and camel races take place on Fridays.

Zellaq on the west coast has several beaches and a sailing club; some Bahrainis have villas here. The southern part of the island contains the oil and gas deposits, and is otherwise barren, with rocks and sand dunes. It is now used as a hunting and hawking area; the industry that the Ruler is encouraging will creep slowly into it as the oil recedes. The highest part of the island, **Jebel Dukhan**, 122m. is in the middle of the oil fields; the whole island can be seen from its summit.

The other islands of the archipelago include **Halat al Suluta** and **Halat al Khulaifat** which are off Muharraq and have some fine old Bahraini merchants' houses. **Nabih Salih** is much favoured by swimmers and water skiers. It is just south of Jufair and is covered with date palms. **Sitra** contains the power stations and de-salination plant, as well as the oil terminal.

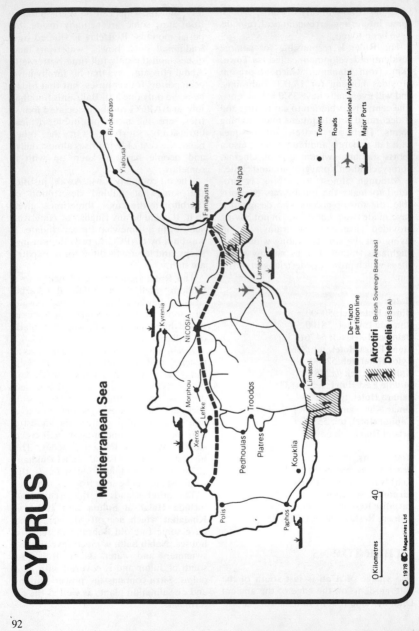

CYPRUS

Mediterranean Sea

Rizokarpaso

Yialousa

Ayia Napa

Famagusta

Larnaca

Kyrenia

NICOSIA

Morphou

Lefke

Xeros

Troodos

Pedhoulias

Platres

Limassol

Kouklia

Polis

Paphos

0 Kilometres   40

• Towns

Roads

International Airports

Major Ports

De-facto partition line

Akrotiri (British Sovereign Base Areas)

Dhekelia (BSBA)

© 1978 © Magazines Ltd

CYPRUS

Cyprus is well on the way to recovering its position as a major Mediterranean tourist destination, with most visitors coming from Lebanon, the UK, Greece, West Germany and the USA. New hotels have been opened since the Turkish invasion of 1974, and these are beginning to make up for the loss of the many major hotels in Famagusta and Kyrenia.

A holiday in Cyprus can take in the capital, Nicosia, and the seaside resorts of Paphos, Limassol, Larnaca and Ayia Napia, as well as the famous mountain resorts around Troodos. There are good hotels, with reasonable rates, excellent Cypriot food and wines, and numerous places of great archaeological and scenic interest.

Tourism is still restricted by the fact that most of the island's hotels before 1974 were in the northern and north-eastern part of the island, now occupied by Turkey. Although tourism is being promoted by Turkey itself, to date this is only resulting in local travel from Turkey to the Turkish-occupied sector of Cyprus. There is no freedom of movement between the two parts of the island, and most of the hotels in Famagusta and Kyrenia stand empty, along with shops, banks, churches and many private houses too.

THE LAND AND THE PEOPLE

The third-largest island in the Mediterranean, Cyprus has an area of 9,851 sq. km. Its maximum length is 240 km. east to west, and greatest north-south width is 96 km. The nearest country is Turkey, a mere 64 km. away, and Cyprus is only 100 km. from the coast of Syria. The Greek mainland is some 800 km. to the west, although Rhodes is only 380 km. away.

The coastline is rocky and indented, with numerous sandy coves and beaches. The north coast is backed by a steep range of limestone hills rising to 1,000 m., but the highest ground is in the mountain massif of Troodos, covered with pine, cypress and cedar trees, reaching nearly 2,000 m. at Mount Olympus. Between the two hill and mountain ranges are the fertile Messaoria plain in the east and the more fertile Morphou basin to the west, and the greatest north-south width is 96 km. The nearest country is Turkey, a mere 64 km. away, and Cyprus is only 100 km. from the coast of Syria. The Greek mainland is some 800 km. to the west, although Rhodes is only 380 km. away.

Nearly 10% of the land area is covered with forest. Another 50% is arable, and used for wheat, barley, potatoes, vegetables and the almost ubiquitous olive tree. There are vineyards on the southern and western slopes of the Troodos mountains, and the valleys support fruit.

The history of Cyprus, as a vulnerable prize for successive conquerors of the eastern Mediterranean, has left its people tragically divided. The Ottoman Turks who occupied the island in the 16th Century came in large numbers, and today their descendants comprise one-fifth of the population, divided by religion, class and social customs from the Greek Cypriot majority.

The problems created by these divisions were never resolved by the British colonial authorities, who ruled from 1878 to 1960. A Greek Cypriot campaign for Enosis, or union with Greece, gathered momentum in the late 1950s, although an international agreement, guaranteed by Greece, Turkey and Britain, gave Cyprus an independence constitution that temporarily shelved the basic inter-communal problems.

Under the presidency of Archbishop Makarios Cyprus managed to avoid full-scale civil war, but in 1963 Turkish Cypriots rebelled and were forced to evacuate mixed villages, and in 1967 there was an even greater separation of the two communities.

In Greece itself the military junta were getting impatient with Makarios's reluctance to bring about Enosis, and in July 1974 they staged a coup to overthrow the Archbishop. This caused bitter fighting between Greeks and provoked a Turkish military invasion in the same week. Moreover the Greek junta in Athens failed to fight the Turks and itself collapsed.

The Turkish forces moved in massively and eventually occupied 40% of Cyprus. The reluctance of the Turkish community to negotiate realistically for another power-sharing formula is based on the bitter experience of the 1960s, when their position and influence (favoured under British rule) had been steadily eroded.

The Turkish invasion displaced an enormous number of Greek Cypriots—over 200,000 according to the United Nations—and many of these have yet to find permanent accommodation. There are also problems for the Turks still in the south and for Greeks unable to leave the north. Significant numbers of Greeks have left for Greece, or other countries, and in the north there has been an influx of mainland Turks. Cyprus may have to put up with its divisions for some time to come.

EARLY HISTORY

According to the evidence of neolithic monuments that still stand near Larnaca, Cyprus has a pre-history dating back to 6000 BC. By 2000 BC the Achaean Greeks had established city-kingdoms on the Mycenean model and introduced the Greek language and way of life.

Cyprus (the Greek word for copper) has long been known for its copper and its forests, and was constantly fought for by the Assyrians, Egyptians and Persians.

Alexander the Great removed the Persians, but the division of his empire after his death meant that Cyprus came under the rule of the Greek Ptolemies who had become rulers of Egypt, and then under the Romans from 58 BC to AD 330, when it became an important part of the Byzantine empire.

In the Middle Ages Cyprus was conquered by Richard I of England, then it passed to the Knights Templar. The Lusignans from France established a feudal kingdom from 1192 to 1489. The Republic of Venice was in control between 1489 and 1571, when the Turks conquered the island and settled much of it.

Turkish control lasted until 1878 when the expansionist policy of Russia led the Turks to cede Cyprus to Britain as a means of defence for the Turkish mainland.

GENERAL INFORMATION

Area: 9,851 sq. km.
Population: 650,000.
Capital: Nicosia.
Government: Independent republic, presidential system. Five-yearly elections. Northern part under Turkish occupation.
Languages: Greek, Turkish, English.
Religions: Greek Orthodox (78%), Sunni Muslim (18%).
Currency: Cyprus pound, divided into 1,000 mils.
£1 sterling=CY£0.743 $1=CY£0.382.
In the Turkish-occupied zone, the Turkish lira is in use.
Time: GMT+2.

HOW TO GET THERE

Travellers may enter the republic only through Larnaca airport, or the ports of Larnaca, Limassol and Paphos. From the point of view of the Greek Cypriot Government entry only through Kyrenia, Famagusta, Karavostassi and Tymbou airport (Ercan) is prohibited as these are under Turkish military control

By air: Larnaca is served by several international airlines and Cyprus Airways. Flights from London, Athens, Beirut and Israel. There are flights from Ankara to Tymbou airport (Ercan) in the Turkish-occupied zone. The airport at Nicosia is used only for diplomatic purposes.

By sea: The main ports in the Government-administered region are Larnaca and Limassol. A car-ferry service operates from Athens, Rhodes and Beirut.

Famagusta is in the Turkish-occupied zone.

Visas and health regulations
Passports are required by all visitors, but visas are not needed by citizens of Austria, Belgium, Britain and Common-wealth countries, Denmark, Finland, France, West Germany, Greece, Iceland, Ireland, Italy, Japan, Luxembourg, Netherlands, Norway, Spain, Sweden, Switzerland, USA and Yugoslavia. Other citizens should apply for visas at Cypriot diplomatic missions abroad.

A smallpox vaccination certificate is required.

Visitors to the so-called "Turkish Federated State of Cyprus" must comply with Turkish travel regulations (*see chapter on Turkey*).

Customs and currency
Personal baggage is permitted free of duty. The import or export of Cyprus currency is forbidden beyond the value of CY£10. Traveller's cheques and foreign currency may be cashed at any bank.

CLIMATE

A healthy climate, with a long dry summer, hot on the coast and bracing in the mountains. Winter is mild, and the sea is usually warm enough for swimming at any time of year. Snow falls in the mountains between December and March.

ACCOMMODATION AND FOOD

Excluding the Turkish-occupied sector there are over 50 hotels, ranging from five-stars (in Nicosia and Limassol) to one-star. The main accommodation centres are Nicosia, Limassol, Larnaca, Paphos and the hill resorts. The inclusive hotel rates are very reasonable by modern standards. Several tour operators offer holiday flats and villas. There are guest houses in the main centres.

The Turkish-controlled part of Cyprus contains most of the island's hotels, but they were still nearly all closed in early 1978.

There are excellent restaurants of all grades throughout Government-controlled Cyprus. Tourist Information Offices in Nicosia, Limassol, Larnaca and Paphos will give details for each town.

TRANSPORT

Buses connect all the towns and villages of the Government-controlled area. Efficient taxi services also connect the main towns; a seat in a shared taxi will usually cost less than CY£1, whatever the distance.

There are car hire services, including Avis, Budget and Hertz; information available from Tourist Information Offices. Driving is on the left side of the road.

BANKS

The main foreign banks are Barclays, Chartered, National Bank of Greece and Grindlays. The local banks are Bank of Cyprus, Hellenic Bank and Cyprus Popular Bank. Banks open 0830-1200 Monday to Saturday.

PUBLIC HOLIDAYS

New Year's Day; Epiphany, 6 January; Greek Independence, 25 March; Orthodox Easter; Labour Day, 1 May; Assumption, 15 August; Christmas.

Festivals: 6 January, Feast of Epiphany; 11-12 February 1978, Limassol Carnival; February, ski competitions at Troodos; 13 March 1978, wine festival in all towns and villages; 22 April 1978, St. Lazarus Icon Procession, Larnaca; 26 May-11 June 1978, International Fair, Nicosia; 18 June 1978, Kataklysmos festival in all seaside towns; June, Nicosia Cultural Festival; 28-29 June 1978, St. Paul's Feast, Kato Paphos; July 1978, Limassol Art Festival; August 1978, Paphos Folk Art Festival; September 1978, Stroumbi Village Wine Festival, Paphos, and (second fortnight) Limassol Wine Festival.

EMBASSIES IN NICOSIA

Australia, tel: 73001; **Bulgaria**, tel: 72486; **China**, tel: 73041; **Czechoslovakia**, tel: 49336; **Egypt**, tel: 65144; **France**, tel: 65258; **West Germany**, tel: 44362; **East Germany**, tel: 44193; **Greece**, tel: 41880; **India**, tel: 43732; **Israel**, tel: 45195; **Italy**, tel: 73183; **Lebanon**, tel: 42216; **Libya**, tel: 49363; **Netherlands**, tel: 45222; **Poland**, tel: 48411; **Syria**, tel: 74481; **Turkey**, tel: 65242; **USSR**, tel: 72141; **UK**, tel: 73131; **USA**, tel: 65151 (information tel: 73143); **Yugoslavia**, tel: 45511.

TOURIST INFORMATION

Cyprus Tourism Organisation, 5 Princess Zena De Tyras Street, Nicosia, tel: 021 44264, Larnaca airport, tel: 041 543 89, Opposite Customs, Limassol, tel: 051 62756, Democratias Square, Larnaca, tel: 041 54322, 3 Gladstone St., Paphos, tel: 061 32841.

NICOSIA

Capital of Cyprus since the 12th century AD, when the coastal cities were being heavily raided, Nicosia is the only inland town on the island. Its palaces, residences and cathedral of St. Sophia date from the medieval rule of the Frankish Lusignan kings. Worth seeing are: Cyprus Museum, Folk Art Museum, the Venetian walls, the Archiepiscopal Palace and the Cathedral of St. John.

Modern Nicosia has modern shops, hotels, cinemas, theatres and night clubs, and is well placed for visiting most of the island's regions. There is also an international conference centre.

Hotels

Cyprus Hilton, five-star, Archbishop Makarios Ave., Box 2023, tel: 64040, tlx: 2388.

Churchill, four-star, Achaeans St., Box 4145, tel: 48858, tlx: 3280.

Philoxenia, four-star, Elenja Ave., Box 4812, tel: 403457, tlx: 2850.

Asty, three-star, Prince Charles St., Box 4502, tel: 73021, tlx: 2618.

Catsellis Hill, three-star, Kasos St., Box 2329, tel: 43114.

Cleopatra, three-star, Florina St., Box 1397, tel: 45254, tlx: 2316.

Excelsior, three-star, Photios Stavrou St., tel: 42062, tlx: 2067.

Kennedy, three-star, Regaena St., Box 1212, tel: 75131, tlx: 2202.

Lido, three-star, Philokypros St., Box 1467, tel: 74351.

Two-star and one-star hotels include **Carlton, Crown, Nicosia Palace, Pisa Tower, Regina Palace, Acropole, Alexandria, Averof** and **Louis**.

LARNACA

A few minutes from the international airport and only half an hour's drive from Nicosia, Larnaca is a pleasant seaside town, of great historical interest. It is on the site of the Mycenean city of Kition, which was the home of Zeno, founder of the Stoic school of philosophy in Athens. Visitors may see the excavations of ancient Kition being conducted in the Kathari section of the town.

One of the most interesting monuments is the Church of St. Lazarus. Also worth seeing are the Phaneromeni megalithic monument, the ancient castle, the Pierides Museum and the Tekke of Ummul Haram (foster mother of the Prophet Muhammad).

In the region of Larnaca is the Khirokitia neolithic site dating back 8,000 years, Stavrovouni Monastery and the interesting villages of Lefkara and Pyrga. Of scenic interest is the Salt Lake near

Visit Cyprus

The island of the Middle East, a land of fruits and flowers and friendly people.

CYPRUS Ideal for: happy holidays, vacations, conferences, shopping.

CYPRUS A perfect combination of sandy beaches, historic cities, pinescented fashionable hill resorts and green valleys. For more information please apply to your travel agent or Cyprus Tourism Organisation, P.O. Box 4535, Nicosia. Telex: 2165 Cytour. Tel: (021) 43374.

Larnaca, with its flamingoes and surrounding woods.

A new beach and yacht marina are
being developed.

Hotels
Sun Hall, four-star, Athens Ave., Box
300. tel: 53341, tlx: 3065.
Four Lanterns, three-star, 19 Athens
Ave., Box 150, tel: 52011, tlx: 2491.
Africa Lodge, two-star, 26 Galileo St.,
tel: 54531.

AYIA NAPA

Although Turkish-occupied Famagusta is
the nearest town, Ayia Napa is easily
accessible from Larnaca. It is a beautiful
fishing village with a medieval monastery, sea caves, windmills, sandy beaches
and clear water. It is an excellent spot for
walks in beautiful scenery. Paralimni is
an atttractive village nearby.

Hotels
Grecian Bay, five-star, under construction in 1977.
Nissi Beach, three-star, Box 11 Paralimni,
tel: 441.
Parneva Beach, two-star, Box 5 Paralimni, tel: 435.

LIMASSOL

A festive and busy town with a history
going back to the ancient kingdoms of
Curium and Amathus, and to the Crusade. Richard Coeur de Lion married
Berengaria of Navarre here and the
Knights of St. John of Jerusalem established their headquarters here in 1291.

In Limassol are the castle, museum,
gardens, zoo and wine factories. In this
highly cultivated district are citrus and
vine plantations and the historic interest
of Episkopi Museum, Kolossi Castle and
the Roman floors and mosaics at Curium.
There are some fine beaches.

Hotels
Amathus Beach, 10 km. east of Limassol,
five-star, Box 513, tel: 66152, tlx: 2683.
Apollonia Beach Yermassoyias, five-star,
Box 594, tel: 65351, tlx: 2268.
Curium Palace, four-star, Byron St., tel:
63121, tlx: 3150.
Pavemar, three-star, 28th October Ave.,
Box 263, Tel: 63535, tlx: 2035.
Two-star and one-star hotels include
Chez Nous, **Pefkos**, **Continental**, **Limassol
Palace** and **Panorama**.

HILL RESORTS

The main hill resorts are Platres, Prodromos, Troodos, Pedhoulas, Kakopetria,
Kalopanayiotis, Moutoullas (with medici-
nal springs), Perapedhi, Omodos, Galata
and Agros.

With snow from December to March,
there is a popular winter season, with
skiing on the heights of Mount Olympus.

The area is endowed with interesting
monuments, monasteries and churches,
but the main appeal is the natural beauty
of the well-forested mountains. Cedar
Valley and the nearby look-out point are
spectacular.

Hotels
PLATRES
Forest Park, four-star, Box 82, tel: 751.
Edelweiss, two-star, tel: 335.

PEDHOULAS
Pinewood Valley, three-star, tel: 353.
Marangos, two-star, tel: 657.

PRODROMOS
Berengaria, one-star, tel: 555.
Alps, tel: 553.

TROODOS
Troodos, two-star, Box 1190 (Nicosia),
tel: 631.

KAKOPETRIA
Makris, three-star, tel: 419.
Hellas, two-star, tel: 450.

Paphos, birthplace of Aphrodite

GALATA
Rialto, one-star, tcl: 438.

KALOPANAYIOTIS
Drakos, **Helioupolis**, **Kastalia**, **Loutraki**, **Synnos**.

PERAPEDHI
Paradisos and **Perapedhi**.

AGROS
Vlachos.

PAPHOS

Paphos is a pleasant seaside resort with a combination of beautiful landscapes and historic interest. The archaeological sites include those of the ancient Greeks, the Romans, the Byzantines and the medieval period.

The town itself (formerly known as Ktima) is colourful and attractively set on a rocky cliff overlooking the sea and the harbour of New Paphos. In the town are: the fourth century St. Paul's Basilica; the mosaics in the houses of Dionysus and Theseus; and the Byzantine Castle of 40 pillars.

Carved out of cliffs are the 'Tombs of the Kings'. Some contain impressive Doric pillars. At a distance of 15 km. east is Old Paphos (known as Koukalia) with the remains of the Temple of Aphrodite, a centre of pilgrimage in the ancient world. Further in the same direction is the legendary birthplace of Aphrodite.

St. Neophytos monastery with Byzantine frescoes and icons is 11 km. north of modern Paphos. Further inland, through Paphos forest, are the two ancient monasteries of Chrysorroyiattissa and Ayia Moni. Also worth visiting are the Cedar Valley and the Spring of Love, near Polis, as well as the monastery of Kykko and the spectacularly-sited tomb of Archbishop Makarios.

Hotels
Paphos Beach four-star, St. Antonios St., Box 136, tel: 33091, tlx: 3202.
Dionysos, three-star, Poseidon St., Box 141, tel: 33414, tlx: 2949.
Axiothea, two-star, Aeolos St., Box 70, tel: 32866.
New Olympus, two-star, 12 Byron St., Box 115, tel: 32020.

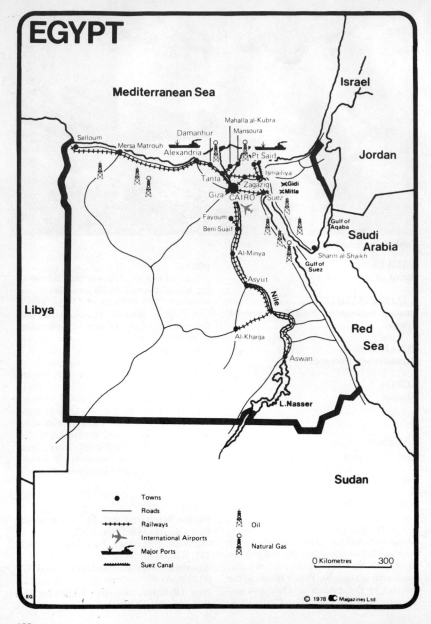

EGYPT

Mediterranean Sea

Israel

Jordan

Selloum

Mersa Matrouh

Damanhur

Mahalla al-Kubra

Mansoura

Alexandria

Pt Said

Ismailiya

Tanta

Zagazig

Gidi

Mitla

Giza

CAIRO

Suez

Fayoum

Beni-Suaif

Gulf of Aqaba

Saudi Arabia

Al-Minya

Sharm al-Shaikh

Gulf of Suez

Asyut

Nile

Libya

Red Sea

Al-Kharga

Aswan

L.Nasser

Sudan

●	Towns
—	Roads
+++++	Railways
✈	International Airports
⚓	Major Ports
~~	Suez Canal
⚒	Oil
⚒	Natural Gas

0 Kilometres 300

EG

© 1978 Magazines Ltd

EGYPT

The land of ancient civilisation, today Egypt is hoping for a great new upswing in its economy. By 1980, production of oil and natural gas could reach 50 million tonnes a year; the Suez Canal is earning more revenue than ever before; there is increasing foreign investment and recently vast reservoirs of water were found in the Western Desert.

Mammoth investment in upgrading hotels and building new ones will enable Egypt to welcome visitors in style. The fantastic pyramids and other monuments and tombs have, for 3,000 years, drawn travellers to Egypt.

Tourists have always enjoyed traditional Egyptian hospitality, and now that the country has shrugged off the gloomy period of the late sixties and early seventies they are assured of comfortable accommodation even in the most remote areas.

Most luxury hotels in Cairo, Luxor and Aswan overlook the Nile with its long-masted *feluccas*. It is the Nile which makes Egypt essentially different from other countries in North Africa.

Egypt's archaeological heritage is second to none, and in addition it has its seething bazaars, and there is the appeal of villages where life moves at the pace of a camel turning a water wheel.

Although it still lacks first-class facilities, the great Delta city of Alexandria retains its romantic, slightly seedy atmosphere of Lawrence Durrell's 'Quartet'. The miles of beaches from here to Mersa Matruh offer an alternative holiday to crowded resorts elsewhere on the Mediterranean.

395 km. south of Suez, Hurghada is one of the world's richest areas for fish and coral, with a luxurious hotel on the Red Sea shore.

The healthy climate of Upper Egypt offers an escape from the European winter. January temperatures average 24°C. 899 km. from Cairo, Aswan straddles the invisible line between the Middle East and Africa. As in Cairo, with its skyscrapers and espresso bars side by side with ancient mosques and camel markets, Aswan combines a glorious past with a dynamic present.

THE LAND AND THE PEOPLE

The Nile divides Egypt unevenly into two and the Suez Canal provides a third division—the Sinai desert. Egypt is bounded by Israel in the north-east, Sudan to the south, Libya to the west and the Mediterranean in the north. The terrain is for the most part flat, arid desert.

Besides the Nile Valley and the Delta, the land is interspersed with oases, often set in depressions in the desert. With the exception of the Qattara Depression in the Western Desert, and Wadi an-Natrun just west of the Delta, these oases stretch from Siwah in the north-west near the Libyan border in a south-easterly broken line—Bahariya, Farafra, Dakhla, Kharga—which forms the main part of

Swansea University
WITHDRAWN FROM STO
Information Services & Syst

the New Valley. Rainfall is confined largely to the northern coast. Greenery is confined to the Nile Valley, the oases, the Delta and to the Mediterranean coast. Temperatures are highest between May and September. In April the hot, dusty, yellowing *khamsin* wind blows. Crops ripen in July and August, and in April and May. Without the blessing of the Nile, Egypt would be wholly, instead of only 96%, barren in its million square kilometres.

The construction of the Aswan High Dam has enabled advances to be made in the reclamation of land and has also tamed and controlled the flood waters, which in the past were often as much a cause of damage as a benefit. The country's 39 million people are crammed into the fertile areas, with the main concentrations at the base of the Delta in Cairo, in the Delta itself and beside the Nile.

The western region lies lower than the east, which has its loftiest peak in Jebel Shayib (2,187 m.). The Western Desert has patches of land rising to 300 m. among tracts of rocky terrain, broken by densely palmed oases.

The area east of the Nile consists of rocky uplands, often hard to penetrate and cross. South of Suez stretches a narrow coastal strip with fine beaches and deep-sea diving. The Delta is of striking lushness, emphasised by the desert, and here alone are trees regularly visible.

As can be expected in a largely agricultural country, the *fellahin* or peasant farmers make up the bulk of the population. They live mainly in the Delta and Nile Valley, frequently debilitated by bilharzia and often in circumstances little changed from their traditional ways of life. Their farming systems have remained the same for centuries; they use the *saqia*, a wooden water-wheel pulled by oxen, and the *shadoof*, the Archimedes screw-technique for pumping water—old fashioned but still effective. Only now is new mechanisation being introduced.

Egyptians have a hybrid background,

reflecting the number of peoples who have crossed and occupied the country. The majority stem from the Arab tribes who settled as a result of the Muslim conquests of the seventh century. More recently Italian, Greek and Armenian communities have settled. These, however, have been seriously reduced in size since 1952, and this has had the effect of changing the cosmopolitan nature of the major cities, Cairo and Alexandria. The Christian Copts number about four million and claim to be the descendants of the original inhabitants, who were an Hamitic people living along the banks of the Nile.

The contrast between the villages and the sophisticated cities remains great, although all the basic amenities of electricity and water are now freely available. Nevertheless, the exodus from the countryside to the cities is increasing.

The 1952 revolution had the effect of curbing such older traditions as polygamy, and women have been brought increasingly into everyday life. The nationalisation of the land cut down the land-owning classes and, at the same time, the drive towards industrialisation led to the development of a new industrial class, matched only by the growth of the administrative classes. The advent of President Sadat to power has done much to stimulate middle-class consumers.

CULTURE

President Nasser, in moments of political stress, used to invoke Egypt's 5,000 years of history and culture as the backbone on which the country and its people could depend. The cultural history is apparent everywhere. There are the well-known Egyptological sites centred mainly in the Cairo area and up and down the Nile, Graeco-Roman remains in Alexandria, Coptic churches in Cairo and Alexandria, and Muslim mosques and houses dating from the earliest period of the Arab invasion to the present day. Nasser's reminder was not really necessary.

The cultural carry-over can be seen reflected in the jewellery, glassware, and other articles which can be bought in *Khan al-Khalili* in Cairo and other tourist centres. Authentic items from digs or mounted fragments of Coptic cloth can be found at the more specialised shops. For the modern orientalist Cairo is still a major centre for the purchase of classical and modern Arabic literature.

Publishing is prolific in Egypt. Newspapers and magazines are numerous. Cairo Radio is one of the most powerful in Africa, broadcasting for long hours and in many languages. Television is watched throughout the country. Egyptian films are the most popular in the Arab world. The theatre has been remarkably lively in plays and musicals. In the urban centres the visitor should have little difficulty in getting around. Besides Arabic, French and English are widely spoken.

Some efforts have been made to preserve traditional dance forms through the Rida troupe, which performs regularly in Cairo and at the Pyramids. The culture of the Nubians, which might have disappeared under the waters of the Nile building up behind the Aswan Dam, has been recorded and partly transferred with these people to their newly located villages in the Kom Ombo area. Old traditions remain deeply implanted in the countryside and the poorer areas of towns and cities.

HISTORY

The Old Kingdom: The uniting of the two kingdoms of Egypt—one in Lower Egypt in the Delta, and the other in Upper Egypt along the River Nile—by Menes in approximately 3188 BC is generally taken to mark the formal beginning of Egyptian

The Sphinx and the Pyramid of Cheops, Giza

history. Government had expanded, particularly under the Pharaoh Zoser, at the beginning of the III Dynasty, to cover the area from Aswan to the Mediterranean. He had the step pyramid built at Saqqara. His successors, especially in the IV Dynasty with their capital at Memphis on the apex of the Delta, were responsible for such technical achievements as the Great Pyramid at Giza.

The Middle Kingdom: After a period of internal troubles, during which the south rebelled, union was restored under Mentuhotep I, and the city of Thebes (present-day Luxor) was founded. The Pharaohs of the XI and XII Dynasties extended their kingdom eastwards and southwards to the Second Cataract in Nubia, reaching their zenith of power in about 2000 BC. From 1788 BC and the beginning of the XIII Dynasty confusion set in, and the Hyksos conquered the land from the Sinai desert.

The New Kingdom: After expelling the Hyksos, the Amenhoteps and Tuthmosis Pharaohs of the XVIII Dynasty, between 1570 and 1320 BC, were able to expand the kingdom into an empire extending to the Orontes, the Euphrates and the Third Cataract of the Nile, 400 km. south of the present frontier. This dynasty left its mark up and down the land, especially around Thebes and through such figures as Amenhotep III and Nefertiti, his queen, and son-in-law, Tutankhamun.

A subsequent decline was offset by Ramses III of the XX Dynasty who defeated the Hittites, but thereafter the empire began to disintegrate. In succession Egypt suffered invasion by the Libyans, Nubians, Ethiopians and Assyrians. Under the Saite rulers of the XXVI Dynasty, between 663 and 525 BC, there was some revival of trade and former influence but, in the latter year, the Persian Emperor Cambyses overran the country. The Pharaohnic era ended in 332 BC with the arrival of Alexander the Great.

Hellenic and Roman Period: The foundation of the new capital bearing Alexander's name marked the beginning of a period of renewed sophistication, and the line of the Ptolemies. But while Alexandria retained a pre-eminence, law and order declined under these rulers, as Egyptians, now second-class citizens in their own country, revolted. The famed Cleopatra gave herself and her country to Julius Caesar, and then to Mark Antony. After the deaths of Antony and Cleopatra, Augustus took possession of Egypt in the name of Rome in 30 BC. For six and a half centuries the Romans used Egypt as their empire's granary and ruled with forceful efficiency.

In time the provincial authority broke down, and about AD 300 the Emperor Diocletian arrived to restore order and reform the administrative system. After his abdication in AD 305 Egypt again fell into confusion, with the land being taken over by landlords forming huge feudal estates.

Christian Period: Christianity had come to Egypt during the First Century AD, and during the Fourth Century Byzantium had replaced Rome as ruler. The Coptic Church was acknowledged during the Fifth Century as being separately established.

Arab invasion: (640-969): An Arab army under Amr Ibn al-Aas invaded Egypt in 640, just eight years after the death of the Prophet Muhammad, and in April 641 Alexandria surrendered. Al-Fustat was established as the capital in part of what is now Cairo. For two centuries Egypt was administered first as part of the Omayyad Caliphate and then as part of the Abbasid empire. Two locally-based dynasties—the Tulunids and the Ikhshidids—ruled between 868 and 969 in near independence from the Caliphate.

Fatimids and Ayyubids: (969-1250): The Ikhshidid rule was overthrown in 969 by invasion from Tunisia. The general Jawhar laid out a new capital beside Al-Fustat, which became the basis for modern Cairo. He also founded the university of Al-Azhar. A familiar pattern ensued of an initial period of prosperity and fine administration before the Fatimid empire began to break up. Its power in Egypt became nominal, and passed to the Arab rulers in Syria fighting the Crusaders. The last Fatimid was deposed in 1171, and Egypt formed part of Saladin's empire. On his death in 1193, his empire was divided among his heirs, and the Ayyubid branch ruled in Cairo.

The Mamlukes: (1250-1517): These were the slave bodyguards of the rulers originally, but their power increased as that of their masters declined. It was from their ranks that rulers emerged after an election or struggle for power. Although an alien element largely exploiting the land for their own ends, they protected Egypt from the Mongols and Crusaders. The numerous mosques and public works of this era indicate Egypt's wealth, but the condition of the country declined from the middle of the 14th Century.

Ottoman Egypt: (1517-1798): Selim I overthrew the last Mamluke sultan in a battle outside Cairo in 1517. In the following period, only Al-Azhar retained its prominence as Egypt sank into obscurity as a province and in a backwater from the main trade routes. The Mamlukes succeeded in reasserting their autonomy later.

The European Era: Bonaparte's arrival in Alexandria and the defeat of the Mamlukes in July 1798 brought Egypt rudely into contact with Europe. The enforced withdrawal of the French was followed by a struggle for power which resulted in a triumph by Muhammad Ali, an Albanian, recognised as sultan in 1805. A passionate believer in the benefits of European sophistication, he encouraged its influences—a trend followed by his successors. Under Ismail the Suez Canal was opened in 1869.

Creeping financial commitments and the consequences of Egypt's first modern nationalist revolt under Ahmed Orabi led in 1882 to the British occupation. Egypt now passed under another set of alien rulers. Men like Lord Cromer and Sir Eldon Gorst may have built Egypt up materially, but did nothing for its national pride. There was an unsuccessful revolt in 1919, and between 1922 and 1939—the former date marking Britain's acknowledgement of Egypt as an 'independent' State—the Wafd Party, the King and Britain competed for control.

The Anglo-Egyptian Treaty of 1936 ended the occupation, but gave Britain the right to station troops in the Suez Canal area. The build-up of dissatisfaction with Egypt's status and with King Farouk, and the 1948 defeat by Israel contributed to the formation of the Free Officers led by Gamal Abdel-Nasser. They seized power on 23 July 1952 and overthrew the monarchy.

Revolution: (1952-70): The nationalist aspirations of this group ran through all their policies. But it was not until 1954 that Nasser was able to emerge fully as leader, having outmanoeuvred General Neguib, who was President and the Free Officers' front man. Political parties were banned and land holdings limited. The British military presence was negotiated to end in 1954.

Nasser's standing in Egypt and the Arab world was consolidated by his leadership during the tripartite attack on Egypt by Israel, France and Britain in 1956, in ostensible reaction to the nationalisation of the Suez Canal.

Between 1958 and 1961, Egypt became known as the United Arab Republic as it entered an unsuccessful union with Syria. This undertaking was only slightly less unproductive than the Egyptian military involvement in Yemen between 1962 and 1967.

During the 1960s Nasser inaugurated sweeping nationalisation to bring the country's economy under state control. The Soviet Union acquired its first major economic foothold by agreeing to finance in 1958 the building of the Aswan Dam, after a Western withdrawal. The dam was built between 1960 and 1970. Egypt's involvement in war with Israel in June 1967 ended disastrously.

The period after that was spent trying to keep the economy expanding while building up expensively the armed forces, and looking for a settlement through the UN resolution of the Security Council of November 1967. An artillery and aircraft war was brought to an end by a US-proposed ceasefire in August 1970. President Nasser died in September after mediating in the civil war between King Hussain's forces and the Palestinian guerrillas in Jordan.

Sadat as President: Nasser was succeeded by his Vice-President, Anwar Sadat, who in May 1971; defeated a challenge to his authority led by a former Vice-President, Ali Sabri. Sadat found the strains of a 'no war, no peace' situation increasingly difficult to control. But in 1972 he expelled the Soviet military personnel and in October 1973 he staged the military action that is now officially known as the 'Victory'. The Israelis were driven from the Suez Canal. With this achievement Sadat set about opening up his country to the West. Commercial and travel restrictions were lifted. Huge loans have flooded in, pricipally from the USA. However, there are severe economic strains in a country where the majority of the people remain poor, dependent on a largely agricultural base, and where there are as yet few prospects of oil wealth on the scale of Saudi Arabia's or Libya's.

ECONOMY

Egypt is primarily an agricultural country. Agriculture provides nearly 30% of the Gross Domestic Product and employs more than half the workforce. Cotton is the major crop and foreign-currency earner, followed by rice, of which Egypt is Africa's major exporter.

The agricultural areas are concentrated in the Delta, along the Nile and around the oases. An important project is the development of the New Valley from underground water sources, and much effort has been put into the slow and costly process of reclaiming land. Egypt also produces wheat, maize, millet, sugar-cane and a wide variety of citrus fruits and vegetables. But it remains a large importer of food, especially wheat—a drain on hard currency.

President Nasser's major undertaking was rapidly to increase the pace of Egypt's industrialisation. To this end, and at considerable cost, large investments have been made in the iron and steel works and industrial zone at Helwan near Cairo. Industrial production has been rising at about 10% a year, and contributes about 20% of the GDP from 15% of the country's labour force. Industrial activity ranges from cigarettes and footwear to the assembly of heavy lorries. Assistance from the Soviet Union was crucial in the major aspects of Egypt's industrial development, particularly at Helwan. Moscow's most massive contribution has been the Aswan High Dam project. Completed in July 1970 after a decade of building, it provides adequate power at relatively cheap prices to ensure the spread of electrification and power for industry. A fishing industry is being developed on Lake Nasser, formed by the waters impounded by the dam.

Extensive exploration in the Western and Eastern Deserts and off shore in the Gulf of Suez has produced finds of oil. Promising quantities of gas have been found in the Delta.

Nasser also altered the face of the Egyptian economy by breaking up the large landholdings and bringing the bulk of economic activity under state control. Under President Sadat, the private sector has been given more encouragement.

Huge development loans have been agreed with the US and Saudi Arabia.

GENERAL INFORMATION

Area: 1,002,000 sq. km.
Population: 39 million.
Capital: Cairo.
Head of State: President Muhammad Anwar Sadat.
Government: The President has extensive powers, but government is also carried out by the Cabinet, the People's Assembly and the single political party, the Arab Socialist Union.
Languages: Arabic, but French and English widely spoken.
Religions: Mainly Islam, but also all shades of Christianity (especially Copts), and the Jewish religion.
Currency: Egyptian pound (£E) divided into 100 piastres (PT) and each PT into 10 millimes. £1 sterling = £E0.756 official exchange and £E1.22 tourist rate of exchange. US$1 = £E0.394.
Time: GMT + 2.

HOW TO GET THERE

By air: There are frequent direct flights to Cairo operated by most major international airlines and Egypt Air from many world capitals. Cairo Airport is situated 22 km. from the city centre. Transport into the city is available. There is an airport tax of £E1 on departure from Egypt.

By road: At present the only access for non-Arab motorists is by sea to Alexandria. They can drive from Alexandria to Cairo and Aswan. From Aswan by steamer to Wadi Halfa.

By sea: There are sailings from many European ports to Alexandria.

Visas and health regulations
Egypt issues transit visas (at consulates) for seven days and entry tourist visas for up to one month. These can also be obtained at Egyptian ports, airports and frontier posts. Collective visas may also be issued on personal passports or on collective passports to groups of tourists organised by travel agencies or persons representing shipping or airline agencies. These groups must stay together. A visitor is required to register with the police or the Ministry of Interior within one week of arrival in Egypt. Hotels or travel agents will normally arrange this.

A certificate of vaccination against smallpox is necessary for all visitors. Visitors coming from areas infected by cholera or yellow fever must have certificates of inoculation. Inoculation against typhoid and paratyphoid is advisable.

Customs and currency regulations
All personal effects, used or unused, are exempt from customs duties and other taxes and dues. Also exempt, though they must be declared, are such items for private use as cameras, radios, recorders, binoculars and jewellery. A copy of the declaration is left with the customs office, and the original kept for submission on departure. The first £20 worth of foods, alcoholic drinks, cigarettes, cigars and medicines bought for personal consumption are not dutiable.

On departure everything bought by visitors holding entry or transit visas may be taken out, provided the total cost of the new articles does not exceed the amount declared by the visitor to be in his possession on entry, and provided the articles are in the nature of gifts or for personal use. Receipts for such purchases should be kept.

Egyptian currency and banknotes may not be taken in or out of the country by tourists, who may exchange unused Egyptian currency into the original foreign currency at the official rate.

There is no limit to the amount of foreign currency that tourists may bring with them in banknotes, travellers' cheques, money orders, bank drafts or letters of credit. On arrival tourists are required to fill in a currency declaration form. Any amount of this declared sum may be exchanged into Egyptian currency through authorised banks or their representatives at the official rate of exchange. These deals must be recorded on this form. On departure tourists may carry with them the balance of the amount declared after deducting the amount officially exchanged and used during the stay in Egypt.

In 1976 a decree was issued that tourists applying for a visa had to transfer or exchange at least £75 or its equivalent in hard currency.

Foreigners leaving the country are permitted to transfer or exchange the hard currency they have not spent after deducting £10 a night. The effect is that these regulations are rarely if ever applied.

CLIMATE

Egypt lies between the Mediterranean and the 23rd parallel north of the equator and is sunny for all but a few days in the year. Rain does not fall on more than 40 days a year, and then only in a few places. Within Egypt there is the contrast between the coastal Mediterranean climate and the hot dryness of the interior. In the desert areas there is a sharp contrast between day and night temperatures.

What to wear
Egypt is an informal country where open-necked shirts are acceptable for business and entertainment—except in predictably self-important establishments. For the summer, the lightest cotton wear is recommended and for winter ordinary woollens and light raincoats.

Health precautions
Egypt is free from diseases that could be met with in normal circumstances, but the chances of stomach upset—especially at the beginning of a visit—are always present. Swimming is best confined to pools or the sea, because of the risk of contracting bilharzia through swimming elsewhere. Fly and insect repellent is advisable, particularly in summer. Hospitals, clinics and chemists are open to tourists and the public every day in most areas.

ACCOMMODATION AND FOOD

Egypt has in the major urban centres accommodation to suit all tourist tastes, with the accent on the higher price range. It has yet to cater for cheaper tours on a large scale. Food is usually a mixture of oriental and international cooking with the emphasis on well-spiced meats and sugary pastries.

Tipping
About 15% on hotel bills and meals and 10% for taxi drivers is expected.

NEW ACCOMMODATION PROJECTS

Egypt is going ahead with ambitious plans to expand accommodation, notably in Cairo.

Cairo's newest hotels are the Nile-side, 600-bed **Meridien** and the motel **Jolie Ville** near the Pyramids. Extensions to the **Mena House** are complete.

Major projects under way are Marriott's 2,200-bed **Omar Khayam**, which will be Cairo's biggest hotel, and a 1,400-room hotel at Heliopolis managed by Sheraton.

Sheraton will also manage a 700-room airport hotel due for completion in 1979.

Shepheards is being renovated. Work has started on the 1,680-room **Inter-Continental** on the site of the former Semiramis, overlooking the Nile, and the

Boulac area in central Cairo has been cleared for the Triad Touristic Centre—an hotel and apartment complex with offices, trade centre, conference hall and restaurants.

Brent-Walker are building an hotel, **El Salam**, in the grounds of El Shams Club in Heliopolis. It will open in July-August 1978.

Then there is the French-managed **Hotel Cairo**, a 1,056-room hotel in Tahrir Square.

The 900-room **Ramses Hilton** in Cairo will open in 1980. Hilton will also manage a 400-room hotel in Port Said.

The 840-bed ETAP hotel, the **Karnak**, is now open in Luxor. A contract has been signed for a 400-bed **Sheraton Luxor**, and a Pyramid Sheraton hotel school.

Sheraton is involved in seven major projects in Egypt. Extensions to the Cairo Sheraton will bring its total number of rooms to 900 and the company is to manage the hotel at Hurghada, the resort with immense tourist potential on the Red Sea.

The former **Red Sea Tours Hotel** will be completely refurbished into a 250-room resort-hotel, especially for diving and other water sports. It will open in mid-1978.

Another Sheraton project is two 90-cabin Nile steamers to begin a service in 1978.

TRANSPORT

Within Egypt transport is extensive and comparatively cheap.

By air: Egypt Air operates flights between the major cities (for information tel: Cairo 976477, 922444, 900554): Cairo-Alexandria (45 minutes); Cairo-Luxor (80 minutes); and Cairo-Aswan (1 hour 45 minutes).

By rail: Good and comfortable rail services are available between Cairo and the major cities and towns.

The railway organisation offers a first-class ticket inclusive of hotel charges at a reduced rate for a round trip to Cairo, Luxor and Aswan from either Alexandria, Port Said or Suez. There are also varying rates for different-sized tourist and student groups. (Information: Cairo 58458.)

By road: Taxis are available in all cities and towns and can accommodate up to five people. Fares are reasonable. Day or long-distance trips can be negotiated at rates which more than compensate for the lack of a formal car hire service. Cars can, however, be hired from the large hotels. Tourists bringing their own cars are required to have a carnet de passage and an international driving licence. (Contact Egyptian Automobile Club, 10 Kasr el-Nil Street, Cairo.)

BANKS

The Central Bank is the bank of issue and government banker. The commercial banks are the Bank of Alexandria, Banque du Caire, Bank Misr and the National Bank of Egypt, all of which have head offices in Cairo and branches in Alexandria and other main towns. They also have branches at Cairo Airport and in the major hotels, where travellers' cheques can be exchanged. Thos. Cook and Son (4 Sh. Champollion, Cairo) is also an authorised foreign-exchange dealer.

Business hours
Banks are open daily (except Fridays) from 08.30 to 12.30 hours and from 10.00-12.00 on Sundays. Shops are mostly open from 09.00 to 13.30 and from 16.30 or 17.00 to 20.00 or 21.00. Government offices are open from 09.00 to 14.00 every day except Friday and national holidays. Commercial offices are open from 08.30 to 14.00 in summer daily

except Fridays, and in winter 09.00-13.00 and 16.00-19.00 except on Thursday afternoons and Fridays. Post Offices are open daily except on Friday. The Central Post Office in Ataba Square in Cairo provides a 24-hour service.

PUBLIC HOLIDAYS

The Muslim holidays fall on different days each year in the Christian calendar. The principal ones observed in Egypt are the Muslim New Year, Mouled el-Nabi (the Prophet's Birthday), Ramadan Bairam (Eid el-Fitr) and Kurban Bairan.

The fixed holidays are: 18 June (Evacuation Day), 23 July (Revolution Day), 23 December (Victory Day). Banks are closed on 1 January and on Coptic Christian festival days.

The Nile Festival is held in December each year at Luxor (Al-Uqsur) and Cairo.

TOURIST OFFICES ABROAD

France: 56 ave d'Iena, Paris 16.
Italy: 19 via Bissolati, Rome.
Lebanon: Hag Hussein el-Eweni bldg, Midan Riad el-Solh, Beirut.
Spain: Alcala 21, Madrid 14.
Sweden: Strandvogen 9, Stockholm.
Switzerland: 11 rue Chantepoulet, Geneva.
UK: 62a Piccadilly, London W1.
USA: 630 Fifth Avenue, NY 10020, New York.
West Germany: 6 Frankfurt AM, Taunusstrasse 35.

FOREIGN EMBASSIES IN CAIRO

Afghanistan: 53 Omar Ebn El-Khattab Street Heliopolis. tel: Cairo 61104.
Algeria: 14 Brazil Street, Zamalek. tel: Cairo 805630.

Austria: 21 The High Dam Street, Dokki. tel: Giza 805898.
Belgium: 8 Abdel Khalek Tharwat Street. tel: Cairo 73632.
Canada: 6 Mohammed Fahmi El-Sayed Street, Garden City. tel: Cairo 23110.
Cyprus: 3 Nabil El-Wakkad Street, Dokki. tel: Giza 814778.
Denmark: 12 Hassan Sabry Street, Zamalek. tel: Cairo 802002.
France: 29 El-Giza Street. tel: Giza 848833.
Greece: 18 Aisha Al-Taymurya Street, Garden City. tel: Cairo 30443.
Iraq: 9 Mohammad Mazhar Street, Zamalek. tel: Cairo 801820.
Italy: El-Salamlik Street, Garden City. tel: Cairo 20658.
Japan: 10 Ibrahim Nagib Street, Garden City. tel.: Cairo 24469.
Jordan: 6 El-Geheiny Street, Dokki. tel: Giza 811753.
Kuwait: 12 Nabil El-Wakkad Street, Dokki. tel: Giza 814791.
Lebanon: 5 Ahmed Nessim St. tel: Giza 845466.
Liberia: 2 St. no. 22, Madinet Al-Awkaf, Dokki. tel: Giza 801956.
Morocco: 10 Salah Eddin Street, Zamalek. tel: Cairo 801269.
Netherlands: 18 Hassan Sabry Street, Zamalek. tel: Cairo 802022.
Norway: 2 Shafik Mansur Street, Zamalek. tel: Cairo 808824.
Saudi Arabia: 12 El-Kamel Mohammad St., Zamalek. tel: Cairo 802073.
Spain: 28 Ahmad Hishmat Street, Zamalek. tel: Cairo 801881.
Sudan: 3 Ibrahim Street, Garden City. tel: Cairo 25043.
Sweden: 4 The High Dam Street, Dokki. tel: Giza 806131.
Switzerland: 10 Abdul Khalek Tharwat St. tel: Cairo 78171.
Syria: 7 Ahmad Sabry Street, Zamalek. tel: Cairo 818106.
Tunisia: 26 El-Gezira Street, Zamalek. tel: Cairo 816940.
Turkey: El-Nil Street, Giza. tel: Giza 843040.

UK: Garden City. tel: Cairo 20850.
USA: 5 America El Latinia Street.
USSR: 95 El-Giza St. tel: Giza 805069.
Yemen: 28 Amin El-Raf'i Street, Dokki. tel: Giza 804206.
Yemen (South): Hasanin Higazy Street, Dokki. tel: Giza 817208.

CAIRO

The sprawl of Cairo stretches north and south along the Nile and contains an untidy combination of local and modern architecture. But it gives this capital of several million people a more individual appearance than many Arab capitals. It has large avenues and squares which contrast with the narrow and twisted streets of the poorer areas. The shops in the main streets are fully stocked, mainly with locally produced goods. Pedestrian and traffic chaos is slowly being brought under control. A fine view of the city may be obtained by mounting the 180 m. tall Tower of Cairo on Gezira.

The Pyramids of Giza are the most famous aspect of Egypt's sights, but only a small part. The three great Fourth Dynasty pyramids of Giza, their surrounding tombs, and the Sphinx, and the step pyramids at Saqqara are only a few of a series which stretch out over a distance of 70 km. as far as El Faiyum. From the pyramids a view across the whole Nile Valley is possible from west to east. The reverse view can be obtained by going up to Saladin's Citadel in the Mokattam Hills. There can be seen the Mohammad Ali and Suliman mosques, both in Istanbul style, Ommayyad mosques and the Guahara Palace museum containing many of King Farouk's ornamental extravagances. In Tahrir Square is the Egyptian Museum, with the finest collection of Egyptological items.

Other museums worth seeing are the Coptic Museum with its collection of objects dating back to the early Christian era, and the Islamic Art Museum, among whose rare objects are notable Koranic manuscripts and Arab ceramics. In Beit el-Kretlia (formerly the Gayer-Anderson museum) are reserved examples of 18th-century styles of living and furniture, bridging European and Oriental influence. In the Abdin Palace Museum King Farouk's lifestyle can be seen.

Among the Islamic monuments to visit are: Al-Azhar University and Mosque, built partly in AD 972; Al-Hussein Mosque in the square opposite; the Sultan Hassan Mosque at the foot of the Citadel with its ceramics and twin minarets; the old-style Ibn Tulun Mosque with its rare minaret mounted by an outside staircase; and the oldest mosque of all, attributed to the first Arab conqueror Amr Ibn al-Aas. There are also some churches worth visiting: the Holy Virgin's Church (also known as the Hanging Church) built in old Cairo about AD 400, the modern Cathedral of St. Mark and, close by at Zeitun, the Virgin's Church.

Hotels
Main hotels
Nile Hilton: Tahrir Square. tel: 811811.
Sheraton: Galaa Bridge. tel: 983000.
Meridien: Corniche el-Nil Street. tel: 845444.
Shepheards: Corniche el-Nil Street. tel: 33800.
Mena House Oberoi: al-Ahram Street, Giza. tel: 8555444.
Cairo International Airport: tel: 966074/6.
Jolie Ville: Desert Road, Cairo. tel: 851226.
Atlas: 2 Bank el-Goumhuria Street. tel: 918311.
Manial Palace: el-Manial Street. tel: 844535.
Cleopatra: Tahrir Square. tel: 970420.
El Nil: Ahmed Ragab Street, Garden City. tel: 22805.
El Borg: Saray el-Gizira Street. tel: 816068.
President: 22 Taha Hussein Street, Zamalek. tel: 816751.

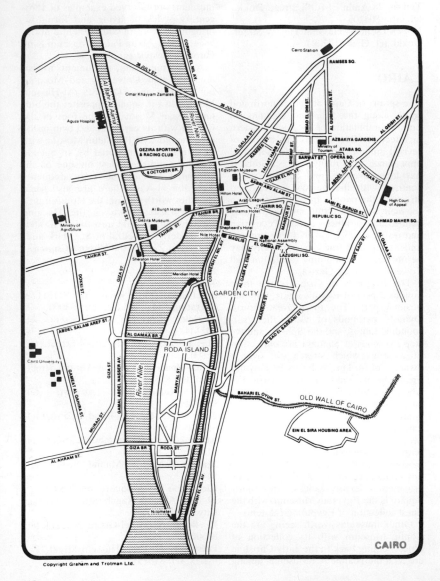

CAIRO

Copyright Graham and Trotman Ltd.

Khan el-Khalili: 7 Bosta Street, Ataba Square. tel: 900230.
Continental: 10 Opera Square. tel: 911322.
Shehrezade: 182 el-Nil Street. tel: 819896.
Cosmopolitan: 1 Ibn Taalab Street. tel: 979220.

Other hotels
Ambassador: 31, 26 July Street. tel: 51022.
Golden Tulip: 13 Talaat Harb Street. tel: 41159.
Gresham House: 20 Talaat Harb Street. tel: 43070.
Lotus: 12 Talaat Harb Street. tel: 970360.
Garden City House: 23 Kamal El-din Salah Street. tel: 28400.

Restaurants
These Cairo restaurants are recommended:
Versailles: 30 Mohammad Sakeb Street, Cairo (Zamalek). Ostentatious, but good cuisine.
Alla el Din: 26 Sherif Street.
Ibis: Hilton Hotel.
Estoril: 12 Talaat Harb Street European food at very reasonable prices.
Grillon: 8 Kasr el-Nil Street. Good French/Italian food.
Lappas: Functional. European food.
Groppy: Talaat Harb Street. Serves good European food at reasonable prices.
Union: 28 July Street. Good European food at reasonable prices.
Sofar: 21 Adli Street. Good Lebanese food.
Munchen: 31, 26 July Street. Typical German food.
  In Port Suez, the **St. James Restaurant**, 23 July Street, serves very good fish at very reasonable cost.
  20 kms. from Alexandria, the seaside **Restaurant Zephyrion**, serves excellent sea food.
  With few exceptions, a meal for two in a good Egyptian restaurant will cost about £12, including a bottle of local wine.

Entertainments
Floor shows and oriental dancing can be seen at the larger hotels, at such places as *Auberge des Pyramides, Covent Garden* and *Arizona* on the road to the Pyramids, and beside the Nile at *Kasr el-Nil* and *Al-Shagara*, and *Fontana* on Roday island.
  There is also dancing and a floor show at *Sahara City*, 12 km. from the Pyramids. There are several theatres, mainly for Arab works, and many cinemas with current western films. Son et Lumiere can be seen at the Pyramids (tel.: 852880), and the Citadel (tel.: 53260).

Sports
At the Pyramids there are two riding schools, and another on Gezira Island. At sporting clubs in Gezira, Maadi and Heliopolis visiting membership can be arranged and swimming, tennis, golf, squash and basketball enjoyed.

Shopping
For tourist goods, the main area is Khan el-Khalili where modern reproductions of antiquities are readily available. Of special value are jewellery, spices and copper, ivory and mother-of-pearl inlaid work. For the keen bargainer with the practised eye genuine antiquities, old Coptic cloth and Muslim relics may be found.

Travel Agencies
Misr Travel & Shipping Co., 1 Talaat Harb Street, Cairo. tel: 29500.
Tourist Services (Egypt Air) Formerly Karnak, 12 Kasr el-Nil Street, Cairo. tel: 59916.
Gabry Travel & Tourist Agency, 1 Talaat Harb Square, Cairo. tel: 40203.
Thomas Cook, 4 Champollion Street, Cairo. tel: 46392.
Eastmar, 13 Kasr el-Nil Street, Cairo. tel: 970445.

American Express, 15 Kasr el-Nil Street, Cairo. tel: 970138.

Hapy Travel & Tourist Agency, 17 Kasr el-Nil Street, Cairo. tel: 55501.

Naawas Tourist Agency, 17 Mahmoud Bassiouni Street, Cairo. tel: 41432.

Kuwait & Arab Countries Travel Agencies, 6 Kasr el-Nil Street, Cairo. tel: 55555.

ALEXANDRIA

If Cairo is Arab Africa, Alexandria is the Mediterranean. The corniche and buildings stretch along the shore, and their layout and the cooler temperatures make Alexandria the natural focus for a mass summer exodus from Cairo. Situated between the sea and Lake Maryut it is Egypt's second-largest city and its main port. In the early days of Christianity it was one of that religion's main centres.

For a glimpse into the monarchical age the museum of the former royal palace of al-Montazah should be visited. For those in search of the past there is the Graeco-Roman museum and Pompey's pillar standing among the ruins of the Serapium Temple. Near the port are the catacombs of Kom al-Shuqafa, dating back to about AD 100. At the northern tip of the harbour entrance, where the Pharos used to stand, is the Fort of Qait Bey. The mosque of Abu al-Abbas al-Mursi, with its high minaret and four domes, dates from 1767 and is the chief Islamic monument.

Alexandria's chief glory is its beaches. Among the best known and most crowded are, from east to west, Al-Maamoura, Al-Montazah, Al-Mandara, Al-Assafra, Miami, Sidi Bishr, San Stefano, Glym and Shatby. These all lie along the corniche, but on the western boundaries of the city are the beaches of Agami and Hanoville.

Hotels

Palestine: Montazah Palace. tel: 66799.

San Stefano: Al-Geish Avenue. tel: 63580.

Cecil: 16 Saad Zaghlul Square. tel: 807532.

Al-Salamlek: Montazah Palace. tel: 65813.

Hanoville: Agami Beach. tel: 800077.

Metropole: 52 Saad Zaghlul Street. tel: 21467.

Agami Palace: Agami Beach. tel: 805555.

Swiss Cottage: 252 Al-Geish Avenue, Glymosopoulo. tel: 62885.

Villa Nana: 558 Al-Geish Avenue, Sidi Bishr. tel: 60527.

Al-Amawi: 7 Al-nasr Avenue, Mansheya. tel: 34761.

Restaurants

The top hotels all have high-class Oriental and Western cuisine. Besides these are: **Zafarian** at Abu Kir (sea food). **Santa Lucia,** 40 Safeya Zaghlul Street, for good European food. **The Elite,** 13 Safeya Zaghlul Street, has good European food, as does the **Pam Pam,** 23 Safeya Zaghlul Street, for the same with music. There are also numerous cinemas and summer theatres.

Sports

Besides swimming and water-skiing facilities, the visitor can without difficulty become a temporary member at the **Smouha** and **Sporting** clubs. Both have a golf course, horse racing, tennis and squash. Membership can also be arranged for yachting, rowing and automobile clubs.

Tourist information

Main tourist office: Saad Zaghlul Square, Ramleh Station (tel.: 25985). Tourists can also obtain information from the Sea terminal office (tel.: 37090).

FROM ALEXANDRIA

From Alexandria the visitor (where permitted by security regulations) should travel west along the coast (by train, bus or private car) to **Sidi Abdel-Rahman**, 127 km. away on this beach is the first class **Hotel Alamein** (64 rooms).

Further along the coast, 290 km. west of Alexandria is the small but expanding port of **Mersa Matruh**, with a seven-km. beach boasted of as one of the best in the world. It can be reached by rail (from Alexandria, tel: 58458), by air (three flights weekly from Cairo, tel.: 872123), and by road from Alexandria. There are two tourist-class hotels: **Lido** and **Rim**.

From Mersa Matruh it is also possible to travel 300 km. south-west to the Siwa Oasis near the Libyan border. In this oasis, where dates, olives and grapes are grown, the village has moved down from a craggy outcrop of rocks to leave a remarkable shell of tall uninhabited buildings on the heights.

The separate and special culture produced by the Bedouin and descendants of slaves brought from central Africa has been sadly eroded in recent years. The remains of the temple of Amun, whose oracle was once consulted by Alexander, can still be seen.

THE RED SEA

One of Egypt's most spectacular tourist regions for those who prefer swimming and sunning to sightseeing.

From **Suez** to **Halayib** on the border with Sudan is a 1,000-km. coastal strip between craggy hills and blue waters rich in fish and coral for the underwater swimmer. In winter it is warm and sunny, and in summer breezes make the heat tolerable. A road runs down the coast. It is now a military area and excluded even to Egyptian non-military personnel.

Two centres have been established. At **Ain Sukhna**, 55 km. from Suez, there is a first-class hotel of the same name. **Hurghada**, 375 km. south of Suez, is the area's best site for underwater photography and

fishing. A first-class hotel of the same name is at **Abu Menkar** five km. away. It is a circular-shaped hotel in the middle of which is a large pool filled with Red Sea fish.

On the road between Suez and Ain Sukhna is **Zaafarana**, the starting point for visits to the monasteries of St Anthony and St Paul.

THE NILE SOUTHWARDS

Travelling up the Nile by steamer is by far the most pleasant way to grasp the significance of this river for Egypt. After the noise and bustle of modern Cairo, the river cruise is not only peaceful but gives a better idea of Egypt's variety as it passes by towns, small villages and sights of traditional life.

For Nile cruise information contact **Eastmar**, 13 Kasr el-Nil Street.

AL-MINYA

This should be the first stop, whether reached by car, train or steamer. It is situated 247 km. south of Cairo on the west bank.

Al Minya is a suitable centre for visiting sites in the area. **Beni Hassan** is 20 km. south of Al-Minya on the east bank. It is best to travel by steamer or car to Abu Korkas and then cross by sailing boat to see a Middle Kingdom cemetery and rock tombs decorated with remarkable paintings of hunting, sporting events, agricultural and military activities.

From Mallawi, 45 km. south of Al-Minya and within a 20-km. radius on the same western bank are **Al-Ashmunein**, with temples and statues from the XIX Dynasty to Christian times, and **Tuna Al-Gabal** with attractively decorated tombs. 16 km. on the east bank is **Tel Al-Amarna**, which was the capital city established by Amenhotep IV (Akhenaten) after renouncing Amun. It contains the tombs of the royal family and nobles carved out of rock.

Hotels
Lotus. Port Said Street. tel: 4541.
Ibn Khaseeb. tel: 4535.
Nefertiti. tel: 3000.

LUXOR

Luxor is a beautifully situated resort 671 km. south of Cairo on the east bank of the Nile. It was known in ancient times as Thebes and was for long the capital.

Hotels
Karnak Etap Hotel. opened 1977.
New Winter Palace. tel: 2222.
Winter Palace. tel: 2000.
Savoy. tel: 2200.
Luxor. tel: 4205.

FROM LUXOR

In the middle of the town is the temple of Luxor with its court of lotus-bud columns. A brief drive along the river bank brings the visitor to the massive temple of **Karnak**, the Great Temple of Amon-Ra.

A short journey across the river by ferry opens the way through fertile fields of sugar-cane, cotton and wheat, to Egypt's most spectacular ancient relics. These include the **Valley of the Kings** and **Valley of the Queens**, containing the frescoed tombs of Tutankhamun, Sety I, Amenhotep II, Ramses II, Ramses III, Ramses VI and Queen Nefertari, as well as the tombs of nobles.

Other sites include the funeral temples of the kings, the Ramasseum of Ramses II, the temple of Medinet Habu, and the ramps and terraces of Queen Hatshepsut's Funerary temple of Deir el-Bahari. To the north and south of Luxor on the same side of the river as the Valley of the Kings, the temples of Dendera and Esna should be visited.

Ministry of Tourism office: tel: Luxor 2215.

ASWAN

This town is a winter resort of considerable attraction, but unbearably hot in summer with the temperature rising to 40°C. It stands on the First Cataract on the border between Egypt and Nubia. The Aga Khan had a villa built here, and his mausoleum perched on high ground dominates part of the river.

Hotels
New Cataract, Abtal el-Tahrir Street. tel: 3222.
Cataract, Abtal el-Tahrir Street. tel: 2233.
Kalabasha, same address. tel: 2666.
Oberoi Hotel, Elephantine Island. tel: 3455.
Abu Simbel, Al-Nil Street. tel: 2888.

FROM ASWAN

The granite quarries of the area from where the Pharaohs of Thebes obtained stone for their statues and monuments contrast sharply with the modern bustle of the **High Dam**. The dam is situated about 8 km. south of the town, along with its earlier counterpart built in 1902 (and heightened in 1912 and 1933).

There are several important sites to be visited from Aswan. Two km. to the south is the classically laid out temple of **Philae**, which is to be saved from the waters of the dam under an arrangement similar to that which saved the Abu Simbel (Abu Sunbul) temples. Forty-five km. to the north, situated on a hill overlooking the Nile, is the temple of **Kom Ombo**. A hundred and twenty-three km. north from Aswan stands the temple of **Edfu** on the west bank. Dedicated to Horus, it is one of the best preserved

Temple of Abu Simbel

temples in Egypt. The town is accessible by road and has a first-class hotel, the Edfu.

Southwards from Aswan are the temples of **Abu Simbel**, hewn out of sandstone cliff then raised above the dam waters and replaced under a Unesco-backed project between 1963 and 1968. It is preferable to fly to Abu Simbel rather than travel by hydrofoil because the Nile waters have swallowed up the villages and vegetation, leaving a largely featureless landscape. The temples were built between 1300 and 1233 BC by Ramses II, four of whose seated statues are at the entrance to one of the temples. The other is dedicated to Nefertari.

Also saved from the waters is the temple of Kalabsha, dating from the time of the Roman Emperor Augustus. It was removed from a site 55 km. south of the dam to a new position just beside it.

Ministry of Tourism Office, Aswan 3297.

EL FAIYUM

The nearest Egypt has to a national park is the El Faiyum area. This is the country's most fertile oasis, situated 125 km south west of Cairo and occupying a huge area amid the desert. It can be reached by road and bus services.

It is striking for the abundance of its greenery, fruits and vegetables, set among streams with waterwheels. Sportsmen are drawn by Lake Qarun, whose waters are full of fish. Between the autumn and spring there is duck shooting. Also in the area are Syllin village with its amphitheatres and mineral water, the Queen's Pyramid and the pyramids of Amenemhat III and Senusert II.

Hotels
Auberge el-Fayoum, on Lake Qarun. tel: Abu Ksah 17.
Pavillon de Chasse, same address. tel: Abu Ksah 16.

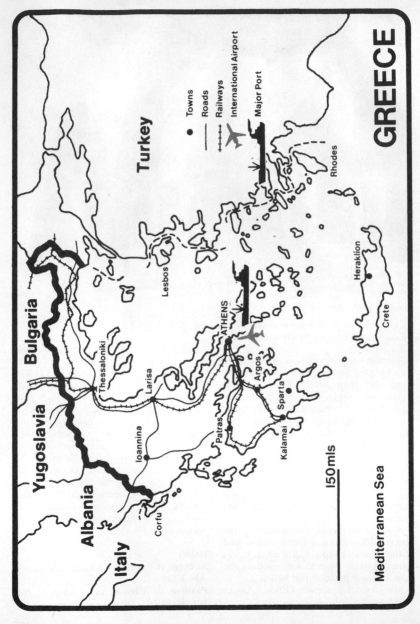

GREECE

Towns
Roads
Railways
International Airport
Major Port

Turkey

Bulgaria

Yugoslavia

Albania

Italy

Thessaloniki

Larisa

Ioannina

Corfu

Patras

Argos

Sparta

Kalamai

ATHENS

Lesbos

Rhodes

Heraklion

Crete

Mediterranean Sea

150 mls

GREECE

Julietta Harvey

The small peninsula at the south-east tip of Europe, called 'Hellas' by its own inhabitants and 'Greece' by everyone else, has always been the meeting-point between East and West: this is apparent in its long history—a history longer and more dramatic than that of any other Western country. Greece stretches across the Balkan Peninsula from the Ionian to the Aegean Sea—including islands on both sides—and as far south as the major Mediterranean island, Crete. And yet the Greeks' attitude to Greece is that it is a land separate and distinct; they consider it so different from other countries that when they travel to Rome, Paris or London, they speak of 'going to Europe' as if Greece were not part of the Continent. In a way they are right; because the Greek civilisation of the past and present is uniquely individual, and also, with the influences from East and West, various and vigorous.

The attractions of modern Greece, like the achievements of ancient Greece, come from a happy and distinct combination of geography and temperament, permeated with a vitality rarely found in other European countries. This is evident in sailing into a Greek port or crossing a Greek border: sounds, smells, movements and colours—the very tempo of life—all conspire to heighten sensibility and intensify experience: this may be the reason why Greece is a place which is not only visited, but, especially revisited.

This vitality derives from the heady mixture, over the centuries, of many peoples and ways of life, reinforced by the Greek passion for travelling. The country is surrounded by water on three sides, and has a long, lacy coast-line (no less that 15,000 km.): it opens up through innumerable ports and harbours to the Mediterranean, to Africa, to Asia, and to the rest of Europe. A Greek is familiar with the Middle East: his language and food, to say nothing of his religion and history, are marked by elements from Turkey, the Holy Land, Egypt and beyond. But he is also familiar with the West where so many of his countrymen have gone to make a new home; and in the West a Greek sees, the co-heirs of his ancient civilisation.

Perhaps because Greeks are great travellers they are also hospitable to other travellers. Their hospitality never ceases to amaze visitors: it used to be a sacred duty among the ancient Greeks, and its tradition has survived long periods of impoverishment; one only hopes that it will survive equally well the touristic prosperity which it has fostered. (It should be said that, through a combination of touristic enterprise and inflation, Greece is not now as cheap as it used to be.)

Part of Greek hospitality is an uncontrollable curiosity about anything foreign. This may disconcert visitors, for whom words like 'privacy' and 'discretion' make more sense than to a Greek; but of course that curiosity is simply another expression of the Greeks' openness to the rest of the world—the attitude of the born traveller, when at home! And one should not forget the close links that Greeks have with the rest of the world, which they have been 'colonising' for centuries.

Greeks are an imaginative and idealistic people who are also quick-witted and practical. The ancient Greeks, who originated and perfected the powers of the mind, did so after a long struggle to reconcile the excesses of passion and emotion with the demands of reason. Ancient tragedies, still very popular with modern Greeks, portray this strife of the Apollonian with the Dionysiac. Modern Greeks face the same predicament: it is apparent in their art and especially in their music. Greece is unique among Western countries in that its traditional music and dancing are not museum-

Traditional Greek dancing

pieces but part and parcel of everyday living; but like the tragedies, Greek music and dancing betray the same effort to harness a passionate exuberance to a poised acceptance of the wisdom of life.

THE LAND AND THE PEOPLE

To describe Greece one must describe the people, because as one of its visitors has put it: 'Greece is more than a place, it is a happening.' But Greek landscape is part of that 'happening' because the forces of nature, friendly and aggressive, are visibly at work. In its variety and unpredictability the landscape fits the character of the people. The adventurousness of the Greek landscape derives from the numerous mountains which form a ribbed, interlaced network covering three quarters of the land. The Pindus range in the north, with jagged granite peaks and wild gorges, offers magnificent views from the winding roads, mountains like Rodope along the Bulgarian border, Olympus—with the highest summit in Greece, 2,917 m.—Ossa and Pelion opposite Olympus, Maenelon in Peloponnessos, have all nurtured communities of a fiercely independent character— much more rugged than the coastal Greeks. Covered with oaks, chestnuts, pines and olives, they are green oases perfumed with herbs in the heart of summer; and in the spring they are carpeted with innumerable varieties of wild flowers.

Greek rivers are too temperamental to be very useful for irrigation; they do not lie in their beds long, wide and calm, but usually tumble down mountains impatiently, now appearing in an unexpected waterfall, now in a hidden spring; they flood in the winter and dry up in the summer. Springs are a great pleasure of the Greek mountains, and to the rain-starved Greeks they always have a very special value. Springs were sacred in ancient Greece; they were protected by deities and were thought to have a special power (the Castalia spring in Delphi, for instance). Their mythology still lingers on in modern Greece, and a Greek village will boast of its spring and of its very special water, rather than of its wine. And yet the Greeks invented Dionysos, the God of wine, and vines spread throughout the land and produce many varieties of wine; but to a Greek the shade of the vine is at least as valuable. There are the deep, dark, green vales between mountain slopes, like the Tempe, crowded with deities in the past and now with folklore. There are the fertile plains and tobacco fields in the north; the steep unapproachable rocks of Meteora in Epirus with monasteries perched on the top; and the cruel rockiness of Mani where people have to bring earth from elsewhere to bury their dead.

The Greek islands are extensions of the mountain chains from the mainland; most of them are simply the tops of mountain ridges. The landscape that prevails in the Aegean islands and southern Greece is unlike any European landscape. There are several islands that are green: Samos, Thasos, Corfu, Lesbos, where the olives and pines reach down to the edge of the sea.

HISTORY

Prehistoric

On the bank of the river Peneios in Thessaly, remnants of tools have been found that are a hundred thousand years old (mid Palaeolithic period). Remains of early man were discovered in a cave, Kokkines Petres in Halkidiki in northern Greece; they date back to some time between 75000 BC and 50000 BC. Signs of the oldest farming and stockbreeding communities, dating from the Neolithic age (7000 to 2800 BC) were discovered in the fertile plains of Macedonia and Thes-

saly. During the same period a Neolithic civilisation also started in a group of islands in the Aegean, the Cyclades. The Cycladic civilisation developed during the Bronze Age (2000 to 1100 BC), as the first Indo-Europeans came from the East with technology (copper, and methods for smelting it) and new ideas: it was the oldest European civilisation. It developed mainly around three centres: the Cyclades, Crete (the Minoan civilisation), and the Greek mainland (the Helladic civilisation).

The Minoan civilisation was related in its last stages to the younger Mycenean civilisation. Around 2000 BC the first known Greek-speaking tribes from the Indo-European group of nations began to descend to the Greek mainland and form settlements. The Minoan civilisation in Crete reached its height in the 15th century BC. In about 1450 BC the nearby island of Thera (Santorini) suffered an enormous volcanic explosion which destroyed Knossos, and other important centres in Crete; the Minoan civilisation began to decline.

But in the meantime (14th and 13th centuries BC) a new civilisation was flourishing on the Greek mainland around Mycenae; it embraced the Aegean and the eastern Mediterranean. The first form of Greek language, 'Linear B', evolved in the Mycenean era. But both the Minoan and the Mycenean civilisations were destroyed by the Dorians, the last Greek tribe, who began their invasion from the north at around 1100 BC.

Recorded history

In the Dark Age that followed (from the 11th to the eighth centuries BC) refugees from the ruined strongholds on the Greek mainland moved east and colonised the Aegean coast of Asia Minor. On the mainland the Dorians formed new centres, mainly farming and stockbreeding communities, which were however turned inwards and stayed isolated from one another; they were gradually to evolve into the self-governing Greek city-states. In Asia Minor the Greek colonies were also developing into independent cities and it was in those cities that in the ninth century BC a new form of writing, the alphabetic, developed and spread gradually over the entire area inhabited by Greeks.

Archaic period (700 to 500 BC)
For several centuries the city-states were to be the bases of Greek political, social, economic and religious life. Uniformity and a sense of national unity irrespective of tribal origins developed; from the year 776 the cities took part in 'sanctified' 'pan-hellenic' athletic games. The city-states had several things in common: strong defences against attack from other rival cities; an acropolis, where temples and other places of worship were concentrated; an *agora* (market-place), the citizens' official meeting-place. They all had a king at the start, then an aristocracy, and then a tyrant. There was a good deal of rivalry amongst the cities, manifest also in peaceful activities: athletic contests, competition in splendour of architecture, art, and religious offerings. Rivalry was perhaps an important principle in the development of their civilisation.

There was a second wave of colonisation from Greece between 750 and 600 BC, and as the colonies were now in close contact with the metropolis, trade moved from the Phoenicians to the Greeks, who now mastered the Aegean and developed a thriving economy. Sparta and Athens emerged as the two principal, and rival, powers.

Classical period (500 to 323 BC)
Rivalries had to be suspended when a new power, the Persians, appeared in the Aegean, threatening Greek supremacy. The Greeks were united under the aegis primarily of Athens and to a lesser degree

of Sparta, and faced the threat victoriously both on land (Marathon 490 BC and Plataea 479 BC) and at sea (Salamis 480 BC). The victories against the Persians contributed greatly to the prestige of Athens and its predominance over the other cities; the Athenian Alliance was formed, democracy was achieved under Pericles, literature and the arts were flourishing: it was the age of philosophy, tragedy, sculpture, architecture, oratory, an age of unprecedented achievement— the Golden Age of Greece (fourth and fifth centuries BC).

But the old rivalry between Sparta and Athens grew stronger, and culminated in the Peloponnesian War (431-404), which crippled both powers and finally ended with the victory of Sparta and her Peloponnesian allies over Athens. Sparta was challenged in its turn by the other city-states, and the strife continued wearing them down economically and politically until they had to give in to the new power that had emerged in the north under Philip of Macedon (Chaeronia 338). Philip was proclaimed the leader of the Greeks, for the campaign against the Persians; the campaign was in fact led by the son of Philip, Alexander, whose conquests reached from Egypt to India.

Hellenistic period (323 to 146 BC)
Greek civilisation spread across the borders of Greece and developed on the Mediterranean coasts: the Near East, North Africa, Italy. But Alexander's vast empire was broken up after his death into smaller kingdoms under his generals. Once again, internal strife, both in mainland Greece and in the colonies among the generals, weakened Hellenism; Athens and Sparta declined. The Romans first appeared in Greece during the third century BC; in 146 BC the Greeks were defeated near the isthmus of Corinth, and most of Greece was incorporated into the Roman empire. Rome learned a lot from

the Greeks, both directly from the mainland, and from the Greek colonies in Sicily and southern Italy—in 'Magna Graecia'. The defeated Greece, Horace wrote, had conquered its coarse master by imposing its culture throughout the Roman Empire.

Roman and Byzantine period (146 BC to AD 1453)

The Romans repaid their debt to Greece by ensuring under the 'Pax Romana' peace and well-being to the Greek cities. Greek remained the official language, and Corinth was now the administrative centre. When in AD 395 the Roman Empire was divided into the Western and Eastern Empires, Greece was incorporated into the Eastern part with Constantinople as the capital. The second most important city was now Thessaloniki, in northern Greece, while Athens and the older city-states dwindled. When the School of Philosophy was closed in AD 529 Athens became a provincial town.

The mainland and islands of Greece were an easy target for the Crusaders in 1204: the land was carved up among the Franks and the Venetians. The Crusades, combined with invasions from the north (by Goths and Slavs), weakened Byzantium until it fell in 1453 to the Ottoman Turks. Under Turkish rule, for almost four centuries, Greece endured its darkest period. The Greeks did however keep alive their national identity, language and religion; in the 18th century they started rebelling, and they fought their victorious War of Independence from 1821 to 1827.

Modern Greece

The European powers recognised Greece's independence in 1832, and chose in the same year Prince Otto I as King of the Hellenes. The new and independent kingdom started recovering the various islands and territories that re-

mained under foreign domination.

After considerable political upheaval, which involved the temporary abdication of King Constantine, Greece, under Premier Venizelos, entered the First World War with the Allies. With encouragement from the Allies, Greece invaded Asia Minor in 1922, but was defeated by the Turkish army under Kemal Ataturk. As a result, a compulsory exchange of populations between Greece and Turkey was agreed, and was supervised by the League of Nations: 1.5 million Greeks from Asia Minor were resettled in Greece (several thousands were massacred by Turkish troops as they were departing), and 800,000 Turks and Bulgarians were repatriated to their respective countries. The King, George II, was deposed in 1923, and Greece was a republic from 1924 to 1935, but unsettled economic conditions and violent political strife with Venizelos as one of the protagonists, resulted in the return of the monarchy.

In 1941, Greece was occupied by Germany. There was however a strong Communist-dominated resistance movement, leading, after the departure of the Germans, to the Civil War between Communist guerrilla bands and royal troops. Due partly to the intervention of Britain (1945), and the United States later on, the Communists lost: the Civil War ended in 1949. There was a succession of governments (the principal ones under Karamanlis and George Papandreou), until the military coup of 1967. In 1974, after seven years of repressive dictatorship, the military regime collapsed, and handed over power to a civilian government headed by Karamanlis. Political parties were allowed to operate freely (including the Communist Party) and in a referendum in the same year the re-establishment of the monarchy was rejected by a large margin. In November 1977 Karamanlis's party was re-elected to power.

CULTURE

The civilisations and cultures that flourished and declined in Greece have a strong presence in modern Greek life, character and landscape. The remains of ancient Greek art are preserved in a developed network of museums; while what survives of ancient architecture is an integral part of the landscape. The white transparency of the ancient marbles competes with that of the rocks about them; the broken columns, surrounded in spring by plants and flowers, are still shaded by Athena's sacred tree, the olive. Ancient Greek amphitheatres, like Epidauros or Philippi, with their magnificent acoustics, are still in use for dramatic productions, for the Greek tragedies especially.

The Christian Byzantine tradition of the country which found rich expression in churches and monasteries, in the medieval icons, the mosaics and the frescoes, remain a live part of contemporary Greek culture because they are still in everyday use for worship. Byzantine art still continues to inspire Greek folk art, Byzantine music is still heard in churches, and influences individual composers. There is an unbroken continuity between Byzantine and modern Greek culture. Religious festivals still remain spontaneous, lively and important events and indicate the people's active participation in their cultural inheritance. But there are particular places where time seems to have stopped, and Byzantine art and architecture make up an imposing world of their own, separated and untouched by contemporary life: the monastic community of Mount Athos, and the deserted medieval town of Mistras.

The Greek summer festival in Athens, Epidaurus, Philippi, with dramatic and musical performances, folk dances, and art exhibitions, is a magnificent expression of the tightly unified and continuous culture of past and present. The audiences of the Greek tragedies see in them contemporary political and social situations; music like that of Theodorakis—a blend of Byzantine and traditional folk music—is inspired by recent Greek history; folk dances originate in ancient Greek dances; the revival of Byzantine iconography is seen in the works of modern artists. Poets and novelists, like Cavafy, Seferis (the Nobel Prize winner) and Kazantzakis, chose Greek topics; they were inspired by and recreated the rich cultural blend of Greece.

In addition to the picturesque island architecture there is the less known architecture of the mountainous areas in Macedonia, Epirus, and the villages of Mount Pelion, with its Balkan and Turkish character, and with its own distinct attractiveness. Folk arts, like rug-making, weaving, embroidery and wood-carving, still thrive in the countryside.

Music and dancing are the most lively expressions of Greek culture, because they are not only part of ordinary family and social life, but also the means through which the people try to make sense of their life, their society and its politics. There has been recently a big revival of popular music in Greece, which is not unconnected with the country's political upheaval.

WILDLIFE

Because of its geographical position between the European, Asian and African continents, Greece enjoys an immense variety of plant life. On the mountains and in the north generally European types of vegetation prevail. There are oaks, chestnuts, varieties of conifers, and firs on the higher slopes; the black-pine forests on Mount Olympus are famous. Evergreen trees and shrubs are found in the lowlands. Oleanders, bays, junipers, and olives spread over the Peloponnese. Planes and poplars grow near the sea, rivers and mountain slopes. Pines, olives and vines grow all over the country, and

Palaeokastritsa, Corfu

innumerable varieties of wild flowers cover the countryside in the spring.

The forests in the north harbour European animals, such as the wild cat, martin, brown bear, roe deer, wolf, wild boar, lynx, fox and hare. Mediterranean animals include the jackal, wild goat, and porcupine, all adapted to the dryness and heat. Among birds there are the pelican, stork, heron, and many northern varieties winter in Greece. Reptile and insect life is varied and ubiquitous.

ECONOMY

The economy suffered a dislocation during the Second World War and the Civil War that followed. Greece is still a relatively poor country agriculturally because of inefficient irrigation and the compartmentalisation of the land. Farming contributes about 20% of the annual national product and manufacturing about 16%. Tourism is obviously an important source of income. Greece produces principally fruit, tobacco, grapes, currants, olives and olive oil; to a lesser degree wheat, sugarbeet, potatoes and tomatoes. Large numbers of sheep and goats are raised.

The country's main industrial centres are Athens, Thessaloniki, Piraeus, Patras, Heraklion. The main manufactures are textiles, food products, chemicals, construction materials, refined petroleum and ships. Since 1950 there has been investment in the infrastructure. On the whole, the value of imports (mainly consumer goods and machinery) is considerably higher than that of exports (food, wine, tobacco, olives and olive oil, and textiles). Greece has been an associate member of the EEC since 1962.

GENERAL INFORMATION

Area: 131,945 sq. km.
Population: nine million.
Capital: Athens.
Head of State: President Karamanlis.
Government: Presidential Republic.
Languages: Greek. *Katharevousa* (Purified Greek) is still used in official legal

documents, while *demotiki* is the spoken language; English is also very widely spoken.

Religion: Christian Greek Orthodox, except for a minority of five per cent who are Jewish or Catholic.

Currency: Drachma. £1 sterling=68.899 drachma. $1=36.05 drachma.

Time: GMT + 2.

Weights and Measures: French metric system. The standard unit of land measurement is the *strema* (=¼ acre). Some liquids (e.g. olive oil) are measured by weight (kilo etc.) rather than in litres.

HOW TO GET THERE

Information about travelling to and within Greece, as well as general information about the country, can be obtained from the National Tourist Organisation of Greece (N.T.O.G., in Greek E.O.T.), which has offices in the main cities throughout the world. Its booklet 'General Information about Greece' is continually revised.

By air: Athens has air links with all five continents, either by direct flights or through intermediate staging points, operated by the major airlines and the Greek line Olympic. There are also direct flights to Thessaloniki, Corfu, Heraklion (Crete), Cos, and Rhodes. There are also charter flights run by most airlines at much reduced prices.

By rail: There are regular lines to Greece, but on the whole they are not ·cheaper than charter flights. There are, however, reductions of 50% for students and school pupils, and 30% for groups exceeding ten persons.

By sea: Regular shipping and ferry-boat lines link foreign ports on the Mediterranean with Piraeus, Corfu, Igoumenitsa, Patras, and Corinth.

By bus: The *Europabus* service of the European railway network ensures road communication between Greece and the rest of Europe. Information on this and the railway service can be obtained from NTOG offices abroad.

There are also provisions for visiting Greece by private means, car, aircraft, yacht.

Visas and health regulations

Visas are not required except for visitors from the following countries: Turkey, USSR, German Democratic Republic, Bulgaria, North Korea, Albania, Chinese People's Republic, Poland, Czechoslovakia, Rumania, Hungary, Yugoslavia, and Cuba. The regulations of the World Health Organisation apply also for Greece.

Currency and customs regulations

Tourists entering Greece need not pay duty on personal effects. Other items may be imported duty-free by special permission, on condition that they are re-exported. One may not, under any circumstances, import firearms, ammunition, narcotics—or parrots! Souvenirs up to a value of 4,500 drachmas can be exported. The export of archaeological objects and works of art is strictly prohibited unless you have a special licence. There is no restriction on foreign currency, but sums of over £200 should be declared on entry.

CLIMATE

From May to October unbroken sunshine is virtually guaranteed throughout Greece; summer showers are sudden and forceful. There is nearly always a light breeze from the Aegean in July and August, the *meltemia*, which mitigates the extreme heat and can make the sea very rough. Most of the rainfall takes place between November and February, in short heavy bursts that are interspersed with long, bright and often warm periods.

Snow is not uncommon on the mountains (where there are skiing resorts) but quite rare in southern Greece. In March and April, though the sea is still chilly, the countryside is covered with flowers—it is the best time to visit Greece! September and October are perfect for bathing and for temperate weather.

What to wear

From May to October, light and cool clothes. For the winter months, December to February, one needs warm clothes—as for an English winter—especially in northern Greece

ACCOMMODATION AND FOOD

Prices for food and accommodation are still low in Greece compared to those in other European countries, but they are not as low as they were a few years ago. There are however off-season reductions of about 20%. There is a wide choice of hotels (from luxury to fifth class), flats, rooms in private houses, youth-hostels, and camping grounds. The local tourist police are very helpful in finding accommodation for visitors; and on most islands the local landladies usually wait for visitors at the wharf advertising their rooms. Look out then for ladies dressed in black. Some of the most popular islands can be full at high season, but Greek beaches are extremely hospitable.

The common complaint about a Greek meal is that it is seldom served hot; but on the other hand (food is not everything, and time is not always money), a Greek meal is seldom hurried. In most Greek restaurants and tavernas, food is served outdoors for the larger part of the year, and in the cool shady yard of a taverna, or on a breezy seafront, a meal can be a real delight.

In Greek restaurants it is customary for clients to visit the kitchen and inspect the food before ordering. But one should

also keep in mind that Greeks like to eat from a variety of dishes at the same time, and that they like to share them: so, where, how and with whom you eat matter as much as what you eat.

Restaurants with pretensions to an 'international' cuisine might prove not very international, but very expensive. A genuine Greek meal in a lively atmosphere, on the other hand, can be found at reasonable prices in the traditional eating-places, the *tavernas* (but not the touristy 'night-club' type).

Greek cuisine is largely Middle Eastern in character: with some imagination you can recognise Turkish or Arabic names of dishes in the Greek menus—halva, dolmades, shish-kebbab, etc. As it originated in a country which could not boast an over-abundance of meat, Greek cuisine uses olive-oil lavishly, and its local vegetables variously and imaginatively. Vegetables tend to be overcooked, but when fresh they are delicious. Greek taste in meat is quite luxurious: the popular kinds of meat are veal—rather than beef—and, in the right season, suckling pig and young lamb. Fish is usually fresh and delicious, but increasingly expensive.

An enjoyable and leisurely way of starting a Greek meal is to have first a variety of starters with *ouzo*, a strong aniseed-flavoured drink, made from grape-stems and usually drunk diluted with water. For starters, one can have *taramosalata* (a fish-roe pate), *melitzanosalata* (aubergine pate), *tzatziki* (yogurt with cucumber), olives, etc. For a main course one should certainly try Greek fish: *barbounia* (red mullet), *tsipoures* (porgy), *synagrida* (bream), *lithrinia* (bass), and, least expensive, *marides* (white-bait). Among meat courses, interesting and not expensive dishes are: *fricasse* (lamb and green vegetables in lemon sauce), *dolmades* (stuffed vine-leaves), *keftedes* (spiced meat-balls), *moussaka* (minced meat with aubergine—a very different dish from what one gets outside Greece), *yemista* (stuffed tomatoes, green peppers, aubergines, or courgettes). Tomatoes still taste like real tomatoes in Greece, so salads—in particular a mixed salad (*horiatiki*, meaning 'peasant' salad)—are delicious. With their meals Greeks usually drink *retsina* (resinated wine). It is on the whole an acquired taste, and it can vary a lot from place to place; when it comes from the barrel and is served cold it is at its best. There are a rich variety of other wines, white and red, all at very reasonable prices. For finishing a meal, peaches, grapes and melons are ideal: full of flavour and cheap. Greek sweets, like all Middle Eastern sweets, are rich and syrupy; they can be obtained at any time in *zaharoplasteia* (pastry-shops).

TRANSPORT

Greece has a highly developed network of air, rail, bus and sea services.

By air: Olympic airways serve the domestic airlines exclusively; they operate lines from Athens to the principal towns on the mainland and islands. There are also local lines between the main towns, and, in the summer months only, between Rhodes and Crete and Carpathos. Airlines to and between islands increase in number all the time.

By rail: There are two railway lines from Athens: one northbound to Thessaloniki, and the Yugoslav and Turkish borders; the other southbound to the Peloponnese and Kalamata.

By bus: There is an efficient bus network all over Greece, with both local and long-distance services. The buses are on the whole comfortable and the prices reasonable. Bus journeys off the beaten track can be quite adventurous; there are still a few pre-war buses surviving, punished daily by bad roads. Such journeys are well worth it, however, especially for those travellers who want to discover the Greece that is unknown to tourist guides. Taxis may be hired at reasonable prices for long-distance trips.

By car: There is a motorway from the Yugoslav frontier to Thessaloniki and Athens, and from Athens to Corinth, and westwards along the northern coast of the Peloponnese to Patras. Other roads vary from the new to mere dirt tracks.

By sea: There is a regular and efficient inter-island shipping service operating mostly out of Piraeus, with a few local services running from Thessaloniki, Kavala, Volos, Patras etc. By planning carefully one can visit several islands within a limited time without having to go back to Piraeus in between. There are several car-ferries operating from Athens to the bigger islands, as well as locally (Kavala-Thassos, Igoumenitsa-Corfu). But because travel agencies tend to act only for certain steamship lines, one should consult also the *Key Travel Guide*.

There are also sightseeing tours organised by ABC Tours, CHAT Tours, and others; and cruises around the islands organised by Epirotiki, Kavounides, Sun and others. Information about them can be found in the *Key Travel Guide*.

There are provisions for chartering a yacht with crew, or an aircraft, for those who can afford it.

BUSINESS HOURS

All banks, bureaux and classified hotels, and some tourist shops, will change money. Banking hours, except Sundays and holidays, are: 0800 to 1300 and 1730 to 1930. Branches with exchange facilities around Syntagma Square in Athens are open for longer hours (0800 to 2100).

General trade shops, food-stores, and chemists are open, with minor seasonal variations, from 0800 to 1300 (1345, May to October), and from 1600 to 2030 (1700 to 2000, May to October). Popular art and gift shops stay open from 0800 to 2030, and those at Monasterake (the 'flea-market') in Athens are open also on Sundays from 0800 to 1500. Kiosks (*periptera*), restaurants, cafes, pastry and dairy shops are usually open all day long, including Sundays.

PUBLIC HOLIDAYS

1 January (New Year's Day); 6 January (Epiphany); Orthodox Shrove Monday; 25 March (National Holiday); Orthodox Good Friday; Orthodox Easter Monday; Ascension Day; 15 August (Assumption of the Holy Virgin); 28 October (National Holiday); 25 & 26 December (Christmas Day and St. Stephen).

EMBASSIES IN ATHENS

Austria: Alexandras 26. tel:821-1036
Belgium: Sekeri 3. tel: 361-7886
Canada: Ioannou Gennadiou 4. tel: 739-511
Cyprus: Irodotou 16. tel: 737-883
Denmark: Kolonaki Sq. 15. tel: 713-012
Egypt: Vass. Sofias 3. tel: 361-8613
France: Vass. Sofias 7. tel: 361-1664
Germany East: Vas. Pavlou 7. tel: 672-5160
Germany West: Loukianou 3. tel: 724-801
Iraq: Amarillidos 19. tel: 671-5012
Iran: Antinoros 29. tel: 742-313
Italy: Sekeri 2. tel: 361-1722
Jordan: Filikis Etairias 14. tel: 728-484
Kuwait: Mihalakopoulou 45. tel: 748-771
Lebanon: Kifissias 26. tel: 778-5158
Libya: Irodotou 2. tel: 727-105
Netherlands: Vas. Sofias 4. tel: 711-361
Norway: Ipsilantou 40. tel: 746-173
Portugal: Loukianou 19. tel: 790-096
Saudi Arabia: Marathonodromou 71. tel: 671-6911
Spain: Vass. Sofias 29. tel: 714-885

Switzerland: Lassiou 2. tel: 730-364
Syria: Vas. Pavlou 18. tel: 672-5577
Turkey: Vas Georgiou. tel: 764-3295
UK: Ploutarhou 1. tel: 736-211
USA: Vass. Sofias 91. tel: 712-951
USSR: Irondou Attikou 7. tel: 711-261

TOURIST INFORMATION

There are National Tourist Organisation (NTOG) information desks in the principal towns; there are offices in Athens at 2 Karayeoryi Servias, 4 Stadiou, and at the airport. There are also numerous travel agents.

ATHENS

Athens is not a marble city, as we imagine the city of Theseus and Pericles to have been; since those days it has had a dramatic history which is visibly conveyed to the onlooker. The Athens of Byzantine times, which had dwindled into a small provincial town, was subsequently sacked by Slavs, dominated by Franks, ruled briefly by Venice, and finally taken by the Turks. In that dark period for Greece, during a siege by the Venetians in 1687, the Parthenon was damaged; later, it was almost destroyed when the Acropolis was turned into a battleground during the Greek War of Independence. When Athens became the capital of the newly independent Greece, a new city was built beside the straggly village that surrounded the Acropolis. After the First World War, at the 'catastrophe' of 1922, over a million Greek refugees from Asia Minor engulfed the city; then haphazard shanty towns appeared all around Athens almost overnight, and were to become the core of today's ugly, sprawling suburbs. The Second World War and the Civil War that followed added to the disaster; and the frenetic building that went on until recently did not help.

And yet, because of its unique landscape and light, Athens remains a beautiful and exciting city. It is surrounded by mountains—Parnis, Penteli and Hymetos—and is built around the sharp-peaked hill of Lycabettus and the rocks of the Acropolis, with a sprinkling of smaller rounded hills—the Nymphaeon hills, the Pnyx, the Areopagus. Plaka, the old quarter of the city crawling up to the Acropolis, is a picturesque remnant of a past world, with beautiful old houses and small authentic tavernas hidden in backyards. It is also the centre of Athenian night-life, with restaurants out on the narrow street, music, dancing, and crowds of people. Plaka is simply a miniature of Athens, which is a crowded, busy, extremely lively and gay city.

The Acropolis
The road towards the Acropolis leads past the classical Theatre of Dionysos and the Roman Odeion of Herodes Atticus (where musical and dramatic performances take place), to the steep path that winds up over the foundations of the earlier cities to the gateway of the Acropolis, the massive Propylaia. The Parthenon, built during the Golden Age of Pericles (fifth century BC) by Iktinus, and decorated by the sculptor Pheidias, is the most important temple of the Acropolis; it was dedicated to the Virgin Goddess Athena. Its strong and simple Doric columns are surrounded by the finer Ionic sculptured frieze, 160 m. long, illustrating the Panathenian Procession. The 92 metopes were also sculptured, with reliefs representing a battle with giants, a battle with amazons, battles with centaurs, and scenes from the Trojan war. A massive gold and ivory statue of Athena (which has not survived) was set up in the interior. When construction was completed, the pedimental sculpture was added, featuring the birth of Athena, and the quarrel between Poseidon and Athena.
To the south of the Propylaea stands the small and elegant temple to Athena Niki, built in the Ionian style. The last temple to be built, also in the Ionian style, was the Erechtheion with its famous porch of Caryatids. These buildings also date from the fifth century BC.

The Acropolis Museum
Among the world-famous and indeed beautiful sculpture exhibited is the unique collection of statues of female figures of the archaic era, the Korae, with the well-known 'archaic smile'.

The Areopagus is a rock standing to the north-east of the Acropolis; there the most ancient political and judicial body in Athens, the council of elders, held its sessions. But the Areopagus was superseded by democracy and the democratic assemblies that were held on the Pnyx, rising above it to the south.

Most of the other visible remains of ancient Athens are to the north and west of the Acropolis: the octagonal Hellenistic Tower of the Winds, Hadrian's Library (Roman), remnants of the Roman agora, all within the jumbled streets of Plaka. The ruins of the Greek agora, the Stoa Attalou, and the perfectly proportioned Doric Hephaisteion, are in the relatively open space beyond. Farther along there are the ruins of the Sacred Gates, the City Walls, and the Ancient Cemetery, the Kerameikos. The list is long, but one should mention also some very important Byzantine monuments. The tiny 11th century church of Ag. Apostoli; Ag. Theodori (also 11th century), one of the most attractive Byzantine churches in Athens; Kaesariane; Kapnidarea. The Monastery of Daphni, 10km. out of Athens, is the most important surviving Byzantine monument: built in the sixth century AD, it is famous for its exceptional craftsmanship and for its mosaics, inspired by classical ideals, which are among the finest in Greece.

Museums
The **National Archaeological Museum**

contains an outstanding collection of masterpieces from excavations throughout Greece: a collection of archaic Kouri (statues of young men) with the 'archaic smile', bronze statues of gods from the classical era, the recently discovered and fascinating frescoes from Santorini which depict colourful and light-spirited scenes from nature and everyday life in the Cretan style. Other important museums are: the **Benakis Museum** (containing a variety of collections from prehistoric to modern times), the **Byzantine Museum**, the **Museum of Folk Art**, and the **National Historical Museum**.

Around Athens

One should visit **Piraeus**, Greece's most important port and one of the largest in the Mediterranean. The main pleasures are Tourkolimano and Passalimani, two small harbours surrounded by colourful tavernas, where you can have a feast at the edge of the sea with music around you in full swing. **Eleusis** is the birthplace of the tragedian Aeschylus; a visitor can see there the Sanctuary of Demeter and the site where the ancient Eleusinian Mysteries were celebrated. At **Cape Sounion** is a temple of Poseidon, which dominates a sharp precipice looking out over the Aegean. One can watch there a magnificent sunset on one side of the temple and at the same time see a huge moon rising on the other.

Hotels

There are many hotels spread throughout the city; only a small proportion of the better class ones are given here. (R=rooms)
In or near Syntagma Square (Constitution Square):
Grande Bretagne, 430 R, overlooking Syntagma Square (Luxury).
Amalia, 130 R, overlooking the National Garden (Luxury).
Electra, 150 R, 5 Ermou Street (first class).
Lycabettus, 6 Valaoritou Street (second class).

In Kolonaki, Pankrati, and towards the American Embassy:
Athens Hilton, 480 R, 46 Leof. Vas. Olgas (Luxury).
Caravel, 470 R, 2 Vas. Alexandrou (Luxury).
Alexandros, 8 Timoleontos Vassou (second class).

In Plaka
Electra Palace, 18 Nikodhimou (first class).
Plaka, Kapnikareas (second class).
Royal, 44 Mitropoleos (third class).

Between Syntagma and Omonoia
Esperia Palace, 185 R, 22 Stadhiou (first class).
Galaxy, 100 R, 22 Akademias (second class).
Metropole, 59 Stadhiou (second class).

Near Omonoia
King Minos, 180 R, 1 Piraeus (first class).
El Greco, 65 Athenas (second class).
Omonoia, 260 R, Plate Omonoias (third class).

Near the Archaeological Museum
Acropole Palace, 130 R, Ikisiokto Oktovriou (Luxury).
Arcadia, 40 and 46 Marnis (second class).
Museum, 16 Bouboulinas (third class).

For further information on hotels, flats and pensions consult the annual directory of the Chamber of Hotels of Greece and the *Key Travel Guide* or the *Blue Guide*.

Restaurants

There are scores of restaurants in Athens, since Greeks themselves eat out most evenings; but they eat late, so restaurants start getting busy only after 9pm. There is international food, not cheap, in all the luxury class hotels; but it is more interesting to eat out, in restaurants which specialise in Greek food (most of them do), or in tavernas. In particular there are: **Corfu** and **Vassilis** in the Syntagma area; **Pyramides,** 21 Philhellinon Street; **Gerofinikas,** 10 Pindarou Street (Kolonaki); **Myrtia,** 35 Markou Mousourou Street; Delphi, 15 Nikis Street; **Floca,** 9 Venizelou; **Platanos,** Odos Diogenous (in Plaka). Most tavernas are open only in the evening; they offer excellent Greek food and a lively, convivial, distinctly Greek atmosphere. There are many tavernas in Plaka which cater mainly for tourists: **Vakhos, Erotokritos, Platanos, Efta Athelfia.** The tavernas on the slopes of Lycabettus (**Pythari, Rodia, Ta Pethia**) and in the area behind the Hilton tend to have a more local atmosphere. In the summer Athenians tend to go farther out in Attica.

Entertainments
There are innumerable cafés and pastry shops (*zacharoplastia*) in Athens. Chatting while watching people go by is a traditional Greek entertainment. There are some fairly good Western-style nightclubs; but the most interesting places, although increasingly expensive, are the *bouzoukia,* where one can hear Greek popular music. Some of the better-known bouzoukia are **Deilina** at Glyfada, **Anamnesis** at Vouliagmeni, **Fantasia** at Keffalinias, **To Prossopo** in Fog. Negri Square, and **Plakiotiko Salone** on Dedalou Street.

THESSALONIKI

The second largest city, Thessaloniki is beautifully placed at the head of the Thermaikos gulf. It was built in the fourth century BC, and its importance grew with its strategic position on the Via Egnatia linking Byzantium and Rome; it became the second city of the Byzantine Empire. It was sacked by Goths, Slavs, Franks and Epirots; it was a Venetian protectorate for a while, and had about 500 years of Turkish occupation. It forms a wide amphitheatre sloping down to the sea from the Byzantine walls on the slopes of Mount Hortiates; on the sea-front there is the 15th century White Tower, and at a higher point in the city the Via Egnatia passes under the Arch of Galerius. The glory of the city is its Byzantine churches, some of them hidden in the old Turkish quarter just below the city walls. The oldest of these churches is Agios Georgios, which began as a Roman Rotunda of the late third century, then became a church, then a mosque, and is now a museum. Others are Panagi Acheropietos (fifth century), Agios Demetrios (fifth century), Agia Sophia (eighth century), and Panagia Halkeon (11th century). Agia Ekaterini (13th century) and Dodeka Apostoli (14th century, with fine frescoes and mosaics) are the prettiest.

Museums
The **Archaeological Museum of Thessaloniki** exhibits some exquisite classical, Hellenistic and Byzantine jewellery. It should be greatly enriched by the very recent (November 1977) discoveries in Vergina of Philip of Macedon's tomb. **Vergina** and **Pella,** a few miles away from Thessaloniki, are important archaeological sites.

Hotels
Mediterranean Palace is the nicest, elegant and old-established, on the sea-front, 120 R (first class).
Makedonia Palace, also on the sea-front (Leof. Kennedy), 295 R (Luxury).
Electra Palace, 5A Plateia Aristotelous, 130 R (first class).
El Greco, 23 Egnatias (second class).
Egnatia, 13 Leontos Sofou (second class).
Capitol, 16 Monasteriou (near the station), 190 R (first class).
Capsis, near the station, 425 R (second class).
Rotonda, 28 and 97 Monasteriou (second class).
A.B.C., Plateia Syntrivaniou, 100 R (third class).
Queen Olga, 44 Vas. Olgas, 130 R (second class).

Restaurants

Thessaloniki has a reputation for good food. A very dependable restaurant is **Olympos Naoussa** on the sea-front (Vas. Konstantinou). Among others are: **Stratis,** also on the sea-front (2 and 27 Vas. Konstandinou); **Perdica,** 40 Vas. Sophias; **Averof,** 17 Singrou. Among the tavernas, **Krikelas** (284 Vas Olgas, on the way to the airport) is the best. Among others are: **Fengaria** and **Xenophon** on Komnenon Street; and **Vlachos,** Plateia Lefkou Pyrgou. There are a good number of very pleasant tavernas by the sea at Aretsou and Nea Krene; their view of the bay is splendid.

Entertainments

There are several very lively *bouzoukia* just outside Thessaloniki, on the road to Agia Triada; **Remvi** at Aretsou has a continental character. Several of the larger hotels have tavernas and nightclubs. The **Kastra** near the city walls are worth the visit, especially for the pleasant view. New tavernas with music and dancing appear all the time, and it is worthwhile exploring them.

Tourist Information

Tourist Police, 10 Plateia Agias Sofias.
NTOG, 8 Aristotelous Street.
Cooks (travel agent), 8 Meg. Alexandrou.
American Express, 5 Plateia Aristotelous.

NORTHERN GREECE

Kavalla is one of the most attractive towns of the eastern part of northern Greece. It is beautifully situated at the head of its bay, and Byzantine walls and the surviving Turkish houses and streets add a lot to its interest and attraction. It is the best base for visiting Philippi, and the main embarkation point for the island of Thasos.

Hotels: Galaxy, Philippi, Okenanis.

Philippi is an ancient Macedonian town with extensive Roman ruins and a fourth century BC amphitheatre, remodelled in Roman times. The theatre is now restored, and is used for performances. The town has a fortified citadel belonging to the Byzantine era.

Marmaras, a village in Northern Greece (Halkidiki Peninsula)

NATIONAL TOURIST ORGANISATION OF GREECE

Mount Athos is the only existing monastic state in Europe, a form of self-governing monastic republic, built on the easternmost of the three prongs of the Halkidiki peninsula as far back as the 10th and 11th centuries AD, the monasteries are treasure-houses of Byzantine icons, manuscripts and imperial gifts of gold and jewellery. Admission is denied to women and to female animals! Permits are issued by the Greek Ministry of Foreign Affairs in Athens, or by the Ministry of Northern Greece at 48 El. Venizelou in Thessaloniki. The Halkidiki peninsula has beautiful unspoiled beaches and is quickly developing into a popular tourist centre especially among the Greeks.

Kastoria, in the western part of Northern Greece, is a very interesting and wealthy old town, delightfully situated on a peninsula reaching into a lake.
Hotels: Xenia Du Lac, Kastoria, Acropolis.

CENTRAL GREECE

Volos: On the Aegean coast of central Greece, Volos is very attractively situated at the foot of Mt. Pelion, running round the gulf. It is very convenient for visiting the charming villages on Pelion, and for crossing to the nearby islands of Skiathos and Skopelos.
Hotels: Palace, 44 Iasonos; **Alexandros,** 3 Topali.

Meteora: In the middle of Epirus there are the monasteries of Meteora, perched on top of gigantic granite spires rising to 1,500 feet. Only seven remain of the 23 built in the troubled 14th century, to provide refuge for religious hermits from the constant violence of the Thessalian plain below. Women should wear skirts when visiting these and other monasteries in Greece. Visitors to Meteora can spend the night at **Kalambaka** (Motel **Divani, Aelikos Astir,** both open all year; **Xenia**).

Delphi: Two thousand feet up on Mt. Parnassus, Delphi is a superb combination of man's and nature's handiwork. The great Temple of Apollo, in which the famed oracle functioned, dominates the sanctuary. The Sacred Way led up to the Temple; there are remnants of other elegant buildings: the Ancient Theatre, still in use today; the Sanctuary of Procnaia Athena; the Stadium for the Pythian games, which included contests among poets, musicians and philosophers.
Hotels: Amalia, Xenia; Vonzas.

Ioannina: Not far from Igoumenitsa on the west coast of Greece, Ioannina is an interesting and attractive town built on a rocky promontory jutting into Lake Pambotis.
Hotels: Xenia, Palladion, Acropole.

THE PELOPONNESE

Ancient Corinth is wonderfully situated on a rocky plateau below the massive peak of Acro-Corinth, with ruins of successive Classical Greek, Byzantine, Frankish, Venetian and Turkish fortifications, and a staggering view. Visitors can stay in modern Corinth.
Hotels: Kypselos, Acropolis, Ephyra.

Mycenae was the centre of the Mycenean civilisation. The prehistoric citadel is surrounded by Cyclopean Walls with two gateways (the famous Lion Gate and the Northern Gate) dating back to the 13th and 14th centuries BC. Among the more important buildings are six royal tombs of the 16th century BC, sanctuaries, dwellings, the Granary, the Mycenean Palace on the crest of the hill, and the House of Columns further east. Outside the walls rise tholos-tombs of the Atridae, among which is the Treasury of Atreus (the Tomb of Agamemnon), the Tomb of Clytemnestra, and the Tomb of Aegisthus.

Epidaurus. Little remains of the Sanctuary of Asclepios, built during the third and fourth centuries BC; but to the south-east of the Sanctuary, among the olives, stands the impressive open-air Theatre of Epidaurus, the best-preserved in the whole of Greece. It is the work of Polycleitos Junior (fourth century BC); it can seat 14,000 and is renowned for its unique acoustics. Attending a performance of a Greek tragedy in it is a breath-taking experience. The museum contains pieces from the Temple of Asclepios, medical and surgical instruments, inscriptions concerning medicines and cures, and sculptures.

Conveniently near Epidaurus and Mycenae there is the elegant aristocratic old town of **Nauplion**, which was the capital of Greece in the first years after the War of Independence. Visitors to Epidaurus frequently stay here.

Hotels: Xenia Palace (Luxury) on Acropyrgion, **Amphitryon, Xenia, Agamemnon**.

Olympia is near the West Coast of Peloponnese. In the midst of majestic towering pines by the river was the principal Sanctuary of Zeus. This is where the first Olympic Games were held in 776 BC, and where they were repeated every four years or more than a millenium. There were also competitions in music, literature and the arts. There are extensive remains of the Altis, the Temple of Zeus, the Altar of Zeus, the Temple of Hora, and the Stadium. The two excellent museums at Olympia contain, among other extremely interesting exhibits, the classical masterpieces: Niki by Paionios and the statue of Hermes by Praxiteles.

Hotels: Xenia, near the Altis; **Neda; Nea Olympia** and **Apollon**, closed in the winter.

Mystra. In southern Peloponnese, along the foothills of Taïyetos stand the ruins of a Byzantine city with its fortress, palaces, mansions, and dwellings of the poor, monasteries and churches. The castle, built in 1249, dominates the surroundings. In upper Mystra stood the palace of the Despots, a rare specimen of Byzantine building. Among the monasteries the Perivleptos Convent contains some of the finest frescoes (end of 14th century). Visitors to Mystra can stay in **Sparta**.

Hotels: Menelaion and **Maniatis** on 65 and 60 Palaiologon Str.

Monemvasia: The decayed Byzantine town of Monemvasia is situated at the seaward end of a forbidding rocky promontory in the southern Peloponnese; it is best reached by sea (from Piraeus).

Hotel: Monemvasia.

THE GREEK ISLANDS

Crete is the largest of the Greek islands and the home of the oldest civilisation in Europe, the Minoan, Its two main centres were **Knossos** and **Phaistos.** Their palaces were built originally around 1900 BC and rebuilt, after they had collapsed in an earthquake, about 200 years later. They were not only royal residences but also administrative and religious centres for the whole district. The interiors of the buildings were decorated with very fine frescoes. The two palaces were destroyed in 1450 BC by the eruption of the volcano on nearby Thera.

The museum in **Heraklion** contains almost all the works of Minoan civilisation that have been discovered—vases, miniature sculptures, metal work, sarcofagi, frescoes.

Crete should be visited also for its extraordinarily beautiful and various scenery—wild mountains, deep gorges, unspoiled beaches, and vast fields with innumerable varieties of wild flowers, many of which are unique to the island. Crete is rich in citrus fruits, bananas, vines, olives and palm trees. Among other places on the island that also deserve a visit are Malia, the Lasithi Plateau with hundreds of windmills, Agios Nikolaos (a picturesque village which is now a rather over-developed international centre), Ierapetra, Mount Ida, Hora Sfakion, Hania, and the Samarian Gorge.

Hotels
Heraklion: Astoria (first class) **Astir** (first class) **Zenia** (first class) **Mediterranean.**
Agios Nikolaos: Minos Beach, 105 chalets (luxury) **Mirabello,** 175 R and 50 chalets (luxury) **Hermes.**
Khania: Kidon Plat. El. Venizelou, **Xenia, Doma,** 124 El. Venizelou.

The Cyclades: Between the southernmost tip of Euboea and the north coast of Crete, the surface of the Aegean is broken by the rocky peaks of a sunken plateau. The Cyclades are dry, rocky islands, and only a few of them are inhabited, but with their clear air and water, their brilliant light and fascinating scenery, they are among the most popular Greek islands.

Thera or **Santorini** is the southernmost island of the Cyclades and the nearest to Crete; it has the most dramatic appearance and history: it suffered since ancient times earthquakes, volcanic eruptions, submersions, elevations and enlargements. The island is a huge dark rock with white houses perched on top; its crescent shape, with high sheer cliffs inside, encloses a gulf in the centre of which is Greece's last active volcano. An early explosion of this volcano destroyed the Minoan civilisation of Crete—Thera itself is thought by some archaeologists to be the original Atlantis. The principal centres on the island are the town of Thera and its port; **Ancient Thera** which dates from the 10th century BC; and the newly excavated site at Acrotiri—it had been buried under volcanic ash and thus remained extraordinarily well-preserved. The exquisite frescoes from Acrotiri are exhibited in the National Archaeological Museum of Athens.

Hotels
In the main town of the island, **Thera:**

Atlantis, Kanaris, Apr. to Oct.; **Panorama** open all year.

Mykonos and **Delos** have to be visited together: Mykonos, an extremely popular international centre, is the jumping-off place for the ruined, silent, ancient island of Delos. Mykonos is brilliantly white, noisy and cheerful; it is famous for its 360 chapels (one for each family), for its windmills, and for its mazes of streets which were designed to baffle the pirates. It is also the home of a growing international artistic colony. Caïques for Delos leave at intervals in the morning and return in the afternoon. **Delos** was an important religious centre from the seventh century BC onwards—festivals and games took place there, and the wealthier cities made offerings and established treasuries on the island. Originally a place of pilgrimage, it became a rich trading port, and under the Romans a thriving slave market; covered with ruins, it is now an awesome sight. Delos is one of the most important ancient sites in Greece and deserves more than one trip with a detailed guide to the place.

Hotels: Leto and **Manto,** open all year; **Theoxenia, Rhenia, Kouneni** closed in the winter.

Also extremely interesting, among other islands of the Cyclades, are **Andros, Kea, Paros, Naxos, Amorgos, Milos,** and **Ios** near Thera.

Hotels on Ios: Chryssi Akti, Armadoros, summer only.

The Dodecanese lie in the extreme south-east end of the Aegean.

Rhodes is the largest and best-known island: its medieval character is evident everywhere, and since it had been a thriving centre in ancient times, there are also many classical ruins. A lot of the buildings on Rhodes date from its occupation by the Knights Hospitallers of St John between 1310 and 1522: they are found especially in the Old City, and

CHRISTINE OSBORNE

Corfu

among them are the medieval Castle of General Masters, which contains a marvellous collection of mosaics from Cos; the magnificent 15th century Inn of Auvergne; the Innes of the Seven Tongues; and the Hospital of the Knights (now an archaelogical museum). The classical sites of Kameiros and the Acropolis of Lindos also deserve a visit. Rhodes, with its warm weather almost all the year round has developed into one of the most popular tourist centres.

Hotels: Grand Hotel (luxury) **Astir Palace** (luxury), **Athena** (first class), **Mediterranean, Chevaliers Palace** and many others.

Other important islands in the Aegean are **Samos** and **Chios** near the Turkish coast; **Lesbos,** a large and fertile island, also near the Turkish coast but further north; the green island of **Thassos** in the northern Aegean, opposite Kavala; **Skiathos, Skopelos** and **Skyros,** the most important of the **Sporades,** strung between Pelion and the northern tip of Euboea; and **Euboea** itself, the second largest island of Greece after Crete.

Very near to, and easily accessible

from Athens, are **Aegina, Poros, Spetsai,** and **Hydra;** the last has an attractive individual character

The Ionian Islands are off the west coast of the mainland. There are seven: **Corfu, Paxos, Lefkas, Ithaca, Kefalonia, Zakinthos,** and—a long way further south—**Kithira. Ithaca** is of course the most important among them historically; **Corfu** the most popular. Its development is concentrated within a small part, and so 90% of the island is still unspoiled; it is green and fertile. The town of Corfu is handsome and elegant, dominated by two Venetian fortresses. The arcaded sidewalks are faced by Rennaissance public buildings.

Hotels
Corfu Palace, Leof. Vas. Konstandinou, with swimming pool (luxury)
Cavalieri, 4 Od. Kapodistriou (first class)
Astir, Od. Donzelot (second class)
Olympic Leof. Megali Donkisis Marias (second class).
Arion (second class)
Corfu Hilton (luxury)
Xenia Palace, summer only (second class)

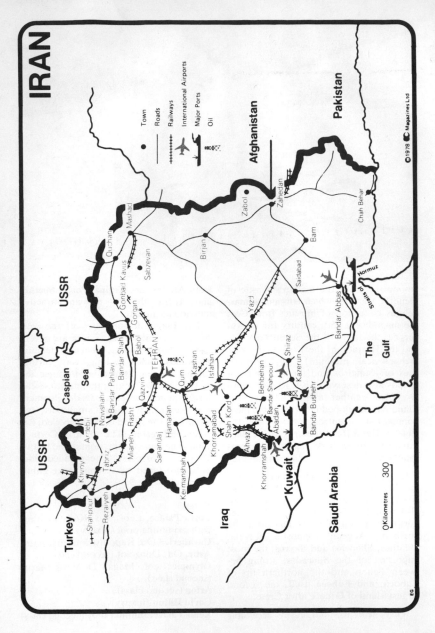

IRAN

Town
Roads
Railways
International Airports
Major Ports
Oil

USSR
Turkey
Iraq
Kuwait
Saudi Arabia
Afghanistan
Pakistan

Caspian Sea
The Gulf
Strait of Hormuz

Khvoy
Shahpour
Rezaiyeh
Tabriz
Ardebil
Nowshahr
Bandar Pahlavi
Rasht
Qazvin
Mianeh
Hamadan
Sanandaj
Kermanshah
Khorramshah
Ahvaz
Khorramshah
Abadan
Bandar Shahpour
Bandar Bushehr
Kazerun
Shiraz
Behbehan
Shah Kord
TEHRAN
Qum
Kashan
Isfahan
Babol
Bandar Shah
Gorgan
Gonbad Kavus
Sabzevan
Quchan
Mashad
Zabol
Zahedan
Bam
Brian
Yazt
Saidabad
Bandar Abbas
Hormuz
Chah Behar

0 kilometres 300

©1978 Magazines Ltd

Pakistan

138

IRAN

Christine Osborne

Iran is a land of stunning contrasts with a host of attractions for tourists, including the mountain and desert landscape, its rich archaeological heritage, beautiful handicrafts, delicious food, first-class hotels and good internal communications. Its only drawback as a prime tourist destination is the surly service afforded visitors in many hotels and major restaurants in the capital, Tehran. Elsewhere there is a welcome for the visitor.

THE LAND AND THE PEOPLE

Iran's 1,648,000 sq. km. extending from the Caspian Sea to the Sea of Oman, are a complete geography lesson in land-use and associated activities.

North of Tehran, the Elburz Mountains form an imposing barrier between the high plateau and the Caspian. The highest peak, Mount Damavand, is 5,671 metres (higher than Mount Blanc).

In the intensely farmed Caspian basin, autumn is the most picturesque season. Babolsar is the centre of Iran's caviar industry. Sturgeon are caught during spawning time: March-May.

West, the Zagros Mountains border Turkey and Iraq, and further barren ranges rise inland from the Sea of Oman.

Central Iran is largely desert, punctured by *qanats*, or irrigation canals. The Dasht-e Kevir, a desert of stones, and the Dasht-e Lut, an ocean of sand, cover an area the size of France.

Contrasts are everywhere: rivers lined with golden poplars, the sudden green of a desert oasis, and in winter the snow-capped Elburz Mountains whose ski-fields are a short drive from Tehran.

Iran's population of 34 million comprises many ethnic backgrounds, but the majority is of Aryan stock. There is variety in religions (although 90% of Iranians observe Shi'ia/Islamic rites) costumes, folklore and building styles.

The Aryans were the first Indo-European peoples to settle in Persia from the north-east; the name Iran stems from Aryana. Fars (whence Persia) was the heart of Aryan country. The Achaemenian empire resulted from the fusion between the Persians and the Medes, who settled further north. This essentially Persian nucleus remained little affected by the numerous invasions.

Today, the tourist will see the enormous variety of Iran's tribes: Turcoman shepherds wrapped in felt cloaks, smock-wearing Kurds and nomadic Qashqai women in eye-catching scarlet robes. Many of these minority groups speak their own language.

The several million Kurds and Lurs who live in the north-west Zagros Mountain region and the Baluch, in south-eastern Iran, lead a way of life quite removed from Farsi. This also applies to the Qashqai of Fars, today slowly settling to sedentary lives, but once numbering some 150,000—constituting the biggest tribe of nomads in the world.

The Turcomans, in north-eastern Iran, came mainly from the steppes. Their women wear flamboyant red scarves and silver jewellery. In the west live the fiercely independent Kurds, and the central-eastern border with Afghanistan is inhabited by Seyyeds, dark-skinned fishermen and livestock breeders.

The Bakhtiari nomads pitch their triangular black tents in remote valleys in the Zagros range. Each winter they migrate south to the fertile Khuzestan and Lurestan plains, but as westernisation in the form of houses, clinics and schools reaches outlying villages more and more tend to settle into new agricultural developments.

Persia was largely a rural society when, in the 10th and 11th centuries, it was invaded by Turkish and Mongol nomads from the steppe country. Large-scale nomadism, which prevailed in much of Iran, was mainly caused by the invasions and not, as is generally thought, by climatic conditions. However in southern Iran, where rainfall is scanty, life was always founded on a nomadic society.

Later the steppe nomads settled in the cooler mountain areas and on the fertile plains. The return to sedentary life has been slow, but as the tribes formed huge nomadic alliances and demanded political representation the process has speeded up. Certainly many reforms of the present Pahlavi dynasty have induced the nomads to fold their tents.

Freedom of worship is permitted throughout Iran. Armenians attend mass in the Isfahan district of Jolfa, Zoroastrians lay their dead in 'Towers of Silence' and a colony of Jews, dating from the Babylonian era, still lives in Hamadan.

Iranian women have a movement headed by the Shah's sister, Princess Ashraf, the first woman to appear unveiled. The Women's Association has over 71,000 members and has established hundreds of child-care and literacy centres all over the country. Its main efforts have been directed towards improving living standards of rural women, but it is now turning its attention to improving the situation of women in Tehran slums.

There are enormous gaps between the elite and poor rural families drawn into the city hoping for a better life.

HISTORY

The Achaemenian dynasty was founded by King Achaemenus, who ruled the Aryan tribes who had settled in the area south of Parsa, in the ninth century BC. Other Achaemenian groups, among them the Medes, had settled the high plateau even earlier. In 722 their capital was Hamadan and their evolution can be traced to the fourth millenium BC.

Cyrus II, who reigned from 559 to 529 BC, is revered as the first to unify and shape the country. Reputed to be a just ruler and tolerant conqueror, he captured Tintyr (Babylon) in 538 BC. The Persian Empire then stretched from Asia Minor and India as far as the Nile. Persepolis was built and a new captial, Pasargade, was founded in the region of Fars.

The next inspired emperor was Darius, who developed the heritage of Cyrus. His famous army of 10,000 men, the 'Immortals', conquered western India, the Black Sea and the Danube coast. They crossed the Red Sea and dug a canal on the present site of Suez, thus linking the extreme frontiers of the Achaemenian empire.

Darius's dream of capturing the Hellenistic capital, Athens, failed when the Persian forces suffered defeat at Marathon in 490. His son, Xerxes, also attempted to conquer Athens but was defeated at Salamis, in 480 BC.

Alexander shared the common dream of a unified world and his aim was to engender Persian participation in the new, still essentially Greek, civilisation. When he died, in 323, an officer, Seleucus, reaped the rewards of this ethnic fusion sought by the great conqueror. But although the 'Hellenised' Persian aristocracy supported the Seleucids, the dynasty survived less than a century.

In 247 BC, the Parthians rose to power, reigning during the rise of the Roman empire. Gradually rejecting Greek influence, they restored Zoroastrianism as the traditional religion, and during this period Persia began to recover its personality.

AD 224 saw the rise to power of the Sassanids from Fars who ruled for four centuries, until the Arab conquest of Persia. While the Sassanids were busy rebuilding Persia, Muhammed was preaching Islam in Arabia. A Persian, Sulman, became one of his prophets and the people gradually became influenced by his teachings, adopting the Shi'ite branch of Islam.

The Arabs finally vanquished the Sassanid forces in the battle of Al-Qadisiyah and Persia was absorbed into the new Arab empire with many Muslim converts chosen as local governors.

The ninth century AD saw a new awakening when the governor of Khorasan, on the Caspian coast, founded a new Persian dynasty. Now, however, began a series of Turkish invasions which continued until the 15th century. Mahmoud el-Ghazhri founded a vast empire, promoting the combined Islamic-Persian civilisation in those countries captured. The Seljuks, his successors, ruled over an area from China to the Bosphorus.

The beginning of the 13th century saw the start of devastating raids by Mongol hordes led by Genghis Khan. Being nomads from the central steppes, they were incompetent to rule and entrusted much local power to the cultivated Persians.

In the closing years of the 14th century, Persia was again invaded, this time by Tamerlane, who split it into several kingdoms. Tamerlane brought the same evils as the Mongols had done over a century previously. Agriculture declined as people fled to the mountains to escape heavy taxes and barbarous treatment, town life atrophied and the country was generally depressed. Yet the kingdom, although administered by the Turks, retained its deep-seated Persian culture.

The 16th century saw the initially glorious rule of the Safavid shahs, but Persia began a decline which was not arrested until Shah Abbas assumed power in 1587. A brilliant ruler and patron of the arts, Shah Abbas set up his capital in Qazvin, but moved the court to Isfahan, which he built into a most beautiful city—*Isfahan nis-i-jhan.*

The Turks withdrew to Tabriz, which Shah Abbas occupied in 1602, going on to reconquer Baghdad in 1623. Under Shah Abbas Persia developed diplomatic and commercial links with Europe. But after two centuries of rule, the Safavid dynasty weakened and Afghan invaders captured Isfahan in 1722.

Persia found a new strength in a non-commissioned army officer, Nadr, a Turcoman who drove the Afghans out in a series of brilliant campaigns. Uzbekestan and Iraq were seized, Delhi was taken in 1739 and Nadr was proclaimed Shah.

After Nadr's death, in 1747, Afghanistan and Persia were soon separated and a new dynasty was founded by the Zands, who chose Shiraz as their capital.

In Turkey the Qajars had become very strong, and in 1779 they took over Persia, electing to rule from Tehran.

European countries were by now experiencing the process of industrialisation and Persia, still a feudal state, became involved in the power struggle, largely Anglo-Russian. In 1907, both powers signed a Persian trusteeship agreement, and on the outbreak of World War 1 Persia was divided into British and Russian zones.

When the last Qajar ruler was deposed, another army man, Reza Khan, founded the Pahlavi dynasty in 1924. The Shah abdicated when the allies occupied Iran in 1941 and he was succeeded by his son, the present Shah, Mohammed Reza Shah Pahlavi.

CULTURE

Iran has one of the richest cultures in the Middle East, a deep-rooted civilisation which has survived repeated invasions and occupation by foreign societies.

Certain art forms are wholly Persian, but art has also been influenced by that of surrounding civilisations. The 13 centuries of Arab occupation saw a fusion with Islamic art.

Elamite art, dating to 2000 BC, testifies to great development in architecture. Bronze reliefs and skilfully worked varnished brick panels were probably used inside the megalithic-type tombs. The first Persian invaders lavishly decorated these tombs. Amlash in particular has yielded splendid vases embellished with domestic animals.

The Sakiz treasure throws valuable light on the origins of Achaemenian art. Gold accoutrements and inlaid ivorywork were discovered in a bronze sarcophagus.

During the Achaemenian period (530-331 BC) art was influenced by countries under Persian sovereignty: Assyria and Babylonia with a certain diffusion of Greek and Egyptian styles. Achaemenian art was primarily directed towards the adulation of the king, seen in splendid bas-reliefs at Persepolis. Typical is the sovereign seated on a throne receiving his subjects. Achaemenian artists were also skilled in depicting animals, including lions and unicorns. There is the majestic bas-relief of the 'Immortals'.

Hellenistic influence is apparent in Parthian sculpture, bas-reliefs depicting hunting scenes and the usual vassals bearing gifts to the emperor.

Early Persian art, by now diluted with various Oriental trends, saw a renaissance under the sassanid shahs, who were great builders of palaces, bridges and other monuments. Palace walls were decorated with lavish frescoes and stucco, and floors were covered in mosaic paving featuring Eastern, Greek and Roman motifs.

The Muslim occupation of Persia contributed fresh ideas and even experts find difficulty in distinguishing Persian from Islamic art of this period. This fusion of styles is reflected in arabesques and geometric patterns, especially in tile decoration on the cupolas of mosques. Mausoleums were also sumptuously decorated.

No better example exists of Islamic-Persian architecture and associated arts than the city of Isfahan. Isfahan is the richest repository of Persian art, its lofty 'Friday Mosque' a veritable museum of nine centuries of work by sculptors and craftsmen. It was built under the Seljuk shahs, but every successive dynasty contributed something. The work of the ornamentalists is most evident in the rich mosaic faience adorning the side walls of the south porch.

Craftsmen excelled in pottery, weaving, sculpture and mosaic work, but it was probably in miniature paintings that Persian art reached a peak. The style developed in the 14-15th centuries, attained its zenith during Mongol rule and maintained a high creative level under the Safavid shahs.

Persian literature has its beginnings in antiquity in poems attributed to the prophet Zoroaster himself. There is little evidence of literature during the Parthian period or in Sassanid Persia, but religious poetry is believed to have been an established tradition.

Again, literature was influenced by Islam. In the ninth century, Persian poetry was enjoyed far beyond the limits of the empire. In poetry the epic was most popular, and in its most classic form

Sheikh Lutfullah Mosque, Isfahan

Persian poetry was characterised by refinement of expression.

After the centuries of Arab rule, literature experienced a revival. The vast heritage of epic legends is combined in the famous *Book of Kings* by Firdausi. A 50,000-couplet masterpiece, it relates the dawn of civilisation and the history of Persia until the end of the Sassanid empire.

Persia has produced some great names in the arts and sciences, including Omar Khayyam, an astronomer and mathematician as well as a poet, and Sadi and Hafiz, the two most cherished poets.

Today, the *naqqal*, or professional narrator, keeps the riches of Persian poetry alive in recitations to the illiterate. Indeed poetry reading is still very much practised in cheaper Persian cafes.

WILDLIFE

Iran has a wide range of wildlife, mainly found in the mountainous north.

Lynx, leopard and Persian cheetahs still exist, but the Persian lion is believed extinct. Red and roe deer, wild sheep, goats and ibex abound in the mountain ranges and in the forests there are bears, wild pigs, porcupines, badgers and squirrels.

Though mainly preferring forest cover, rabbits, hares, jackals, foxes and wolves are distributed throughout the country. In the deserts wild asses are found.

Iran also boasts a variety of bird life. Birds classified as game and subject to strict laws are: pelicans, cormorants, herons, egrets, storks, flamingoes, ducks, geese, swans, birds of prey (eagles, falcons, vultures, etc), pheasants, partridges, snowcocks, quails, cranes, rails, crakes, waders, gulls, terns, sandgrouse, doves, kingfishers, woodpeckers and all passerines.

The Caspian Sea is noted for many varieties of sturgeon, white fish, pike, catfish, perch and salmon. Northern streams abound in brown trout and some 200 species of fish inhabit the Persian Gulf, plus shrimp, lobster and turtles.

Iran has strict conservation laws governing not only unlawful hunting and fishing in protected areas, but also pollution of rivers and lakes and mutilation of trees.

Hunting and fishing licences are divided into three categories: ordinary for birds and vermin (excluding wild pig), general (birds and mammals) and fishing. heavy fines are imposed for any violation of the game laws. Information on seasons and cost of licences is obtainable from the *Department of Environmental Conservation*.

Wildlife Parks
Mohammed Reza Shah Wildlife Park in the districts of Bojnord, Gorgan and Shahrud.
Des Wildlife Park in Dezful.
Dasht-e-Naz Wildlife Park in Sari.
Karkheh Wildlife Park in Dezful.
Tandoureh Wildlife Park in Khorasan.
Khoshkedaran Wildlife Park in Mazandaran.
Kolah Ghazi Wildlife Park in Isfahan.
Bamou Wildlife Park in Shiraz district.
In addition are some 50 protected regions and rivers.

ECONOMY

Anyone familiar with Iran a few years ago and returning now would be amazed at its transformation, and even the least-forewarned first-time visitor could not fail to be surprised at its modern development.

Particularly since the implementation of the Fifth Plan (1973-78) Iran has made an immense leap to catch up with the industrialised nations of the 20th century. Thousands of kilometres of roads have been laid, new ports and airports built and dams and irrigation channels made. Schools, clinics and women's centres have been constructed in remote rural villages and industrial centres sited outside major towns.

Land reform, the first of the 12 principles of the 'White Revolution', is proceeding. Agricultural co-operatives have been formed with credit supplied at low interest for mechanisation and fertilisers.

Today agricultural production represents about 20% of Iran's GNP, with the emphasis of further planning on supplying industry with primary products and satisfying local demand. The main products farmed are cotton, rice, tea, tobacco, wheat, fruit and sugar beet. New crops are sugar-cane in Khuzestan, and the Jiroft and Minab plains along the Sea of Oman are earmarked for intensive farming.

Until these plans become effective and there is a greater switch from traditional methods to mechanisation, Iran will continue to rely on imported foods, a burden of some $1bn.

Oil is the reason for the economic transformation of Iran from an agricultural state (until the 50s) to a country with a sound industrial base. Per capita income has risen from $100 to $1,600 per annum. Although less than the budgeted figure, Iran's 1975 oil revenues amounted to $18-19bn.

Iran is estimated to have some nine billion tonnes of oil reserves. On 1974 levels, it could maintain production for about 30 years. As a world oil exporter, it is second to Saudi Arabia, and as a producer it occupies fourth place.

In the tourist sector, the number of new hotel beds is being increased to 21,950 (de luxe), 20,500 (average) and 47,750 (inexpensive) to accommodate the expected 925,000 visitors to Iran in 1978.

The industrialisation of Iran, from essentially small craftsmen to industrial mass production, is in full swing. Begun in the 1930s, but remaining static for some time in its initial stages, it gained pace in the 1960s until today it employs 35% of the total labour force (excluding the oil sector).

The oil industry, spearheaded by NIOC, continues to develop towards total self-sufficiency in production, refining and transportation. Special attention is now being given to the petro-chemical and steel industry with the construction of additional blast furnaces. There is growing utilisation of Iran's vast natural-gas reserves, estimated to be 5,500 billion cubic metres. Natural-gas exports by long-distance pipelines will become Iran's second most important product. Over 13bn.c.m. will be supplied annually to the USSR, from 1981, and further industrial expansion will be in the processing of liquefied natural gas.

However, despite Iran's apparently healthy economic position, there are signs that it may soon confront deficits, resulting from its construction and industrialisation policy, since initially non-oil exports develop only slowly as a source of foreign exchange.

Bottlenecks, rather than financial restraints, have caused delays in implementing certain key aspects of the Fifth Plan. There are shortcomings in infrastructure: roads; inadequate port facilities for example result in long delays.

Equally serious is the continuing shortage of locally trained technicians so that Iran, for the time being, will need to rely on foreign experts.

GENERAL INFORMATION

Area: 1,648,000 sq. km.
Population: 34,100,000 (1975).
Altitude: Central plateau has an average altitude of 1,000 m. The highest altitudes are in the north, where the volcanic peak of Mt. Damavand rises to 5,700 m.
Capital: Tehran.
Head of State: H.I.M. Mohammad Reza Pahlavi, Shahanshah of Iran.
Government: Monarchy, with legal political activity limited to a single party.
Languages: Persian (Farsi) is the most widely spoken language.
Turkish is understood in the north-west and Arabic in the south-west. Business-

men and government officials usually speak English or French and some German.
Religions: 98% Muslim (90% Shia and 7% Sunni). Other religious communities include Christians, Jews and Zoroastrians.
Currency: Iranian monetary unit is the rial (IR), but tomans are used in every-day life (one toman equals 10 rials). £1 = 133IR. $1 = 70.55IR.
Time: GMT + 3½ hours.

HOW TO GET THERE

By air: Aircraft arriving from Europe land at Tehran-Mehrabad. The national airline, Iran Air, provides regular connecting flights to London, Paris, Frankfurt, Geneva, Istanbul, Rome, Moscow, Kabul and the Gulf emirates and operates both a one-stop (London) 707 flight from New York to Tehran five days a week, and a non-stop jumbo 747SP flight from New York to Tehran twice a week. Tehran is served by most of the major airlines, including Air France, British Airways and PanAm. Abadan also has an international airport.

By sea: Khorramshahr (near Abadan) on the Persian Gulf is the biggest port. Some freighters which stop there take passengers. P&O (Cargo Division) do occasional trips from Britain, via Suez and Kuwait. Hellenic Lines sail from the States and occasionally stop at Iran.

By road: The Asian Highway provides 2,000 km. of two-lane asphalt highway from the Turkish border at Bazergan and the Iraqi border at Qasr-e-Shirin to the Afghan border at Tayebat. The road from Tehran to the Pakistani border is under construction from Kerman to the border. An alternative entry into Iran from Ankara, which avoids the mountain passes is via Aleppo (Syria) and Baghdad (Iraq) and thence to Kermanshah (Iran), but this includes a bad stretch of 400 km. and requires two supplementary visas, which can be obtained at Ankara.

Motorists' Organisations: Touring and Automobile Club of Iran: 37 Varzesh Avenue, Tehran, tel: 48342. An international driving licence is recommended. In Iran, insurance is required for the length of stay and must be obtained at the first large town inside Iran (e.g. Tabriz, when coming from Turkey). A carnet de passage (issued by the AA or RAC for UK drivers) is compulsory for any car staying in Iran for longer than one month.

By rail: To Istanbul by express from London or Paris, and then to Hydarpasha, from where there are trains to Tehran four times a week.

By bus: There are air-conditioned buses travelling on roads from Turkey. There is a regular bus service from Munich to Tehran, which takes eight days. For further information contact Touring Bureau, Starnberger Bahnhof, Munich, West Germany.

Visas and health regulations
British passport holders do not require a visa for entry or exit. US and Canadian citizens do require visas, obtainable from an Iran embassy or consulate. Tourists who arrive by air from countries where there is no Iranian consulate can obtain a 15-day visa at Abadan or Tehran airport. A three-month visa can be renewed for an equal length of time at Service for Foreign Residents, Farah Jonoubi Avenue, Tehran. Smallpox vaccination is required, and cholera inoculations are advised. From about April to October visitors to the Caspian area should take precautions against malaria.

Currency and customs regulations
Money can be changed at banks, or at the Tehran bazaar, where there is a slightly higher rate for banknotes, but not for travellers' cheques. Money can also be changed at the big hotels, the airports and the frontier posts of Bazargan and Khosravi at the official rate. Cash and travellers' cheques can be exchanged for local money. Duty-free items for tourists entering Iran include personal effects. Visitors are also permitted to bring 200 cigarettes or an equivalent in tobacco products and a bottle of alcoholic drink without paying duty. It is forbidden to export antiques that are older than 100 years. Visitors should make sure the word 'modern' is on the bill for all items.

CLIMATE

The temperature in Tehran ranges from a maximum of over $38°C$ ($100°F$) to a minimum of $-14°C$ ($7°F$) with January temperature averages $3°C$ ($38°F$) and July-August temperature averages $29°C$ ($84°F$). Humidity is low, but the nights stay hot and dry in summer. There is usually a short rainy season in the spring and early winter, but no rain between the end of April and the beginning of October. In winter there are heavy snowfalls. In mountain regions there are extreme changes of temperature. The Gulf and Caspian areas are extremely hot and humid and the winters are mild.

What to wear
In summer extremely light clothing is necessary—dresses and suits of cotton, linen, or silk. Women need to dress discreetly bearing in mind that Iran is an Islamic country. Shorts should not be worn, and trousers are preferable to very short skirts. Women should wear a scarf in mosques and other religious buildings. In winter very warm clothes are needed. Coats, hats and warm shoes should be taken.

Health precautions
Drinking water is quite safe in most large towns, but it should be asked for specifi-

cally at hotels, as the tap water may taste unpleasant. In rural areas it is wise to drink only tea and soft drinks. Public baths are a great Iranian institution. There are good hospitals in Tehran.

ACCOMMODATION AND FOOD

There are many Western-style hotels in Iran but it is wise to book well in advance, in the tourist centres of Isfahan, Shiraz and especially Tehran. The accommodation ranges from de luxe hotels with all amenities, four-star hotels with all comforts and three-star hotels, slightly less equipped but still comfortable, to two-star hotels, which are clean and give satisfactory service.

In the provinces there are hotels of variable standards, and Ministry of Tourism Inns (or *Mehmansara*).

The restaurants in Tehran and in all the big cities serve international cuisine. There are many local-style restaurants, the most typical being the Tchelo-kebabi, which specialises in *tchelo-kebabs* with many variations. Rice is the main base for Iranian dishes, but meat, vegetables, yoghurt, bread and cheese are also used a great deal. In Tehran and Tabriz, the Armenian eating houses serve sandwiches and vodka. There are tea houses in the villages which serve skewers of meat with bread and soup.

Along the Caspian Sea fish is the staple food. The sturgeon is caught under government licence and good caviar is available there, though it is not particularly cheap.

Tipping: Hotels, restaurants and nightclubs usually add a service charge of 15%; extra tipping depends on the quality of service. Small tips can be given for room service (10-20 Rs), porters (10 Rs) barbers and hairdressers (30-50 Rs), mosque guide (10-15 rs). Tipping is not expected in tea houses of unclassified hotels, and taxi drivers need not be tipped.

TRANSPORT

By air: There are several flights a day by Iran Air to the large cities such as Tabriz, Isfahan, Shiraz and Mashad. Domestic flights cover all major tourist towns and provincial capitals.

Iran Air: Villa Avenue 44, Tehran, tel: 911578/76; Ferdowsi Avenue, Tehran, tel: 911575; Braim Sunshine, Block 15, Shahpour Avenue, Abadan, tel: 2145/6. Local offices also in Ahwaz, tel: 25146; Bandar Abbas, tel: 3233; Bushehr, tel: 698; Isfahan, tel: 28200, 28292; and Shiraz, tel: 23111.

By road: There are about 50,000 km. of roads, of which some 14,000 km. have asphalt or paved surfaces. The dirt roads and tracks are of varying quality, depending on whether they have been levelled or not and on the weather. It would be wise to check with the Touring and Automobile Club in Iran, 37 Varzesh Avenue, Tehran, on the condition of the roads, as they change from one season to the next. Buses, which are comfortable, and of a reasonable standard, run frequently all over Iran. This is the most popular way of travel for Iranians, and the cheapest. There are stops for rest rooms and refreshments. The main companies are TBT, Mihantour, Levantour, Iran Tourist, Iran Peyma and Adel.

Taxis are plentiful; local customs allow eight to 10 people in each vehicle. A price should always be agreed upon before the start of the journey.

By rail: The rail network is linked to Europe through Turkey as well as the USSR via Tabriz in Azerbaijan, beside serving some faraway provinces such as Kerman, Khorasan (Mashad) and Khuzistan (Khorramshahr). The Caspian line ends at Gorgan. The first-class accommodation and sleepers are excellent in every respect. There are two categories of trains: expresses and regulars.

BANKS

More than 40 foreign banks have representative offices in Tehran, including: Bank of America NT and SA, Bank of Tokyo, Banque de Bruxelles, Banque de Paris et des Pays-Bas, Bayerische Vereinsbank, Berliner Bank, Chase Manhattan Overseas Corporation, Commerzbank, Deutsche Bank, Dresdner Bank, Midland Bank International, Vereinsbank in Hamburg.

There are also 28 Iranian banks, all of which have offices in Tehran.

Business hours
Banks: 0730-1300/1700-1900 Saturday to Wednesday and 0730-1130 Thursday (summer); 0800-1300 and 1600-1800 Saturday to Wednesday (winter).
Shops: 0800-2000 Saturday to Thursday, 0800-1200 Friday (winter); 0800-1300 and 1700-2100 Saturday to Thursday, 0800-1200 on Friday (summer).
Government offices are usually open from 0800-1400 hours (Saturday to Wednesday) and 0800 to either 1200 or 1300 hours (Thursday). All ministries and government offices close on Fridays.
Offices: From 0800-1700 in winter with variable afternoon hours, and from 0800-1300 hours and 1800-2000 hours in summer. Many offices are closed on Thursday afternoon and most on Friday.
The bazaars close at sunset.

PUBLIC HOLIDAYS

The Iranian year starts on 21 March. During the New Year holiday, which runs from 21 to 25 March, all government offices and most business firms are closed. The following are public holidays

in Iran with fixed dates: the Iranian New Year, 21-25 March; Sizdah, the 13th day of the year, 2 April; Anniversary of the Constitution, 5 August; birthday of the Shah, 26 October. In addition there are at least 25 Muslim national feast days or religious holidays with changeable dates each year.

EMBASSIES IN TEHRAN

Afghanistan: Pahlavi Avenue.
Algeria: Avenue Roosevelt (Nord), rue no 8, No. 13.
Austria: Takhte Jamshid, Forsat Avenue.
Bahrain: 31 Avenue Vozara.
Belgium: Avenue Takhte Tavous, 41 Avenue Daryaye Noor.
Canada: Takhte Jamshid, Forsat Avenue, PO Box 1610.
Denmark: Copenhagen Avenue 13.
Egypt: 123 Avenue Abassabad, Avenue Park, PO Box 22.
Finland: Avenue Gandhi, corner of 25th Street.
France: France Avenue.
Germany: (West): Ferdowsi Avenue.
Greece: Kheradmand Avenue, Kucheh Salm no. 43.
India: N. Saba Avenue, no 166.
Iraq: Avenue Pahlavi.
Italy: France Avenue 81.
Jordan: Bukharest Avenue, no. 16th Avenue no. 55.
Kuwait: Maikadeh Avenue, 3-38 Sazman-Ab Street.
Lebanon: Bukharest Avenue 16th Street, no. 43.
Morocco: Avenue Nader Shah, rue Afshine no. 1.
Netherlands: Takhte Tavous, Near Pahlavi Avenue, Rue Moazami.
Oman: Avenue Abbas Abad, Avenue Bukharest, 17th Avenue no. 10.
Portugal: Rodsar Avenue, no. 41.
Qatar: Avenue Abbas Abad, Avenue Television, Second Avenue 14-16.
Saudi Arabia: Avenue Aban, PO Box 2903.

Spain: Fisherabad Avenue, Khoshbin Street 29.
Sudan: Avenue Ghandi, rue 21, no. 5.
Sweden: Takhte Jamshid Avenue, Forsat Avenue.
Switzerland: Pasteur Avenue.
Syria: Avenue Muhammad Reza Shah, Avenue 34, no. 9.
Tunisia: Abbas Abad, Avenue Park No. 131.
Turkey: Ferdowsi Avenue, no. 314.
United Arab Emirates: Avenue Vozara, 8th Street.
UK: Ferfowsi Avenue.
USA: Takhte Jamshid Avenue, Roosevelt Avenue.
USSR: Churchill Avenue.
Yeman Arab Republic: Avenue Bukharest, rue 6, no. 23.

TOURIST INFORMATION

Ministry of Information and Tourism: 174 Elizabeth Blvd, Tehran. Publications available from them are: Iran Travel News (monthly), Monthly Statistics Bulletin, brochures, guide books, road maps, posters, etc.

TEHRAN

The capital has a population of well over three million and is a modern city in nearly every sense of the word, with up-to-date shops, traffic fumes, noise, impersonal high buildings and extensive suburbs. But there are places of architectural interest, including the Golestan Palace, near the bazaar, which acts as a museum of royal wealth, and the Shahyad Monument, constructed in 1971 in modern Persian style. The Sepahsalar Mosque, completed in 1830, has eight minarets from which the city can be viewed. Museums include the Archaeological Museum, the Decorative Arts Museum and the National Arts Museum, and there are several cooling parks and gardens.

Outside Tehran there is some fine scenery. Only 8 km. south is *Rey*, with early monuments. Further in the same direction is *Varamin* (40 km. from Tehran). West of Tehran is *Qazvin* (150 km.) on the Asian Highway, an ancient city full of mosques and shrines. A mountain resort is *Shemshak* (100 km.).

Hotels

De luxe
Aria Sheraton, 204 rooms, Kh. Pahlavi tel: 683021, tlx: 212798.
Inter Continental, 416 rooms, Kh. Iran-Novin, tel: 656021, tlx: 212300.
Park, 270 rooms, Kh. Hafez, tel: 644121, tlx: 212466.
Royal Tehran Hilton, 544 rooms, Kh. Pahlavi, tel: 290031, tlx: 212510.
Tehran International, 340 rooms, Kh. Kourosh-Kabir, tel: 840081, tlx: 212700.

Four-star
Commodor, 138 rooms, Kh. Takht-Jamshid, tel: 669611, tlx: 212630.
Exelsior, 50 rooms, Kh. Pahlavi, tel: 665596.
Imperial, 86 rooms, Kh. Takht Jamshid, tel: 649310, tlx: 212521.
Kings, 86 rooms, Kh. Pahlavi, tel: 89661, tlx: 212675.
Marmar, 72 rooms, Kh. Sepahbod-Zahedi, tel: 830083.
New Naderi, 100 rooms, Kh. Naderi, tel: 312056, tlx: 212704.
Semiramis, 82 rooms, Kh. Roosevelt, tel: 825145, tlx: 212331.
Sina, 200 rooms, Kh. Takht-Jamshid, tel: 663291, tlx: 212599.
Tehran Palma, 200 rooms, Kh. Shahreza, tel: 661851.
Tehran Tower, 72 rooms, Kh. Pahlavi, tel: 835051, tlx: 212832.
Versailles, 95 rooms, Kh. Pahlavi, tel: 895661, tlx: 212877.

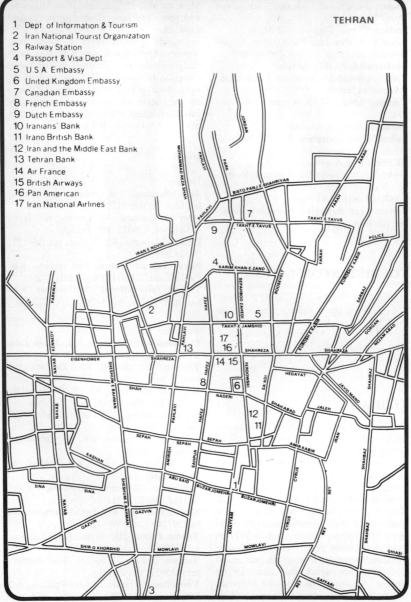

TEHRAN

1 Dept. of Information & Tourism
2 Iran National Tourist Organization
3 Railway Station
4 Passport & Visa Dept
5 U.S.A. Embassy
6 United Kingdom Embassy
7 Canadian Embassy
8 French Embassy
9 Dutch Embassy
10 Iranians' Bank
11 Irano British Bank
12 Iran and the Middle East Bank
13 Tehran Bank
14 Air France
15 British Airways
16 Pan American
17 Iran National Airlines

Copyright Graham and Trotman Ltd.

Victoria, 88 rooms, Kh. Pahlavi, tel: 890051, tlx: 212710.

Three-star
Ambassador, Kh. Villa, tel: 894966.
Atlantic, Kh. Takht-Jamshid, tel: 890286.
Caspian, Kh. Takht-Jamshid, tel: 834066.
Continental, Kh. Villa Kh. Sepand, tel: 891184.
Elizabeth, Elizabeth Blvd, tel: 650533.
Evin, Parkway, tel: 291021.
Kian, Kh. Zartosht, tel: 653236.
Miami, Kh. Pahlavi, tel: 625670.
Naderi, Kh. Naderi, tel: 313610.
Rudaki, Kh. Arfa, tel: 666314.

AZARBAIJAN— THE WESTERN GATEWAY

This province borders Turkey, Iraq, and the Soviet Union and for most overland travellers is the first taste of Iran. It has mountains and fertile valleys and the great salt lake of Rezaiyeh.

The first town on the Highway is **Maku** (which has a Tourist Inn and smaller hotels), from which various ancient sites, including Armenian churches, can be explored.

Rezaiyeh town, about 20 km. from the western lake shore, claims to be the birth place of Zoroaster and its mosque was built on the site of an important fire-temple. The bazaars contain beautiful hand carved inlaid woodwork.

Tabriz, is the second-largest city in Iran and is linked with Tehran (640 km.) by daily rail, air and bus services. It has a four-star International Hotel, a Tourist Inn near the railway station, a tourist camp in a public garden and a number of reasonable hotels around the town centre. The covered Qaisariyeh bazaar dates back to the 15th century and offers carpets, rugs, silks, leather goods and jewellery, there is some fine cooking in Tabriz too.

Tabriz has the ruined but restored Blue Mosque, completed in 1465 in the reign of Jahan Shah, when the city was the capital of Iran. There are two museums. From Tabriz there is a 218-km. journey to **Ardebil**, skirting Mount Sabalen (4,800 m.) associated with Zoroaster's vision of the holy scriptures. Ardebil has the beautiful mausoleum of Shaikh Safieddin, buried there in AD 1334; the town has a Tourist Inn and small hotels. From Ardebil visitors can drive to **Astara** on the Caspian Sea, and then on to **Bandar Pahlavi, Rasht** and **Tehran.**

THE 'GOLDEN TRIANGLE'

The ancient cities of **Hamadan, Kermanshah** and **Khorramabad** form the corners of the Golden Triangle of Ancient Persia, in the west of modern Iran, near the Iraqi border. This 'Triangle' contains the city of **Hamadan** itself—the summer capital of Cyrus the Great; the treasure mounds of Nush-e Jan, Baba Jan, Godin, Giyan, Ganj Dareh, Harsin, site of the 'Lorestan Bronzes'; the ancient potters' village of Lalajin; the temple of Artemis; the grottoes of Taghe Bostan and the bas-reliefs of Bisotun.

The Silk Route to China and the Royal Road of the Achaemenians also passed through the Triangle. There is pleasant rolling hill scenery in this part of Iran, interspersed with the enigmatic mounds (or *tappeh*) that house ancient treasures.

Hamadan (which has three main hotels) does not reveal much of its ancient history, except the 'Stone Lion' dating from the time of Alexander, the 'Mausoleum of Esther and Mordecai' which is now in fact thought to contain the remains of a different Jewish queen, Shushan Dokht, wife of a Sassanian king, Yazdegerd (around AD 400). The village of **Lalajin** is 24 km. from Hamadan; it produces millions of pieces of pottery every year.

Kermanshah (with four main hotels) is

a good base for visiting **Taghe Bostan**, 9 km. to the north, with its grottoes and bas-reliefs on the cliffs. **Bisotun**, 'The Mountain of the Gods', with a bas-relief 60 metres above the ground showing the deeds of Darius is, 32 km. from Kermanshah. Unfortunately for the average visitor it is only visible from a distance, but there are several other extraordinary reliefs on the mountainsides in this region.

The Seleucid temple of Artemis at **Kangavar**, 31 km. from **Sahneh**, consists of massive fallen columns, which are being reassembled. They are thought to have been damaged by an earthquake. The **Kangavar Valley**, 10 km. east of Kangavar, is rich in remains going back to 6000 BC. The most accessible and revealing excavated site is Tappeh Godin (on the road to the pleasant town of **Touisserkan**—which has a good hotel).

ISFAHAN

A former capital city of Persia (in the 11th or 13th and 16th to 18th centuries) Isfahan is still a central feature of the country, located midway between Tehran and Shiraz. It has a moderate climate, with an altitude of 1,500 m. on the Zayandehrud river plain; it is protected from southern winds by the Zagros mountains and it receives cool northern breezes in spring and summer.

Isfahan has a central square unmatched in elegance and spaciousness anywhere in the world. It is seven times the size of the Piazza San Marco in Venice, and puts the grandeur of the surrounding palaces and mosques into appropriate proportions.

Among the most rewarding features of Isfahan are its mosques, palaces, bridges, gardens and trees. The Friday Mosque—Masjid-e Jomeh—is one of Iran's finest buildings, with something from every era of Persian architecture. The Shaikh Lotfullah Mosque has an exquisite dome, and the 17th century King's Mosque—Masjid-e Shah—is famous for the stalac-

tite effect of its northern entrance. Other sights are the Ali Qapu Palace, the Seosepol Bridge with its 33 arches, the Chehel Soton (columned palace) and the Khiaban-e Chadar Bagh (four gardens' avenue).

The bazaars of Isfahan take travellers completely from the outside world and immerse them in an age-old rhythm of life, an atmosphere full of the market-cries of vendors, the hammering of the coppersmiths, the activities of carpet-weavers, silversmiths and cloth printers, the grilling of kebabs and the preparation of spices. The distinctive artifacts include carpets, rugs, pottery, embroidery, hand-printed cloth, jewellery, silver, brass and copper.

Hotels

De luxe
Shah Abbas, 134 rooms, Kh. Shah Abbas, tel: 26010-7.
Koroush, 133 rooms, Farah Blvd, tel: 40230.

Three-star
Ali Qapu, Kh. Chahar-Bagh, tel: 31282.
Iran Tour, Kh. Abbas-Abad, tel: 35976.
Pol, Ayenekhaneh Blvd, tel: 43950
Daryush, Kh. Chahar-Bagh Pahlavi, tel: 35468.

SHIRAZ (FARS PROVINCE)

One of the great ancient cities of Iran. Craftsmen from Shiraz helped the building of ancient Persepolis in 550 BC. The city was always prosperous and grew to fame in the 18th century when Karim Khan Zand made it his capital. Among the historic buildings are Masjid-e Jame (Friday Mosque, begun in AD 894), Masjid-e Now (New Mosque, begun in the 12th century), Shah Cheragh (King of Light Shrine, a pilgrimage centre with fine mirror work) and Narenjestan-e Qavam (the Orange Grove). There are

Ruins of Persepolis

beautiful gardens.

Shiraz has an international arts festival in the first week of September, which concentrates on theatre, music and dance from East and West. Shiraz artifacts on sale in its many bazaars and shopping arcades include Qashqai tribal carpets, mats, tablecloths, inlaid woodwork, gold, silver, glass and ceramic work. All these handicrafts are on display at the new Iran Handicraft Centre in the city.

Flying to Shiraz takes less than two hours from Tehran. The bus takes about nine hours.

Persepolis, 50 km. from Shiraz, is the ceremonial seat for the Achaemenians, built on an enormous platform carved out of the Kuhe Rahmat. Darius the Great began the project in 521 BC. His son Xerxes and successors added to its palaces and halls. This was the setting of the 2,500th Persian Empire Anniversary celebrations in October 1971. Nearby is Naqshe Rustam, with rock-cut tombs and a Zoroastrian temple. **Pasargade**, 80 km. north of Persepolis, is in the plain of Morghab, capital of Cyrus the Great.

Hotels
Kourosh, de luxe, Parke Farahnaz, tel: 28001.
Park, four-star, Chahar Rahe Zand, tel: 21426.
International, four-star, Kh. Ghasredasht, tel: 38780.
Mehmensara, three-star, Kh. Foroodgah, tel: 21021.

KHUZISTAN

The scene of early Persian civilisations dating back to 8000 BC, Khuzistan has several archaeological sites of great interest. **Haft Tappeh**, north of Ahwaz, includes more than a dozen burial mounds and the remains of the Elamite city of Tikni (1500 BC). **Choga Zanbil** has the remains of an important religious centre dating back 3,000 years. **Shush** (Susa) has a museum that has gathered impressive samples of architecture and remains from several eras. It is also the site of Daniel the Prophet's tomb.

THE CASPIAN COAST

The towns of the coast most popular with holidaymakers are **Ramsar, Babolsar, Nowshahr** and **Bandar Pahlavi**.

Hotels

AMOL
Masoud, tel: 2205. **Bozorg Amol**, tel: 2533. **Sadaf**, tel: 4450.

BABOLSAR
Casino, tel: 4060. **Metropole**, tel: 9982. **Motel**, tel: 4551. **Khazar**, tel: 9909. **Villa 12**, tel: 9903.

BANDAR PAHLAVI
Sepeed Kenar, tel: 3031. **Grand**, tel: 2266. **Iran**, tel: 2524.

BEHSHAHR
Ashraf, tel: 469. **Razeghi**, tel: 61.

CHALUS
Chalus, tel: 3030. **Shokoufeh**. **Takhte Jamshid**, tel: 2371. **Orkideh**.

GORGAN
Miami, tel: 2627. **Haghighat**, tel: 2371. **Saadi**, tel: 3432. **Taslimi**. **Villa**, tel: 4525. **Zhilla**, tel: 4642.

LAHIJAN
Mehmensara, tel: 2858. **Abshar**, tel: 2866. **Iran**, tel: 2285.

MAHMOODABAD
Fanuse Darya. **Golden Bell**. **Parauru**.

NOWSHAHR
Puchini, motel, tel: 8650. **Nowshahr**, tel: 8200. **Sahra**, tel: 8266.

RAMSAR
New Ramsar, four-star. **Khazar**.

RASHT
Iran, tel: 23035. **Ordibehesht**, tel: 22210. **Pamchal**, tel: 26022. **Asia**, tel: 23330. **Carvan**, tel: 24262. **Fars**, tel: 25251. **Ferdowsi**, tel: 22443. **Iran Javan**, tel: 22362. **Keyvan**, tel: 22967. **Kian**, tel: 25665. **Park**, tel: 24915. **Zibasara**, tel: 24000.

SARI
Mehmensara, tel: 3070. **Mazanderan**, tel: 4112. **Sari**, tel: 4077. **Nader**, tel: 2357.

SHAHSAVAR
Diana, motel. **Gol**. **Jahane Now**. **Marjan**. **Nadji**.

KHORASAN

A huge province in the east of Iran, stretching between the Elburz mountains and the Great Kevir desert. Khorasan means 'the land of the rising sun'. It was from here that Persian culture spread to central Asia and here also occurred the great revival of learning in the Islamic era. The cities of Toos and Neishabur became centres of calligraphy, poetry, philosophy and science.

Mashad is today the most populous city in Khorasan, It used to be a crossroads of caravan traffic on the Silk Route to China, but it was modernised earlier this century, with avenues and parks. The Sacred Precincts and the old bazaar now exist separately from the modern city. The bazaar is full of hidden alleyways, backstreet turquoise workshops and carpet factories. Up to four million pilgrims and tourists visit the city and shrine each year.

The courtyards, mosques, libraries and colleges surrounding the holy shrine in Mashad have been built under successive rulers over an immense expanse of time. For non-Muslims, entrance to the 'Sacred Threshold' itself must be applied for through the Ministry of Tourism's local office.

A sun dried village in the province of Khorsan.

About 130 km. west of Mahad is the ancient town of **Neishabur**, home of Omar Khayyam, poet, mathematician and astronomer. His tomb is a principal tourist attraction.

Toos, 30 km. north-east of Mashad, is where Persia's 11th century poet Ferdowsi was born and died.

The main roads to Khorasan province are the northern route, through Gorgan and the Caspian region, and the southern route, which follows the ancient Silk Route, passing many historic ruins, shrines and mosques.

Hotels
Hyatt, four-star, Farah St. **Iran**, three-star, Khosravi-Now St., tel: 28010. **Apadana**, tel: 21581. **Kourosh**, tel: 23955. **Amin**, tel: 28114. **Amir**, tel: 21300. **Pars**, tel: 23201. **Tehran**, tel: 40091. **Bulvar**, tel: 32031. **Park**, tel: 25893. **Bakhtar**, tel: 43787. **Sepid**, tel: 29053. **Sina**, tel: 29333. **Kasra**, tel: 21415.

KERMAN

In the southern desert region, the city of Kerman was founded by the Sassanid King Ardashir I. Turks and Mongols occupied it successively until the Safarid dynasty, when it became prosperous for a while, though it was subsequently destroyed in the 18th century. However the most exquisite architecture of the Friday Mosque, built in 1348 and restored by the Safarids in the 16th century, has survived to display its stunning beauty, proportions and decoration. Kerman is full of mosques. It also has a fine shady garden and a ruined citadel said to have been built by Ardashir. There are five hotels.

KISH ISLAND

In the Persian Gulf lies an island that is becoming a millionaires' paradise resort, being developed with 500 luxury villas and ultra-modern hotels. The first hotel to open was the **Shayan**, managed by the French PLM. There will be golf, riding, polo and all water sports, and the island will be linked to Paris by fortnightly air services. The November to April winter season will be popular with the jet-set tourists.

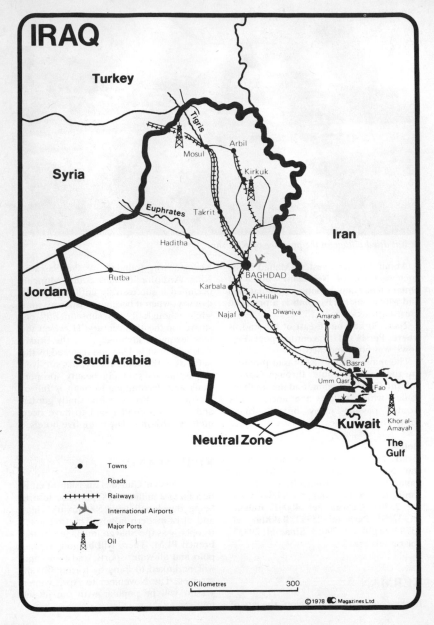

IRAQ

Turkey

Syria

Tigris

Mosul

Arbil

Kirkuk

Euphrates

Takrit

Haditha

Rutba

Jordan

Karbala

Al-Hillah

Najaf

Diwaniya

Amarah

BAGHDAD

Iran

Saudi Arabia

Basra

Umm Qasr

Fao

Kuwait

Khor al-Amayah

Neutral Zone

The Gulf

● Towns

—— Roads

++++++ Railways

✈ International Airports

⚓ Major Ports

🛢 Oil

0 Kilometres   300

©1978 Magazines Ltd

IRAQ

Judith Perera

Iraq is a country of contrasts both in its landscape—with hills, mountains, deserts and marshes—and its people, who are ethnically and religiously diverse. A relatively rich country with a long, chequered history Iraq is with justification called the cradle of civilisation.

Its present Islamic culture is the latest in a long series of cultures which have dominated the region, and it still boasts the remains of the great cities that ruled past civilisations like Ur, Babylon and Nineveh. Considerable trouble is taken to preserve and show to advantage the historical remains of these past cultures and most of them are easily accessible by road or rail. The northern mountains and southern marshes are interesting for their wildlife, and the north in particular is renowned for its mineral water springs.

The main language spoken is Arabic, but English is taught as a second language and is widely spoken. There are also some minority languages like Kurdish, Syriac and dialects of Turkish and Persian.

THE LAND AND THE PEOPLE

The central feature of Iraq is its two major rivers the Tigris and the Euphrates—its ancient name of Mesapotamia is Greek for 'land between the two rivers'.

Yet although these rivers traverse the length of Iraq, from the Turkish and Syrian borders in the north to the Gulf in the south, it is a country of contrasting scenery with distinctly different regions.

The north-east is a mountainous region—the highest peak, the Hasarost, being 4000 m. This is almost a temperate zone with abundant rainfall and snow in the winter months. The lower slopes of the mountains are cultivated to grow fruit, vegetables and tobacco.

This area is inhabited predominantly by Kurds who constitute about 15% of the total population of Iraq. They speak their own language and have preserved their own distinctive way of life. The area also includes small numbers of Assyrians (about 40,000) who speak a form of Syriac, Yazidis (65,000) who also have their own language and Turkomans (about 100,000) who speak a Turkish dialect. The Assyrians live mainly in the foothills of the mountains where the rainfall is less. With the help of irrigation, however, they produce cereals as well as vegetables.

The west of Iraq is a sparsely populated desert and semi-desert zone where nomadic tribes roam living off their herds of camels, goats and sheep. Rainfall is minimal here and the summers very hot. In places the underlying rock protrudes through the sand and scrub and it is from this that present-day Iraq—meaning cliff—gets its name. The people of this area are essentially the same Arab tribes which inhabit the eastern parts of Jordan and the north-eastern parts of Saudi Arabia.

The majority of Iraq's population, however, is concentrated along the two rivers. This area is relatively fertile, although rainfall is slight falling mainly in the winter months. The rivers flood regularly in spring especially in the south where they flow several feet above the surrounding plain, raised on the levels of silt which they deposit.

The central plains north of Baghdad are well irrigated, sometimes on the basis of systems which are thousands of years old, and many crops are produced including cereals, vegetables and cotton. South of Baghdad the severe flooding has re-

Malwiya Samarah Town

IRAQI CULTURAL CENTRE

sulted in areas of both marshland and desert. Yet in the areas which have been drained and irrigated, dates, citrus fruits, cereals (including rice) and cotton are grown. Date cultivation is concentrated mainly in the area of Basra. Winters in the plains are mild but summers are hot and very humid.

It is in the southern marshlands that the much-photographed 'Marsh Arabs' live. They are concentrated mainly in the area of Al-Chebayish just before the Tigris and the Euphrates join together in the Shatt al-Arab waterway which takes them to the Gulf. The area was once well cultivated, but in the seventh century it was flooded leaving only the higher areas above water. There are now more than 1,000 islands each supporting a few houses and the only form of transport is the *mash houf*—a small boat made of reeds. The 12,000 inhabitants of this area have constructed artificial islands of papyrus and mud and bridges now connect some of the islands.

In general, however, the people of the central plains are Arabs but of very mixed ancestry. They are mostly Muslim, but are divided between the two main sects of Islam—the Sunni and the Shi'a. The Sunni are mainly in the northern areas and are from the wealthier sections of society, while the Shi'a are concentrated in the south. There are in addition some 400,000 Christians of various sects scattered throughout Iraq.

Iraqi society therefore has not only substantial ethnic minorities, but also religious minorities. The Kurds and Turkomans, for example, although distinct ethnic groups, are Sunni Muslims, while the Assyrians are Christian. The Yazidis, on the other hand, have a religion of their own which includes pagan as well as Islamic and Christian elements. Although this adds to the diversity of Iraq it also causes problems. The Kurds, for instance, have been seeking an independent Kurdistan for centuries, and the

Shi'a feel that they are an underprivileged group, as the ruling elite is Sunni.

HISTORY AND CULTURE

The history of civilisation in what is now Iraq is at least 6,000 years old. Legend would suggest that it is even older, for it locates the site of the Garden of Eden at Al-Qurna, where the Tigris and Euphrates rivers join to form the Shatt al-Arab, and 120 km. north-west of Baghdad, excavations have revealed signs of settlement dating back to 7000 BC.

The first well-known settlers, however, were the Sumerians, whose city states based on a sophisticated agricultural economy were flourishing around 3500 BC. The sites of two of these cities, Ur and Uruk, can be seen near Nasiriya which is between Baghdad and Basra.

By 2300 BC the empire began to collapse with the entry into the area of various Semitic tribes. Ur flourished briefly again in 2100 BC but was finally sacked by the Amorites, another Semitic tribe from Arabia. After several centuries of disunity, a new empire was forged by the Semitic King Hammurabi whose capital was Babylon. The city, however, was sacked by the Hittites in the 17th century and the focus of power moved northwards.

The Assyrian empire based on the northern city of Nineveh lasted from about 1400 BC until about 600 BC and at its height extended as far south as Egypt. The remains of the great Assyrian cities of Nineveh, Nimrud and Ashur can still be seen in the hills some 400 km. north of Baghdad.

Nineveh was sacked in 612 BC by a combined revolt of the peoples subjected to the Assyrians' harsh rule and Babylon came into its own again. King Nebuchadnezzar reconstructed the city and built the famous hanging gardens, and his Chaldean Empire reached its peak in about 570 BC. Babylon subsequently fell to the Achaemenian Persians and then to

Hatra in northern Iraq

IRAQI CULTURAL CENTRE

Alexander the Great. After his death in 323 BC, however, it ceased to be an important political centre, but the ruins of its later glory are still standing some 59 miles south of Baghdad.

Subsequently Iraq fell under the sway of the Seleucids and the Parthians. The Parthian Persians and then the Sassanids held the area against the Romans and then the Byzantine Empire until 637 AD when the Arabs fired with the new religion of Islam invaded the region.

The first centre of Islamic civilisation was Damascus under the Umayyad dynasty, but in 750 AD the Abbasids became dominant with the support of the Shi'a in Iraq and the centre of Islamic power was transferred to Baghdad—a new city built for the purpose. This was the era of Caliph Haroun al-Rashid of the *Thousand and One Nights* who encouraged the flowering of Arabic culture. Most of the beautiful mosques built during this period are still standing, many of them with gold domes and minarets. But perhaps the most renowned of Iraq's Islamic attractions are the Shi`a shrines at Karbala and Najaf.

Gradually areas at a distance from Baghdad began to break away from the Abbasid Empire and it became weaker until the final blow was struck by the Mongol invasions of the 13th century. Iraq then ceased to be of any importance and was conquered by the Turks in the 16th century. As the Ottoman Empire began to decline the various areas of present-day Iraq enjoyed considerable local autonomy and by the early 19th century the Western European powers were showing an interest in the region.

Arab nationalism began to have some influence by the end of that century and during the First World War the British used this to persuade the Arabs to fight against the Turks who had ruled them for so long. The promised independence never came, however, and Iraq found itself a British mandated territory. A series of Anglo-Iraqi treaties followed under which Britain safeguarded its interests while giving Iraq more and more nominal independence. But there were recurring problems over borders and with the various ethnic minorities.

Modern Iraq began in 1958 with the overthrow of the 'monarchy' which Britain had imposed on the country. There followed a series of fairly bloody coups d'etat ultimately bringing to power the Baath Party which rules today.

The biggest problems the country has faced in the past 25 years have been border tension with Iran, which was finally settled in 1975, and the rebellion of the Kurds in the north who were seeking autonomy. Some nominal autonomy has now been granted but it is not considered satisfactory by most of the Kurdish population. Large-scale revolt has ceased for the time being however, as the Kurds were badly defeated after Iran stopped backing them in 1975.

Because of its long and varied history, Iraq is a culturally rich country. There is much to see dating from as far back as the Sumerian civilisation through the succeeding civilisations to the Islamic culture which predominates today. The people vary from the Marsh Arabs of the South to the nomads of the West and the Kurds in the north with their brightly coloured and distinctive clothes.

Crafts which are still followed include copper work and the weaving of carpets. A more recent occupation, however, is making copies of the ancient statues and engravings of past civilisations for sale mainly to tourists. The copies are usually of very good quality and are often made from casts of the original.

ECONOMY

Iraq's economy is based on oil and agriculture. Oil is the country's principal source of wealth and all its oil resources are now in government hands. Agriculture, nevertheless, still employs more people than any other sector of the economy and much of Iraq's attention is focused on river control and irrigation. Barley, wheat, lentils and linseed are the main winter crops and rice, dates, tobacco and sesame the main summer crops. Dates are Iraq's main export, leaving aside oil. The industrial base is being developed but not as fast as other oil-producing countries like Iran or Algeria. There is less need, as Iraq is essentially under-populated and is potentially a rich agricultural country provided its irrigation problems can be solved.

GENERAL INFORMATION

Area: 438,446 sq km.
Population: 10,765,000.
Capital: Baghdad.

Head of State: President Ahmad Hassan al-Bakr.

Government: Republic. Power is in the hands of a faction of the Arab Baath Socialist Party.

Language: Arabic.

Religion: Over 90% of the population are Muslims. There are small Christian communities in all the principal towns and a very small Jewish community in Baghdad.

Currency: The Iraqi dinar (ID) is divided into 1,000 fils. £1 = 0.565 ID. $1 = 0.2899 ID.

Time: GMT +3.

HOW TO GET THERE

By air: Iraqi Airways operates direct flights from London and other European cities on most days of the week. The following international airlines operate scheduled flights to Baghdad airport: Aeroflot, Air France, Air India, Alitalia, Austrian Airways, British Airways, EgyptAir, Iranian Airlines, KLM, Lufthansa, MEA, PIA, Saudi Arabian Airlines, SAS, Swissair, Syrian Arab Airlines, Poland Airlines, Japan Airlines.

By road: Iraq is linked to Kuwait, Jordan, Syria, Iran and Turkey.

By sea and rail: Basra, Iraq's seaport connects the country with the Far East and Europe. P&O/Strath services operate a passenger/cargo service.

The Orient Express connects Iraq with Europe through Syria and Turkey.

Visas and health regulations

A valid passport with an entry visa obtainable from Iraqi consular offices abroad is required. A certificate of religion is also necessary. Usually a written invitation to visit Iraq from a government organisation is demanded before a visa is issued. Applications should be made well in advance as delays sometimes occur in obtaining visas.

Visitors need a valid international certificate of vaccination against smallpox,

Baghdad

and visitors are advised to be vaccinated against cholera and typhoid.

Currency and customs regulations

It is forbidden to export Iraqi bank notes. Foreign currency has to be declared on entry and it is not allowed to export sums in excess of the amount declared on entry.

Visitors are allowed to take, free of duty, one litre of spirits and 200 cigarettes or 50 cigars or ½ kilo of tobacco. Travellers' personal effects are not subject to customs duty.

CLIMATE

The central and southern areas of the country are characterised by a cold winter and long, dry summer. From May till the end of September it is excessively hot with no rainfall and temperatures are between 38°C and 49°C. In Basra the humidity is high thoroughout the summer and the nights are hot. From October to April the weather is usually dry and warm during the day, while from December to March the nights are cold. Rain falls normally between October and April.

What to wear

In summer, lightweight clothes are essential and headgear and sunglasses are advisable. From the end of October to mid-April medium-weight clothing is required.

ACCOMMODATION AND FOOD

Hotel prices are government-controlled and a single room with bath in a first-class hotel costs ID 8. Because of the heavy pressure on hotel accommodation, it is advisable to arrange for advance booking. The prices of restaurant meals is also government-controlled. A meal in a first-class restaurant costs from ID 2 to ID 4

(excluding drinks). Restaurants serve both oriental and European dishes. Popular Iraqi dishes are *Kubba*, a special preparation of wheat known as *Borghul* is mixed with minced meat, flattened, and pieces stuffed with meat and filled with nuts, sultanas, spices, parsley and onion. They are formed in the shape of flat platters or round balls, then boiled and ready to serve; *Dolma*, made from stuffed vine leaves, cabbage, lettuce, onions, eggplants, marrow or cucumbers. The stuffing is made of rice mixed with minced meat and spices; *Tikka*, small chunks of mutton on skewers grilled on a charcoal fire; *Quozi*, a small lamb boiled whole and then grilled. It is usually stuffed with rice, minced meat and spices, and served on a large tray heaped with rice; *Masgouf*, this is fish from the Tigris, which is cooked right on the river bank, fresh from the river.

TRANSPORT

By air: Iraqi Airways operates regular air services between Baghdad, Basra and Mosul.

By road: All major towns are connected by metalled roads, and there are regular bus services from Baghdad and other main cities. The fare from Baghdad airport to the main hotels in town is ID 2. It is advisable to negotiate the fare before the start of the journey. Self-drive facilities are available.

By rail: The Iraqi Republican Railways run regular passenger and goods services. There are three main routes: Baghdad-Basra; Baghdad-Kirkuk-Irbil; Baghdad-Mosul-Tel Kotchek.

BUSINESS HOURS

On Friday all government offices and business concerns are closed. Govern-

Ali Baba fountain, Baghdad

ment offices: Summer: 0800 to 1400 Saturday to Wednesday and 0800 to 1300 Thursday; Winter: 0830 to 1430 Saturday to Wednesday and 0830 to 1330 Thursday. Shops and businesses: Summer: 0800 to 1400 and 1700 to 1900 Saturday to Wednesday and 0800 to 1300 Thursday; Winter: 0830 to 1430 and 1700 to 1900 Saturday to Wednesday and 0830 to 1330 Thursday; Banks: Summer: 0800 to 1200 Saturday to Wednesday and 0800 to 1100 Thursday; Winter: 0900 to 1300 Saturday to Wednesday and 0900 to 1200 Thursday.

PUBLIC HOLIDAYS

New Year's Day, 1 January.
Army Day, 6 January.
14 Ramadhan Revolution, 8 February.
Prophet's Birthday, 20 February.
Nawruz Day, 21 March.
Labour Day, 1 May.
Republic Day, 14 July.
Republic Day, 17 July.
Eid al Fitr, 3-6 September.
Eid al Adha, 10-13 November.

Muslim New Year, 2 December.

EMBASSIES IN THE CAPITAL

Algeria: Karradat Mariam. Tel: 32181.
Austria: Aqaba bin Nafi Square. Tel: 99032.
Belgium: Sa'adoun Par. Tel: 69301.
Denmark: Alwiyah. Tel: 93058.
Egypt: Karradat Mariam. Tel: 34127.
France: Karrada Dakhil-Kard el-Pasha. Tel: 96061.
Germany, Federal Republic of: Masbah Square. Tel: 92027.
Greece: 52 Street, near Al-Wahtiq Market. Tel: 96729.
Holland: Sa'adoun Park-Nidhal Street. Tel: 87175.
Iran: Karradat Mariam-Haifa Street. Tel: 33095.
Italy: Alwiyah-Nidhal Street. Tel: 95143.
Japan: Masbah. Tel: 95156.
Jordan: Karradat Mariam. Tel: 33185.
Kuwait: Karradat Mariam-Haifa Street. Tel: 33151.
Lebanon: Masbah-Hussam el-Din Street. Tel: 99019.

Libya: Mansour—the main Mansour Street. Tel: 518590.
Morocco: Karradat Mariam. Tel: 38151.
Qatar: Masbah. Tel: 96144.
Saudi Arabia: Safa al din al Hilly Street. Tel: 20036.
Spain: Masbah. Tel: 92851.
Sudan: Masbah. Tel: 99007.
Sweden: Nidhal Street. Tel: 95391.
Switzerland: Karradah al Sharkiah. Tel: 98170.
Syria: Masbah Square. Tel: 95130.
Tunis: Mansour. Tel: 517786.
Turkey: Safa al din al Hilly Street. Tel: 20021.
UK: Sa'adoun Street. Tel: 99001.
United Arab Emirates: Mansour. Tel: 515206.
USSR: Karradat Mariam-Haifa Street. Tel: 34350.
Yemen Arab Republic: Masbah. Tel: 96027.
Yemen, People's Dem. Republic of: Al Mansour. Tel: 51138.

TOURIST INFORMATION

Baghdad International Airport, Tahrir Square, Baghdad. Tel: 60237.

BAGHDAD

Baghdad, the capital of Iraq, houses almost a fifth of the whole population. It was originally built on the western bank of the Tigris, but has now grown and covers both banks connected by a number of bridges. Much of the city is of recent construction with modern office blocks and hotels but the old bazaars are still there—in particular the copper market where beautifully decorated copper utensils can be bought, and the silk market where both silk and wool are for sale. Persian and Iraqi carpets are also sold here.

Baghdad boasts no less than seven museums as well as a national gallery of modern art. There are innumerable buildings of historic interest in and around the city including a large number of exquisite mosques. In particular there are the ruins of the Abbasid Palace and the Mustansiriya College, possibly the oldest university in the world.

Hotels
Ali Baba Hotel, Sa'adoun Street. Tel: 92395.
Andalus Palace Hotel, Sa'adoun Street. Tel: 91069.
Baghdad Hotel, Sa'adoun Street. Tel: 8889031.
Al-Abbasi Palace, Sa'adoun Street. Tel: 94386.
Ambassador, Abu Nawas Street. Tel: 8886105.
Khayam Hotel, Sa'adoun Street. Tel: 96176.
Carlton Hotel, Aqaba Bin Nafi Square. Tel: 96091.
Dar Al Salam Hotel, Sa'adoun Street. Tel: 96151.
Saharah Hotel, Andalus Square. Tel: 90003.
Orient Palace Hotel, Masbah. Tel: 96785.
Ramses Hotel, Mushajar Street. Tel: 8882160.
Diwan Hotel, Sa'adoun Street, near Nasr Square. Tel: 8889961.

Restaurants
Sarab, Nidhal Street. Tel: 90156.
Farouq, Damascus Street. Tel: 32475.
Strand, Masbah Street. Tel: 92788.
Golden Nest, Unknown Soldier Square. Tel: 93857.
Fawanees, Sa'adoun Street. Tel: 90522.
Golden Plate, Abu Nawas Street.

Nightclubs
Moulin Rouge, way to Rashid Camp. Tel: 90809.
Embassy, Al Masbah. Tel: 95971.
Baghdad, Rashid Army Camp Street. Tel: 97945.
Select, Sa'adoun Street. Tel: 99848.
Semiramis, Sa'adoun Street. Tel: 99728.
Al Khayam, Salhiyah. Tel: 34200.

Martyr's mosque in Baghdad

BASRA

Basra is the biggest city of the south and is situated on the banks of the Shatt al-Arab about 60 km. from the Gulf and about 600 km. south of Baghdad, to which it is linked by rail, road and air. It is the centre of date production and is on the edge of the desert. It has been called the Venice of the east because of its numerous canals, but is primarily important as Iraq's only direct link with the sea. It is from Basra that Sinbad of *A Thousand and One Nights* is said to have started his seven journeys. Nearby is Al-Qurna, said to be the site of the Garden of Eden where there is a famous old tree called Adam's Tree. Basra also has several shrines dating back to the early days of Islam.

Hotels
Shatt al-Arab Hotel. Tel: 7263.
Ur Hotel, Ashar. Tel: 217730.

MOSUL

Mosul is the main town of the north and is situated on the eastern bank of the Tigris some 500 km. north of Baghdad. It is linked by rail to Syria and Turkey and is an important centre of trade and communications. The distinctive building material used in Mosul is limestone set in a gypsum cement and alabaster. In the past it was famous for making muslin which is derived from the town's name. Its museum houses some Assyrian and early Islamic items, and there is also the 13th century palace of Qara Sarai as well as the old mosque of Nabi Jirjis.

Hotels
Station Hotel. Tel: 3083.
Rafidain, Wadi Hajar. Tel: 71121.
Idara el-Mahaliya, Cornish Street. Tel: 71151.

KIRKUK

The other important northern town is Kirkuk which assumed greater importance after oil was found in 1927. One of the strangest sights near the town is the Eternal Fires—the endless burning of natural gas seepages which are believed to be the burning furnace of the Old Testament which Daniel had to face. Kirkuk also boasts a castle dating from Ottoman days.

Hotels
Kirkuk, City Centre. Tel: 6614.
Station, Railway Station. Tel: 2566.

ARBIL

Arbil, also in the north, is believed to be the oldest, constantly inhabited city in the world. It is first mentioned in 2000 BC, as Arbileam and later became famous as Arbella in the fourth century BC. It shows various stages of habitation throughout history and in recent years has become a tourist and holiday centre.

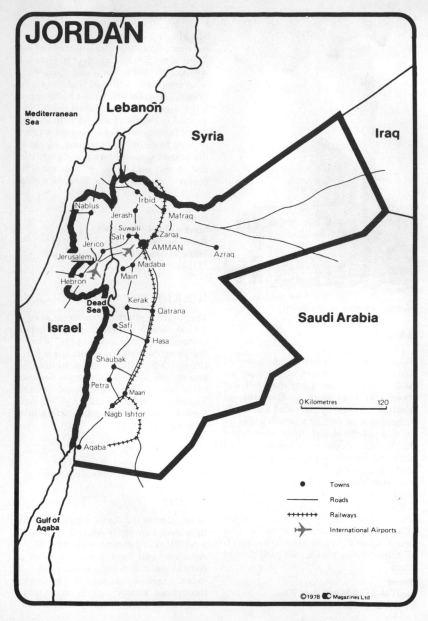

JORDAN

Mediterranean
Sea

Lebanon

Syria

Iraq

Nablus

Irbid

Jerash

Mafraq

Suwaili

Salt

Zarqa

Jerico

AMMAN

Azraq

Jerusalem

Madaba

Hebron

Main

Dead
Sea

Israel

Kerak

Qatrana

Safi

Hasa

Shaubak

Petra

Maan

Nagb Ishtor

Saudi Arabia

0 Kilometres   120

Aqaba

Gulf of
Aqaba

●	Towns
—	Roads
++++++	Railways
✈	International Airports

©1978 ▄ Magazines Ltd

JORDAN

Christine Osborne

Although Jordan is a small country, there are many things to see and do. You can ride a horse through ancient Petra, have coffee with desert Bedouin or swim over coral reefs in the Gulf of Aqaba.

Jordan's dry climate has preserved its ancient cities, Crusader castles and sacred shrines. All are easily visited from the capital, Amman. The only problem in sightseeing in outlying areas is the lack of facilities at many historic sites.

Jordan, however, is exceptionally clean. Many people speak English and are friendly and hospitable. The country also produces attractive souvenirs.

THE LAND AND THE PEOPLE

Desert covers nearly 80% of Jordan's surface area. The capital, Amman, is situated at a height of 800m. on a high plateau extending 324 kms from Syria to Ras en Naqb in the south.

The country is linked north-south by two parallel roads, the Kings Highway and the Desert Highway. The former descends from Amman south through spectacular Wadi Mujib to Petra. The Desert Highway, 324 kms long, is the main thoroughfare from Amman to Aqaba on the Red Sea.

North-west of Amman are undulating hills, some forested, others under cultivation. South-west is the Dead Sea depression, 400m. below sea-level, the lowest level on earth. The River Jordan flows through this valley which is the agricultural heart of Jordan.

Trans-Jordan was a sparsely populated, primarily Bedouin patriarchy, ruled from its creation in 1921 by the Emir Abdullah, second son of the Sherif Hussein of Mecca—a Hashemite descendant of the Prophet.

The total population is 2.75 million, including the West Bank. 76% is urban, 29% rural with nomadic tribes accounting for about 4%. About half a million of the population of East Jordan are classified as Palestinian refugees and are supported by the United Nations Relief and Works Agency. A further quarter of a million people were displaced by the events of 1967.

The majority of people are Muslim, but a relatively large Christian minority has settled in Amman.

HISTORY

The Jordan Valley is considered by many historians to be the original site where man began a sedentary life.

Positioned between the Arabian deserts and the Mediterranean, with this fertile valley belt, it was natural that Jordan saw the passage of both travellers, and invaders.

Caananites, Egyptians, Babylonians, Persians, Greeks, Romans, Byzantines, Crusaders and ultimately European powers, have occupied and quarrelled over Jordan.

Severe desert conditions forced the original settlers, the Caananites, onto the eastern Mediterranean littoral. Migrations from the Arabian peninsula continued throughout the Bronze Age. Some historians maintain that famine in the Land of Canaan drove the descendants of Abraham into Egypt, about 1700 BC, but that in 1560 BC the Egyptians expelled their Hyksos, shepherd overlords and enslaved the Israelites who were led back to Canaan by Moses.

Amid the ruggedly beautiful scenery of Mount Nebo, Moses indicated the rich river Jordan valley. Obeying, the Jews moved to Jericho and into Palestine. In 1000 BC King David moved capital from Hebron to Jerusalem.

In 578 BC the Babylonians occupied Jerusalem until freed by Cyrus the Great in 538 BC; under Persian rule, the Jews were allowed to return. Alexander the Great imposed Hellenistic civilisation on the region but it was not conquered by another empire until the Roman imperial expansion, which sacked Jerusalem in AD 70. Thereafter Roman civilisation was forced upon the peoples. Last to fall under Roman domination were the industrious Nabataeans in their rocky stronghold of Petra, in south-west Jordan.

Roman rule continued until the fourth century when the Emperor Constantine adopted the Christian faith and Jordan became a province of Byzantium.

Jerusalem was again conquered by the Persians in the seventh century. This time Christians were massacred and their churches destroyed. However the occupation lasted only two decades. By now the Arabs had grown powerful, defeating the Byzantine rulers and introducing Islam.

In 1099, the Crusaders attacked Jerusalem, capturing the city and building their famous fortresses along the profitable caravan routes from Arabia.

The Christian knights suffered defeat by Saladdin in 1187, but shortly after, Ayyubite rule ended when the Mamelukes invaded Jordan and Syria, remaining until 1516.

It was then the Ottoman Turks who invaded the Holy Land, imposing a harsh regime which lasted until the Arab revolt of 1916.

Under command of the Hashemite Sherif of Hedjaz, in co-operation with Colonel Lawrence, the Arabs laid siege to Turkish troops, driving them out of the region.

Allied victory over the Germans and Turks was declared in 1918 and the Arab world was split into British and French mandates.

In 1917, the Balfour Declaration declared the country which had been Arab for centuries, a home for the Jews who, at that time, constituted only 7% of the population.

Palestine was made a British mandate, Trans-Jordan was devised and the son of the Sherif, Abdullah, made first head of state.

After the 1948 war with Israel, Trans-Jordan occupied part of Palestine and the holy sites of Jerusalem. In 1951, parliamentary representatives from both West and East Banks formed a constitution for a united Jordan.

In 1967, Israel conquered the West Bank and Jerusalem which is now considered by Jordan as occupied territory.

CULTURE

Since time immemorial, Jordan has been the camping-ground of Bedouin tribesmen. A rugged desert life normally precludes creative activities, but the Jordanian Bedouin women weave striking robes—usually black and embroidered in colourful geometric designs around the neck, sleeves and hem. The traditional styles are displayed in the Folklore and Costume Museum in Amman.

The Western trend for Oriental fashion has seen a small cottage industry develop. The robes may be bought in Amman's *souk*; those sold in Aqaba, made by the Bedouin in Wadi Rum, are entirely hand-sewn.

Of local handicrafts made by sedentary peoples, Jordan is noted for mother-of-pearl objets d'art, olive wood ornaments, in particular religious artifacts, metalwork and leatherware.

Ethnic music resembles Middle Eastern music elsewhere. The main instruments in the *takht*, or orchestra, are the three-stringed *rababa*, or violin, the *qanun* which resembles a small harpsichord, the *oud*, or Islamic lute usually made from gazelle horn and percussion implements such as the *riq*, *tablah* and *daff*.

The country's rich archeological heritage is seen in such sites as *Petra*, *Jerash* and *Madaba*.

Petra

CHRISTINE OSBORNE

ECONOMY

The loss of the West Bank in 1967 created acute economic problems for Jordan. Its major agricultural area gone, it suddenly found itself host to 400,000 refugees which severely curtailed normal development.

Growth was further inhibited by Israeli raids which saw Jordan direct large sums into military spending. Confidence also weakened following the confrontation with local Palestinian organisations.

Other factors contributed to the depressed state of the Jordanian economy in the late sixties and early seventies: the drain of skilled labour to developing countries, particularly the Gulf States, has led to a shortage of locally trained technicians; the reluctance of foreign companies to invest in the country because of high labour costs has seen rising unemployment with an estimated 715,000 workers migrating. Although remittances from migrants make up a major part of Jordan's foreign exchange earnings (about $360 million in 1976), the result is that Jordan is now a labour importer.

The shape of the economy is seen in the distribution of labour: 60% in the civil service, including 680,000 in the armed services and 40% in agriculture.

Traditionally, Trans-Jordan was an agricultural economy until 1948, exporting cereals, fruits and vegetables to Palestine and abroad, via Haifa.

As the country is largely desert, agriculture was concentrated in the Jordan Valley, particularly in what is now 'occupied territory'. The Jordan Valley Development Plan (1973-1982) is consequently aimed at upgrading agriculture and living standards on the East Bank. By increasing mechanisation and irrigation of holdings, the plan aims to increase the quantity and quality of produce, thereby reducing the trade deficit.

Phosphate mining (mainly in al-Hasa) is Jordan's only heavy industry; 1976 phosphate exports totalled 1.6 million tons.

Light industries are the manufacture of plastics, paints, leatherware, cigarettes, cement, soft drinks, batteries and worsteds.

Spending by Arab visitors and tourists benefited the economy considerably more than exports. In 1976, it exceeded $190 million.

The main aim in the tourism and antiquities sector of the Five Year Development Plan 1976-80, is to upgrade existing facilities, develop potential attractions and prolong the length of stay of visitors.

Emphasis is on encouraging private investment in the accommodation and allied section of the tourist industry with the government offering nine years tax exemption and full repatriation of foreign capital.

Another important goal is to preserve Jordan's rich archaeological heritage, in particular Petra. The Ministry of Tourism and various bank groups have devised a $13 million plan for its protection involving building watersheds to protect the monuments from run-off, resettlement of the Bedouin living in the city, constructing a visitors centre, horse stables and making improvements to the existing hotel.

Further in the Five Year Plan, the government intends acquiring private land of archaeological interest and encouraging excavations by international organisations.

To finance this section of the plan, JD24 million ($73 million) is to be spent by the government and through private resources and foreign loans. Some $330 million has been committed in aid and loans, largely from the United States, Saudi Arabia, Abu Dhabi and Kuwait.

The economy was also assisted by the events in Lebanon although inflation greatly increased as a resullt of property speculation and the accommodation squeeze.

Today there are signs that Jordan, albeit with continued aid, may soon begin to reduce its balance of payments deficit.

$196 million in Euro-dollar loans was raised in the first six months of 1977 which indicates Western confidence in the country's economic stability.

WILDLIFE

Jordan is not greatly endowed with wildlife.

In forested hills north-east of the Dead Sea and around Jerash and Ajlum live squirrels, badgers, wild boar and goats.

East of Amman, Azraq oasis is a stop-over for many varieties of migratory birds on their flight from Europe to India and Africa.

Mammals are sparsely distributed in the desert and cobble conglomerate areas of central, western and southern Jordan.

These are normally desert gazelle, fox, the sand rat, hares and jerboa.

The Gulf of Aqaba is rich in marine life, being especially noted for coral.

GENERAL INFORMATION

Area: The Kingdom of Jordan covers 95,396 sq. km. and has borders with Syria in the north, Israel in the west, Saudi Arabia in the south and Iraq in the east.

Population: At the end of 1971 the population was estimated at 2.57 million of which 1.83 resided in East Jordan, 0.74 million in West Jordan (under Israeli occupation since June 1967). About half a million of the population of East Jordan are officially classified as refugees from Palestine, while a further quarter of a million people are estimated to have been displaced by the events of 1967.

Head of State: King Hussein Ibn Talal.

Government: Constitutional Monarchy. National Assembly suspended. Power in hands of the King.

Languages: The official language is Arabic, but English is widely spoken.

Religion: The majority of the population is Muslim, but there is a sizeable Christian minority.

Currency: The Jordanian Dinar (divided into 1000 fils) is the unit of currency. £1=0.578JD. $1=0.312JD.

Time: GMT + 2. Summer time (May-Aug) GMT + 3.

HOW TO GET THERE

By air: ALIA, the Royal Jordanian Airline, has three weekly flights from London, Paris, Rome, Copenhagen, Frankfurt, Madrid, Bangkok to Amman; four weekly flights from Athens, and two weekly from Cyprus. Other airlines which fly to Amman are: MEA, KLM, Lufthansa, Alitalia, Aeroflot, British Airways, Egyptair. There is an airport service tax of JD2 for passengers embarking from abroad.

By road: From Europe through Turkey and Syria, there are good road conditions all the way to Amman. Taxis and buses run daily between Beirut, Damascus and Amman. There is also an overland road linking Amman to Baghdad.

By rail and sea: By train, the Orient Express from Istanbul to Beirut via Aleppo, or through Aleppo to Damascus and then to Amman. By sea, Jordan's only port is Aqaba on the Red Sea. Cargo vessels arrive from Europe and Asia, and some carry passengers, but there are no scheduled passenger lines which call at Aqaba. The nearest sea port is Beirut.

Visas and health regulations

A valid passport with an entry visa is normally required for a visit to Jordan. Visas are available at Jordanian embassies abroad. Tourist visas are also obtainable at points of entry.

Cholera vaccinations and smallpox vaccinations are required of arrivals from infected areas.

Currency and customs regulations

There is no restriction on the import of foreign currency, which can be readily exchanged locally. There is a limit of JD100 in local currrency both for import and export. Tourists are not required to declare the currency carried by them and on departure may take out any foreign currency without limits.

Each visitor is allowed to take in 200 cigarettes, one bottle of spirits, one box of cigars. Articles for personal use such as portable typewriters, cameras etc, are admitted free of duty.

CLIMATE

The summer, May to September, is hot and dry, but pleasantly cool in the evenings. The Jordan Valley (400m below sea level) is warm during the winter months and extremely hot in the summer. Rain falls during the months November to March.

What to wear

Clothes should be lightweight for summer and sun hats and sun glasses are also advisable. In winter warm woollens, coat, and raincoat are necessary.

ACCOMMODATION AND FOOD

Hotels offer a wide range of accommodation, both de luxe hotels and small inn type pensions or hostels. Prices vary according to class ranging from JD5 for a double bedroom to JD19.50 in the de luxe Jordan Intercontinental hotel.

There is a large number of restaurants which offer both European and Oriental dishes. Typical Jordanian dishes are *musakhan*, chicken in olive oil and onion sauce roasted on Arab bread, and *mensaf*, whole stewed lamb with yoghurt served on a bed of rice.

Water is generally safe to drink and alcoholic beverages are freely available.

TRANSPORT

Jordan has an excellent network of roads and all cars drive on the right. The service taxi (sharing) is a popular mode of transport providing regular daily runs along set routes within towns and throughout the country. Bus transport is also available both within Amman and to most outlying districts.

There are scheduled weekly flights from Amman to Aqaba (50 minutes).

TOURIST INFORMATION

Tourist Authority office. King Hussein Street. Amman. tel: 42311-7.

BANKS

Arab Bank, Faisal Street, Amman. tel: 38161

Al Ahli Bank, Redah Street, Amman. tel: 25126

Al Aqari Bank, Post Office Square, Amman. tel: 36357

British Bank, King Hussein Street, Amman. tel: 36175

Central Bank of Jordan. King Hussein Street. Amman. tel: 30301

Cairo Amman Bank, Shabsough Street, Amman. tel: 39321

Chase Manhattan Bank, Jebel, Amman. tel: 25131

City Bank, Faisal Street, Amman. tel: 38959

Grindlays Bank, King Hussein Street, Amman. tel: 30104

Industrial Bank Development, Jebel, Amman. tel: 42217

Jordan Bank, Faisal Street, Amman. tel: 24348

Mashrek Bank, King Hussein Street, Amman. tel: 24161

Rafidain Bank, King Hussein Street, Amman. tel: 24365

Business hours

Most Muslim businesses close on Fridays, while Christian-owned businesses close on Sundays.

Government Offices: Saturday-Thursday 0800-1400.

Business Hours: May-October 0800-1300—1530-1930. November-April 0830-1330—1500-1830.

Banks: Saturday-Thursday 0800-1330. Cashiers close at 1230.

Shops: Saturday-Thursday 0800-1300—1500-1800.

PUBLIC HOLIDAYS

National Holidays: 1 May, Labour Day, 25 May, Independence Day, 11 Aug, King Hussein Accession to the throne, 14 November, King Hussein's birthday.

Religious Holidays: 20 February, Prophets Birthday, 3-6 September, Eid al Fitr. 10-13 November 1978, Eid al Adha, 2 December, Hijra New Year.

EMBASSIES IN THE CAPITAL

Algeria: Jebel Amman. tel: 41271
Belgium: Jebel Amman. tel: 44683
Egypt: Jebel Amman. tel: 41375
France: Jebel Amman. tel: 41273
Germany: Jebel Amman. tel: 41351
Greece: Jebel Amman. tel: 41361
Iran: Jebel Amman. tel: 41281
Iraq: Jebel Amman. tel: 39331
Italy: Jebel Webdeh. tel: 38185
Kuwait: Jebel Amman. tel: 41235
Lebanon: Jebel Amman. tel: 41381
Morocco: Jebel Amman. tel: 41451
Oman: Shmeisani. tel: 61137
Qatar: Jebel Amman. tel: 44331
Saudi Arabia: Jebel Amman. tel: 30195
Spain: Jebel Amman. tel: 22140
Switzerland: Jebel Amman. tel: 44416
Syria: Jebel Amman. tel: 41392
Turkey: Jebel Amman. tel: 41251
United Arab Emirates: Jebel Amman. tel: 44368
UK: Jebel Amman. tel: 41261
USA: Jebel Amman. tel: 44371

USSR: Jebel Amman. tel: 41229
Yemen: Jebel Amman tel: 42381

AMMAN

Jordan's capital city with a population of 750,000 people. Biblically known as Rabbath-Ammon, and Philadelphia in Roman times, the city lies on seven hills that are dotted with Ammonite, Moabite, Greek, Byzantine, Roman and Islamic remains. The most impressive sight is the second century AD Roman amphitheatre in the middle of the city. Although it has been recently restored, the greater portion of the amphitheatre is original.

The Citadel (Jebel el Qalat) towers over the city, and is the home of the Jordan Archaeological Museum whose exhibits include the relics dug up in the process of building modern Amman and from other sites within the Kingdom.

Amman is a new town which grew up at a rapid pace in the past 30 years. The layout of the city is modern and spacious.

The *souk* area is in the heart of the city and includes scores of small shops and kiosks.

Hotels
Jordan Intercontinental, (de-luxe) Jebel Amman. tel: 41361
Grand Palace, (first class) University street. tel: 61121
Philadelphia, (first class) Roman Theatre Square. tel: 25191
Jordan Tower, (first class) Shmeisani. tel: 61161
Granada, (second class) Jebel Amman. tel: 38031
Shephard, (second class) Jebel Amman. tel: 39197
Firas Wing, (second class) Jebel Webdeh. tel: 22103
Hisham, (second class) Jebel Amman. tel: 42720
Merry Land, (second class) King Hussein street. tel: 30217
Al Ghusein, (second class) Jebel Hussein. tel: 65178

Roman amphitheatre at Amman

ROYAL JORDANIAN EMBASSY

City Hotel, (second class) Prince Mohammad street. tel: 42251
Caravan, (second class) Abadali.
tel: 61195
Canary, (second class) Jebel Webdeh.
tel: 38353
Select, (second class) Jebel Webdeh.
tel: 37101
Al Cazer, (second class) Al Hashimi
street. tel: 36304
Saladin, (second class) Al Amaneh
street. tel: 24508
Amman Grand Hotel, (second class) Jebel Amman. tel: 44528
Continental, (second class) Basman
street. tel: 23161
Palace, (third class) Mango street. tel:
24326
New Park, (third class) King Hussein
street. tel: 21166
Karnak, (fourth class) King Hussein
street. tel: 28125
Lords, (fourth class) King Hussein street.
tel: 22167

Restaurants

There is no shortage of good eating
places in Amman. Most restaurants offer
a mixed menu of European and Oriental
dishes. The following is a selected list of
the best places to eat:
Elite, Jebel Webdeh. tel 22103
Omar el Khayyam, Prince Mohammad
street. tel: 42910
Le Terrace, Shmeisani. tel: 62831
Flying Carpet, Shmeisani. tel: 62181
Jordan, Prince Mohammed Street. tel:
38333
Le Cesar, Jebel Webdeh. tel: 24431
Babalu, Jebel Amman. tel: 41116
Jabri, King Hussein Street. tel: 24128
Seven Seas, Prince Mohammad street.
tel: 44085
Estanbouli, Jebel Amman. tel: 28212

Entertainments

Sporting events in the **Hussein Youth
City**, motor and go-kart racing sponsored
by the Royal Automobile Club, municipal and hotel swimming pools, and
nightclubs.

There are swimming pools and tennis
courts at, the **Hussein Youth City**, the
Orthodox Club, the **Royal Automobile
Club**; there are also courts at the **YWCA**
and swimming pools at the **Intercontinental** and **Philadelphia** hotels.

Night Clubs

Venus Club, Jebel Amman. tel: 37236
Le Cesar, Jebel Weibdeh. tel: 24431
Le Prive, Jebel Abdoun. tel: 44880
Flying Carpet, Shmeisani. tel: 25141
Wagon Club, Jebel Abdoun.
Intercontinental Hotel, Jebel Amman.
tel: 41361

JERUSALEM AND THE WEST BANK

Since the war of June 1967, East Jerusalem and the West Bank have been under
Israeli military occupation. Previously
this was Jordan's main tourist attraction.

Arab **Jerusalem** (al Kuds al Sharif)
posseses the world's greatest religious
shrines sacred to Christians, Muslims and
Jews. Within the boundaries of al Haram
al Sharif (the Noble Sanctuary) stands the
beautiful Dome of the Rock and the Al
Aksa Mosque dating from the Ommayad
period. Close to al Haram al Sharif stands
the Western (Wailing) wall, the last remnant of the Temple and the most sacred
of Jewish shrines. Here also stands the
Church of the Holy Sepulchre, built and
often rebuilt on the site of Christ's cruci-
fixion, and the Via Dolorosa, the narrow
pathway where Christ carried his cross to
Calvary. Outside the walled city are the
Garden of Gethsemane and the Mount of
Olives.

In **Bethlehem**, south of Jerusalem lies
the birthplace of Christ marked by the
Church of the Nativity.

Hebron (al Khalil), south of Bethlehem, is an ancient town with the famous
al Ibrahimi mosque and the tombs of
Abraham, Isaac and Jacob and their
wives.

Nablus (Samaria) lies north of Jerusalem and is the home of 350 surviving Samaritans. Jacobs Well stands at the entrance of the City; there are also numerous biblical sites such as Herod's Temple of Augustus and a Roman tribunal, stadium and theatre.

Jericho (Ariha) is half an hour's drive from Jerusalem and lies 400m. below sea level in a landscape of salt encrusted desolation. Nearby on the river Jordan is the spot where John the Baptist baptised Jesus Christ. A few kilometres away lies the **Dead Sea**, the lowest body of water in the world.

Visiting the West Bank

Visitors to Jordan are allowed to travel in group tours across the river Jordan into the Israeli-occupied West Bank and then return to Jordan. Group tours are organised by local Jordanian travel agents in Amman. Holders of non-Arab passports travelling as individuals are permitted to make a one-way trip across the river Jordan and then have to continue their trip via Israel.

JERASH

Just over 30 minutes by car from Amman to the north, over the scenic hills of Gilead in Jerash, lies a town of great historical interest. It is probably the most beautifully preserved Graeco-Roman city in the world and lay for hundreds of years beneath the sands before excavation and restoration began in the 1920s.

The most impressive sight is the Great Oval Forum, with a wide street of columns which lead towards the towering columns of the temple of Artemis. There are also the remains of several baths and pools, three theatres, and the triple arched gateway built in AD 129 to celebrate Hadrian's visit to the town.

AQABA, PETRA AND WADI RUM

Aqaba lies at Jordan's southernmost tip

on the shores of the Red Sea, and is the country's only seaport. It is set against a rugged background of mountains, but the golden beach and blue waters are inviting to eyes that have seen nothing but desert on the journey there.

As a fun resort, Aqaba has much to offer; there is swimming in the Red Sea all the year round (in winter the temperature rarely falls below 200C), also snorkeling, skin and scuba diving, boating, fishing and water skiing. The underwater scenery, which can be viewed through glass-bottomed boats, has coral formations and tropical fish.

A new airport is connected by regular weekly flights to Amman 325km. away (55 minutes flying time). There is also a regular taxi and bus service to Amman and vice versa.

Petra, 262km. south of Amman was inhabited by the Nabataens from about 3000 BC. Temples, palaces and tombs are everywhere hewn out of the mountain side. The most magnificent scene is that of the Treasury. Although within easy reach of Amman, a day trip to Petra can be tiring. The only transport into Petra itself is by horseback, and it is a three-hour journey from the highway to the site. The visitor enters Petra through a *siq*, or a narrow defile, between walls towering 70m. overhead. The sights provide excellent photography.

There is a Government rest house and restaurant just outside the entrance to Petra. A hotel camp inside the ruins also has overnight facilities.

Two hours drive from Petra behind the mountains which surround Aqaba is **Wadi Rum**, the desert with the valley of the moon landscape. It is a large valley with eerie black and red crags and pink sands.

Hotels
Holiday Inn, (de luxe) Aqaba. tel: 2426
Coral Beach, (first class) Aqaba. tel: 2056
Nazzal's Camp, (dormitory style) Petra.

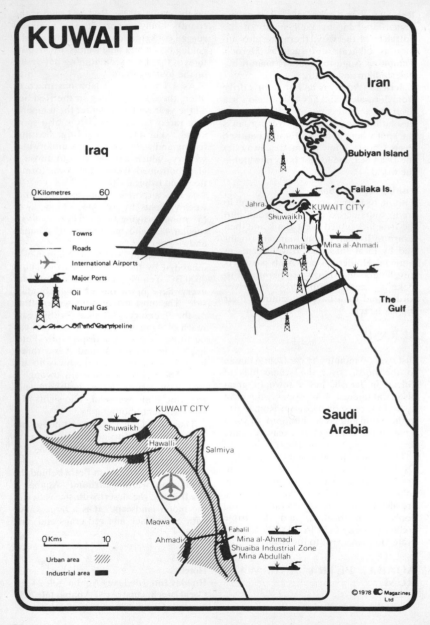

KUWAIT

Iran

Iraq

0 Kilometres 60

Bubiyan Island

Failaka Is.

Jahra
Shuwaikh
KUWAIT CITY

Ahmadi
Mina al-Ahmadi

Towns
Roads
International Airports
Major Ports
Oil
Natural Gas
Oil and Gas pipeline

The Gulf

Saudi Arabia

KUWAIT CITY
Shuwaikh
Hawalli
Salmiya

Maqwa
Ahmadi
Fahalil
Mina al-Ahmadi
Shuaiba Industrial Zone
Mina Abdullah

0 Kms 10
Urban area
Industrial area

©1978 Magazines Ltd

KUWAIT

Rosalind Mazzawi

Kuwait is a country for the businessman, but not for the tourist. Visas are never issued for tourism alone, although visitors' passes are obtainable for those staying with relatives and friends. The information presented in this chapter will therefore be useful only to that sizeable body of people who go to Kuwait for commerical or family reasons.

THE LAND AND THE PEOPLE

Seen from the air, the land is sand-coloured, with a paler brown lacy edge of shore, and green-blue shallow sea, becoming bluer farther out. As the plane circles to descend, the new high buildings of Kuwait City become more evident, and the water is seen to be patterned with the wakes of oil tankers, cargo ships, a few dhows and a multitude of tiny pleasure craft. Kuwait was the first Gulf country to reap oil riches, and therefore it is today the most technologically advanced.

Oil was first thought to be present in 1914. Subsequently oil was drilled and shipped out by the Kuwait Oil Company (a partnership between the Anglo Persian Oil Company (UK) and Gulf Oil (USA) from 1938). This small country contains two of the largest oilfields in the world, Burgan and Magwa, their reserves being 62 billion barrels. In 1975 it produced 1.84 million barrels a day.

The vast quantity of oil exported has resulted in a high per capita income for the citizens of the country, and a huge influx of consumer goods, foreign executives and workers, and the construction of hospitals, housing, highways, schools, a university, and all kinds of commerical buildings and hotels. There are cinemas, restaurants and shops in abundance: almost anything produced on the globe is available in Kuwait, at a price.

Kuwait City is today a bustling American style metropolis, with many US and Japanese automobiles. Arabic is the language of the country, and most Kuwaitis wear their national dress—long white *dishdashas*, with pockets for money and cigarettes, and white headcloths, either with *agals*, or black ropes, to secure them, or draped as turbans.

Kuwait, and Kuwait Airways, the national airline, both prohibit the sale and consumption of alcoholic liquor. This is in accordance with Islamic precept, and is a convention to respect. Unfortunately it has had the result of most prohibition laws, in increasing the black market trade, particularly in spirits. Many Westerners working in Kuwait spend a disproportionate amount of time, effort and money in ensuring a supply of liquor for themselves.

Arab tradition does not include 'drinking' as a means of spending time, though 'sitting' is perhaps more common. People on the verandas in front of their houses in the late afternoon, after the siesta, call passing acquaintances to sit with them. This friendly invitation is common throughout the Arab world.

Outside Kuwait City, the prosperous suburb of Shuwaykh extends along the sea coast; farther to the south are Fahaheel and Ahmadi. The latter was an oil town originally designed to provide living quarters for Europeans employed by KOC; nowadays it is somewhat less insular. For the people of Kuwait are an ancient seafaring and merchant people; for thousands of years their *dhows*, *boums*, and *baggalas* plied up and down the Gulf, and went as far as Indonesia and Zanzibar with the trade winds.

Kuwait was a shipbuilding centre until about 1950: since then the flood of modern wealth and technology has overwhelmed the country so that skilled craftsmen who were trained to construct the wooden dhows prefer to become mechanics, run shops or work in the oilfields. Some of the ships may still be seen in Gulf waters, but they are mostly in private hands or preserved as relics of the past, as in the Qatar museum.

Unfortunately for the traditionalists, the ancient mud-brick buildings of Kuwait City have almost all been knocked down and replaced in the rush to modernise. The sky, the sea and the land remain the same, but now the desert is lit at night with the oil flares, and in the day the silver pipelines bearing the oil are seen criss-crossing the sands to the three refineries and the ports.

The Sabah family have ruled in Kuwait since 1776; the present Amir, Shaikh Jaber al-Ahmed al-Sabah, succeeded his uncle in 1978. There is a Majlis, or National Assembly, of 50 members, who were elected by male Kuwaiti citizens over 21. All laws had to be approved by both the Amir and the Assembly. The executive power is vested in the Council of Ministers. It may seem obvious to say that only Kuwaiti citizens may vote, but about 55% of the population is non-Kuwaiti, and therefore does not possess the vote. Some are European-skilled

A Kuwait boum

technicians and executives, but most are Palestinians and Jordanians.

Kuwait has its own university, founded in 1966, with 4,500 students in Faculties of Arts, Commerce, Education, Law and Science. New petroleum, engineering and medical colleges opened in the academic year 1976/77. Education is free from kindergarten to university for all Kuwaitis, who also receive free textbooks, medical treatment and an allowance for food and clothing. Scholarships are given for Kuwaitis to study abroad subjects not offered by the university: in 1975/76 there were 2,787 Kuwaiti students outside the country. Government scholarships are also given to students from Arab, African and Asian states to study in secondary schools and the university in Kuwait.

Medical treatment is free and universal for Kuwaiti citizens, and for non-Kuwaitis in government service. Most of the large companies have comprehensive health services for their foreign employees, and the hospitals are excellent. Visitors may be treated free in emergencies, but the Kuwaiti health service works rather in the other direction, sending citizens to the UK and the US for specialised medical treatment, paid for by the Kuwaiti Government.

A great deal of money is invested overseas and a sizeable income is derived from these investments. (KD 60 million in 1972/73). The Kuwait Fund for Arab Economic Development was founded in 1961, and now has an authorised capital of KD 1,000 million. By February 1976 KD 301 million had been approved as loans distributed. It is intended to help the poorer Arab countries, and (since 1974) all developing countries.

GENERAL INFORMATION

Area: 17,656 sq. km.
Population: 995,000 (1975). This includes expatriate inhabitants, who number 391,266.
Between 1970 and 1975 the annual population growth rate was 6.1%.
Capital: Kuwait City.
Head of State: The Amir: Shaikh Jaber al-Ahmed al-Sabah.
Government: The Amir appoints the Prime Minister, who appoints the ministers, who are responsible to a 50-member National Assembly, elected by adult male suffrage. The Assembly was dissolved on 29 August, 1976 after the Amir had stated that it had 'exploited democracy and frozen government legislation for private gain'.
Languages: Arabic. English is widely spoken.
Religion: Islam is the State religion. There are Christian, Bahai, Hindu and Parsee Minorities, which have their own places of worship.
Currency: Kuwaiti Dinar=1,000 fils. US$1=KD 0.287. £1 sterling=KD 0.497.
Time: GMT + 3.

HOW TO GET THERE

By air: Kuwaiti Airways from London. Many other airlines call there, including British Airways, Swissair, Air France, Lufthansa, KLM, SAS, Alitalia, Iberia, TWA, MEA, Aeroflot.

By road: Overland from Beirut and Amman on pipeline route, or from Tripoli, and Homs, across the Syrian desert to Baghdad and Basra: thence by steam launch or sailing boat (no scheduled services) or by road.

By rail: Through Iraq to Basra: thence by steam launch or sailing boat.
Note: Most travellers arrive by air, or overland in private cars.

Visas and health regulations
Business visas are given upon application

with supporting documents from local sponsor.

Tourism is not encouraged. Visitors' visas are available with invitation and confirmation from the person to be visited. Vaccination against smallpox and cholera is required. Persons coming from countries where yellow fever is endemic must have inoculation certificates. TAB vaccination is not required, but is recommended.

Currency and customs regulations
Any amount of currency may be freely imported and exported. Personal effects and trade samples are admitted without duty, but the import and consumption of alcohol is strictly forbidden. For capital and consumer goods imported a customs duty of 4% ad valorem is levied.

CLIMATE

Kuwait is located in the desert zone and has a continental climate. Throughout the year, this climate produces wide variations in temperature, sparse rainfall and occasional dust storms.

Winter (December-February): Generally mild. Temperatures can sometimes dip to zero centigrade when winds come from the north-west; south-east winds bring warm spells. Occasional rainfall is sometimes accompanied by thunderstorms.

Spring (March-May): Very pleasant with cool nights and warm days. Warm air is carried by prevailing southerly winds and cooled by occasional rains.

Summer (June-September): Hot with some cooling at night. July and August are particularly hot with temperatures occasionally reaching 50°C. There are a few dust storms, and the light warm sea breezes increase the humidity

Autumn (October-November): Warm to hot in October and mild to cool in November. Nights are cool. There are variations in humidity and temperature with occasional light rains towards the

end of the season.

What to wear
Men: Summer: short-sleeved shirt and light trousers. Tropical suit for more formal occasions. Air-conditioning is universal and can be too cold. Sweater and raincoat for winter, but heavy suits are rarely, if ever, worn.

Women: Trousers and hip-length loose shirts or tunics with sleeves—or maxi-dresses. Cotton is much cooler than man-made fabrics; it is advisable to wear clothes that cover as much of the body as possible. Tight clothes are uncomfortable and unsuitable.

ACCOMMODATION AND FOOD

There are some excellent and expensive hotels. Reservations must be made well in advance and confirmed.

Hotels
Kuwait Hilton, P.O. Box 5996, tel: 533000, tlx.: 2039.

Kuwait Sheraton, 261 rooms (200 more under construction), P.O. Box 5902, tel: 422055, tlx: 2106.

Golden Beach, 37 rooms, P.O. Box 3483, tel: 439521.

Bristol, 110 rooms, P.O. Box 3531, tel: 439281, tlx: 2061.

Sahara, P.O. Box 20461, tel: 424121, tlx: 2102.

Universal, 120 rooms, P.O. Box 5593, tel: 425361.

Messilah Beach, P.O. Box 3522, tel: 613466, tlx: 2215.

Carlton, P.O. Box 3492, tel: 423171, tlx: 2064.

Prices range from KD 30 a night for a double room to KD 9.

Other hotels, such as the **Hyatt Regency Kuwait** are under construction.

Food is plentiful and varied as it is imported from all over the world. The big hotels serve both European and Arab food. The Universal has a Chinese restaurant.

TRANSPORT

Private car, taxi, service taxi (shared), bus (operated as round town service by Hilton Hotel).

BANKS

The State bank is the Bank of Kuwait and the Middle East, managed by the British Bank of the Middle East under an agreement negotiated in 1971. There are various commercial banks financed by local capital; the most important are the Al Ahli (a share of which is held by the French Credit Lyonnais), National Bank of Kuwait, the Gulf Bank and the Commercial Bank of Kuwait.

A souk in Kuwait

The National Bank of Kuwait is one of the world's most important financial institutions. Assets of commercial banks more than doubled between 1970 and 1975. With the growth of new shareholding companies in the Kuwaiti economy, 72 million shares, worth approximately KD 300.5 million were traded in 1976.

Banking hours: 0830-1200.

PUBLIC HOLIDAYS

The Muslim holidays are calculated according to the lunar calendar and therefore change each year. They are four days at the end of the fasting month of Ramadan, which in 1978 falls on 5 August and four days of Eid al-Adha on 11 November. The Prophet's Birthday is another movable feast. Also celebrated as public holidays are Christmas Day, Easter Day, Kuwait National Day (25 February) and both Western and Muslim New Year's Days.

FOREIGN EMBASSIES IN KUWAIT

Algeria, Argentina, Bahrain, Bangladesh, Belgium, Brazil, Bulgaria, China People's Republic, Egypt, France, Gabon, German Federal Republic, Greece, Hungary, Indonesia, Iran, Iraq, Italy, Japan, Jordan, Kenya, Lebanon, Libya, Malaysia, Mexico, Morocco, Netherlands, Oman, Pakistan, Poland, Qatar, Romania, Saudi Arabia, Spain, Sudan, Sweden, Switzerland, Syria, Tunisia, Turkey, United Arab Emirates, UK, USA, USSR, Yemen—North, Yemen—South, Yugoslavia, Zaire.

INFORMATION

Information may be provided by the Ministry of Information—Mubarak al-Kabir St., Kuwait.

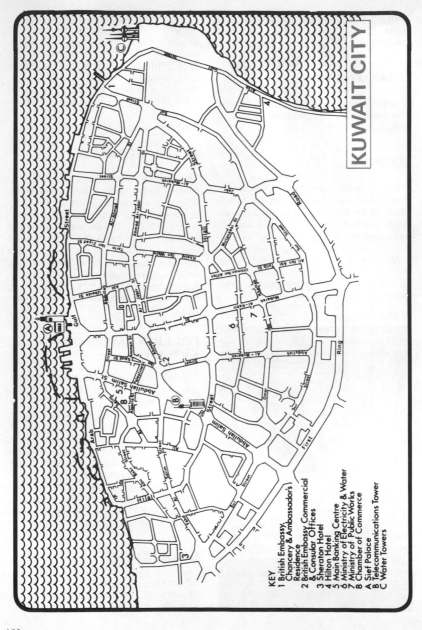

KUWAIT CITY

KEY
1 British Embassy,
  Chancery & Ambassador's
  Residence
2 British Embassy,Commercial
  & Consular Offices
3 Sheraton Hotel
4 Hilton Hotel
5 Main Banking Centre
6 Ministry of Electricity & Water
7 Ministry of Public Works
8 Chamber of Commerce
A Sief Palace
B Telecommunications Tower
C Water Towers

WHAT TO SEE IN KUWAIT

The old port and dhows are worth visiting.

Tourist Towers on the Gulf opened in 1977: one is a water tower and the other, 200 metres high, a theatre, night club and revolving restaurant.

There is a colony of artists who have studios in an old merchant's house, beautifully restored, on the bay. Nearby is the **Kuwait Historical Museum**, which has models of boats, artifacts, pottery, seals and coins. Most of these were found on the coast. A fine series of Kuwaiti postage stamps portrays some of them. Falaika may be visited, the launch trip taking about an hour.

At Jahra on the Basra road there is a boat-building centre, where *boums* and *jambuks* are still constructed in the traditional way, although they are mostly to be used for pleasure trips, rather than trading, pearling or fishing.

South of Kuwait City the road leads to Fahaheel, now a residential town, then to Ahmadi which is the settlement for the expatriate employees of the Kuwait Oil Co. The atmosphere is very British, though it is more cosmopolitan than formerly. Neat little houses are set in attempts at gardens which need continual watering.

Mina al-Ahmadi is one of the oil ports, the other being Mina Saud. They have immensely long jetties stretching out into the sea to a depth feasible for modern supertankers. The oil pipes run along these jetties and are hooked to the tankers for loading.

Sports: Many sports are available including all water sports, swimming, sailing, skin and scuba diving, power-boating (especially popular in Kuwait). Riding clubs flourish in the winter months: tennis and football are played, and the Sheraton Hotel has a health club and

Tourist Towers

gymnasium.

Amusement: Several cinemas show recent films, two theatres put on amateur productions—some showing great talent—and the artistic life of the country is developing.

Shopping: All basic and most luxury goods are available, in boutiques, or small general stores often run by Indians or Pakistanis. There is much demand for tape recorders, cassette players, hi-fi equipment and the latest in freezers, refrigerators, air-conditioners and automobiles. Many Kuwaiti women wear the latest Paris fashions, but they usually go to Paris to buy them. Only their jewellery is from the Arab world—until 1975 most of it coming from the gold *souks* of Beirut.

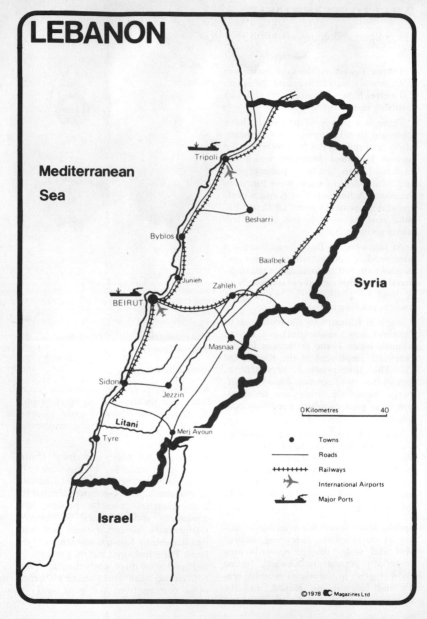

LEBANON

Mediterranean

Sea

Tripoli

Besharri

Byblos

Baalbek

Junieh   Zahleh

Syria

BEIRUT

Masnaa

Sidon

Jezzin

0 Kilometres   40

Litani

Merj Ayoun

Tyre

● Towns

Roads

++++++ Railways

✈ International Airports

⚓ Major Ports

Israel

©1978 Magazines Ltd

LEBANON

Rosalind Mazzawi

In the year 1978 Lebanon was one of the most precarious places on earth in which to live; it is also still one of the most beautiful. This paradox has several possible explanations: the Levant coast has always been one of the chief crossroads of the world, and the stretch of coast between Tripoli and the Gaza strip has invited invaders, refugees, sellers, and merchants since 2000 BC. The particular problems of the past two years are hard to disentangle, but if we describe the land, then the people, and examine their history briefly, the reader may begin to make some sense of what seems totally senseless destruction.

THE LAND AND THE PEOPLE

The traveller approaching by sea sees the tops of the mountain ranges, and especially Jebel Sannin, rising above the sea horizon. Gradually the slopes and the coastal plain, covered with buildings, emerge, and then the serried mass of Beirut's buildings and harbour. For a stranger, arriving by sea or air, the first impression can be one of total confusion, but it soon sorts itself out. The country is half the size of Wales; but like Wales, if stretched out flat would cover a much greater area.

There is a warm and humid coastal plain where citrus fruit and bananas are cultivated—in places the plain is five or six km. wide; in others less than a kilometre, in which a main road, a railway, and an almost continuous trail of small houses have to fit, besides the crops. There are also marvellous vegetables, lettuces, radishes, and beans grown in tiny patches, two metres square, irrigated daily and having high yields. The lower slopes of the mountains bear grapes, apricots, plums, peaches, figs, olives, and patches of barley, often on terraces painstakingly cut out and cultivated. This is quite well-watered country, because the mountains are of porous limestone, and the heavy winter rainfall on the seaward slopes of the Lebanon range soaks into them, and then emerges as springs half way down the mountains. Over the centuries these have been tapped, tamed, and led on to the terraces or into the villages also situated at the halfway mountain mark.

Four of the five *mohafazat*, or provinces, of the country, Akkar in the north, Kesrouan and Chouf in the centre, and south Lebanon have the configuration of coastal plain, well watered slopes, and mountain summits where little grows except some apples. The famous cedars also grow high in the mountains, but most are recent replants. Only at the village of the cedars high above Tripoli in the great semicircle of the Kornet es Saouda, where snow lingers all the year round, is a forest of the ancient cedars of the Lord. About 25 are over 1000 years old: with the redwoods of California they are the slowest growing trees on earth. Most of the cedars of Lebanon seen in European parks are from 18th century plantings.

Lebanon has always welcomed and encouraged visitors, but for the past few years conditions have been too precarious for the package tour participant.

The traveller from Beirut to Damascus travels up a steep highway to the highest pass on the Lebanon range, Dahr el Beidar. From the top there is an incredible view of the mountain sloping down to the flat, patchwork Bekaa valley, and the barren, rainless slopes of the Anti-Lebanon mountains beyond which lies the frontier with Syria. The Bekaa, the fifth *mohafazat*, is the richest agricultural region of the whole Levant, and has been so since Roman times when it was one of the chief granaries of the Empire. The Litani river flows through the Bekaa to water it, and at the southern end a large dam and artificial lake have been constructed to provide electric power, and modern irrigation system for the plain. The fruits and vegetables, some of the most delicious in the world, are more than the country can consume, and until the civil war were exported daily to the Gulf countries and Saudi Arabia, by air or by refrigerated truck.

Lebanese have traditionally sought their fortunes overseas, usually as merchants, in North and South America, West Africa, and more recently in the Gulf. The natural resources of the country are few, and the enterprise of the citizens is one of its greatest assets. Lebanese who have made their fortunes overseas and are able to return home to live in some style, intend to keep their money, and not pay it to the Government in taxes. Public and social services are therefore minimal, and while some citizens are quite rich, the Government is poor, being unable to pay its employees

adequate salaries. They are obliged to find unofficial ways of making ends meet.

Lebanon is the only country in the world whose population is composed exclusively of minorities. These are various sects of Christians, two varieties of Muslims, and the Druse, who are different again. Rivalry between the various sects, each with different foreign affiliations, has led to conflict in the past, and is one, though not the only, cause of the recent civil war.

The Christians are Catholic, Orthodox, and Protestant. the Catholics are subdivided into Latin (or Roman) Catholics, Chaldeans, Greek Catholics and Maronites. The Latin Catholics are, to a foreigner, the usual variety found all over the world, but they are few in Lebanon, and most are of foreign descent, with European connections and closely linked to the Franciscan order—who were made custodians of the Holy Places (Terra Sancta) after the Crusades. Their Bishop is usualy an American or Italian Franciscan, and they follow the liturgy and customs of the Western Church. Since the Vatican Council decreed that mass must be said in the vernacular of the country the two principal Latin churches in Beirut, St.Louis and St. Francis, have regular Sunday Masses in French, Arabic, English, Italian, German and Spanish, and occasionally Polish.

The Chaldeans are a small offshoot of the Nestorians who reunited themselves to Rome in 1553 by acknowledging the supremacy of the Pope whilst keeping their own liturgy and customs. The Greek Catholics are a larger body, who broke away from the Greek Orthodox Church in 1760, and rejoined Rome under the same conditions. They permit clerical marriage before ordination as do the Maronites. But marriage is a bar to preferment in the Church because the archimandrites and Bishops are almost always chosen from members of the celibate monastic orders.

The Maronites are a turbulent sect,

whose Patriarch has his residence at Bkerké—just north of Beirut. Their founder was a monk of northern Syria, St. Jean Maron, who founded a religious order in the sixth Century AD which attracted many followers. Gradually they spread to Lebanon, built monasteries, and after the Muslim invasions of the seventh century withdrew to their mountain fastnesses refusing conversion, or indeed any contact with the Muslim enemies. They have a traditional alliance with France, dating from the 12th century; in 1182 they acknowledged Papal supremacy in return for independence in liturgy and canon law. In 1585 a Maronite College was set up in Rome. Many Maronites emigrated to North and South America in the late 19th and early 20th centuries. The communities in the Diaspora are both prosperous and full of patriotic feeling, at a distance, towards their ancestral home. They have always sent money home, and some, after 20 or 30 years away (especially in West Africa) return to their mountain villages, build comfortable houses, and seek to end their days prosperously and peacefully. Maronite political intransigence has lasted until today, and is to some extent responsible for the recent troubles.

HISTORY

The people of Lebanon make up its history and that history is long and turbulent. The cities of the sea coast Byblos, Tyre and Sidon are familiar from Egyptian history and from the Old Testament.

Lebanon was in ancient times Phoenicia, when the harbours were great trading centres, and Phoenician ships carried goods all over the Mediterranean. The cities of Carthage in what is now Tunisia, and Massilia (Marseille) in present day France were founded by Phoenician traders, and after the rise of the Roman Empire Phoenicians remained the sharpest merchants.

Beirut, then called Berytus, was a considerable Christian town with a university famed for its law faculty. Roman and then Byzantine rule endured until the Muslim conquests, when the mountain people remained Christian, and most of the coastal inhabitants became Muslim. The Arab empire endured until the Crusades when Norman military power established itself for almost two hundred years in the Levant, between 1099 and 1271. Then the Turks took over, and ruled in gradually increasing somnolence, until Napoleon's invasion of Egypt in 1799, when the Muslim world began to rediscover the West. Muhammad Ali Pasha came to power in Egypt in 1820, and brought Palestine, Lebanon and Syria under his hegemony. The victorious campaigns were fought by his son Ibrahim Pasha, a talented general, and it was only when the British, Austrians and Russians defended Beirut in 1840 by sending a fleet that the Egyptians were stopped.

In 1841, 1845 and 1860 three separate bouts of civil strife, mostly between Druse and Maronites, took place; in the 1860 troubles the Turks who were nominally in control openly aided the Druse, and conflict spread to Damascus where about 11,000 Christians were slaughtered. Finally, the European powers decided to intervene, along with Turkey A joint French Turkish force was sent to Beirut to restore order, and on 9 June 1861 an organic statute for Lebanon (le grand Liban) was signed in Istanbul between the European Powers and the Ottoman Government. It remained in force until the Turkish empire crumbled in 1917, and made Lebanon an autonomous Mutasarrifiyah of the Ottoman Empire. The Mutasarrif was a Christian and the inhabitants were officially permitted the free exercise of their religion, allowed to ring church bells, and have public religious processions. French educational influence became ever stronger, and when the Ottoman Empire was carved up, at the end of the First World War, the

French received the mandates for Syria and Lebanon.

The Syrians bitterly resented French hegemony, but Lebanon became for a time almost a province of France. It became fashionable for many Lebanese to disclaim Arab antecedents, loyalties, and the language; instead, they referred to themselves as Phoenicians and sent their children to French schools where the elementary history books began 'Nos Ancêtres les Gaulois. . . .' The French did their best to impose their culture and civilization in Lebanon, as they had done in Algeria, and were in some ways more successful, because of the so-called 'religious' link. But this ephemeral success was due to the Levantine desire for assimilation to European rather than Muslim Arab culture, reinforced by the Maronite community's fear of being swamped, persecuted, and even wiped out. This is a totally irrational fear, for Christian minorities today live unmolested in most Muslim countries, as do Muslim minorities in Christian lands. But it has borne bitter fruit in Lebanon today.

The Greek Orthodox have been long established in Lebanon, and Syria, and their traditional alliance is with Russia, the religious link before the 1917 Revolution having continued for political reasons ever since. The enormous St. George Hospital in Beirut was built with a long term loan from the Moscow Narodny Bank, and all the medical equipment was donated by the USSR. Russian, Greek, and Arabic are languages in liturgical use in the Orthodox Church.

There are far fewer Protestants than other Christians in Lebanon, but they have an importance out of proportion to their numbers, because the American University of Beirut was founded by American Protestant missionaries in 1872, and always attracted Protestant teachers. The best schools in Lebanon are still either French and Catholic, or English/American and Protestant. There are also fringe Protestant sects, and an Anglican church in Beirut. It is under the jurisdiction of the Anglican Bishop in Jerusalem.

The Armenians must be discussed separately, because although they are all the same race of Indo-Europeans from Turkey, they can be Protestant, Gregorian (Orthodox) or Catholic. Indeed Cardinal Agaganian, who died in 1968, was Prefect of the Oriental Rites in Rome, and widely considered 'papabile'. The Armenians took refuge in Lebanon in 1918/20 after many of them were massacred in Turkey and Northern Syria by Ottoman Turks. They are an industrious and cultured people, excellent craftsmen and musicians, and also talented bankers and financiers who have contributed largely to the prosperity of Lebanon and its pre-eminence until 1974 as a world banking centre.

Islam is divided into two sects, the Sunni and the Shi'a. Generally speaking, the western part of North Africa, Egypt, Syria and of course the Arabian peninsula Islam is Sunni: representing the orthodox and legalistic aspects of the Faith; the eastern countries of Iraq and Iran are mostly Shi'a, and this is directed more toward the mystical face of Islam. It believes in holy men and women as minor prophets and even miracle workers, and the Sufi way of life is stronger. Sunni and Shi'a are both strongly represented in Lebanon. The old Muslim families of Beirut and Tripoli are Sunni, dating from the time of Ottoman hegemony before 1860, and the Shi'a are found in the poorer areas, southern Lebanon and the northern Beka'a. They are now probably the largest community, and are becoming more prosperous, although still ruled by feudal land lords. Many from south Lebanon emigrated to West Africa or the Americas, and made considerable fortunes there; they exercise a certain amount of political influence at home. At present their leader is the Imam Moussa Sadr, a remarkably able man of Iranian origin (his Iranian passport has recently been taken away) but Arab sympathies.

The Druse are found in the mountains of Lebanon, in the Djebel Druse in Syria, and in northern Palestine. They call themselves Muwahiddin (Unitarians) or Bani Ma'aruf (the Sons of Knowledge); the word Druse now generally used comes from one of the founders of their faith, a Persian called Darizi. Since they practice *takiyah*, or concealment of their faith, little is known about it by outsiders, although copies of their sacred books were abstracted in the early 19th century and may be found in the Vatican and Bodleian libraries. Not all the Druse are versed in the religion: there is a class of initiates, known as the Akl or Juwayhid, who meet on Thursdays to discuss both religious and community affairs. About 10% of the Druse are initiates, and admission is subject to strict tests. The first Druse were converts from Islam; their Deity is the indivisible source of Light, both spiritual and physical. They believe in reincarnation and far sight, and have many well-documented examples to prove it. The moral code is strict, and Druse women who marry outside the community are still ostracised. The Druse mountain villagers are very hospitable, and the villages exceedingly clean; they are good farmers and when they emigrate especially to the US usually do well.

The country officially became an independent republic in 1946, and has, ever since, been plagued with the problem of its citizens all wanting their independence at once. The National Pact is an unwritten agreement between the various communities providing that the President of the Republic shall be a Maronite Christian, the Prime Minister a Sunni Muslim, the Speaker of the Chamber of Deputies a Shi'a Muslim, and the Foreign Minister a Greek Orthodox Christian, and so on. The Parliament, or Chamber of Deputies, has 99 members, each community being represented according to its strength in the country. However, no official census has been taken since 1946,

because it would almost certainly show that the Shi'a Muslims were the largest in numbers, and the Maronites fewer than they claim. So the deputies became less and less representative. Since 1946 there have been six Presidents of the Republic, each one holding office for seven years, without the right of re-election. In 1958 Camille Chamoun tried to change the constitution and seek re-election. Civil strife broke out and lasted for about eight months, until Fouad Chehab, a former Commander-in-Chief of the army, was elected. When his mandate expired Charles Helou took over peacefully and retired gracefully and constitutionally in 1970. He was succeeded by the more belligerent and ambitious Suleiman Frangié, who comes from Zghorta in north Lebanon. This small town is divided into two clans, the Frangié and the Douaihi, who have carried on a blood feud since time immemorial. Both sides have the reputation of shooting their opponents, or outside intruders, first, and asking questions afterwards. Thus a certain expectation of toughness preceded Frangie into office, and it was hoped that he would cut the Gordian knot of corruption and bureaucratic inefficiency which has always bedevilled the Lebanese Government. He did make some effort, at the beginning of his term, but outside complications became too strong for him.

The Palestinians, during the early 1970's, exacerbated Lebanese community rivalry by bringing in a new political element. The PLO (Palestine Liberation Organisation) has its headquarters in Beirut, and is the master mind of the Resistance. Many militant Palestinians also lived either in the UNWRA camps which ring the city, or, having prospered to a certain extent, in Beirut apartments. Many went to work in the Gulf, having received good schooling in the establishments set up by UNWRA. Others found jobs in Lebanon, although there were always problems over work permits because most did not possess Lebanese nationality. Between 1948, the year of the exodus from Palestine, and 1955 when the Lebanese rules became much stricter, a good many Christian, and fewer Muslim Palestinians obtained the much coveted Lebanese identity card. This was deliberate Government policy to increase the number of Christians.

The vast majority of Palestinians are entirely involved in the cause, which has nothing to do with religious rivalry and everything to do with national feeling. Children were brought up to sing patriotic songs about 'Palestine is our homeland and we shall return';.the Palestinian map and flag were prominently displayed in all classrooms, and gradually guerilla forces, the Fedayeen, were trained in the camps of Lebanon, Syria, Jordan, and the Gaza strip to attack and infiltrate enemy territory, Israel. The reader of any newspaper over the past five years will be familiar with accounts of 'incidents' and 'reprisals'. The Lebanese Government gave official lip service and support to the Palestinian cause, and indeed wished that they would go back to Palestine. But as the Palestinians became more and more vociferous friction grew. The real cause was economic, the prosperous and comfortable Lebanese, the 'haves', suddenly found themselves faced with a group of people, the 'have-nots', who could be pitied and helped as poor refugees, but not treated as equals when they improved their status, because they were too lean, hungry, and idealistic. The Maronites were the most ferociously opposed to the Palestinians: the recent civil disturbances began in April 1975 when a bus carrying some Palestinians returning from a comrade's funeral passed near a Maronite church, where a Maronite politician was addressing a meeting. The bus was attacked and all its passengers massacred.

During 1975 and 1976 half of Beirut was destroyed, the country was torn apart, and at least 30,000 people killed. For about six months no public services functioned and the airport was closed.

Order was restored by the Arab peace-keeping forces—mostly Syrian—who entered the country in June 1976 and occupied Beirut in November. They are still there. Many private citizens who left the country during the worst of the troubles have returned; a brave effort is being made to pretend that reconstruction is taking place and tourism will again be possible. But in fact Lebanon has been divided; right-wing Maronite Christians have withdrawn to an enclave north of Beirut, centred on the town of Jounieh, with its own airport at Hamat near Batroun. The Left-Nationalist-Palestinian alliance controls the area of Tarik el Jdeideh to the west of Beirut.

The problems have not been settled; an uneasy peace is broken by frequent machine-gun rattles at night, and kept alive by armed Syrian patrols. The Palestinians regard Sadat's peace initiative towards Israel with the deepest suspicion, and feel strong enough to oppose the Maronites, who openly declare their solidarity with Israel, and show it in south Lebanon. Their behaviour is an invitation to attack; it seems incomprehensible until the historical causes are realised. Since 1860 the ruling caste in Lebanon had been Maronite. Maronites had the best education, the best jobs, the best Government posts, and spoke condescendingly of 'ces Arabes'. They showed all the snobbery and arrogance of the French in Algeria. As Lebanon was drawn into the increasing wealth and progress of the Arab world, the Maronites had to join the Arab community. They turned from sneers to shots, and their vaunted devotion to religion evidently did not extend to a knowledge of that phrase of scripture: 'A house divided against itself cannot stand'. The recently canonised Maronite monk, St. Charbel, might have some difficulty in recognising his followers.

The agriculture, the scenery and the night life of Lebanon form the country's permanent attractions, and time and economic necessity may perhaps heal the wounds which now gape open. The Lebanese are traditionally the middlemen of the Mediterranean, especially during the past 20 years, of the oil rich Arab countries. It is very difficult for the rest of the Arab world to manage without the port of Beirut, the banking facilities of the city, and the pleasures which a hedonistic society offers to its visitors, in a language and an idiom that they understand. Night life—clubs, restaurants, bars and the casino—has been one of the country's chief sources of income, and both those who organise and those who patronise it are loathe to see it in abeyance. Much business has been transferred to Athens, to Baharain, to Egypt and to London, but once the facilities are restored, most of it will come swooping back.

GENERAL INFORMATION

Area: 10,400 sq. km.
Population: 2,784,000 (1973 estimate; no official census has taken place since 1950). This includes 188,000 Palestinians.
Capital: Beirut.
Head of State: President Elias Sarkis.
Government: Republic, with Council of Ministers responsible to 99 member Chamber of Deputies. President has rarely used veto on parliamentary decisions.
Languages: Arabic is the official language of the country, but French is almost as widely used. Many people have a good knowledge of English.
Religions: Both Islam and Christianity, in all imaginable varieties, are found; total freedom of worship exists.
Currency: Lebanese Lira, or pound divided into 100 piastres. £1 = LL5.68; $1 = LL2.99.
Time: GMT + 2.

HOW TO GET THERE

By air: In September 1977 Beirut Airport was served by the following airlines: Aeroflot, Air France, Alia, Austrian Air-

lines, Balkan Bulgarian, British Airways, CSA, Cyprus Airways, Egypt Air, Iberia, Interflug, KLM, Kuwait Airways, LOT, Lufthanasa, MALEV, MEA, Royal Air Maroc, Sabena, Swissair, Tarom and TWA. British Airways, Iraqi Airways, MEA, and TMA operate scheduled cargo services.

By road: It is quite possible to drive to Lebanon from Europe, through Turkey and Syria, via Aleppo and Homs to Tripoli, and along the coastal road to Beirut. Alternatively, from Damascus over the mountains there is a first class highway.

By rail: It is possible to reach Beirut by rail from Aleppo; two diesel cars, known as the 'automotrice' make the journey once a day in each direction. The time is 10 to 13 hours, depending on frontier delays and other unpredictable circumstances. This is a slow but picturesque and informative way of approaching the capital.

By sea: The following shipping lines serve Beirut for both cargo and passengers. SOL Maritime Services Ltd., 140 A Franklin Roosevelt avenue, POB 1682, Limassol, Cyprus, tel: 63993, telex: 2882. Serves Greece and Cyprus. London office: Sol Shipping Ltd., 100 Tottenham Court Rd., London W1, tel: 637/4551, telex: 24825.
Black Sea Shipping Co., Latoschkina St. 1 Odessa, USSR, and 1 Potemkintsev Sq., Odessa, telex: 447. London office: CTC Lines, 1-3 Lower Regent Street, London SW1, tel: 930-5833, telex: 917193. This shipping line runs two services from Odessa, one via Bulgaria, Turkey, Greece and Cyprus to Syria, Lebanon and Egypt; the other directly from Odessa to Syria, Lebanon and Egypt.
Alexandria Shipping and Navigation Co., 557 El Horria Avenue, POB 812, Alexandria, Egypt. Drive on/drive off car

ferry between Alexandria, Beirut and Limassol.

Demline, Modern Building, Al Arz Street, POB 1416, Beirut, Lebanon, tel.: 290261, telex: Dem 20227. London Office: Demline Mangement (UK) Ltd., Cotts House, Camomile St., EC3, tel.: 283/1234, telex: 8814641. Serves Lebanon, Greece and France.

Egyptian Navigation Co., 2 El Nasr St., Alexandria, Egypt, tel.: 800050, 503, telex: 4131 UN. Other offices in Cairo, Port Said and Suez.

Lebanon Eastern Trading & Transport Co., Fattal Building, Port St., Beirut, tel.: 252650. Serves Egypt, Syria, Labanon, Greece and Italy.

London Alexandria Navigation Co. (London) Ltd., 35 Piccadilly, W.1. tel.: 734/2634.

Visas and health regulations

Visas are required by all visitors except citizens of Arab countries. There are several categories: Transit visas, valid for 15 days from date of issue, allowing one entry and exit. Tourist or visitors' visas, valid for six months and allowing two entries. Business Visas, granted on presentation of a letter from the firm which an individual represents, valid for six months and allowing multiple entries. A 48-hour visa is issued by the immigration authorities at the airport to travellers arriving from places where there are no Lebanese representation; it can be converted to an ordinary visa at the police headquarters. The visitors' visa may become a Visa de Sejour for up to a year upon application.

Vaccination for smallpox is obligatory for everyone; inoculation against cholera and yellow fever is required for travellers coming from areas where these diseases are endemic. TAB is not obligatory, but is advised.

Currency and customs regulations

Up to 500 cigarettes and one litre of alcohol may be imported duty free. Firearms require a licence to be obtained previously. All narcotics are strictly forbidden. Currency of any kind may be freely exported or imported; Lebanon is a free market.

The traveller arriving by car should normally possess a triptyque or carnet de passage en douane issued by the Automobile Club of the country in which the car is registered. Travellers should also have international driving licences and arrange for comprehensive insurance, although this is not compulsory. It is possible to obtain temporary admission documents at the frontier. either a Fiche d'Entré valid for up to three months, or a Fiche d'Admission Temporaire valid for six months and extendable for up to two years. However, to obtain this a refundable deposit or bank guarantee will be necessary. Petrol is reasonably cheap, and driving is on the right. Good road maps are available at bookstores or petrol stations. It is possible to rent self drive cars from Avis, EuropCar, or smaller local firms; and best to enquire which are operating at present at one of the larger hotels. Driving in Lebanon is hazardous, requires strong nerves, considerable skill, and a continued use of the horn.

CLIMATE AND WHAT TO WEAR

There are four distinct seasons in Lebanon, spring, from March to May, summer, from June to September, autumn, October and November, and winter which begins in December and usually lasts half way through March. In winter there is a good deal of rain which turns to snow on the mountains; it is damp and drafty everywhere and normal winter clothes are required, with raincoats, umbrellas, and sweaters being necessary. Spring and autumn are both mild and pleasant, lightweight suits are suitable for both sexes. Summer is hot and humid on the coast, and cooler in the mountains; the lightest clothes are required, with a wrap for the mountain resorts. Cotton is always preferable to artificial fibres, and loose garments are far better than tight skimpy ones. Lebanon has always been renowned for its social and night life, visitors should therefore bring with them at least one set of clothes suitable for formal entertaining.

Health precautions

One of the best hospitals in the Arab world, the American University Hospital, is situated in Beirut. There is also a French hospital, the Hôtel-Dieu, and many private establishments, as well as doctors in private practice. All medicines may be obtained from the numerous pharmacies, which take it in turns to maintain a 24 hour service. Visitors may suffer from minor stomach upsets; suitable medication is easily available. Those susceptible should avoid unpeeled fruit or vegetables. The water is normally safe to drink, but local bottled water is available also.

ACCOMMODATION AND FOOD

There are many hotels in Beirut and in the towns of Tripoli, Sidon, on the coast, and Chtaura, Zahleh and Baalbek in the Bekaa. At Beiteddine, where the Presidential summer residence is located, another old palace of the Amir Fakhreddine has been restored to its original state with great care and expense, and opened just before the civil war as a luxurious mountain annex to the Phoenicia Intercontinental. The ski resorts of Cedars, Laklouk, Faraya and Zaarour all have hotels used by skiers in winter, and those in search of mountain peace and coolness in summer. The chief summer resorts are Aley, Bhamdoun, Sofar, Brummana, Beit Mery, Bikfaya, and Dhour Choueir, and all have hotels or guest houses open during the four month summer season.

Good Arab food is available every-where. Particular to Lebanon is *kibbe*, made of lamb, or sometimes fish pounded to a fine paste with *burghol*, or cracked wheat, and served raw, or baked in flat trays in the oven, or rolled into golf-ball sized pieces and fried. *Arak* is the national drink, but Lebanese wine is also excellent; there is a long tradition of the monasteries owning vineyards and making wine. The best varieties are Chateau Musar (white), Ksara (red), and Domaine des Tourelles (rose).

In Beirut there is every kind of national restaurant, French, Italian, German, Austrian, Scandinavian, Greek, Chinese, Japanese, Indian, Malaysian, Spanish and Filipino. The best restaurants for Arabic food are **Al Ajameh** in the *Souk Tawileh*, and **Al Barmaki** at the beginning of Rue Hamra. The town of Zahleh, in the Bekaa, lies on the banks of a river, the Bardoni, and the upper part of the town on a rocky gorge lined with cafes on either side of the river. People go there to spend a whole day on Sunday, or a long evening in the summer; they eat, drink, talk, smoke narghileh, and generally relax. It is a great place for families.

TRANSPORT

The traveller without his own car may get about the country by bus, by service, or by private taxi. Buses are cheap, picturesque, and not very comfortable; it is preferable to have some knowledge of Arabic to enjoy the trip. 'Service' taxis run on the same principle as Turkish 'dolmas'; they operate both in Beirut, and from Beirut to Damascus, Aleppo, and Amman, as well as to towns and villages within Lebanon, on definite routes. Fares are fixed, and the passengers pay for their seats. Before engaging a private taxi it is advisable to fix the fare first, a tip is not necessary except for an exceptional service. Tour companies run buses to the main tourist attractions, Baalbek, Byblos, the Cedars, Sidon, and

Beiteddine. At present it is not possible to visit Tyre.

BANKS

Lebanon has been one of the chief banking centres in the world, and a great deal of money had been deposited in the 76 banks which hold operating licences. There are no exchange control regulations, and it is permitted to hold numbered anonymous accounts. As well as the banks, there are many money changers in the commercial districts, who carry out all exchange and transfer operations. Bank opening hours are 0830 till 1230, but some remain open until 1500. Money changers operate from 0900 till 1330, and 1530 till 1800.

PUBLIC HOLIDAYS

The usual Muslim, and Western Christian public holidays are observed, as well as:
22 March Founding of the Arab League.
30 April Labour Day.
6 May Martyr's Day.
22 November Independence Day.
31 December Foreign Troops Evacuation Day.

EMBASSIES IN BEIRUT

Afghanistan: Rue Rachidin, Tallet el-Khayyat.
Algeria: Jnah, opposite Coral Beach.
Bahrain: Sami Fouad Hamzeh Bldg., Bir Hassan.
Belgium: Centre Verdun, Rue Dunat.
Canada: Rue Hamra, Centre Sabbagh.
Egypt: Rue Ramlat el-Baida.
France: Rue Clemenceau.
German Dem. Rep.: Ave de Paris.
German Fed. Rep.: Rue Hamra, Imm. Arida.
Greece: Rue de France.
Iran: Jnah, Imm. Sakina Mattar.
Iraq: Jnah, The Phare Eden Roc.

Italy: Rue Makdissi, Imm. Cosmidis.
Jordan: Rue Verdun, Imm. Belle-Vue.
Kuwait: Bir Hassan, The Stadium Roundabout.
Libya: Jnah, Imm. Cheikh Abdallah Khalifé Al-Sabbah.
Malta: Achrafé, Rue Marian Geahchan, Imm. Varkés Sarafian.
Morocco: Corniche Masraa, Imm. Chamat.
Qatar: Dibs Bldg., Chouran Street.
Saudi Arabia: Rue Bliss, Manara.
Spain: Ramlet el Baida, Imm. White Sands.
Sudan: Rue Mme Curie, Imm. Minkara.
Switzerland: Ave. Perthuis, Imm. Achou.
Tunisia: Ramlet el-Baida, Imm. Rock and Marble.
Turkey: Bir Hassan.
United Arab Emirates: Jnah, Face Eden Rock, Imm. Wafic Tabbara.
UK: Ave. de Paris, Ain el-Mreisse.
USA: Ave. de Paris, Imm. Ali Reza.
USSR: Rue Mar Elias el-Tina.
Yemen Arab Rep: Blvd. Khaldé-Quzai, Imm. Ingénier Ryad Amaiche.
Yemen People's Dem. Rep: Ramlet el Baida, Imm. Ramlet el Baida.

TOURIST INFORMATION

The National Council of Tourism in Lebanon, Bank of Lebanon Street, PO Box 5344, tel: 340940 Beirut.

BEIRUT

Until the civil war Beirut was one of the busiest and most prosperous cities of the Mediterranean. Reconstruction of the destroyed port and city centre is now beginning, but needs time. The modern town was never beautiful, but had a spectacular setting on the sea, with Mount Sannin, snow-capped for five months of the year, rising directly behind it.

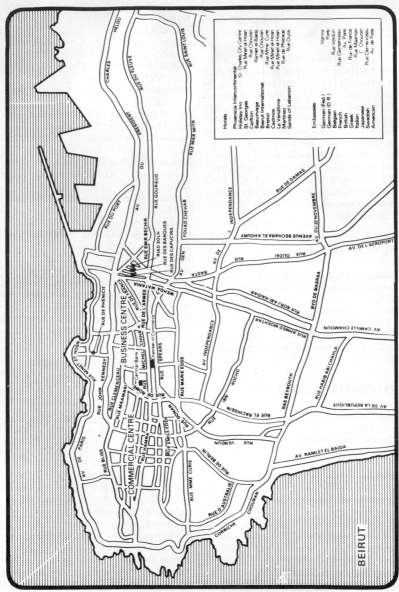

Hotels

Phoenicia Intercontinental
Holiday Inn
St Georges
Carlton
Beaurivage
Beirut International
Bristol
Cadmos
La Vendôme
Martinez
Sands of Lebanon

St Charles City Centre
Rue Minet el-Hosn
Rue Chouran
Ramlet el-Baïda
Rue Chouran
Rue Mme. Curie
Rue Minet el-Hosn
Rue Minet el-Hosn
Rue de Phénicie
Rue Ouzai

Embassies

German (Fed.)
German (D.R.)
Belgian
French
British
Greek
Italian
Japanese
Swedish
American

Hamra
Paris
Rue Verdun
Rue Clemenceau
Av. Paris
Rue de France
Rue Mazraan
Chouran
Rue Clemenceau
Av. de Paris

BEIRUT

Copyright Graham and Trotman Ltd.

There are five universities, the American, always known as the AUB, the French Universite St. Joseph, the Lebanese University, the Beirut Arab University, and Beirut University College. The last used to be an all-female establishment, under the name of Beirut College for Women. When it became co-educational it changed its name, though not its US Protestant affiliations. There is an active intellectual life, with British, French, German, Italian, and US cultural institutes, which all possess good libraries and put on plays, concerts, and exhibitions. There is also a National School of Music and an Academy of Fine arts.

There are many cinemas, showing the latest European, American and Indian films, as well as those made in the Arab countries.

Shops in Beirut contain every possible variety of foreign goods, as well as local manufactures.

The night life is well known, and the *Casino du Liban* unique in the world, because of its spectacular site at Maamaltein, about 25 km. from Beirut, and the alliance of gambling facilities to both indoor and outdoor restaurants, a night club with floor shows rivalling those of Las Vegas, and a theatre where plays with the original London or Paris casts are given, or concerts by renowned performers.

Hotels

Four star A
Beau Rivage, Ramlet Baida, P.O. Box 105013, tel: 303120/1.
Beirut Carlton, Gen. de Gaulle Avenue, P.O. Box 3420, tel: 300240.
Beirut International, Gen. de Gaulle Avenue, P.O. Box 6110, tel: 300016/17.
Bristol, Mme Curie Street, P.O. Box 1493, tel: 351400/9.
Cadmos, Minet el-Hosn, P.O. Box 4654, tel: 365870/2.
Martinez, Phoenicia Street, P.O. Box 6203, tel: 367810/11.

Vendôme, Minet El Hosn St. tel: 369280/1.

Four star B
Atlantic, Ramlet Baida, tel: 300147/9.
Beirut Commodore, Lyon Street, tel: 350400/20.
Cavalier, Hamra Street, tel: 353001/5.
Continental, Gen. de Gaulle Avenue, tel: 311015.
Coral Beach, Jnah, tel: 317200/4.
Du Roy, Chatila Str., Raouché, tel: 233099.
Excelsior, Minet el-Hosn Str., P.O. Box 113816, tel: 367400.
King's, Chouran, tel: 297501/3.
Méditerranée, Chouran, tel.: 220050.
Melkart, Ramlet Baida, P.O. Box 3456, tel: 306910/1.
Napoléon, Makdissi Street, tel: 340207/9.
Pavillon, Hamra Street, P.O. Box 8242, tel: 350160/2.
Riviera, Avenue de Paris, tel: 362480/2.
Rodin, Roustom Pacha Str., tel: 363170/1.
Royal Garden, Lyon Street, P.O. Box 155873, tel: 350010.

Three star A
Alexandre, Adib Is'hac Street, P.O. Box 6861. tel: 332286.
Astra, Hamra Street, tel: 346600/1.
Atlas, Mme Curie Street, tel: 360530/1.
Bedford, Jeanne d'Arc Str., Hamra. tel: 340600.
Cedarland, Abdel Aziz Street, tel: 340233/4.
Dolphin, Gen, de Gaulle Ave., tel: 301208.
Federal, Australie Street, tel: 315077.
Marble Tower, Makdissi Street, tel: 346260/1.
Marhaba, Ayoub Tabet Str., Shourant, tel: 340020/2.
Marly (Le), Hamra Street, tel: 340230/1
May Flower, Sidani Street, tel: 340680.
Orient Prince, Mme Curie Street, tel: 340030/1.
Plaza, Hamra Street, tel: 346070/4.

Three star B

Biarritz, Karawan Street, Verdun, tel: 300020/2.

Charles, Roustom Pacha Street, tel: 368790.

Concorde, tel: 350190/2.

Embassy, Makdissi Street, tel: 340814/5.

Lord's, Ardati Street, P.O. Box 9054, tel: 346200/1.

Mozart, Ardati Street, tel: 346410.

Napoli, Hamra Street, tel: 346040/1.

Sunrise, Avenue de Paris, tel: 362320/1.

Triumph, Mme Curie Street, tel: 350490/1.

Vestales, Tannoukhine Street, Hamra, tel: 342273.

Two star

Mace, Hamra Street, tel: 344626/7.

Mochrek, Makdissi Street, tel: 345772/3.

New Hamra, Hamra Street, tel: 346046/8.

One star

Park Lane, Abla Street, tel: 347860/1.

St. Lorenzo, Hamra Street, tel: 348604/5.

OTHER TOWNS

Tripoli is the second city of Lebanon; it is divided into two parts, the port and the town outside. They are joined by 2 km. of road which runs amongst orange plantations; in spring the scent of the blossoms is almost unbearably fragrant, and serves to disguise other, less agreeable fishy and oily odours. For just north of the town is the IPC pipeline terminal, bringing the oil from Mosul. There is also an oil refinery, one of the two (the other being at Zahrani, south of Sidon) that supply the needs of the country. Tripoli has a provincial charm and cachet; excellent Arabic sweets and patisseries flavoured with orange flower water are made here, and a good many people work in the port or as fishermen.

Sidon is much smaller, and of interest

to the visitor principally for the Crusader sea castle built at the end of a causeway largely from stones taken from the remains of Roman buildings. It is the centre of the richest agricultural part of the coastal plain, and its markets are full of the most delectable vegetables and fruits.

Tyre is at present out of bounds for the ordinary visitor because of the uncertain political situation in South Lebanon; the remains of the ancient city are immense and impressive. The ancient chariot-racing circus has been perfectly preserved, and several plays and festivals have been held there in recent years. The modern part is a small fishing town, but remains on the harbour floor show how vast it once was.

Byblos is reputed to be the oldest town in the world; it was certainly a flourishing port in the time of the Phoenicians and the Egyptians, and has relics from these times, as well as Byzantine ruins and a Crusader castle and church. The harbour is still a resort of fishermen and pleasure craft—recently also of unofficial weapons importers. Here ancient tombs jostle modern restaurants, and artifacts dredged from the sea floor decorate the port walls.

Beiteddine in the Chouf mountains, between Beirut and Sidon, is the site of the palace built by the Emir Beshir, Prince of the Druses, in the early 19th century. It is now the official residence of the Lebanese President in summer, and the public may visit the courtyards, gardens, and state rooms. Both the palace itself, and the drive there are one of the most interesting excursions for the visitor.

Baalbek, is one of the best preserved temples of the Roman world still in existence. It is a complex of several temples, forming the City of the Sun, at the far end of the Bekaa plain. A book written in 1926 describes it as 'the great Roman temple encircled by the mountains, towering above a grove of tall and gently waving poplars. I should doubt if

The harbour at Byblos

there were another place on earth where natural and man made beauty coincide as at Baalbek. Too often beautiful scenery is barren of beautiful architecture, while the great creations of man languish in negligible surroundings. But in this one spot nature and man have simultaneously achieved the infinite. Baalbek was the Greek Heliopolis, or City of the Sun, and though the Roman temples are dedicated to Jupiter and Bacchus, it still belongs, in spirit, to the sun. The six soaring columns of the temple of Jupiter beyond are sand-coloured, washed by the sun, and look like pillars of sunlight solidified, sunlight harnessed and brought to earth in tangible form, captured from the solar system to stand as a lasting monument to man's love of warmth and light.'

SPORTS

Swimming, sailing and water skiing are, as might be expected, much practised in Lebanon. We have already mentioned the various snow skiing resorts; all have ski lifts and instructors; the sport grows yearly in popularity. There is a race course in Beirut, and horse riding is possible at several clubs near Beirut, in Sidon, and in the Bekaa, which is ideal horse country. The best horses, however, are bred in the Akkar region, a flat wind-swept plain to the north of Tripoli, bordering upon Syria. Tennis and golf may be played, and in Beirut there are several 'keep-fit' studios, of which Silhouette, rue Hamra, tel: 340076, and Sheri-Lynn, rue Madam Curie, tel: 243620, are the best known.

ARTS AND CRAFTS

Lebanon is best known for its pottery, glass-blowing in various jewel colours, and metal work. At Jezzine in the mountains beyond Sidon animal bones are carefully carved into cutlery inlaid with metal and enamel, and shaped like birds. There are also weavers who make rugs, materials, and traditional Arab garments like abayas and Kaftans. Much beautiful embroidery is done in the Druse and Christain mountain villages, and can be purchased. Antiquities are sometimes available, but export licences are needed, and it is very difficult to be certain if they are genuine.

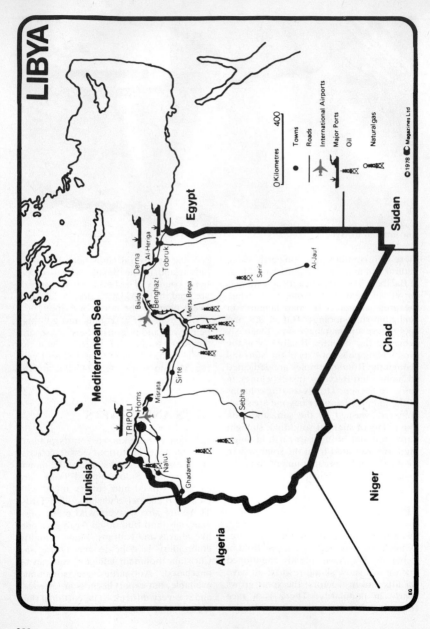

LIBYA

Libya's dramatic Roman ruins, its long and uncrowded beaches and its Saharan oases make it an attractive country to visit. Despite its vast area, Libya has a population of not much more than two million. Throughout history, civilisation has clung to the narrow coastal strip, while the forbidding Sahara lurked behind. But in the past two decades the desert has begun to yield a massive oil wealth—to the tune of $8bn a year—bringing sudden changes to the whole country, in the economy, in social developments and especially in political attitudes. These changes also affect the traveller.

The Government's present priorities have meant that there is no official tourist encouragement. Entry formalities have become more stringent, and include insistence that visitors' passports should have all the essential information printed in Arabic. This can be done by a Libyan embassy, but there may be delays before a visa is issued. Occasionally the Libyan authorities will not allow unmarried women to enter the country.

Since the 1969 revolution most foreign businesses have been expropriated or have been made to close, including some restaurants and shops, specifically those that had been owned by Italians or Jews. There has also been a steep rise in the cost of living, and there is little chance of spending much time in Libya on a small budget. But there is excellent accommodation both Tripoli and Benghazi, the ruins of Leptis Magna, Cyrene and Sabratha are magnificent, the people are still hospitable and the coastal Mediterranean climate is still ideal for a holiday.

THE LAND AND THE PEOPLE

Most of Libya's huge area of 1,759,400 sq. km. consists of desert, and all its frontiers are desert frontiers, from Tunisia and Algeria in the west to Egypt in the east, with the Sahara extending across the southern frontiers with Niger, Chad and Sudan. There are almost 2,000 km. of Mediterranean coastline, and a strip of this is cultivated: in the west from Zuara to Misurata—where a large iron and steel smelting complex is being built—and along the coast from Marsa Susa to Benghazi in the east. Inland parts of the hilly terrain of the Jebel Nefusa, in the former province of Tripolitania, are cultivated. In Brak, in what was known as the Fezzan, extensive agricultural development is taking place.

In the uplands of the old province of Cyrenaica, the Jebel Akhdar (Green Mountain) the vegetation is more lush. The gargantuan sheep farm at Kufra, in the deep south-east, has become Libya's prestige agricultural symbol though it has its drawbacks (the cost of raising, feeding and maintaining is so high that by the time a carcass reaches Tripoli it has to be sold at about LD250).

With the exception of 'sand sea' like the Calanscio, and the Saharan mountains of the Tibesti, there are oases scattered throughout Libya, the most accessible being Ghadames on the Algerian border and Sebha—the developing capital of the southern province. Both are served by regular flights from Tripoli. Other important oases are Ghat, Kufra and Jaghboub.

The population of two million is tiny considering Libya's size and is concentrated mostly along the coast. Away from the coastal road and its offshoots communications were bad until the 1969 revolution, but since then infrastructure has been uppermost in all three development plans. New, wide highways have been, or are being, built to ease land communications. The long coastal road runs from the Egyptian border to the Tunisian frontier and provides a through road that connects Cairo, Alexandria, Benghazi, Tripoli, Tunis, Algiers and Casablanca. There are regular buses, and taxi services, between the two principal towns, Tripoli and Benghazi, and the interior, and scheduled Libyan Arab Airlines flights to all large towns and important oases.

The rural people have traditionally been mostly nomadic shepherds, but since the discovery of oil in the late 1950s there has been a steady drift to the towns, which has created problems of inadequate shanty settlements around Tripoli and Benghazi, but most of these have now been demolished and replaced with apartment buildings built by the Government and sold at a nominal price.

Ethnically and culturally, Libyans are almost entirely Arab, with an admixture of Negroes in the south and indigenous Berbers in the west. Although the Berber language is still used in certain settlements, such as Sorman, Arabic is the language of the whole country. Foreign residents form a large minority, many being temporary expatriates, such as Egyptians (250,000) on contract as technical advisers, doctors and teachers, British and American employees of oil companies and various others working as doctors, engineers, pilots and university lecturers. Since the rapprochement with the Soviet Union in 1974 there has also been a large influx of East bloc personnel in all strata of economic life. The Italian residents who formed a substantial community, particularly in the former province of Tripolitania, between the end of the Second World War and the 1969 coup, were expelled in August 1970.

CULTURE

Most Libyans trace their ancestry to the tribes known as the Beni Hilal and Beni Suleim, who came from Arabia in the 11th century AD, passed into Upper Egypt and then were encouraged by the Fatimid Caliphate to reconquer Tripolitania and Tunisia from the Berbers, who had managed to assert their independence against the descendants of the original Arab invaders—the followers of Amr Ibn al-As in the seventh century. These two nomadic tribes put an end to almost all settled life in Libya for many centuries, with the exception of Tripoli and Benghazi. Pastoralism became the norm. This still applies to much of the life in the Eastern province which is still a nomadic or semi-nomadic society.

There is a more settled farming community in the Western province, and it was here that the Italian colonists found some measure of co-operation (rather than the guerrilla warfare of the Cyrenaicans) during the 1920-40 period. Tripolitanians have gradually become detribalised, whereas Cyrenaicans are still largely aware of their tribal roots, even in the towns. This is the most obvious difference between the two sides of the natural frontier of the Sirtic desert which divides the two.

It was the Cyrenaican Bedouin who most firmly embraced the ascetic teachings of the Senussi movement. This sect, founded by the grandfather of ex-King Idris (Muhammed Ali al-Senussi), migrated from Morocco and Algeria into Cyrenaica during the second quarter of the 19th century.

Libyan culture is a provincial manifestation of the culture common to all Arab countries. There have been no outstanding writers, and the characteristic poetry is in the oral tradition of the Bedouin. Art and architecture show themselves in mosques (though even the best of them, such as the Ahmad Pasha Karmanli in Tripoli, do not compare with the best of the Arab world), in calligraphy, and in such crafts as woodwork, leather, rug-making and metal-engraving. The music, again, is of the simple traditional kind associated with all nomadic Arabs, and there have been some official efforts to preserve and present it through radio programmes and concerts.

In general, Libya is culturally conservative, and this is in keeping with the devout tradition of Islam as it is known in the country, and also with the slow spread of literacy. The growth of education during the past 20 years, from primary to university level, will continue to be important.

HISTORY

The Phoenicians were the first civilised people to settle in Libya. In the eighth century BC the three cities of Oea (later to be known as Tripoli), Leptis Magna and Sabratha were founded in addition to Carthage, which became the capital of the Western Phoenician Empire. Greek settlers from the Aegean came to Cyrene in the east in the middle of the seventh century BC and soon established the rest

of the Cyrenaican Pentapolis or 'five cities': Euhesperides, Tokra, Tolmeta and Apollonia. The Pentapolis was united in a federation under the protection of the first of the Ptolemaic pharaohs, Ptolemy Soter, towards the beginning of the fourth century BC. After the defeat of the Carthaginian empire western Libya became a Roman province, and under the Emperor Augustus Leptis Magna and Sabratha in particular expanded and flourished. At the same time Cyrenaica was united with Crete as a Roman province for administrative purposes.

The decline of Rome brought raids on its Libyan cities from native inland tribes such as the Austuriani and Vandal invasions. Later, during the mid-seventh century came the Islamic conquest under the Arab general, Amr Ibn al-As—later consolidated by the Beni Hilal and the Beni Suleim already mentioned. The Roman cities were abandoned and fell into ruin and were buried in the sand until the arrival of archaeologists in the 20th century.

Spaniards and others sporadically dominated the Libyan coastal strip for several centuries, until eventually in the 16th century the Ottoman Empire took over, administering the area loosely from Constantinople. Sometimes local families established virtual autonomy under the Ottomans; one such was the Karamanli dynasty which ruled Tripoli during the 18th and early 19th centuries—the period of the 'Barbary pirates'. In 1801 President Jefferson sent American warships to Tripoli in an attempt to subdue the pirates' raids.

By the beginning of the present century, Italy was eager to take part in the general European expansion into Africa. Libya, feebly administered and badly defended by the Turks, was an obvious goal, and in 1911 Italy invented a diplomatic excuse for invading the country. Landings were made a few kilometres west of Tripoli and at Homs, Benghazi and Derna.

In the 1930s a vast Italian colonial scheme got under way. Thousands of Libyans were dispossessed of their land and extensive farm settlements were begun for peasants brought in from Sicily and southern Italy, particularly in what was then Tripolitania and the Cyrenaican Jebel Akhdar. This was stopped by the Second World War, during the first years of which Libya became a battleground for Italian, German and British troops. At the end of the war Britain was administering western and eastern Libya and France the south. Under the United Nations, Libya was granted independence on 24 December 1951, with Idris, the leader of the Senussi sect, as king.

In the early years of independence Libya concluded military and economic agreements with Britain and the US, to bolster up its financial instability. But in the late 1950s the international oil companies were granted exploration concessions, and soon Libya became one of the largest suppliers of oil in the world, one of its chief advantages being its comparative closeness to European markets.

In September 1969 a military coup overturned the Government of King Idris and the Libyan Arab Republic was established under the rule of Colonel Muammar Qaddafi and a 12-man Revolutionary Command Council. The RCC sought closer ties with other Arab countries, particularly Egypt, and a diminution of European—especially Italian—and American influence. Most foreign firms were expropriated, and a Federation of Arab Republics was agreed with Egypt and Syria. The FAR, however, came to nothing. In 1974 Libya and Tunisia decided to merge, but this also fell through.

In March 1977, in an attempt to establish Hellenistic fundamentals of democracy combined with extreme Islamic principles, a Jamaharyia was declared. Libya is now officially known as the Socialist People's Libyan Arab Jamaharyia (state of the masses).

ECONOMY

Libya's economic and political fortunes float on a sea of oil, which is being extracted from the desert at a rate of 2.4 million barrels a day. At the present rate of production it should last for another 36 years. Once listed by the World Bank as one of the poorest countries in the world with the fewest economic possibilities, Libya has now the highest per caput income in Africa ($4,440 in 1974) and foreign-exchange reserves in excess of $3,523 million. Plans for extensive development in every sector of the economy have been drawn up as a result of the new-found wealth. Since the 1969 revolution there have been three development plans. The third, launched in January 1976, is known as the Plan of Socio-Economic Transformation; it ends in 1981.

Since the introduction of the first development plan agricultural production has increased, industry has expanded and dramatic improvements have been made in housing, roads, electricity, water supplies, health and social services. But a serious problem is the lack of skilled manpower at every level. Large numbers of Egyptians now fill managerial posts and much of the labour force is made up of Tunisians, Algerians and Palestinians. Education and training of Libyans is a priority but it will take up to the end of the current development plan to train sufficient numbers for the oil industry alone. Nevertheless, under a Petroleum Law of 1955 up to 75% of the oil companies' work force must be Libyan.

After the revolution Libya nationalised most foreign-owned oil companies operating on its soil. But in recent years it has allowed new ones to start operations on a partnership basis with the Libyan National Oil Corporation.

The main oil-producing region is the eastern sector of the country, although new and promising deposits have recently been discovered in western Libya. Pipelines in the east lead to terminals at Mersa Brega, Ras Lanuf, Mersa Hariga and Zucitina. The country's first refinery, at Zawia, 35 km. west of Tripoli, was inaugurated in September 1974 and has a capacity to distil 120,000 barrels of crude oil a day; a second is under construction in Tobruk and is expected to go on stream in late 1978 with a daily production capacity of 220,000 barrels. Plans for a third refinery at Misurata have been temporarily shelved. Natural gas is another important export: the gas liquefaction plant at Mersa Brega is the biggest of its kind in the world, with a capacity of 345 million cubic feet a day.

GENERAL INFORMATION

Area: 1,759,400 sq. km.

Population: 2,257,037 (1974 est.).

Altitude: Sea level to 4,000m (Tibesti mountains in extreme south).

Head of State: Officially Libya has no head of state, but Colonel Muammar Qaddafi as Secretary-General of the General People's Congress and leader of the revolution, is regarded as the *de facto* President or 'Chairman'.

Government: On 3 March 1977 Libya became a Jamaharyia (a state of the masses). Simply defined, it is an attempt to combine the ancient Greeks' *demos* system coupled with the principles of Islam. The Government is elected by the General People's Congress, whose members are elected by popular committees. Popular committees are the basic unit of administration. Members are elected in villages, towns, government departments, private companies, ports, hospitals, airports etc. and in turn select their own members to sit in the Congress.

Date of Independence: 24 December 1951. Independence Day is no longer observed, but Revolution Day on 1 September is.

Languages: Arabic (official); English and Italian are spoken in the towns. All public notices and signboards are in Arabic script.

Religion: Islam.

Currency: Libyan dinar (formerly pound), divided into 1,000 dirhams (formerly millimes). 0.587 dinars=£1 sterling; 0.289 dinars=US$1.00.

Time: GMT + 2.

Electricity: 125V in the Western Province. 220V in the Eastern Province.

HOW TO GET THERE

By air: Libya's main airport is Tripoli, situated 34 km from the capital. A new terminal building was opened at the end of 1977, replacing the obsolete Second World War hangar which had served as a terminal since the 1940s. Transport is available from and to the airport at a charge of 500 dirhams. A Libyan Arab Airlines coach to the airport normally calls at all the principal hotels, but it is advisable to confirm this with either LAA or hotel reception.

Benina airport serves Benghazi and is situated 20 km. from the city. Plans for a new terminal have been designed and invitations for international tenders are expected to be issued during the first quarter of 1978. Libyan Arab Airlines connect Tripoli and Benghazi with hourly flights.

There are daily flights connecting Benghazi, Tripoli and Rome; twice weekly with London; once weekly with Frankfurt; twice weekly with Athens; five days a week with Cairo; twice weekly with Paris; thrice weekly with Tunis (Tripoli only—continuing once weekly to Algiers and once a week from Tunis to Casablanca). There are also flights twice weekly to Malta; twice weekly to Zurich and twice weekly from Cairo to Damascus and Jeddah.

Airlines serving Libya include Aeroflot, Air Algérie, Alitalia, CSA, Air Malta, British Caledonian, KLM, Saudi,

Lufthansa, Swissair, Tunis Air, TWA, UTA, Alia and Balkan.

By sea: Several shipping lines operate services from Europe to Libya. A car ferry operated by Linea Grimaldi sails regularly from Genoa to Tripoli and Linea Tirrenia run a similar service from Naples to Tripoli and Benghazi.

By road: The main coastal road runs through all Libya's towns on the Mediterranean. Non-Arab citizens should check beforehand whether they may cross the border from, or into, Egypt. If not, they can fly from Cairo to Tripoli via Benghazi or take a boat from Alexandria, although sailing is not recommended.

Vehicle owners should have a carnet de passage or tryptique. There is an embargo on certain makes of car. Check with a Libyan diplomatic mission. There are bus and taxi services from towns in Tunisia.

Visas and health regulations
All visitors must have a valid passport and visa. UK visitors should obtain a visa from the Libyan Embassy in London, supplying two photographs, a smallpox certificate (inoculation against cholera is also advisable). A visa costs £4. A regulation in force since 1972 makes it compulsory for all visitors to have the essential information in their passports printed in Arabic. This is normally done by the passport issuing authority, and can take several days.

Entry visas will not be issued at the frontier for visitors arriving direct from countries where there is a Libyan diplomatic or consular mission (ie UK, US, Belgium, France, Greece, Italy, Spain, Switzerland, West Germany, Cyprus, Malta, Tunisia, Algeria, Chad, Iraq, Morocco, Nigeria, Saudi Arabia, Syria, Japan, Turkey, Lebanon, Venezuela, Brazil, USSR). Most international airlines serving Libya will not accept passengers on flights to Libya from these countries unless they possess a Libyan visa.

Visas are normally valid for entry within 90 days of issue and for a stay of up to one month. In certain circumstances an extension of one month can be obtained from the Department of Immigration in Tripoli or Benghazi. All visitors should register with the immigration authorities within seven days; otherwise there may be difficulties in leaving. Visitors going on to other African or Mideastern countries should make sure of their other necessary visas before arrival in Libya.

An international certificate of vaccination against smallpox is essential; inoculation against cholera is necessary for those arriving from other Middle Eastern and African countries.

Customs and currency regulations
For short-stay visitors, all general personal effects for private use are exempt from duty. Liquor is forbidden and will be confiscated. Visitors may export locally made goods up to LD150 in value.

On entering or leaving the country a visitor should not have more then LD20 in Libyan banknotes. There is no restriction on foreign currency on entry and departure. It is essential to keep the currency declaration form filled in on arrival.

CLIMATE

The coastal zone has a Mediterranean climate with almost constant sunshine and a very slight rainfall between November and February. The heat in summer (average maximum 30°C) is intensified by the humidity and occasionally by the hot dry *ghibli* wind. In winter it is warm by day and cold at night. Spring (February-May) is generally considered the best time. In the desert there are extremes of temperature throughout the year (intense heat by day and cold at night).

Clothing and health precautions

Fairly warm clothing is needed in winter, light clothing in summer.

There are no hazards to health in the main towns, and the tap water is quite safe to drink. Visitors venturing into remoter areas should be inoculated against typhoid.

ACCOMMODATION AND FOOD

Tripoli and Benghazi have comfortable, modern hotels. Cheap accommodation is not easy to find.

Since alcohol was banned by the Government in 1969 many restaurants have closed, and those that have stayed open are very expensive. The hotel restaurants, although not very good, are thus virtually the only eating places. The increasing cost of living has unpleasantly surprised most visitors in recent years.

Tipping

A tip of 10%-20% is usually included in hotel and restaurant bills. Porters are paid 50 dirhams for each item, but they may ask for more. Taxi drivers are not tipped.

TRANSPORT

By air: Libyan Arab Airlines provide fast and frequent internal services between Tripoli, Benghazi, Sebha, Beida, Mersa Brega, Tobruk, Misurata, Ghadames and Kufra. LAA operate an hourly shuttle between Tripoli and Benghazi.

By road: The main through road follows the coast from west to east. It has recently been resurfaced and widened. The other main roads are: Al Qaddahia-Sebha (850 km.), Garian-Jefren (73 km.), Tarhouna-Homs (73 km.), Mersa Susa-Ras Hilal-Derna (84 km.), Tobruk-Jaghboub (285 km.). Driving is on the right hand side of the road. Since 1969 all signboards not in Arabic script have been removed. Normal and super grades of petrol are available throughout Libya.

There are frequent bus and taxi services between Tripoli and Benghazi (at

Central Bank in Tripoli

least a 12-hour trip). A seat in a taxi costs between four and five dinars. A minibus service operates from Benghazi to To-bruk. Within Tripoli and Benghazi a taxi costs a minimum of 500 dirhams. However, all fares should be agreed beforehand.

Car hire: Tripoli: *Alta Rentacar*, 124 Sh Imgarief. *El Rahila*, Sh Omar Mukhtar. *Otal*, 10-16 Sh Ikball. Car hire is also available in Benghazi. The normal charge is about LD4 a day.

BANKS

Bank of Libya, head offices, Sh Gamal Abdel Nasser, P.O. Box 1103, Tripoli; and Sh Omar Mukhtar, P.O. Box 249, Benghazi. Other banks: Masraf al-Jam-houria, Masraf al-Wahda, National Commercial Bank, Umma Bank, Sahara Bank. Branches in Tripoli, Benghazi and smaller towns.

Business hours
Banks, Government departments and major businesses close on Friday (the official weekly holiday) and work on Sundays. Major businesses, notably oil companies, usually close on Saturdays, and some on Sundays as well.

Banks: Winter: 0900 to 1300. Summer 0800 to 1230; and 1600 to 1700 Saturday and Wednesday.

Hours for other business and Government offices fluctuate considerably.

PUBLIC HOLIDAYS

Holidays vary from year to year according to the Muslim calendar. If a holiday falls on a Friday the following day is observed. The main Muslim holidays for 1978 are: Prophet's birthday, 20 February; Eid al-Fitr, 3-6 September; Eid al-Adha 10-13 November; Muslim New Year, 11 December. The fixed holidays are: British Evacuation day, 28 March;

Sudanese National Day, 25 May; US Evacuation Day, 11 June; Egyptian National Day, 23 July; Revolution Day, 1 September; Italian Evacuation day, 7 October.

EMBASSIES IN TRIPOLI

Algeria: Sharia Qayronan 12.
Austria: Sharia al Amir Abdulkadir.
Belgium: Abu Ubaida Ibn Al Jarah.
Egypt: Sharia Bin 'Ashur.
Finland: Sharia Mustafa Kamel.
France: Sharia Huper.
Greece: Sharia Jalal Bayar, 18.
India: Sharia Mahmud Shaltut.
Iraq: Sharia Nasser.
Italy: Sharia 'Oran 1.
Kuwait: Sharia Bin Yassir.
Lebanon: Sharia Bin Yassir.
Malta: Sharia Bin Ka'ab 13.
Morocco: Sharia Bashir al-Ibrahim.
Netherlands: Sharia Jelal Bayer 20.
Saudi Arabia: Sharia al-Qayrounan.
Spain: Sharia al-Jazayri.
Sudan: Sharia Donato Suma.
Sweden: Sharia Mugaryef.
Switzerland: Sharia Jeraba.
Syria: Sharia Muhammed Rashid Rida.
Tunisia: Sharia Bashir al-Ibrahimi.
Turkey: Sharia al-Fatah.
United Arab Emirates: Sharia Ben Ashur.
UK: Tariq al-Fatah.
USA: Sharia al-Nasr.
USSR: Sharia Solaroli.
Yemen Arab Republic: Sharia Ubai Ibn Kaa'b 36.
Yemen, People's Democratic Republic: Sharia Bin 'Ashur.

TOURIST INFORMATION

Tourist Department, Sh Adrian Pelt, by the seafront. Travel agents were all nationalised in June 1977. Some hotels have their own tourist information offices.

TRIPOLI

Tripoli is the biggest town in Libya, and has a population of over 700,000, if the governorate of Tripoli, which covers considerable areas to the west, east and south, is included.

It is the chief port, and under the present Government has become the capital in name as well as in fact. Though it was founded by the Phoenicians and developed by the Romans as one of three principal cities of the province, along with Sabratha and Leptis Magna, there are now few traces of its origins; the only Roman monument is the arch of Marcus Aurelius in the old city, which dates from the middle of the first century AD.

The Tripoli of today is mainly a product of the Italian occupation, though the large castle by the harbour dates partly from the 16th century and a few of the mosques are as old. The layout of the city is modern and pleasantly spacious. Unfortunately the magnificent corniche has been spoiled because it has now become an open-air port warehouse.

The most interesting part is the old city, beginning at the castle and stretching through many market alleyways, or *souks*. The castle itself houses a good museum with sections devoted to prehistory, archaeology, ethnography, epigraphy and natural history. There are splendid views from the battlements. Photographers, however, are advised not to take pictures of the port. In the *souks* weavers, coppersmiths, goldsmiths, leatherworkers and all kinds of stall-keepers are active.

Hotels

Shati Al-Andalus, tourist village 9 km. along the Zawia Rd, tel: 71392.

Tajoura, tourist village on coastal road, Tajoura.

Al Shati Beach Hotel, de luxe, Hay Al-Andalus, tel: 71641, Box 6678.

Uaddan, first class, Sh. Sidi Isa, tel: 30041.

A street in Tripoli

Kasr Libya, first class, Sh. Sidi Isa, tel: 31181, Box 727.

Mediterranean, first class, Sh. Omar Mukhtar, tel: 43016, Box 6607.

Atlantic, Sh. Sidi Dargout, tel: 30115.

Marhaba, Sh. Sidi Ben Imam, tel: 36464.

Al-Kabier, Sh. Al-Fath, tel: 33578.

Al-Nasr, Maidan Al-Swehly, tel: 36478.

There are about 30 other hotels of varying standard in the capital.

Restaurants

Besides the restaurants in the hotels, these include the **Excelsior** (behind the Grand Hotel) and the **Caravan** and **Le Paris** which are five minutes' walk from the Beach Hotel. The **Wadi al-Rabee** restaurants are perhaps the finest; there is one opposite the People's Palace and another next to the Beach Hotel.

Entertainments

All night clubs were closed about a year before the revolution, and alcohol is forbidden by law. There are several cinemas, but no regular theatre or concert-hall. Good swimming, but better almost anywhere outside Tripoli itself rather than at municipal beaches. Football, golf, horse-racing, ten-pin bowling, and tennis.

BENGHAZI

The chief town of the Eastern province, Benghazi has a population of 350,000. Its first settlement was by Greek colonists, at Euhesperides in the north-eastern outskirts of the present town. This was abandoned by the third century BC, and modern Benghazi lies partly above the Hellenistic and Roman towns of Berenice. There are no obvious signs of these settlements, except confused traces of Berenice at the cemetery of Sidi Kreibish.

Unlike Tripoli, Benghazi was badly damaged during the Second World War, and there are not many surviving buildings from the Turkish and Italian periods of domination. Those there are lie chiefly within the old city, beyond the Maidan Baladia.

Hotels

Omar Al-Khayyam, de luxe, Sh. Gamal Abdel Nasser, tel: 4420, Box 2148.
Kasr Al-Jaziera, de luxe, Sh. Ali Wouraieth, tel: 2144, Box 285.
Atlas Al-Siyahi, first class, Sh. Letewesh.
Al-Anis, first class, Sh. Omar Ben Al-Khattab, tel: 3256, Box 561.
Al Madina, Sh. Lingi, tel: 4818.
Al-Kebir, Sh. Abdel Moniem Riad.

Sahara desert

F.A.O. PHOTO

Kasr Al-Nile, Sh. Ahmed Rafik Al-Mahdawi.

There are about 12 third or fourth class hotels.

Restaurants
Besides the restaurants in the hotels, there are only two worth mentioning: the **Palace** and **Vienna.**

Entertainments
As in Tripoli, the night clubs have been closed. Foreign films are shown at the Berenice and Rex cinemas. There is no theatre or concert hall. At Fuiyahat there is a small zoo. There is no museum at present, though one is planned. The best swimming is outside the town at Mnjerr along the coast road to the east.

Shopping and markets
The chief shopping streets are Sharia Gamal Abdel Nasser and Sharia Omar Mukhtar, and in the *souk* area beyond the Maidan Baladia, which is a smaller version of the Tripoli *souk*.

OTHER TOWNS

On the Tripolitanian coast are **Zawia**, **Homs' Misurata** and the ruins of **Leptis Magna** and **Sabratha**. **Leptis Magna** (123 km. east of Tripoli) has remains dating from the fifth century BC. It appears to have been a leading city in the second century BC and shortly after the Roman destruction of Carthage in 146 BC it became part of Roman Africa. In the second century AD, under the Emperor Septimius Severus, himself born in Leptis Magna, the city flourished. The present ruins display a fine series of public buildings, the most magnificent being the theatre.

Sabratha (76 km. west of Tripoli) also dates from the fifth century BC, but it adopted the Roman city pattern later than Leptis Magna. The Graeco-Roman

Roman ruins at Sabratha

theatre has been restored; it faces the sea and accommodates 5,000 spectators. There are also small baths and temples. South-west of Tripoli (760 km.) is **Ghadames**, accessible by road or air, and aptly known as the 'pearl of the desert'.

In the Eastern province are the towns of **Beida**, **Derna** and **Tobruk**. Among the ruins in this area are those at **Cyrene** (244 km. east of Benghazi) in a green and beautiful setting. **Cyrene**, which is the only locality where it snows in Libya, was founded in 630 BC by Greek immigrants, and the city and surrounding colony flourished for nearly 1,000 years. An earthquake in AD 364 destroyed much of it, but the Sanctuary of Apollo, the Roman baths, the Greek theatre, the temple of Zeus, the house of Jason Magnus and many Greek tombs cut out of solid rock can still be seen. There is also an early Christian church with interesting mosaic work. Other sites in the region are **Susa Apollonia**, **Tolmeta Ptolemais**, and **Tocra**. There are excellent publications 'on Libya's ruins.

There are hotels in **Beida, Cyrene (Shahat), Ghadames, Homs, Sebha, Tobruk** and **Derns**. For details and information on hotels, consult the Libyan diplomatic mission before travelling to Libya or your hotel in Tripoli or Benghazi.

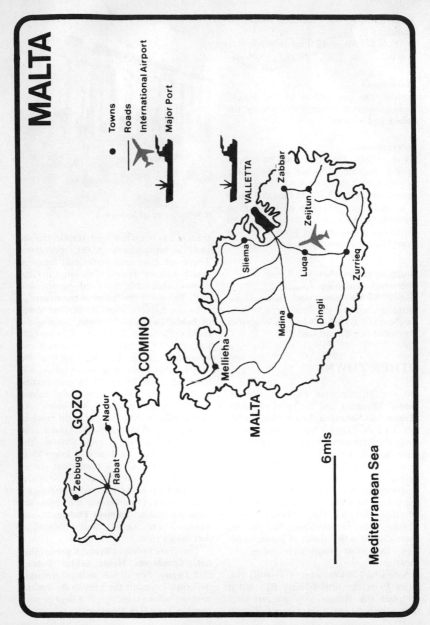

MALTA

Terence Mirabelli

Malta is situated practically in the centre of the Mediterranean Sea, at the convergence of the maritime communications routes between major Mediterranean ports. The republic of Malta is made up of four islands: Malta, with an area of 246 sq. km. is the most heavily populated and the largest. It is 27 km. long by 14.5 km. wide with a maximum height of 244 m. at Dingli Cliffs in the south.

The island, which is predominantly soft globigerina limestone, slopes in a north-easterly direction. Malta is also the most built-up of the islands and is the economic and administrative centre.

The second most important island in the archipelago and about a quarter of the size of Malta is Gozo—14.5 km. long by 6.4 km. wide, covering an area of 67 sq. km. on which a population of 26,000 live. Gozo differs from Malta in that it is lunar in landscape with more hills and valleys, showing off terrace farming at its best. However, agriculturally, culturally and economically Gozo is about five years behind Malta. And although only a 20 minute ferry trip from Malta the island is nevertheless a favourite holiday resort for the Maltese and foreign visitors.

The island of Comino boasts a population of 35 and is only 2.6 sq. km. in area and lies between Malta and Gozo. The islet of Filfla, south of Malta, is just a big uninhabited rock which until recently was used by the British armed forces for bombing practice.

The islands' coasts are predominantly rocky and between them the three major islands sport no more than half a dozen sandy beaches. The Government did consider importing sand from Libya to develop more beaches, but desert sand eroded by wind is soft and fluffy and forms air pockets and is quite unlike sea-eroded, tightly packed beach sand. Desert sand was brought to Malta for testing and was strewn on beaches, but it floated away whenever waves broke.

The Maltese islands are islands of contrast, old and new blend in a way that is complementary to both. It is possibly the only country in the Mediterranean basin where the visitor can see a prehistoric temple and within half an hour wander through a surrealist church.

Besides the dockyard, which stretches across three towns—Vittoriosa, Cospicua and Senglea—tourism is the second largest industry in the republic. In the Government's current seven-year development plan, the industry figures high on its list of priorities.

A new runway was inaugurated in October 1977 to allow five Boeing 707s or McDonnell Douglas DC8s and four B727s to operate simultaneously. A modern terminal complex is being built at Siggiewi to cater for the estimated one million passengers a year.

Coupled with improved travel facilities the hotel industry has also been given all possible assistance by the Government, and the country's hotels and holiday flats cater for all pockets and tastes. Malta's low cost of living, good healthy climate—the islands enjoy freedom from fog, snow, frost and bitter winds with average winter temperatures of 13.7°C and summer temperatures of 22.6°C—hospitable and friendly people and its accessibility make it a favourite as a base of operations with businessmen and companies operating in the Middle East, and for oilmen to come to for a short holiday between stints in the desert—some come from as far afield as Iran and Nigeria.

The Government's boast that Malta is a bridge between Europe and North Africa is not an idle one—although the Maltese themselves disagree. Between AD 870 and AD 1090 Malta was an Arab fiefdom while a thousand years before it had been a Phoenician colony.

HISTORY AND CULTURE

The Levantine and Arab influence still remain in Malta—the language is semitic in origin with approximately 80 per cent of it being Arabic and the remaining 20 per cent romance. The irony is that an Arab can understand a Maltese but not vice versa.

Practically all Maltese speak English while the older generation also speak Italian. Physically the Maltese are akin to the Sicilians while many still have Arabic surnames such as Zahra and Saliba.

However, with the overthrow of the Arabs in AD 1090 by the Norman Count Roger, the predominantly Catholic population of Malta eradicated all traces of Moorish conquest and the sole reminder are some coins in the National Museum.

Notwithstanding their language, the Maltese regard themselves as Europeans and their good relations with the Arab world today are more of a political tactic than an ethnic awakening.

Culturally the islands are a pastiche. Folklore and customs have evolved from the islanders stoical Catholicism, the Arab period and their subsequent occupation by the Order of St John. Most national dances depict manual labour principally farming and fishing—and the struggle against the Arabs and Turks. The fight against the Ottoman Turks is epitomised by the *parata* which is performed publicly every May during a carnival by school children. The *parata* represents the Great Siege of Malta of 1565 by the Turks and their subsequent defeat by the Order of St John.

However, the highlight of traditional life are the village *festas* celebrating a parish's patron saint. The *festas* are normally held the Sunday after the saint's feast day except when the feast falls on a public holiday or on a Sunday. Religious processions are held followed by firework displays—with each parish trying to outdo its neighbour in noise. And with more than 70 *festas* a year, most of which are in summer, Malta can become a very noisy place.

Religious life climaxes on Good Friday with processions in the capital, Valletta, and Mosta. Persons who have made vows can be seen walking barefoot or chained and carrying heavy wooden crosses during the processions. The visitor who naively interprets this pious devotion with theatricism is very much mistaken. The Maltese are zealots when it comes to their faith. Their piety and puritanism is exemplified in plays written by their dramatists.

Since 1971 the Government has been a great promoter of national arts. Most plays staged at the Manoel Theatre—built in 1731 and believed to be the oldest in Europe—were of British and Italian origin. Now more plays in Maltese are being produced, both on stage and television. Also, many painters and sculptors who would otherwise have remained un-

Marsaxlokk, a fishing port on the south coast of Malta

known have come to the attention of the public thanks to the Government's policy of promoting Maltese artists.

Because it is a country which is naturally isolated from both Africa and Europe traditions have died harder than elsewhere. But the easy happy-go-lucky lifestyle of the Maltese is being eroded, Malta is accelerating into the 20th century culturally. The cumbersome, but quaint, national costume has been discarded in favour of simpler garb. The *ghonella* is, or rather was, a black overskirt with the back lifted and pulled over the head as a hood and worn to hide the face and as a head cover in church. The *faldetta*, as the headpiece is known, was wrapped round a board a yard long over the head. The *ghonella* and *faldetta* are occasionally worn by elderly women in Gozo, but hardly ever in Malta.

The *Dghajjsa*, a Maltese version of a gondola, is also disappearing. Until the introduction of the motor car, transport round the Grand Harbour was by *dghajjes*, or water taxi.

Many Maltese accept that today's pace

of life will inevitably mean the disappearance of their traditional values and they are trying to slow-down the pace so that they can acclimatise themselves to modernism on their own terms.

ECONOMY

The principal source of income is the £14 million paid annually for the use of military facilities by British forces. A further £14 million is spent by servicemen and their dependants. However, with the termination of the Military Facilities Agreement (MFA) in March 1979 Malta has had to look elsewhere for its revenue. Attempts to explore for oil offshore have proved fruitless so far.

In its plan to earn enough foreign exchange to pay for massive and growing imports once the MFA expires, the Government insists that these earnings must come from activities in manufacturing, shipbuilding and repairing, tourism and agriculture.

215

To achieve this goal the Government has embarked on wholly-owned or joint venture projects with local firms and foreign corporations and governments.

The prinicipal industries are the dockyard—which is also the largest single employer—tourism and agriculture. With the assistance of Communist China, Malta is constructing a shipbuilding yard and with Arab financial aid it is developing Marsaxlokk bay as a port.

GENERAL INFORMATION

Area: 316 square kilometres (Malta 246, Gozo 67, Comino 2.6).
Population: 320,000
Altitude: 244 metres at Dingli Cliffs in the south of Malta.
Capital: Valletta.
Head of State: President Anton Buttigieg.
Government: Republic within the British Commonwealth. Two-party democracy.
Date of Independence: 21 September 1964. Republic declared on (Friday) 13 December 1974.
Language: Maltese and English.
Religion: Roman Catholic.
Currency: Malta pound. £1 = £M0.760. $1 = £M0.3963.
Time: GMT + 1. GMT + 2 in summer.
Electricity: 240v AC, 50 cycles.

HOW TO GET THERE

By air: Malta is served by its own national carrier, Air Malta. A levy of £M1 is payable by all departing passengers. Transit passengers and infants under two are exempt. Air Malta flies to and from Amsterdam once a week, twice a week from Brussels, once a week from Cairo, twice a week from Frankfurt, 12 times a week from London, once a week from Manchester, twice a week from Paris, six times a week from Tripoli, three times a week from Tunis, once a week from Vienna, once a week from Zurich. Yu-

goslav Airlines, JAT, flies to Malta once a week, British Airways flies to Malta from London 10 times a week and once weekly from Manchester, UTA flies from Nice once weekly, Alitalia flies from Rome twice a week and once from Catania, Libyan Arab Airlines flies twice a week from Tripoli.

By car: Visitors wishing to take their cars to Malta do not require either the Carnet de Passage or the Triptique. A declaration will, however, be required on importation that the vehicle will not be disposed of in Malta unless import duty is paid.

Regarding third party insurance, tourists are advised to extend the validity of their Green Card to include Malta. If they do not do this they can easily take out a policy on arrival in Malta covering their stay on the islands.

By sea: Several shipping companies have regular sailings from the principal European ports. There is a daily ferry service to and from Catania, Messina and Reggio with roll-on roll-off facilities for vehicles.

Visas and health regulations
Holders of European, US, Uruguayan and Libyan passports and Citizens of the Commonwealth do not require visas to enter Malta. For nationals of other American, African and Asian countries a visa is required. Requests for a visa should be addressed to the Maltese diplomatic mission abroad, if there is none in any particular country, the British Embassy represents Maltese interests.

Visitors require a certificate of vaccination only if travelling from an infected area.

Currency and customs regulations
No limits on imports.
Export: Maltese currency notes and or Sterling bank notes up to £M25 per person. Other currencies, including travellers cheques, letters of credit etc, by

residents of countries in the Sterling area up to £M250 per person, by non-Sterling area residents up to £M100 per person or up to the amount already imported and declared to Customs on arrival.

Customs officers may apply a flat rate of 25 per cent on all non-commercial goods, provided the goods value does not exceed £M40. Cigarettes, tobacco and spirits are excluded. Visitors may bring 200 cigarettes or 250 grammes of tobacco, one bottle of spirits and one bottle of wine. Perfumes are permitted in reasonable quantities.

TRANSPORT

All towns and villages are linked to Valletta by a frequent bus service. The various routes are indicated by three colours. Sky blue, light green and red. Destination boards are also found on the front and side of the buses.

Taxis: All taxis in Malta are supposed to have taxi-meters, but these are so seldom used that it is far safer to agree on a price before getting into a taxi.

Karrozini: The karrozini is slowly vanishing and the few that remain are mostly for the benefit of lovers and tourists. Like taxis it is wise to agree on the tariff before boarding.

Dghajjes: These are gaily painted boats that ply the Grand Harbour. It is recommended, here again, to come to an agreement over the price before going afloat.

Car hire: The price for the hire of a car in both Malta and Gozo is very reasonable, usually about £M1.55 to £M3.50 a day. Petrol, on the other hand, is very expensive.

BUSINESS HOURS

0830 to 1245 and 1430 to 1730 Mondays to Friday. 0830 to 1300 Saturday. During summer, that is from 16 June to 30 September, offices are open from 0730 until 1330.

Shops: 0900 to 1300 and from 1530 to 1900 Monday to Saturday.
Banks: 0830 to 1230 Monday to Friday, and from 1700 to 1900 on Friday. 0830 to 1200 Saturday.
Government departments: 0745 to 1230 and 1315 to 1715 Monday to Friday during the winter. And from 0730 to 1330 Monday to Friday in summer.

PUBLIC HOLIDAYS

New Year's Day, Feast of St Paul's Shipwreck 10 February, Feast of St Joseph 19 March, Good Friday, May Day 1 May, Carnival—three afternoons only— not yet announced, Feast of the Ascension 19 May, Feast of Corpus Christi, Mnarja 29 June, Feast of the Assumption on 15 August, Commemoration of the Two Sieges and Regatta Day 8 September, Feast of All Saints 1 November, Feast of the Immaculate Conception 8 December, Republic Day 13 December, Christmas Day 25 December.

TOURIST INFORMATION

Malta Tourist Office, 1 Kingsgate Arcade, Valletta. Branches of the department of information are situated in some local police stations on the island.

ACCOMMODATION AND FOOD

Hotels

Class De Luxe
Corinthia Palace, De Paule Avenue, San Anton, Attard. tel: 40301. Bedrooms 160.
Dragonara, St. Julian's. tel: 36421. Bedrooms 202.

The President's or Royal throne

Grand Hotel Excelsior, Great Siege Road, Floriana. tel: 23661. Bedrooms 150.
Grand Hotel Verdala, Inguanez Street, Rabat. tel: 74901. Bedrooms 164.
Malta Hilton, St. Julian's. tel: 36201. Bedrooms 204.
Phoenicia, The Mall, Floriana. tel: 21211. Bedrooms 114.

Class 1A
Cavalieri, Spinola Bay, St. Julian's. tel: 36255. Bedrooms 89.
Preluna, 124 Tower Road, Sliema. tel: 34001. Bedrooms 200.
Ta' Cenc*, Sannat, Gozo. tel: 76819. Bedrooms 46.

Class 1B
Dolmen, Qawra, St. Paul's Bay. tel: 73661. Bedrooms 121.
Golden Sands, Golden Bay, Ghajn Tuffieha. tel: 73961. Bedrooms 118.
Metropole, Dingli Street, Sliema. tel: 30188. Bedrooms 77.
Ramla Bay, Marfa. tel: 73521. Bedrooms 55.

Salina Bay, Kennedy Drive, Salina Bay. tel: 73781. Bedrooms 100.
Tower Palace, Tower Road, Sliema. tel: 37271. Bedrooms 45.

Class IIA
Capua Court, 60 Victoria Avenue, Sliema. tel: 34081. Bedrooms 69.
Castille, St. Paul's Street, Valletta. tel: 23677. Bedrooms 26.
Comino*, Comino Island. tel: 76171. Bedrooms 98.
Eden Rock, 117 Tower Road, Sliema. tel: 35575. Bedrooms 31.
Hyperion, Qawra, St. Paul's Bay. tel: 73641. Bedrooms 58.
Le Roy, Hughes Hallet Street, Sliema. tel: 36495. Bedrooms 24.
Marina, Tigne Sea Front, Sliema. tel: 36461. Bedrooms 66.
Mellieha Bay, Ghadira, Mellieha Bay. tel: 73841. Bedrooms 214.
Plevna, 2 Thornton Street, Sliema. tel: 31031. Bedrooms 45.
Sliema, 59 The Strand, Sliema. tel: 36314. Bedrooms 50.

St. Julien, Dragonara Road, St. Julian's. tel: 36271. Bedrooms 55.
Tigne Court, Qui-si-sana, Sliema. tel: 32001. Bedrooms 71.
Villa Rosa, St. George's Bay, St. Julian's. tel: 30041. Bedrooms 83.

Class IIB
Crown, 166-167 Tower Road, Sliema. tel: 31094. Bedrooms 36.
Delphina, 72 Dragonara Road, St. Julian's. tel: 33356. Bedrooms 31.
Elba, 52 New Street, Sliema. tel: 36418. Bedrooms 12.
Imperial, Rudolph Street, Sliema. tel: 30011. Bedrooms 77.
Meadowbank, Tower Road, Sliema. tel: 34015. Bedrooms 35.
Mistra Village Aparthotel, Xemxija Hill, St. Paul's Bay. tel: 73295. Bedrooms 10.
Osborne, 50 South Street, Valletta. tel: 23656. Bedrooms 43.
Panorama, Valley Road, New Street, Mellieha. tel: 73511. Bedrooms 21.
Patricia, New Howard Street, Sliema. tel: 36285. Bedrooms 35.
Riviera Martinique, Ghajn Tuffieha. tel: 73426. Bedrooms 15.
Sa Maison, 22 Marina Street, Pieta. tel: 20714. Bedrooms 40.
Xara Palace, 1 St. Paul's Square, Medina. tel: 74001. Bedrooms 19.

Class III
Adelaide, 229 Tower Road, Sliema. tel: 31622. Bedrooms 24.
Astra, 127 Tower Road, Sliema. tel: 31081. Bedrooms 36.
Belmont, Mrabat Street. St. Julian's. tel: 33077. Bedrooms 25.
Cote D'Or*, Golden bay, Ghajn tuffieha. tel: 73961. Bedrooms 22.
Cumberland, 111 St. John's Street, Valletta. tel: 27732. Bedrooms 16.
Duke of Edinburgh, 114 Race Course Street, Victoria Gozo. tel: 76468. Bedrooms 32.
Lion Court, 9 Nursing Sisters Street, St. Julian's. tel: 36251. Bedrooms 11.

Olympic*, Paceville Avenue, St. Julian's. tel: 31766. Bedrooms 18.
Seabank, Mellieha Bay. tel: 73116. Bedrooms 10.
* *Closed in Winter*

Restaurants

An enormous range of foods and types of cooking is to be found in Malta, both the person with simple tastes and the gourmet are well catered for. In Malta you will find restaurants to suit your pocket and satisfy your palate but not your bank account.

Different types of cooking are to be found in the Maltese islands, for example, there are several foreign restaurants as well as some with a full range of local dishes.

Although surrounded by alternatives, traditional Maltese cooking continues to thrive. The best and most popular local specialities are:

timpana—made from a fat and succulent type of macaroni, minced meat, eggs, aubergines, cheese, onions, and tomato purée; *bragoli*—beef olives; *lampuki pie*—a fish pie which is first fried then put with onions, tomatoes, olives, cauliflower, capers and then baked in a case of pastry; *rabbit pie*—is one of the most favourite Maltese dishes; *qaqoċċ mimli*—artichokes stuffed with anchovies, olives, chives, parsley; *qarnita*—a cuttlefish or octopus stew with olives, nuts, raisins, onions, tomato purée and wine; *minestra*—a thick vegetable soup; *ravjul*—a Maltese version of the Italian ravioli; *soppa ta'l-Armla*—(widow's soup) a very unusual dish containing fresh cheese, vegetables, eggs, and herbs. It is very popular during Lent; *Qara baghli mimli*—marrows stuffed with minced meat, tomato purée and dressed with semolina and sliced baked potatoes; *bzarahdar mimli*—stuffed green peppers with anchovies, olives, parsley, and breadcrumbs; *brungiel mimli fil-forn*—aubergines stuffed with minced meat, grated cheese, and eggs and baked; *ross fil-forn*—baked rice with peppers, minced meat, tomato purée, and grated cheese.

Pastizzi are a great favourite, they are either cheesecakes or peacakes. The *gbejna* is a typically Maltese cheese made from sheep's milk; visitors may not like them at first taste, but the flavour 'grows' on you.

VALLETTA

Very few cities, let alone capitals, can be precisely dated. Malta's capital can. The foundation stone was laid at 2 p.m. on 28 March 1566. The plans of Valletta—named after Grand Master Jean de la Valette of the Order of St. John—were drawn by Michelangelo's assistant, Franceso Laparelli, within three days of his arrival in Malta.

Valletta was designed to deny an en-emy the strategic high terrain of Mount Sciberras. Unfortunately for the Order the peninsula's value was realised too late; during the Great Siege of 1565 when the Ottoman Turks invaded Malta and placed their cannons on Mount Sciberras and bombarded at will the Order who were defending the towns of Vittoriosa and Cospicua.

The Auberge de Castille dominates the landward approach to Valletta and is the most ornate building in the city, it is now the Office of the Prime Minister. The other auberges, although less splendid, are a fine example of what later was to become known as traditional Maltese architecture. In fact, most of Valletta's buildings are rather ugly on the outside but once within them they can be ex-tremely beautiful.

The Co-Cathedral of St. John, for example, appears to be a total architec-tural failure when looking at its exterior but its interior is a masterpiece. The

The Auberge de Castille, Valletta

TERENCE MIRABELLI

magisterial palace also gives the same impression but within its large halls and corridors are beautifully decorated and sculpted.

Because Valletta is limited by its topography it gives the appearance of being claustrophobic and in summer the heat can be quite oppressive. It is for these reasons that not many hotels have been built there although the city teems with restaurants.

It is, however, an excellent shopping centre although Sliema can now boast a better quality range.

Valletta is for sightseers only, its lack of hotels and beaches do not make it a visitor's temporary residence.

SLIEMA

While Valletta is the administrative capital of Malta, Sliema is its heart. During summer its corniche is packed by strollers and its beaches full of beautiful bikinied women tanning themselves. Sliema is the St. Tropez of Malta, albeit on a very modest scale.

Sliema is a relatively new and unplanned town, it is also architecturally ugly—a pastiche of traditional design coupled with the cold but functional styles of today. Nevertheless, it is a favourite holiday resort with all amenities.

It is also saturated with hotels of all standards, restaurants to please all tastes and discotheques and night clubs to suit all pockets.

Sliema has grown so rapidly that it now ranks as a city—a Maltese city is roughly the size of a small European town—and it now has two suburbs, St. Julian's and Paceville.

St. Julian's is a pretty residential area looking out over the sea, just beyond it is Paceville the 'in-place'.

Paceville exists for the visitor. Although an unattractive place it does boast Malta's only casino and some of the finest hotels in the Mediterranean. Dotted between hotels are fashionable boutiques, 'with-it' public houses, eating houses and night clubs.

BEACHES AND RESORTS

Islands conjure visions of long, wide, sandy beaches backed by luscious palm trees—not so in Malta. The islands have no trees. The few that there are were planted by the Order of St John over 300 years ago and in recent years by the government in a drive to afforest the islands.

Luxurious sandy beaches are also rare in Malta. There are only eight: Paradise Bay, Ramla Bay, Mellieha Bay, Armier, St. Paul's Bay, St. George's Bay, Ghan Tuffieha and Golden Bay. Most of these are situated in the north of Malta. The other beaches are all rocky but many have small sandy patches.

Gozo has one notable sandy beach, Ramla Bay. Flanking the beach there is a cave in which Ulysses was supposed to have rested during his Odyssey. Xlendy Bay is mostly a rocky beach but has a tiny strip of sand. It is probably the most picturesque beach in the Maltese archipelago.

All the beaches named are easily accessible. In summer buses operate regular services to them from Valletta and Sliema.

Not all beaches, however, have towns or villages nearby. St. Paul's Bay is possibly the most popular and offers the most amenities. There are several night clubs and a host of restaurants but not many hotels. Mellieha is a more attractive town sited atop a hill which affords a magnificent panoramic view of northern Malta and Gozo.

In Gozo Xlendi resembles a Norwegian fjord. Steep banks and deep water that allow luxury cabin cruisers to moor make this resort the most attractive and also the most secluded of Maltese beaches.

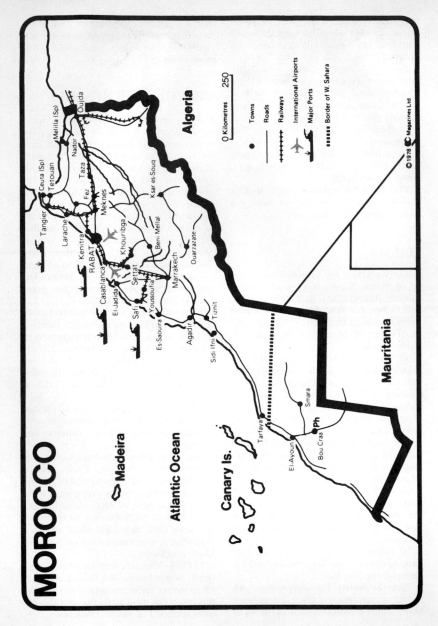

MOROCCO

Madeira

Atlantic Ocean

Canary Is.

Algeria

Mauritania

Tangier
Ceuta (Sp)
Tetouan
Melilla (Sp)
Nador
Oujda
Larache
Fez
Taza
Kentra
Meknes
RABAT
Khouribga
Ksar es-Souq
Casablanca
El-Jadida
Settat
Beni Mellal
Safi
Youssoufia
Marrakech
Ouarzazate
Es Saouira
Agadir
Tiznit
Sidi Ifni
Tarfaya
El-Ayoun
Bou Craa
Smara
Ph

0 Kilometres 250

Towns
Roads
Railways
International Airports
Major Ports
Border of W. Sahara

© 1978 Magazines Ltd

MOROCCO

Serving as a land bridge between Africa and Europe, and between the Maghreb and Black Africa, Morocco has clung to its cultural integrity in the face of numerous onslaughts. It is the strength and persistence of tradition, both Berber and Arab, that makes the country so extraordinarily enticing.

From its mountains sprang Morocco's religious zeal, military finesse and monarchs; the coastal cities and plains added the strengths of commerce, the arts and worldly refinements. The four imperial cities—**Fez**, **Marrakesh**, **Meknes** and **Rabat**—are a fascinating amalgam of ancient buildings with intricate stonework and bustling *souks* where snake-charmers and acrobats amuse the crowds and merchants sell the famous craftwork—carpets, leather, jewellery. Throughout the countryside the *moussem* pilgrimages give occasion for exotic music and dance.

Behind Marrakesh rise the impressive Atlas mountains where winter skiing is becoming popular while others swim off the beaches of Agadir. Farther north the attractive summer resorts draw ever more visitors. Across the mountains to the south lies the forbidding but fascinating Sahara.

Moroccans have an undeserved reputation for pestering and cheating the tourist. Since the majority are peace-loving citizens going about their honest business, there is no reason to be intimidated or angered by the few children and youths who persistently offer their services in the hope of making a few dirhams. You will learn how to handle this minority in your own way. Avoid showing impatience, but any hesitation on your part will be ruthlessly exploited. If you decide to ask someone to help you find your way or to lead you to a particular stall or shop you should be prepared to pay a small tip for the service.

As everywhere else in the world, always carry your money, passport, etc, as securely as possible when walking in a crowd. Girls should avoid travelling or walking unaccompanied. Although English, Spanish and French are widely known, only an Arabic speaker can expect genuine contact with the people of this complex and fascinating country.

THE LAND AND THE PEOPLE

Vivid contrast is the only feature 'typical' of Moroccan landscape: arid desert is set against a backdrop of snow-capped mountains; bare rock neighbours, a gay patchwork of fields, all in a country the size of France on the north-western tip of Africa. The spine of the country is the High Atlas, a range of mountains which seemed to the ancients to be the pillars holding up the sky at the end of their Mediterranean world. Nestling between this barrier and the Atlantic are the fertile plains which nurture Morocco's urban heartland.

The cliffs and beaches of the northern Mediterranean coast, largely inaccessible for lack of roads, greatly resemble the Spanish hills across the water. Their strategic position, especially the ports of Tangier and Ceuta commanding the Straits of Gibraltar, have made them a constant bone of contention and indeed Spain still retains the two enclaves of Ceuta and Melilla. Rising behind the coast are the green, rounded and well-watered Rif mountains.

Separated from the Rif by the Taza Gap, the main corridor into Morocco from the rest of North Africa, the Middle Atlas sweeps up from the south. These mountains rising over 3,000 m. are partly covered with a woodland of pine, holm oak and cedar and partly with open pasture broken up by small lakes.

There are two ski resorts here above Meknes for in winter the Atlas mountains are snow-covered. Beyond, stretching parallel with the coast are the red, sandstone peaks of the High Atlas, towering to Toubkal at 4,165 m. Their north face resembles the Alps but the bare stony slopes of the southern face are a true prelude to the desert.

Living as they do at a historical crossroads, most Moroccans are an inextricable mixture of Berber, Arab, Negro and Spaniard. Although not written, the language of the original Berber inhabitants is still widely spoken in the mountains where they retreated from invaders. The mountain people continue their traditional pastoral life and magnificent craftwork while those on the Saharan side of the mountain have a long history as camel caravaneers across to West Africa.

In the cities the overriding language and culture is Arabic although there is living evidence of the great racial mixing that has gone through the centuries. Moroccan hospitality is legendary and the people generally are grave and laconic but friendly.

CULTURE AND HISTORY

The Muslim religion is almost universal and many factors common to North Africa will be found: cannons signal the hour of sunset during the month of Ramadan; as the feast of Eid el Kebir approaches single sheep for the family sacrifice will be seen tied to lamp-posts; the dispatch and welcoming home of Mecca pilgrims brings out rejoicing friends. The government maintains the mosques—most of which non-believers are forbidden to enter—and the law of the Prophet still determines national issues.

Innumerable brotherhoods, or *zawia*, which share a particular school of learning and special customs, form influential clubs in the cities. Others have spectacular rites, like the wild annual dancing of Aissawa in Meknes. Other occasions for feasting and dancing are the *moussems*, annual pilgrimages to a local *koubba*—a small square white building over the grave of a holy man.

At the festivals dress is an important element: all wear beautiful embroidered cloth and bedeck themselves with impressive silver, gold, iron or copper ornaments set with semi-precious stones. Even the city gentleman in his western suit will often wear a covering *djellaba*. In the countryside normal dress for a man is a *serwal*—trousers loose at the hips tapered to hug the calves—and a shirt. Women the same, often richly embroidered but invisible because the whole is covered by a *kaftan*, a long loose robe, plain or fancy, which buttons down the front.

Music stems from two main streams: the Andalusian style of the court, set to refined Arabic poetry and accompanied by stringed instruments; and the Berber music of the countryside played on flutes, tambourines and percussion, reflecting some influence from infectious Negro rhythms. The National Festival every May in Marrakesh brings together all the music and dance of the various regions: from Rif come exciting warlike dances and the great fantasia spectacle of men charging on horseback waving muskets; the *ahidou* dance of the Middle Atlas and the more Negro-influenced *ahouach* of the High Atlas. From the south come the dances of the desert such as the famous erotic *guedra*, performed at Goulimine, where a woman works herself into an ecstatic trance with sinuous movements of hand and body as her shawls slowly work loose.

Art and craft in Morocco, more rigidly even than in other Muslim countries, follow the religious prohibition against the representation of animals, and the foreigner is immediately struck by the abstract, geometrical quality of all design. Yet, within this limit, the range is immense and the skill of the craftsmen great. Best known are the rugs and tapestries from the High and Middle Atlas mountains and the regions of Marmoucha and Chichaoaua. Buy these in Marrakesh or Rabat if you cannot get to the mountains.

Woven blankets come from Azemmour. Brocades and silks, *djellabas* and *kaftans* are a speciality of Fez. Leatherwork is best in Meknes, including handmade shoes and the floppy open-ended heel-less slippers known as *babouches*. Jewellery comes from Tiznit, Ouarzazate and the south; pottery from Sale, Safi and Fez; muskets, sabres, daggers, copperware, trays, vases from each of the four imperial cities; and marquetry tables and chessmen from Essaouira.

Architecture—at its best in Fez and Marrakesh—glories in intricate mathematical patterns of stone lattice-work in interior courtyards, contrasting with the high exterior walls which provide privacy for all dwellings, great or small. The main public buildings are mosques, dating from the mid-12th century onwards; beautifully decorated *medrassa* (singular: *medersa*), schools or colleges where students gathered in a courtyard at the feet of their teacher; and royal palaces.

Morocco's basically Berber society has at different times come into contact with Carthage, Rome, the ancient kingdoms of the Upper Niger, nearby Spain and Portugal and finally French colonists. But undoubtedly the most lasting influence was the seventh century invasion of Muslim Arabs. This religion, its intellectual inspiration and the periodic reform movements led by zealous desert prophets have determined the changes of custom and dynasty throughout its history.

The Berber people's origin is not definitively known but their language shows strong similarities to Tuareg and ancient Libyan. There were three main Berber groups: the Masmouda, an agricultural, egalitarian people; the Sanhaja, known later as the fearsome 'Veiled Men', camel-riding nomads, traders and conquerors

The Kairouin Mosque, Fez.

PETER FRAENKEL

225

of the desert; and the Zenata, horsemen of the steppe and high plateaux.

From the sixth century BC the Phoenicians and their colony Carthage in Tunisia were establishing trading posts from Melilla to Sala (near Rabat) and in the next century even sailed right down the Atlantic coast, perhaps beyond Senegal. Their great Mediterranean rivals, the Romans, in the last century BC began to extend not only trade with the Berbers but a protectorate over some of their princes and by AD 40 had established direct rule over the province of Mauritania, covering the country as far south as Sala and centred on Volubilis, near Meknes.

Byzantines, Vandals and great confusion followed the fall of Rome until the arrival in AD 683 of Arab conquerors, aflame with the new militant faith of Islam. The bitter pacification took 25 years and many Berbers retired to the mountains for safety, but during the eighth century all became converted to Islam and those in the lowlands accepted much of Arab culture too.

The independent Sanhaja Berbers conducted increasing caravan trade with ancient Ghana (in Senegal and Mali), bringing back gold and some slaves to Sijilmassa (near Erfoud) and Zagora, the great terminals of the most westerly Saharan camel route. The *emir* (ruler) of Sijilmassa, after a pilgrimage to Mecca tried with the aid of the missionary Abdallah ibn-Yasin to impose a stricter, more ascetic form of Islam on his people. Both men were driven out but in the desert they gathered about them a new sect, the Almoravids who, true to Islamic ideals of the *jihad* (holy war), began to spread their reformed faith by the sword. By 1060 their leader Yusuf ibn-Tashfin had taken all of Morocco, founded Marrakesh as his capital, and continued to rule there for 50 years. He conquered as far as Algiers; in 1085 he crossed into Andalusia in Spain and the next year sacked the capital of ancient Ghana.

The association with Andalusia was the most lasting; remaining of vital importance until the fall of the Moorish kingdom of Granada to Christian conquerors in 1492. It was an intellectually fertile association, too, a bridge between Arab and European learning.

The Almoravids were in their turn ousted by followers of a new prophet originating at Tinmel in the Atlas mountains and following the Almohad doctrine. Despite unceasing attacks in Spain and, from Sicily, on their own coast by Christians, the Almohads began building the historic cities which stand today—for example the mosques of Yakub al-Mansour (1184-1199) remain at Seville in Spain, and at Marrakesh.

Moorish ships were gradually losing control of the western Mediterranean to the Christian countries and by the 15th century the Portuguese had even established Atlantic trading posts at Safi, El-Jadida, Essaouira and Agadir and were setting out to bypass Islamic middlemen in Europe's trade both with West Africa and India. At the same time, Granada fell and Moroccan political unity disintegrated.

The Christian presence on the coast touched off another religious revival and led to reunification in the mid-16th century under the Saadi dynasty with their capital once more at Marrakesh. In addition to driving out the Portuguese and attacking Spain, they sent an expedition in 1591 to Songhai, then the great empire on the upper Niger, but in fact destroyed rather than captured the valuable gold trade—from then on the eastern trans-Saharan routes were the more frequented.

Amid continuing threat from Europe, another ascetic reforming movement originated at Sijilmassa in the mid-17th century to bring in the present Alaouite dynasty and a return to international prestige under Moulay Ismail (1672-1727), a tireless, far-sighted statesman, who from his capital at Meknes gathered a huge army of negroes and Europeans as well as Berber. He pacified Morocco, drove out the Portuguese and English interlopers, reduced Spanish possessions to Ceuta and Melilla and kept the Turks at bay in Algeria. He opened up diplomatic relations with many countries including Louis XIV's France and impressed the ambassadors with his magnificent receptions.

By contrast with Egypt, the 18th and 19th centuries brought no move towards modernisation or industry. With the influx of more and more European traders and explorers and the French conquest of Algiers in 1830, traditional Morocco became too important to be left alone but too expensive to be fully conquered, and was caught in the net of late 19th century imperialism. Facing Gibraltar, Tangier became a boisterous international city and centre of intrigue and vice. Spain acquired a protectorate over much of the north at the cost of dealing with determinedly independent Rifian warriors. France took the centre and south, built Casablanca as a modern port and fostered the production of wine and citrus crops for European markets.

The dismemberment of Morocco, the presence of hundreds of thousands of French and Spanish settlers, and the introduction of alien ways spurred a nationalist and a religious revival. It went partly underground during the Second World War as Vichy France clung to control but re-emerged with the 1944 Allied landings. Its focal point became Mohammed V, of the Alaouite dynasty going back several centuries, an effective rallying-point of traditional and modern forces. First exiled by France and then recalled in the face of mounting unrest, he took the country into independence in 1956 in a monarchy uneasily perched above conflicting interests. His death brought to the throne King Hassan II in 1961, then a young man of 31.

As king, Hassan II has struggled to reconcile the many diverse political religious, economic and local forces. His shrewd attempts to play the political game while keeping the monarchy and its extensive powers intact have been only partially successful and he has had to defend himself against the radical Left as well as against the traditional Right. Hassan's monarchy was first seriously challenged from the Left by the late Ben Barka, mysteriously assassinated in Paris in 1965; then in June 1971 he survived a palace revolt and in 1972 an abortive coup led by army officers.

Hassan's standing as national leader received a boost with the annexation of part of the Western Sahara in 1976, after negotiations with Spain, which formerly controlled that territory. But Morocco is having to fight hard against a determined struggle by the Polisario guerrillas in the Sahara. The conflict between Morocco and Algeria has intensified over the issue.

ECONOMY

Morocco has much fertile soil, a varied climate and in the mountains considerable mineral resources, some tapped for centuries, like copper and iron; more important now are phosphates. Yet standards of living vary greatly, by social class and region.

Export crops in colonial times were almost entirely grown by settlers but, although some remain, many of the large estates have been either taken over or broken up and redistributed to Moroccans. None the less most of the land consists of small subsistence holdings. The main crops are wheat, barley, maize, citrus fruits, for export, vegetables and olives.

In its efforts to industrialise, Morocco is almost self-sufficient in textiles, cans much of its own fruit, and has factories for car assembly, soap, cement, etc. Minerals account for 40% of exports and most of these are phosphates of which the country has the largest deposits in the world. If Morocco succeeds in keeping the Western Sahara there are similarly vast reserves of phosphates there too.

Receipts from tourism help to produce a favourable balance of payments. Also of use are remittances from the many Moroccans who work in Europe.

GENERAL INFORMATION

Area: 400,000 sq km.
Population: 17 million.
Altitude: Sea level to 4,000 m. (High Atlas Mts.).
Capital: Rabat.
Head of State: King Hassan II.
Government: Monarchy. The Chamber of Representatives consists of 90 members elected by direct suffrage, 60 members chosen by electoral colleges representing chambers of Commerce and Industry and professional groups, and 90 others elected by urban and rural councils. Opposition parties have boycotted recent elections.
Languages: The Moroccan dialect of Arabic, French and Spanish widely used in the towns.
Religion: Islam. There are Christian and Jewish minorities.
Currency: The Moroccan dirham (H), divided into 100 centimes. £1 = 8.10 dirham; US$1 = 4.351 dirham.
Time: GMT.

HOW TO GET THERE

By air: There are international airports at Tangier, Rabat, Casablanca, Fez, Marrakesh and Agadir, all linked by direct flights with European cities. Royal Air Maroc flies from Brussels, Geneva, Frankfurt, New York, Montreal, Lisbon, Cairo, London, Madrid, Marseille, Milan and Paris as well as from Algiers, Dakar, Las Palmas and Tunis.

British Airways and British Caledonian operate regular flights from London, Ali-
talia from Rome, Air France from Paris, Sabena from Brussels, Iberia from Madrid, Pan American from New York (via Lisbon). Other international airlines serving Morocco: Air Afrique, Aeroflot, Balkan, CSA, Gibraltar Airways, Ghana Airways, Air Mali, Tunis Air.

Tangier-Boukhalf airport is 12 km. from the town; there are buses to and from the air terminal. Casablanca-Nouasseur airport is the external flight airport for that city and is connected by bus to Casablanca-Anfa, the airport for internal flights.

By road: Morocco is most often approached from Spain and France. It is perfectly feasible to drive along the coast of Spain, take the ferry at Algeciras, Malaga or Gibraltar, visit Morocco and then return to Europe by an alternate route. The ferry services mentioned below carry cars. There is also access from Algeria (at Oujda). Motorists need international or Moroccan motor insurance, an international driving licence and log book, plus yellow headlamps for night driving within the country.

Visitors entering from Gibraltar can hire a car there for use in Morocco; this works out cheaper than hiring a car in Tangier, Rabat, etc. (For details on car hire companies in Morocco see the section on *Transport*.) Coming in by road or rail (see below) means taking the daily two-hour ferry connecting Algeciras, Gibraltar, and Malaga to Tangier.

By sea: There are daily passenger and car ferries from Gibraltar, Algeciras and Malaga to Tangier and Ceuta, operated by Bland Line, Transmediterranea and Limadet.

Southern Ferries sail about once a fortnight from Southampton to Tangier (via Lisbon). Other companies sail from Marseille to Tangier and Casablanca.

By rail: One of the most leisurely ways to visit Morocco is by train. There is a direct connection from Paris, via Bordeaux, Madrid, Algeciras and ferry to Tangier, continuing on to Casablanca. There are regular services from Oran in Algeria to Fez, Meknes, Rabat and Casablanca.

Visas and health regulations

A valid passport is necessary for entry to Morocco; visas are not required by citizens of the following countries: UK, US, Australia, Austria, Belgium, Canada, Denmark, Finland, France, West Germany, Greece, Iceland, Ireland, Italy, Luxembourg, Netherlands, New Zealand, Norway, Spain, Sweden, Switzerland, Algeria, Argentina, Bahrain, Brazil, Chile, Egypt, Ghana, Guinea, Indonesia, Iran, Iraq, Ivory Coast, Japan, Jordan, Kuwait, Lebanon, Liberia, Libya, Madagascar, Mali, Mexico, Monaco, Nigeria, Oman, Peru, Philippines, Puerto Rico, Qatar, Saudi Arabia, Senegal, Syria, Tunisia, Venezuela, Yemen and Yugoslavia.

Visitors from all these countries can stay in Morocco for up to three months; should they require an extension of stay they must register with the police. Citizens of other countries who arrive without the necessary visa can obtain a permit for 72 hours' stay provided they hold a ticket for the continuation of their journey.

International certificates of vaccination against smallpox, cholera and yellow fever are only required for visitors arriving from infected areas. Smallpox and typhoid vaccination is, however, recommended for all visitors.

Currency and customs regulations

There is no restriction on the amount of foreign currency brought into Morocco. Officially a declaration of unused foreign currency should be made before departure, though the regulation is rarely observed.

It is illegal to take Moroccan currency into or out of Morocco (foreign exchange controls exist at all customs points), but it is difficult to re-exchange Dirhams for foreign currency, so it is advisable to change only small amounts of foreign currency at a time.

Visitors may take in, free of duty, 200 cigarettes, 50 cigars or 400 gms. of tobacco, and one bottle of wine or spirits, as well as personal effects (camera, tape recorder, typewriter, camping equipment, etc.)—usually limited to one of each item per person. Firearms and ammunition may be imported subject to a licence issued by the Police Department in Rabat.

CLIMATE

Morocco experiences all four seasons but to a different degree in each part of the country. Winter in Tangiers and the north is damp, rainy and chilly, but pleasant with temperatures around 22°C in Agadir, while there is snow and skiing in the High Atlas. Spring is the best time for Marrakesh when its flowers and fruits blossom, summer for Rabat and the Atlantic Coast, when temperatures soar around 38°C in the south. The autumn, particularly September and October, brings temperate climates and light rains to much of the country.

What to wear

In the summer lightweight clothes are essential. At other times of the year (and all the year round in the mountains) some warmer clothes are necessary, especially for the cool evenings. Take good walking shoes or desert boots for the mountains and trips south. Morocco remains a highly traditional, conservative and religious country. Mini-skirts and similar attire are inappropriate outside beach areas.

Few hotels require formal dress for evening meals, although one suit or cocktail dress is a good idea if you plan to attend major social events. Sunglasses, lotions, and some sort of hat or sombrero are useful in the south.

Health precautions
Private medical practitioners and good public hospitals are available in Casablanca; fair to middling elsewhere. The tap water is drinkable in the cities, but bottled mineral waters, the excellent local wines and bottled beers are widely available.

ACCOMMODATION AND FOOD

Morocco has a wide range of hotels, from luxury (five star) to the very cheap. The Government rigorously grades hotels and has fixed maximum prices for those with four stars or less. The free *Hotel Guide* is available from the National Tourist Office in London, New York, Paris or local tourist offices in each city.

Reservations are not a problem at any time of the year, except at the more luxury hotels. While there are price-savings in booking full board (*pension complete*), this means missing some fine restaurants in the cities, and demi-pension may be preferred, allowing one meal besides breakfast inside the hotel.

There are also holiday villages (at Agadir, Al Hoceima, Asilah, Cabo Negro, Marrakesh, M'Dio, Ouarzazate, Restinga-Smir, Sidi Harazem, Fez, and Tangier), youth hostels (at Asni, Azrou, Casablanca, Ifrane, Marrakesh, Meknes, Rabat and Tangier) and camping and caravan sites (at Agadir, Al Hoceima, Azemour, Asilah, Arbaoua, Casablanca, Daiet er Roumi, El Jadida, El Ksiba, Essaouira, Fez, Imouzzer du Kandar, Goulmima, Goulimine, Guercif, Ifrane, Kenitra, Marrakesh, Meknes, Mohammedia, Oujda, Rabat, Ras el Ma, Restinga-Smir, Safi, Tangier, Taza and Tetouan).

Morocco means good food. Its national cuisine is superb especially when eating in restaurants with traditional decor. The national dish is *couscous*, a combination of boiled chicken or lamb with semolina and vegetables. Other national favourites include *mechoui*, roasted lamb, *pastilla*, a flaky pigeon pie, and various sorts of *tajine* stews with a lamb or poultry base. Moroccan red wine is strong and can be excellent and cheap but green mint tea is the distinctive national drink.

Good restaurants are to be found everywhere—not only in the leading hotels but also tucked away in the side streets and bustling alleys of the *medinas*, the traditional walled cities. In the cities there are numerous restaurants serving French, Italian or Spanish dishes. Meals vary in price from the very cheap to the expensive.

TRANSPORT

By air: Internal services connect Casablanca, Rabat, Fez, Tangier, Tetouan, Oujda, Al Hoceima, Marrakesh and Agadir.

By rail: The railway is slightly less expensive than a bus, a bit slower, and a very good bargain. Best bet is the daily train service from Casablanca to Tangiers, leaving at 0800, and arriving at 1400 to connect with the car ferry to Spain. There are also daily rail services from Casablanca to Marrakesh, Rabat, Fez, Meknes, and onwards to Oujda and the Algerian border. Seats must be reserved on first and second-class carriages.

By road: The road system is one of the best in Africa, linking all the main towns. The surface is good but care must be taken in the mountains. The tracks in the south should not be attempted without proper desert travel precautions.

Near the bus depots collection taxis shuttle between the cities whenever there is a car-load. They are faster and slightly more expensive than bus or train; also more dangerous. Metered taxis within

Market day in Morocco's Atlantic village of Asilah.

the city are of two kinds: *petit* taxis are usually painted red and offer the cheapest service but do not carry baggage as do the larger and more expensive taxis.

Hitch-hiking is also good, although you may wish to carry a national flag or sticker so that drivers will know that you are a visitor. The *Compagnie des Transport Marocains* (CTM) is a real bargain with regular and rapid bus services to all parts of the country. Fares and schedules are available from CTM bus depots in Casablanca, Rabat and elsewhere.

Car hire: Avis, BEA, Car Hire Centre International, Hertz and Lane's in London will arrange for cars to be delivered in Gibraltar or Tangier.

The following companies have offices in Tangier, Casablanca or other main towns: Bland, Cartours, Intercars, Marloc, Maroc Union Location, Locoto, Otoloc, Promaroc, Scal (Avis) and Starc (Hertz).

BANKS

Banque Marocaine du Commerce Exterieur, 241 Boulevard Mohammed V, Casablanca.

British Bank of the Middle East, 80 Ave Lalla Tacout, Casablanca, and 18 Bd. Mohammed V. Tangier.

Arab Bank Limited, 174 Bd. Mohammed V. Casablanca.

Business hours

Sunday is the weekly holiday.

Government Departments: Winter: 0830 to 1200 and 1430 to 1800 Monday to Friday, 0800 to 1300 Saturday; Summer: 0830 to 1200 and 1600 to 1900 Monday to Friday, 0800 to 1300 Saturday.

Businesses and Shops: Tangier: 1900 to 1200 and 1600 to 2000; Rest of Country: 0900 to 1200 and 1500 to 1800.

Banks: Winter: 0815 to 1130 and 1415 to 1630 Monday to Friday; Summer: 0830 to 1130 and 1500 to 1700 Monday to Friday.

PUBLIC HOLIDAYS

Eid al Fitr, 3-6 September.
Eid al Adha, 10-13 November.
Muslim New Year, 2 December.
Labour Day, 1 May.
Anniversary of the Green March, 6 November.
Independence Day, 18 November.
Fête du Trône, 3 March.

There are local festivals or *moussems* throughout the year in different parts of Morocco, generally varying according to the Muslim calendar. A major annual event is the National Folklore Festival in Marrakesh in May.

EMBASSIES IN RABAT

Austria: 2 Rue de Tedders.
Belgium: 6 Avenue de Marrakesh.
Denmark: 5 Avenue de Marrakesh.
Egypt: 31 Zankat El Jazair.
France: Avenue Mohammed V.
Federal Republic of Germany: 7 Rue Mohammed El Fatih.
Greece: 9 Rue de Kairouan.
Iraq: 6 Avenue de la Victoire.
Italy: 2 Rue de Secou.
Jordan: 21 Avenue de France, Aqdal.
Kuwait: 44 Avenue Pasteur.
Lebanon: 5 Rue de Tedders.
Libya: 1 Rue Lavoisier.
Netherlands: 38 Rue du Tunis.
Norway: 20 Avenue As-Saouira.
Portugal: 45 Rue Maurice Pascouet.
Spain: 3 Rue Mohammed al Fatih.
Syria: 27 Rue d'Oqbah, Agdal.
Tunisia: 6 Avenue de Fez.
UK: 28 Avenue Allal Bin Abdallah.
USA: Avenue de Marrakesh.

TOURIST INFORMATION

National offices of Tourism:
Rabat: 22 Avenue d'Alger. tel: 21252.
Agadir: Av. du Prince Heritier Sidi Mohammed. Tel: 2894.

Casablanca: Place des Nations-Unies. tel: 20909.
Fez: Boulevard Hassan II. tel: 23460.
Marrakesh: Place Abdelmoumen Ben Ali. tel: 30258.
Meknes: Place de la Grande Poste. tel: 30508.
Tangier: 29 Boulevard Pasteur. tel: 38239.

TANGIER

As Africa's closest port to Europe, Tangier has always been an outpost of both continents. Yet as well as being a distinctly international city with numerous banks and a famous casino, it remains essentially Moroccan with its *souks*, mosques and ruins.

Old Tangier, overlooking the port, is the most interesting part of the town. It adjoins the Gran Socco—the focal point and market place—near which run the main streets and shopping centres of Rue de Belgique, Boulevard Pasteur and Boulevard Mohammed V. In the old town stands the Great Mosque built by Moulay Ismail in the late 17th century. The *Kasbah*, previously the administrative quarter and royal palace, contains fine buildings and the Museums of Moroccan Art and Antiquities, which are worth a visit.

The beaches just to the east of the city are very popular. The climate in Tangier is both healthy and warm. 11 km. to the east is Cape Malabata, with a lighthouse and excellent views of the bays and straits. 11 km. to the west is Cape Spartel with a lighthouse and beaches nearby.

Hotels
Five Star
Hotel les Almohades, Ave. de l'Armee. tel: 360.25-28.
Hotel el Minzah, 85 Rue de la Liberte. tel: 158.85.

Hotel Intercontinental, Parc Brooks, Blvd. de Paris. tel: 360.53.
Hotel Rif, Ave. d'Espagne. tel: 359.10.

Four Star
Hotel Chellah, 47-49 Rue Jeanne d'Arc. tel: 363.88.
Grand Hotel villa de France, 143 Rue de Hollande. tel: 31475.
Hotel Rembrandt, Blvd. Mohammed V. tel: 387.71.

Three Star
Hotel Miramar, 168 Avenue des Far. tel: 302.34.
The Residence Aloucia, Hotel Olid and Hotel Becerra are modest, inexpensive and centrally situated.

Restaurants and nightlife
Tangier offers tremendous variety in its eating places. There is the best in cooking from all over the world: French, Spanish, Italian and Russian as well as excellent Moroccan.

A Moroccan restaurant which seduces the newcomer with its food, wine, excellent music and daring dancers is the Mamounia Palace in the Kasbah. One of the few remaining night clubs is the el Piano, which boasts a fire-eating magician and snake charmers. Many of the best known night-spots have closed down in recent years in the face of competition from the all-in package tour hotels.

EXCURSIONS IN THE NORTH

Tangier is an excellent departure point. Good roads and cheap buses lead 99 km. to the Spanish enclave and duty-free town of Ceuta, known to the Moroccans as Sebta, where from Mount Hacho there is a spectacular view of the Straits of Gibraltar. The former Spanish Moroccan capital of Tetouan is 59 km. from Tangier with a fine *medina* and an exciting, visitable School of Arts and Folklore where 300 students learn weaving, leather and woodwork, sculpture and tapestry design.

60 km. south of Tetouan is the mountain town of Chaouen, home of the proud

Charming Rif mountain village of Chaouen in Morocco.

CHRISTINE OSBORNE

Rif people, and known for its mineral water springs, rug factory, and its good **Hotel de Chaouen**.

The region east of Tangier, from the Mediterranean coast to the Rif mountains, is the least developed for tourism. Lacking major beaches, it offers instead a number of interesting hamlets.

Lixus (82 km. from Tangier), an ancient place with mysterious megalithic, Phoenician and Roman ruins, lies on a hillside just north of **Larache** (87 km. from Tangier), a Spanish-style fishing port with 17th century Stork Castle. Hotels: **Hotel Hesperis** (Four Star). **Hotel Espana** (One Star).

FEZ

Although no longer Morocco's capital, this city is the country's dominant cultural and spiritual centre. Set in a hollow between mountain ranges, it has the oldest university in the world and more reminders of its past glories than any other Moroccan city—ancient mosques, palaces, colleges, gateways and shrines—while it remains busy, bustling and colourful.

The most famous mosques and *medrassa* (colleges) are in Fez el Bali—the old city. The El Kairouyyin Mosque is the largest in Morocco, having been enlarged and added to since its foundation. It contains some very beautiful craftsmanship.

In this district, too, are various markets specializing in different trades—groceries, spices, tanning, pottery and weaving. The entire *medina*, with its teeming population and medieval atmosphere, is the largest in Morocco and one can get easily lost—it is advisable to hire a guide.

In Fez El Jedid is the remarkable Dar El Makhzen, the Sultans' Palace, which covers about 200 acres, a vast and beautiful structure without parallel in Africa. Also to be seen are the gateways Bab Es Siba, and Bab Segma. There are some

fine mosques including the el Azhar Mosque and the Fez El Jedid Mosque.

Among the local festivals are the students' *Moussem* of Sidi Ben Ali Harazem in July and the *Moussem* of Sidi Ali Ben Ghalib in October.

Hotels
Five Star
Palais Jamai, by the medina, formerly a palace. tel: 343.31.
Hotel des Merinides, Route Fez Nord. tel: 345.56.
Hotel Holiday Inn, Ave. des Far. tel: 230.06.

Four Star
Hotel Ramada, Ave. Allal Ben Abdellah. tel: 230.97.
Hotel Zalagh, rue Mohammed Diouri. tel: 255.02.

Three Star
Grand Hotel, Blvd. Chefchaouni. tel: 255.11.

Two Star
Hotel de la Paix, 44 Ave. Hassan II. tel: 250.72.
Hotel Tanger Fez, Place de la Gare. tel: 224.36.

Restaurants
The **Palais de Fez** is well known and specializes in Moroccan dishes. It is in the *medina* near the Kairouyyin Mosque and has also a boutique of Moroccan arts and crafts. It would be wise to book a table in advance (tel: 347.07).Less expensive is the **Dar Saada**, also in the *medina*. For the budget-conscious, the **Bouayoud** near the Bab Boujeloud serves good food at reasonable rates. A great variety of restaurants will be found along the Blvd. Mohammed V catering for all tastes at reasonable prices.

Shopping
Brocades and silks, *djellabas* and *kaftans* are a speciality of Fez markets. The

Tourists enjoy a traditional Moroccan lunch in the Palais Mnebhi Restaurant in Fez.

CHRISTINE OSBORNE

National Leather and Textile Institute is an excellent place to buy wallets, handbags, bookbindings and engraved cushions known as *pouffes*. Apart from the *medina*, where one should bargain for everything, there are very good carpets at the **Maison Moulay Rachid**. There is a permanent exhibition of arts and crafts at the **Palais de Fez** restaurant.

MEKNES

Once the imperial ciy of the 17th-century Alaouite dynasty, Meknes is still a rich market town, with some very impressive buildings and ruins.

Founded by the Meknassa, a Berber people, in the 11th century, many of the buildings date from the 13th and 14th centuries. The Alaouite Sultan Moulay Ismail made Meknes his capital in the 17th century and constructed the vast Dar el Kebira palace complex now known as the Ville Imperiale, and often compared with Louis XIV's Versailles. It was damaged by an earthquake in 1755.

Commercial life nowadays takes place in the new city. The old city is divided into the *medina* and the Dar El Kebira complex which should be entered by the large and impressive Bab Mansour gate. Once inside there are numerous ruins to wonder at: the *Roua*, or stables, which used to house 12,000 horses; the Kouba El Khiyatine, where foreign ambassadors were received; the *Heri* (granaries); the Jardins d'Assai; the reservoir which irrigated the palace gardens; and the Mausoleum of Moulay Ismail.

From Meknes it is only about 30 km. to the famous Roman ruins at **Volubilis**. The walls date from the second century AD, but many of the other buildings are older. There are numerous oil mills (which indicate that the surrounding area was once covered with olive plantations) a bakery, a forum, a triumphal arch, impressive colonnades and mosaics.

Hotels
Five Star
Hotel Transatlantique, rue Berthelot. tel: 200.02.

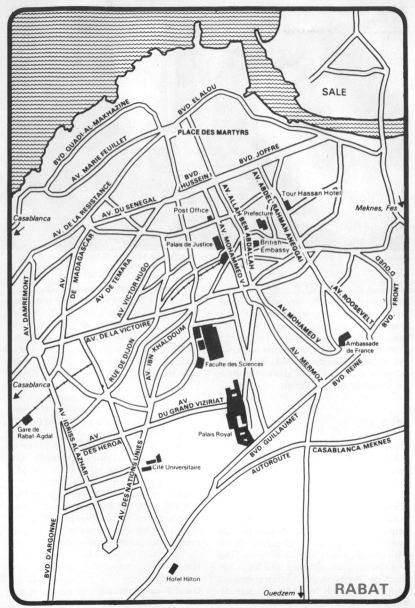

SALE

Casablanca

BVD. QUADI-AL-MAKHAZINE

AV. MARIE FEUILLET

BVD. EL ALOU

PLACE DES MARTYRS

BVD. HUSSEIN I

BVD. JOFFRE

AV. DE LA RESISTANCE

AV. DU SENEGAL

Post Office

Tour Hassan Hotel

Meknes, Fes

AV. ALLAH BEN ABDALLAH

AV. ABDEL. RAHMAN ANEGGAI

Prefecture

Palais de Justice

British Embassy

AV. MOHAMMED V

AV. DE MADAGASCAR

AV. DE TEMARA

AV. VICTOR HUGO

AV. DAMREMONT

BVD. D'OUED

AV. ROOSEVELT

BVD. FRONT

AV. DE LA VICTOIRE

RUE DE DIJON

AV. IBN KHALDOUM

AV. MOHAMED V

AV. MERMOZ

Faculté des Sciences

Ambassade de France

BVD. REINE

Casablanca

AV.
DU GRAND VIZIRIAT

AV. IDRISS AL AZHAR

AV. DES HEROA

Gare de Rabat-Agdal

Palais Royal

BVD GUILLAUMET

CASABLANCA-MEKNES

AUTOROUTE

AV. DES NATIONS UNIES

Cité Universitaire

BVD. D'ARGONNE

Hotel Hilton

Ouedzem

RABAT

Copyright Graham and Trotman Ltd.

Four Star
Hotel Dar Essaada, Mekens Plaisance. tel: 208.37.

Three Star
Hotel Palace, 11 rue du Ghana. tel: 223.88.
Hotel de Nice, Zankat Accra. tel: 203.18.

Restaurants
Hacienda, Fez Road. tel: 21092.
Gambrinus, Zenkat Omar ibn Ass. tel: 20258.
Roi de la Biere, Ave. Mohammad V. tel: 21421.

Nightclubs
Cabaret Oriental, Avenue des FAR
Roi de la Biere, Ave. Mohammed V. tel: 21421.

RABAT

Although Rabat has over a thousand years of history, it has been a major city only since the beginning of this century when the French made it the administrative capital, replacing Fez. It stands on the southern bank of the Bou Regreg river mouth and commands a fine position overlooking the Atlantic.

Connected by a road bridge, the sister-city of **Sale** faces Rabat across the river mouth. Although differing in history and appearance they complement each other well; Rabat—predominantly modern, spacious and sprawling; Sale—traditional, compact and retaining its historical atmosphere.

The Museum of Moroccan Arts is housed in the Oudaia Kasbah; the Museum of Antiquities contains fine Roman bronzes from Volubilis; the ruined mosque at Chellah, to the east of the city, contains ancient tombs, beautifully engraved in Arabic script, and surrounded by a peaceful relaxing garden. When the King is in residence at the Rabat Royal Palace, on certan Friday mornings there is an impressive ceremony accompanying his visit to the mosque for prayers—a display of tradition by a Head of State that is without equivalent elsewhere.

Hotels
Five Star
Hotel Rabat-Hilton, Aviation-Souissi. tel: 72151.
Hotel de la Tour Hassan, 26 Rue Abderrahman Annega. tel: 214.01.

Four Star
Hotel Balima, Ave. Mohammed V. tel: 216.71.

Three Star
Hotel Royal, Ave. Hadj Mohammed Torres. tel: 211.71.

Restaurants
The large hotels serve good Moroccan and European food. Other restaurants are:
L'Oasis, 7 Rue al Osqofia. tel: 22185.
Diffa Room, Hotel Tour Hassan. tel: 21401.
Kabbaj Palace, Ave. Temara. tel: 34241.
Le Corral, 55 Rue Patrice Lumumba. tel: 81320.

Nightclubs
Aquarium, Bd. Mohammed V.
El Farah, Tour Hassan Hotel. tel: 21401.
Hilton Hotel Night Club. tel: 72243.
La Cage, Place Bremond. tel: 21334.

CASABLANCA

Casablanca (pop. 1.5 million) is the principal port and commercial and industrial centre. Its downtown broad boulevards and office-buildings have a totally European quality. Its small *medina* and numerous curio shops have higher prices but more choice than those elsewhere.

The Government-operated Maison de l'Artisanat, across from the Hotel Marhaba, has fixed prices, guarantees of quality, and will ship goods home.

The outskirts of the city are ringed by massive *bidonvilles*, shanty towns of new urban-dewellers eking out a precarious existence. Their children in rags seek out tourists.

It is a place for doing business, arranging your trip, and enjoying fine food. The coast road, reached by public bus, has several good but crowded beaches, and excellent seafood restaurants. Most of the nightlife and outdoor sports are also found along the corniche, including discotheques catering primarily for tourists.

Hotels
Five Star
Europamaroc, Place Mohammed V. tel: 222.57.
Hotel El Mansour, 27 Ave. des FAR. tel: 265.11.
Hotel Holiday Inn, Place Mohammed V.

Four Star
Hotel Marhaba, 63 Ave. des FAR. tel: 667.31/2/3/4/5/6.
Hotel Anfa Plage, Blvd. de la Corniche. tel: 582.42.
Hotel Transatlantique, 79 Rue Colbert. tel: 60761/2/3.

Three Star
Hotel Bellerive, Blvd. de la Corniche. tel: 583.83.
Hotel Washington, Blvd. Rahal El Meskini. tel: 697.77/8.
Hotel Majestic, 57 Ave. Lalla Yacout. tel: 609.51/2/3.
Hotel Excelsior, Place Mohammed V. tel: 622.81/2.
Hotel Windsor, 93 Place Oued El Makhazine. tel: 788.74.

Two Star
Hotel Suisse, Blvd. de la Corniche. tel: 581.19.

Restaurants
The larger hotels have good restaurants with Moroccan and European food and along the coast road there are a number of excellent seafood restaurants: **La Mer**, **Petit Rocher**, **Le Cabestan**, **A Ma Bretagne** and **Le Clapotis**. For Moroccan specialities try **Al Mounia** which is considered one of the best albeit expensive. A restaurant with a sumptuous oriental setting the **Sijilmassa**, specialises in Moroccan cuisine. Also recommended is the **Rissano** in Rue Poggi.
Al Mounia, Ave. Prince Moulay Abdallah. tel: 22686.
L'etoile Marocaine, 107 Rue Allal Ben Abdallah. tel: 27881.
Topkapi, Blvd. de la Corniche. tel: 5851.
Balcon 33, Ain Diab. tel: 58355

Nightclubs
The Rissani, Rue Poggi. tel: 79332.
The Sijilmassa, Ain Diab. tel: 58233.

COASTAL RESORTS

The area around Rabat and Casablanca has the most popular resorts, the best known being **Mohammedia**. North of here the water is colder while the beaches in the south around Agadir are perfect even in winter. Between Agadir and Casablanca are long deserted sandy beaches, but ocean currents are strong.

Kenitra is an important port founded by the French in 1913; the most interesting spot is 11km south of the town at Casbah de Mehdiya. Hotels: **Hotel Mamora**, three star, **Hotel Embassy**, three star, **Hotel Europe**, three star, **Hotel Rotonde**, two star, **Hotel Astor**, two star.

Skhirat Plage (27 km. from Rabat) is a popular seaside resort and the site of a magnificent royal palace. Its luxury hotel is the **Amphitrite**.

Mohammedia is the main seaside resort for both Rabat and Casablanca. It boasts of two luxury hotels (**Miramar** and **Samir**) a casino, 18-hole golf course and yachting.

El Jadida has Portuguese fortifications. Hotels: **Hotel Marhaba**, four star, **Hotel de Provence**, one star.

An exceptionally good tiny resort is **Oualidia**, with a lagoon providing safe bathing, underwater goggling, and two excellent inexpensive hotels, the **Hippocampe** and **La Lagune**.

Safi is a fishing port and up-and-coming industrial town, but it retains a traditional beauty with its medina, ancient Portuguese fortress and palace and potters' workshops. Hotel: **Hotel les Mimosas**, three star.

Essaouira is becoming very popular as a resort, for its beautiful beach and charming, almost Mediterranean appearance. It is an ancient port dating back to pre-Roman times. The fish market has a constant and fresh supply, particularly of sardines. Hotels: **Hotel des Iles**, four star, **Hotel du Mechonar**, two star, **Hotel du Tourisme**, one star.

The **Chalet de la Plage** restaurant serves excellent seafood.

AGADIR

The approach from Essaouira to the southern resort of Agadir is spectacular with mountains on the left and the sea on the right. The long bay is bordered by beaches of fine white sand where it is possible to bathe in December because of the exceptionally good weather. Because of similar climates the vegetation here is like that of the Canary Islands.

The city's beautiful surroundings belie a tragic reality: Agadir was destroyed by an earthquake in 1960 in which 15,000 people died. The town has now been rebuilt, a modern and well-planned resort with a perfect climate for holidaymakers throughout the year.

Hotels
Five Star
Hotel Marhaba, Ave. Hassan II. tel: 26.70.

Four Star
Hotel Atlas, Blvd. Mohammed V. tel: 32.32.
Hotel El Oumnia, B.P. 316 Agadir. tel: 33.51/2.
Hotel Mabrouk, B.P. 338 Agadir. tel: 26.06, 26.29.

Three Star
Hotel Kamal, Ave. du Prince Heritier Sidi Mohammed. tel: 28.17.
Hotel Salam, Blvd. Mohammed V. tel: 28.21, 21.20.

One Star
Petite Suède, Ave. Hassan II. tel: 28.79.

Restaurants
La Pampa, Ave. Prince Sidi Mohammed. tel: 2831.
La Miramar, Blvd. Mohammed V. tel: 2673.
Le Kasbah de Tafraout, Ave. de Far. tel: 3895.
Le Cactus, 5 Ave. Prince Moulay Abdallah.

EXCURSIONS IN THE SOUTH

Travelling due south of Agadir one reaches the towns of Tiznit, Goulimine, Sidi Ifni and Tan Tan. Inland is Tafraoute set in the midst of the Anti-Atlas mountains, the last range before the barren wastes of the Sahara. It is unwise to venture anywhere near the disputed Western Sahara until the war there comes to an end.

Tan Tan is the limit of the tarred road and of the bus route.

Tafraoute is a verdant jewel set in a rough and rocky waste. The buildings stand pink in contrast to the green palms and other fruit-bearing trees. It has a three star hotel, the **Grand Hotel du Sud**.

On the road from Agadir to Marrakesh is **Taroudant**, an old walled town in the Sous valley with the High and Anti-Atlas

ranges rising to north and south.
Hotels: Gazelle d'Or, five star, **Hotel
Salam**, four star, **Hotel Taroudant**, two
star.

MARRAKESH

Once the capital of Morocco, which derives its name from this fabled city,
Marrakesh still pulsates with energy. It is
a meeting place of Berber, Arab and
African, and the Djemaa El Fna square
still provides daily evidence of these three
cultures with its endless entertainment by
snake-charmers, story-tellers, acrobats,
fire-eaters and musicians amid the general hubbub.

Situated at the foot of the High Atlas
range, Marrakesh is a city, encampment
and oasis all in one. In this beautiful
setting some major dramas in Moroccan
history have been acted out. It was
founded in the 11th century by the Al-

Minaret of the great Koutoubia Mosque.

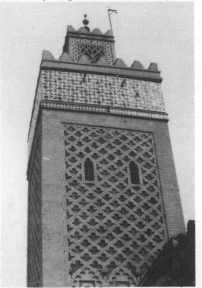

CHRISTINE OSBORNE

moravid dynasty, and many of the early
buildings still remain.

If one is a stranger to the city it is
advisable to employ a guide. Among the
principal structures to see are the city
walls, which were originally erected in
the 12th century to replace a thorny
stockade; they still follow the original line
though they have been repaired throughout the centuries. Of the most impressive
gates the Doukkala, El Makhzen, Aghmat, Aylen and the El Debbagh are
Almoravid in origin, and the Aguenau is
Almohad.

Marrakesh has several ancient
mosques. The site of the 12th-century
Koutoubia Mosque is marked by a tall
minaret, 230 ft. high and perfectly
preserved.

Hotels
Five Star
Hotel Mamounia, Ave. Bab Jdid. tel:
323.18.
Hotel Es Saadi, Ave. Quadissia. tel:
310.11.
Holiday Inn (Motel), B.P. 808 Marrakesh. tel: 300.76.

Four Star
Hotel Marrakesh, Place de la Liberte. tel:
310.51.
Hotel les Almoravides, Arset Djebelakhdar. tel: 251.42/3/3.
Ramada-Inn (Motel), rue Haroun-Rachid. tel: 307.62.

Three Star
Hotel El Maghreb, Ave. des Remparts.
tel: 309.99.
Grand Hotel Tazi, rue Bab Agnaou. tel:
221.52.
Hotel Koutoubia, 51 Charii Mansour
Dehbi. tel: 309.21.

Restaurants
La Maison Arabe, 5 rue Derb Ferran. tel:
22605.
Dar es Salaam, Derb Riad Jedid. tel:
23520.

Riad, Arset El Maach quarter. tel: 25430.
Gharnata, Derb Arfo, Riyad Zitoun Jedid. tel: 25216.
La Taverne, 23 Bd. Mohammed Zerk-
touni. tel: 31035.
Bagatelle, 107 Rue Yougslavia. tel:
30274.

Nightclubs
Oriental, Av. Mohammed V. tel: 22545.
Flash, Av. Mohammed V.
The Fantasia, Marrakesh Hotel.

Entertainments
The folklore festival of music and dancing
is the major event of the year and takes
place in May. Troupes come together
from all over Morocco to exhibit their
arts: troubadours, acrobats, singers and
dancers—and the festivities last for 15
days. Every night in the city's famed
market square snake charmers, jugglers
and acrobats perform and afterwards you
can relax in one of the many bars or
night-clubs.

Shopping and markets
There is tremendous activity in the craftsmen's *souks* where the carpet merchants
spread out their wares before admitting
tourists: Chichoua carpets of geometric
designs on a pink background, Glaoua
rugs which have black stripes amid rain-
bow colours and the warm coloured Ait
Ouazguit. Here there are also the shoe-
makers, leather-workers and the cloth
dyers. Here too you will discover fine
silverware, brass and pottery, handbags
and jewellery.

EXCURSIONS FROM MARRAKESH

From Marrakesh one can visit the pleasant wooded **Ourika Valley** where there
are three hotels: **L'Ourika** (three star),
Ramuntcho and **La Chaumiere.**

At the ski-resort of **Oukaimeden** 80
km. into the mountains are the **Hotel**

Ancient fort in Goulmina

Imlil, (three star), and the **Hotel Chez
Juju**.

Long drives lead up and over the Atlas
passes to the remote towns of **Zagora**,
Ouarzazate, **Tineghir**, **Ksar el Souq** and
Erfoud. Each has one excellent Government-operated hotel, as well as less expensive facilities. Erfoud has a colourful
festival of dancing and folklore in mid-
October. Not to be missed is the graceful,
undulating women's dance, a show-stop-
per when performed abroad by the Moroccan National Dance Company.

Each oasis is inhabited by a Berber
tribe or clan with its distinct styles of
dress and its own *kasbah*, fortress with
imposing brick towers, daily markets,
holy places, and distinctive crafts.

241

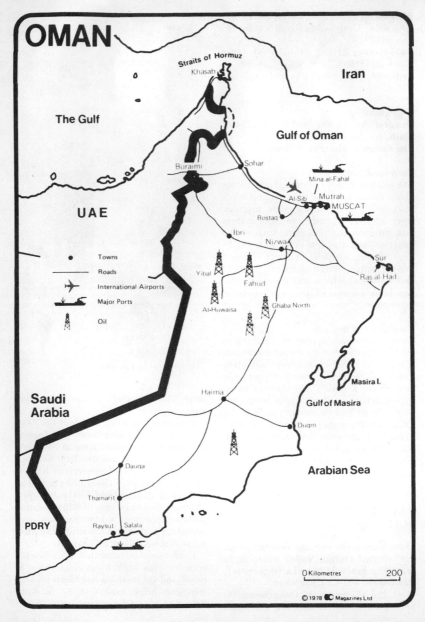

OMAN

Straits of Hormuz

Khasab

Iran

The Gulf

Gulf of Oman

Buraimi   Sohar

Mina al-Fahal

Al-Sib   Mutrah

UAE   Rostaq   MUSCAT

Ibri   Nizwa

Sur

Yibal   Ras al Had

Fahud

Al-Huwaisa   Ghaba North

Towns
Roads
International Airports
Major Ports
Oil

Masira I.

Haima   Gulf of Masira

Saudi
Arabia   Duqm

Arabian Sea

Dauqa

Thamarit

PDRY   Raysut   Salala

0 Kilometres   200

© 1978 ⓒ Magazines Ltd

OMAN

Barbara Wace

It is a pity that though, both geographically and historically, Oman is one of the most interesting countries on the Arabian Peninsula, entry for foreigners is severely restricted. No tourists are allowed, and visas are only granted, with few exceptions, to employees of firms working for the Sultanate, advisers and businessmen. Though a country with a long, proud history, Oman has been in a long period of isolation. When he succeeded his deposed father in 1970, Sultan Qaboos was faced with the task of bringing his country into the mainstream of the 20th century, while fighting a war in Dhofar, his southern province, against left wing guerrillas of the Popular Front for the Liberation of Oman (PFLO). The war is now over, and Oman has already made great strides in development. An infrastructure of hotels and services is being built up, and perhaps it will not be too long before the Sultanate will provide an exciting new destination for the more discerning traveller.

THE LAND AND THE PEOPLE

Oman, on the southeast corner of the Arabian Peninsula, has an area of 300,000 sq. km. and a coastline of over 2,700 km., stretching from the South Yemen border in Dhofar, in the south, up to the United Arab Emirates in the north, which also divides it from the Musandam Peninsula, a rocky, isolated promontory pointing up into the Strait of Hormus.

The Hajir mountains divide Oman, forming a backbone reaching from the Musandam Peninsula across to the south-eastern part of the Peninsula, and these mountains are divided into two parts by the Sumail Gap. To the east of the high Hajir mountains lies the Batinah coast, a fertile, narrow plain, about 160 miles long, peopled by those who have had contact with the outside world for centuries, descendants of Asian merchants, Baluchi traders, Arabs from other countries, a mixed population of different ethnic origins, more outward looking than the tribesmen of the interior, cut off by geography from the world. The Batinah with its long beaches and many date palms, is intensely cultivated. Shepherds and goatherds gather under the shade of the palms. Fishermen bring in huge catches, going to sea in traditional *berasti* boats or *dhows*. Behind loom the mountains dominated by the Jebel Akhdar, the Green Mountains, 3,300m. high, and inhabited by fierce tribesmen who were loyal in the past to the Imam. Sohar, long ago the capital, was an important trading port in Oman's history.

Beyond the other end of the Batinah is

Muscat, the capital, surrounded by mountains, and the natural harbour on whose steep cliffs sailors through the centuries, including Nelson when he was a midshipman, have cut or painted their names in huge letters. A new port at Mutrah, twin city to Muscat and the commercial centre, has been built, Mina Qabous, and with Ruwi, recently grown from a small village with a military airport and ancient fort into a busy urban centre, comprises what is known as Greater Muscat.

Dhofar, the southernmost province, emerging even more recently from isolation because of war, is divided from the north by another huge desert, a vast area of stone and sand, with the Empty Quarter stretching to the west. Dhofar is even more beautiful than the Batinah and the mountains of the interior of the north. Here too there is a coastal plain, with dramatic mountains behind, and Salalah, the main town and capital of the province beside the Indian Ocean. The monsoon brings rain, mist and drizzle, and the resulting green. The climate is sub-tropical, frankincense was grown and exported from here for centuries, the Kuria Muria islands lie out to sea, and the whole area is one of great beauty. In Salalah are found many black Omanis, who left Zanzibar, controlled by Oman until the revolution in the 1960s, and now have settled in this lush country. Like the Shihu in the Musandam, they speak a different dialect. In the interior of Oman can be found nomadic Bedus.

Dress varies in Oman, due to this ethnic variety. Most men wear a long *dishdash*, a white shirt, covered sometimes with a cloak. The distinctive Omani curved dagger, the *Khanjar*, is treasured by all, and worn at the waist, tucked into a cartridge belt. Omanis usually wear turbans, often of brilliantly coloured Kashmir wool, sometimes white cotton. Women wear the black cloak outdoors, called an *abaya*, but the Baluchis sport brilliantly coloured cotton dresses. Many

Omani man wearing a Khanjar

go unmasked, but there are others, particularly in the more puritan interior, who stick to the stiff, black masks.

A distinctive feature of Oman, as of the other Arabian countries, is the extensive irrigation brought by the Persians centuries ago, the *falaj*.

HISTORY

Archeologists now working in Oman have discovered evidence that part of the civilisation was probably pre-Arab. By the second century BC due to its extremely important position at the place where the Indian Ocean and the Arabian gulf meet, it had become an important Arab area, with trade to many areas even as far as China. It was one of the first areas to embrace Islam during the lifetime of the Prophet. The Ibadi sect was entrenched, and Imams were elected until the seventh century.

In the 16th century the Portuguese led the Europeans to attack this important coastal area, to protect their trade routes to India and the Far East. Muscat and

Sohar were both conquered, and evidence of this is still to be seen in the two great Portuguese forts, Jalali and Mirani, which guard the entrance to the harbour of Muscat and dominate the city to this day. There was civil war in the 18th century; only ended when Ahmad Bin Said, elected Imam by both sides in this tribal controversy, and the ancestor of the present Sultan, came to power. From then, until Sultan Qaboos became Sultan, the country was known as Muscat and Oman, but then the name was changed to Oman, to make clear that the coastal community, Dhofar and the tribal interior, were all one kingdom.

From the end of the 18th century until today ties between Oman and Britain have been close, beginning with a treaty in 1798. The present Sultan's father put down a revolt of tribal factions loyal to the Imam in the interior, and a dispute over the Buraimi settlements was settled. Britain backed the Sultan in the dispute with Saudi Arabia over Buraimi, and in the Dhofar War, and Iran and Jordan also sent in troops.

WILDLIFE

Probably one of the most interesting animals in Oman is the Arabian *tahr*, which lives in north Oman, and nowhere else in the world. It is so shy it is seldom seen; it belongs to the goat family, and looks like a gazelle, with a thick coat in winter. Over-hunting has made the gazelle very rare, and the Sultan is taking steps to protect this and other threatened species. Foxes, wild cats, panthers, wolves, hyenas, porcupines are all found in Oman, and there is a rare black hedgehog, as well as many different sorts of bats, huge lizards, a distinctive spiny mouse, and many rare butterflies. The Bedu catch locusts, and eat them—you can see mounds of them in the *souks* of the towns when they have swarmed. The camels of the Batinah Coast are famous, and horses are bred in Oman too, with

much interest being taken in them by the Sultan. There are many rare birds, including flamingos, duck, geese, herons. There is plenty of marine life, and the seas abound in fish. Beautiful shells can be found on the miles of sands.

ECONOMY

Oil was discovered, and began to be exported during the lifetime of the previous Sultan, but it was not until the present Sultan came to power that great use was made of it in developing the country. Now that the Dhofar war is over, great strides are being made to bring Oman into the mainstream of modern life—there is a Development Plan, started in 1976, and due to end in 1980, which looks forward to an annual growth of 12.6% in GNP.

It is hoped to stop the country's dependence on oil in which it is not so rich as some other Gulf countries, and to diversify the economy, so that mineral research, fishing and agriculture are now of great importance. Road building projects have vastly improved communications, and there are plans for many more, to open up the interior. As well as the new port at Mutrah, there is now another completed near Salalah in Dhofar, at Raysut. Social services, health care, and above all education (there are now over 200 schools, contrasted to three when he became Sultan) are top priorities in the Sultan's plans, and experimental farms are studying how the fertile areas can be made more profitable.

GENERAL INFORMATION

Area: 300,000 sq. km.
Population: 600,000 (official estimate: 1.5 million).
Capital: Muscat.
Head of State: Sultan Qaboos bin Said.
Government: Power in the hands of the Sultan.

Language: Arabic. English is generally known in business circles.

Religion: The majority of the population is Muslim following the Ibadi rite. About a quarter of the population however are Sunnis.

Currency: The Rial Omani (RO) is the unit of currency; it is divided into 1000 Baizas.

£1 = RO 0.662 $1 = RO 0.345.

Time: GMT + 4.

HOW TO GET THERE

By air: Gulf Air, and British Airways operate through flights from London to Seeb International Airport, 40 km. from Muscat. There are regular flights between Muscat and Paris, Amsterdam, Larnaca and Athens, and to Karachi, Bombay, the Far East and Australia, and to Middle East capitals such as Beirut, Amman, Cairo. International carriers include: MEA, Kuwait Airlines, Royal Jordanian Airlines, Pakistan International Airlines, Air India, Saudi Arabian Airlines, Iran Air, Somali Airlines, PIA.

By sea: P&O operate the 'Dwark' between Gulf ports, Bombay and Karachi, calling at Muscat irregularly. P&O also operate cargo services with limited passenger accommodation from UK ports to Oman. Details from P&O General Cargo Division, Beaufort House, St Botolph Street EC3.

Visas and health regulations

Anyone travelling to Oman should obtain a visa from the Omani Embassy in the country where they are.

Applicants who already have connections in the Sultanate must attach to their application forms a letter from the firm or Government Department they wish to visit in Oman in which it gives name or names of the persons who will be visiting Oman, the dates of their arrival in Oman and the duration of their stay there. Only in certain special cases, telexes will be accepted in lieu of letters.

British applicants who do not already have connections in the Sultanate will have to produce a letter from The Arab British Chamber of Commerce, P.O. Box 4BL, 26A Albemarle Street, London, W1. (tel: 01-499 3400).

No application without the letters mentioned will be accepted. The application form is in triplicate with three passport size photographs and usual letter of recommendation from the company or firm.

A No Objection Certificate is required for persons going to the Sultanate of Oman on a visit to relatives or friends, to be obtained through friends or relatives in Oman. Visas for NOC holders are granted within 48 hours, and for others within three days, but sometimes it takes longer. The consular section of the Embassy of the Sultanate of Oman, 64 Ennismore Gardens, London, SW7 is open from 0930 to 1330 Monday to Friday. An Israeli visa on a passport automatically cancels the Omani Visa. Visa from the Embassy costs £6. The Arab British Chambers of Commerce charges £4.34 for their services, unless the applicant is already a member.

Vaccination certificates against cholera and smallpox required, TAB injections are advisable.

Currency and customs regulations

There are no restrictions on the amount of foreign currency which may be taken into or out of Oman. Personal effects are allowed in duty free but it is forbidden to import alcohol.

CLIMATE

Very hot and humid in summer, with June-July midday temperatures sometimes as high as 40°C, particularly on the coast where humidity is sometimes 85%. Muscat has 70cm average rainfall; in Nizwa it is higher while in Salalah the light monsoon rain falls from June to

September. The best time to visit the area is from November to March.

What to wear
In winter light wool, with a jacket or shawl for the evenings is suitable clothing. For the rest of the year, loose cool clothes are absolutely necessary, preferably cotton. To avoid offending local customs, men should not wear shorts and women's dresses should cover the knees, preferably with long sleeves. When slacks are worn, shirt or top should cover the hips.

TRANSPORT

Visitors are not permitted to travel into the interior or farther up the coast than Sib, about 50km. from Muscat without prior permission from the Ministry of the interior. Gulf Air flies daily to Salalah in Dhofar, but passengers must obtain permission in writing from the Ministry of Information (Greater Muscat, PO Box 600) and book a seat well in advance.

Taxis operate between the airport and Mutrah/Muscat and inside the main towns. Prices should be negotiated first. Hotels have hire cars.

BANKS

Arab Bank Ltd PO Box 991 Muscat, tel: 722831
Bank of Credit and Commerce Int. SA PO Box 840 Muscat, tel: 701007
Bank of Oman, Bahrain and Kuwait, PO Box 920 Muscat, tel: 722966
Banque de Paris et Pays-Bas, PO Box 425 Muscat, tel: 722740
British Bank of the Middle East, PO Box 234 Muscat, tel: 701007
The Chartered Bank Ltd, PO Box 210 Muscat, tel: 722279

Business hours
The weekly holiday is Friday. Government Offices: 0730 to 1400 Saturday to Wednesday, 1730 to 1300 Thursday;

Dhofar province

Banks: 0800 to 1200 Saturday to Wednesday, 1800 to 1130 Thursday; (opening times one hour later during Ramadan). Business establishments: Variable between 0830 to 1330 and 1600 to 1800 Saturday to Thursday.

PUBLIC HOLIDAYS

Prophet's Birthday 20 February
Ascension of the Prophet 1 July
Eid al Fitr 3-6 September
Eid al Adha 10-13 November
National Day 18 November
Birthday of Sultan Qaboos 19 November
Muslim New Year 2 December

EMBASSIES IN MUSCAT AND MUTRAH

Egypt: PO Box 3969, Muscat
France: PO Box 591, Muscat
India: PO Box 177, Muscat
Iran: PO Box 702, Muscat
Kuwait: PO Box 890, Muscat
Pakistan: PO Box 1005, Mutrah
Qatar: PO Box 802, Muscat
Saudi Arabia: PO Box 873, Muscat
United Arab Emirates: PO Box 335, Muscat
UK: PO Box 300, Muscat
USA: PO Box 996, Muscat

ACCOMMODATION AND FOOD

Hotel accommodation is short and it is advisable to book well in advance and reconfirm before arrival. Prices as in other Gulf areas, are high. A 10% service charge, plus 5% municipal tax is usual. Tipping is not necessary.

Most visitors eat in their own hotels, but a few restaurants are appearing.

Hotels
Intercontinental Hotel, Qurum, opened

end 1977. Box 1398 Mutrah. tel: Muscat 600500; Telex: 3491. London reservation office tel: 01-491 7181. 308 rooms, 20 cabanas.

Al Falaj Hotel, Ruwi. PO Box 456 Muscat. tel: 702311; Telex: MB 229. About 10km. from central Muscat, between airport and Muscat, off Ruwi-Muttrah Road, with simpler annexe off Ruwi High Street. First top hotel built in Oman. 250 rooms.

Gulf Hotel Qurum, PO Box 4455, Tel. 734660; Telex MB 416. About 20km. from centre Muscat, ten minutes from Ruwi, off Seeb road. 122 rooms on hill overlooking sea.

Ruwi Hotel, Ruwi, PO Box 5195. Tel. 702244, Telex MB 456. About 10km. from central Muscat on Ruwi-Muttrah road. 99 rooms.

Mutrah Hotel, Mutrah, (in outskirts). PO Box 4525. Tel. 701711. Telex 226. Only 68 rooms but central position 5km. from Muscat centre an advantage.

Restaurants
The Palm Tree, Ruwi. Unlicensed, it serves Kebabs, homous and Arab specialities.
The Taj, Mutrah, tel.: 702532, serves Indian food.
Al Qurun, near Gulf Hotel.
Airport Hotel, Seeb Airport, tel.: 610418, licensed and serves both European and Arab food.

Hotels in Salalah, Dhofar
Holiday Inn, PO Box 8870, Salalah. Tel.: 46 17 77. Telex: 7638 Holisalm. London reservations office 01-722 7755. Recently opened, resort type hotel, 8km. from Salalah International Airport, 3km. from centre of Salalah. Approx. 100 rooms, 20 villa suites.
Salalah Hotel. Tel.: 451. first hotel in Dhofar, consisting of villas, totalling 20 rooms.

Leisure activities
Swimming in hotel pools, or vast stretch-

es of beach. Sailing is becoming popular. Fishermen will negotiate to take out passengers. There are camel races sometimes on national holidays. There is plenty to buy in the colourful *souks*, though the one in Salalah has been pulled down and the sellers now line the road. Maria Theresa dollars are still to be found, silverware, copper, ornate Omani daggers and knives, traditional Omani Khunjar pottery, woven cloth. Also many modern and electrical goods. There is an excellent small museum in Muscat, and many visistors enjoy studying the old carved doors which still remain. The long empty beaches are covered with beautiful shells.

There is radio and television, with no advertisements.

Longer visits, with permission, can be made to ancient forts such as the one at Nizwa, Bahla, or So, to beautiful mountain and desert country for bathing and picnics, roads improve all the time. There is some night life in the best hotels, with live bands, barbecues, cinema performances, etc.

There is a huge new police stadium at

Camel racing

Wattayeh, near Muscat, and on the birthday of Sultan Qaboos there are dramatic displays before huge crowds of 30,000 and more. Camel and horse races are organised in various places on holidays too. Soccer is popular. Ports and fishing villages are interesting. Dhows and other local craft still to be seen.

THE OMAN MUSEUM

The Oman Museum is housed in a small building in Information City at Qurum, a few kilometres along the coast north-west of Muscat. It houses attractive modern displays covering Oman's archaeology, history and traditional culture. It aims to encapsulate, in a limited space, the culture and history of a complex society, and it does this in a series of five thematic exhibitions dealing with archaeology, the land and its people, Islam architecture and arts and crafts. Recently a small extension has been added to exhibit the results of the latest archaeological and other investigations, which are being carried out in the country.

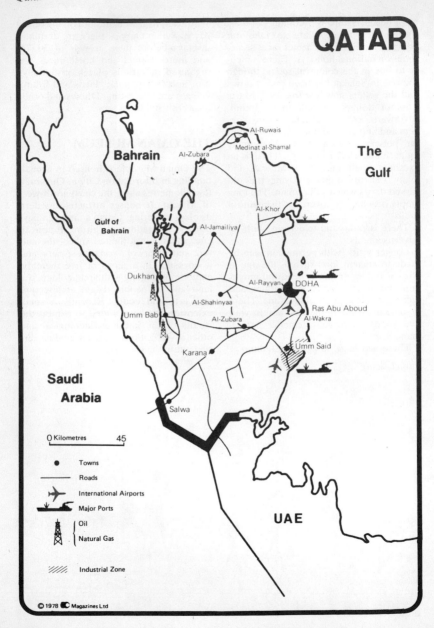

QATAR

Bahrain

The Gulf

Al-Ruwais

Medinat al-Shamal

Al-Zubara

Gulf of Bahrain

Al-Khor

Al-Jamailiya

Dukhan

Al-Rayyan · DOHA

Al-Shahinyaa

Ras Abu Aboud

Umm Bab

Al-Zubara

Al-Wakra

Saudi Arabia

Karana

Umm Said

Salwa

0 Kilometres 45

● Towns

Roads

✈ International Airports

⚓ Major Ports

Oil

Natural Gas

UAE

////// Industrial Zone

© 1978 ◖ Magazines Ltd

QATAR

Christine Osborne

The Arabian Gulf state of Qatar does not grant tourist visas, but bona fide businessmen are welcome. The small, arid peninsula has little of touristic interest. Its few attractive old Gulf-style fishing communities have been replaced by modern towns. But in the north, near Zubara, is the historically interesting Qalit Marir fortress. Near Al-Ruwais is the largest captive oryx herd in Arabia. It may be visited with special permission.

The capital, Doha, has an excellent National Museum. It exhibits the old ways of life and traces the country's development since the discovery of oil. Qatar has miles of unspoilt sandy beaches for bathing and fishing. The main drawback is that there are no Western-type facilities outside Doha and these are largely centred on hotels.

THE LAND AND THE PEOPLE

The people of Qatar are of Arabian stock, a result of mainland migrations, largely in search of water. The first migration crossed from Kuwait in the 1870s and a second took place at the end of the 19th century when Al-Ihsa tribesmen moved to Qatar during the period of Wahibi expansion in mainland Arabia.

Qataris belong to three main Arab tribes: the Awamir, the Manasir and the Banu Hajir. Today's population estimate of 900,000 is misleading since more than half are migrant workers from the Indian sub-continent.

80% of the population live in Doha with a large concentration in Umm Said, Qatar's developing industrial zone. Doha is situated on the mid-east coast. It is small enough to be crossed on foot in 15 minutes.

Dukhan is a self-contained oil town on the west coast. Umm Said is south of Doha.

Qatar's second town, Al-Khor, largely rebuilt, lies north of Doha. In the north is Al-Ruwais, a former large fishing community.

CULTURE

Although Qatar cannot be said to be without culture, many of its old desert traditions have been radically altered since the discovery of oil.

The few Bedouin still living in tents weave rugs for use as curtains and blankets. Their tents are also woven from camel-hair, interspersed with strips of linen. It is unlikely that any are woven today.

Traditional Qatari music resembles other Gulf music, the most usual instrument being the three-stringed fiddle or *rababa*, small hand-drums and oryx horn flutes.

Qatar is experiencing the explosive transition period brought by oil and in the towns the people are caught up in a type of pseudo-Western culture in which the cinema predominates. But there is a strong theatre movement aimed at producing indigenous plays.

HISTORY

Qatar is known to have been inhabited by primitive man by the discovery there of relics dating from 4000 BC. As the country has a desert climate unsuitable for farming and is surrounded on three sides by sea, it is likely that the Qataris have always involved themselves in the fishing and pearling trades.

During the period of colonial expansion, Qatar was an important maritime éntrepôt on the east-west spice, silk and slave routes.

The principal source of income, from pearling, was halted when Japan introduced the cheap cultured pearl. But Qatar received new life with the discovery, in 1940, of oil.

On 3 September 1972 treaty arrangements with Britain were annulled and Qatar became a fully independent sovereign state.

WILDLIFE

There are few wild animals in Qatar owing to the scarcity of food and water. Those which survive have developed particular characteristics not seen in the same species in more temperate climates. The rare desert wolf, the sand fox and hare have evolved very large ears, and the hare and sand rat have bristle-like hairs on their feet to facilitate movement through the sand. The three-toed jerboa is native to Qatar.

ECONOMY

Although the Government is attempting to diversify industry, Qatar's economy is still founded on oil, which was discovered near Dukhan. Exports began in 1949. Today the main fields are Al-Bunduq, which is shared with Abu Dhabi, and Idal-Shargi, which was formerly operated by Shell.

In 1976 Qatar assumed 100% ownership of the Qatar Petroleum Company (QPC) and in 1977 it assumed control of the Qatar Gas Company.

In the World Bank preliminary assessment for 1975, Qatar was placed the third-richest state in the world per capita on an estimated calculation of some 45,000 indigenous Qataris sharing an oil income of some $25 bn. a year.

On current production levels of 475,000 barrels a day, Qatar's oil reserves should last another 40 years. Provisional estimates assess its natural gas deposits at between 40 and 60 bn. cubic feet

Qatar's 1976 budget was £580 m. of which £376 m. was allocated for heavy industry. Some major projects are a natural gas liquefaction plant of capacity 6,200 barrels a day, a £290 m. petrochemical plant to begin production in 1979 at a rate of 300,000 tons of ethylene a year and a steel mill to commence production in 1978 of 400,000 steel billets annually.

Other projects cover fertilisers, flour and cement, and light industry plans include the manufacture of paints, plastics, leatherware, metal containers, industrial cleaners and the packaging of foodstuffs.

As a desert country, Qatar faces acute problems in becoming self-sufficient in basic foods. In the 1,562 acres under cultivation the main crops are tomatoes, aubergines, squashes, marrows, cabbages, barley, citrus fruits and dates. At Umm Qarah poultry farm it is planned to raise a million chickens annually and to produce enough eggs to meet 80% of local needs. Sheep and dairy cattle farming has begun on bore-water-irrigated land near the border with Saudi Arabia.

GENERAL INFORMATION

Area: Qatar is a peninsula of 10,360 sq. km.
Population: Estimated at 900,000.
Capital: Doha.
Head of State: Shaikh Khalifa bin Hamad al-Thani.
Government: An independent sovereign state with a 20-member advisory council under a Prime Minister and the Emir.
Date of Independence: 3 September 1972.
Language: Arabic. All educated Qataris speak English.
Religion: Islam, primarily Sunni Muslim.
Currency: Qatari riyal (QR) divided into 100 dirhams. £1=QR7.56; $1=QR3.95.
Time: GMT +3.

HOW TO GET THERE

By air: Qatar is served by the following airlines: Air France, Air India, Alia, British Airways, EgyptAir, Gulf Air, Iran Air, Iraq Air, Kuwait Airways, MEA, PIA, Saudia, Syrianair and Yemen Airways.

Taxi fare Doha Airport to town centre, QR 20. There is no departure tax from Qatar.

By sea: Ships from various parts of the world dock at Doha. There is no regular passenger service.

By road: By 1978 the final sealed-road section on the trans-Arabian Highway should be completed, making it possible to drive to Qatar from either Kuwait, Saudi Arabia or Abu Dhabi, although this last sector is still unsealed.

Visas and health regulations
British nationals by origin do not require a visa, but a no objection certificate must be applied for and obtained from the *Immigration Department, Ministry of the Interior*, PO Box 2433, Doha, Qatar, Arabian Gulf.

Visa application forms should be obtained from a Qatar embassy; three photographs required; fee £3.75.

Vaccination and inoculation against smallpox and cholera are compulsory.

Customs and currency regulations
No alcohol may be imported. Unlimited cigarettes. No limit on amount of currency taken in or out.

CLIMATE

The climate is dry, hot and with excessive humidity in summer, June-September. Average winter temperature is 16°C.

What to wear
Dress is casual, with consideration for Islamic custom. In winter a coat is necessary at night.

Most visiting businessmen wear suits by day. A tie is necessary at night

ACCOMMODATION AND FOOD

Doha has one luxury hotel, the **Gulf Hotel** (PO Box 1911, tel: 25251, tlx: Doha 4250). Western visitors may obtain alcoholic beverages in its Coral Room Restaurant and Room 501.

Other hotels are the adjacent **Oasis** (PO Box 717, tel: 4551, tlx: 4214), overlooking West Bay, the **Carlton Hotel** and the second-class **New Doha Palace** (PO Box 710, tel: 26131, tlx: 4263) in central Doha. The remaining hotels cannot be classified.

The Gulf Hotel serves very good Middle Eastern and European food. The

Choose **MEA** to Qatar or any of the other main business centres in the Middle East.

Wherever you travel on our extensive network you'll be well looked after all the way.

MEA
the natural
choice airline

other hotels serve European and local Anglo-Indian-type food.

Qatari food is similar to that found elsewhere in the Gulf, with chicken and lamb rice dishes accompanied by Arabic bread, yoghurt and salad.

Doha has few western-style restaurants. Hotels apart, there are only the **Rendezvous, Massis, Strand, Popeye** plus **Kentucky Fried Chicken** and **Wimpy**. The airport restaurant is good.

TRANSPORT

Qatar has no internal air services. Its major towns are linked by a good road network: Doha-Dukhan Road 81 km.; Doha-Umm Said Road 35 km.; Doha-al-Shamal road north, 124 km. There is no public bus service. Taxis are available with the price agreed beforehand.

Car Hire: *Rent-a-Car*, tel: 28100/26649; *National Motors Hire Service*, tel: 23868; *Al-Sada Co-op Co.*, tel: 5037/29494.

BANKS

Al-Fardan Banking and Finance, PO Box 339. Arab Bank, PO Box 172. Bank Almashrek Sal, Box 388. Bank of Oman Ltd., PO Box 173. Bank Saderat Iran, PO Box 2256. Banque de Paris et pays Bas, PO Box 2636. British Bank of the Middle East, PO Box 57. Chartered Bank, PO Box 29. Commerical Bank of Qatar, PO Box 3232. Euroseas Banking Co. Qatar Ltd., PO Box 2524. Citibank, PO Box 2309. Grindlays Bank Ltd., PO Box 2001. Qatar National Bank SA, PO Box 1000. United Bank Ltd, PO Box 329.

Business Hours
Government Departments: 0730-1300, Saturday to Thursday.
Private businesses (shops and offices): 0930-1230, Saturday to Thursday, and 1530-1900, Saturday to Wednesday.

Contractors: 0800-1400, Saturday to Thursday, and 1500-1700 Saturday to Wednesday.
Post Office: 0730-1230 and 1500-1700, Saturday to Thursday.
Banks: 0800-1200, Saturday to Thursday.

PUBLIC HOLIDAYS

1 January, 30 June (half-year closing) 3 September Independence Day, 5 August, Ramadan commences, 3-6 September, Eid al Fitr (moveable according to the end of Ramadan) 3-5 days, 10-13 November Eid al-Adha (moveable), 2 December, Muslim New year, 31 December (half-yearly closing).

EMBASSIES IN DOHA

Egypt: PO Box 2899, tel: 25136.
France: PO Box 2669, tel: 25216.
India: PO Box 2788, tel: 21145.
Iran: PO Box 1633, tel: 5052.
Iraq: PO Box 1526, tel: 22894.
Japan: Tel: 25152.
Jordan: PO Box 2366, tel: 25146.
Kuwait: PO Box 1177, tel: 5227.
Mauritania: PO Box 3132.
Morocco: Tel: PO Box 3242.
Oman: Tel: 29113.
Pakistan: PO Box 334, tel: 25117.
Saudi Arabia: PO Box 1255, tel: 27144.
Somalia: Tel: 5758.
Sudan: PO Box, 2999, tel: 25156.
Tunisia: PO Box 2707, tel: 21694.
UK: PO Box 3, tel: 23991/2.
USA: PO Box 2399, tel: 87701.
West Germany: Tel: 29720.

TOURIST INFORMATION

Information on Qatar is obtained from the Ministry of Information in Doha.

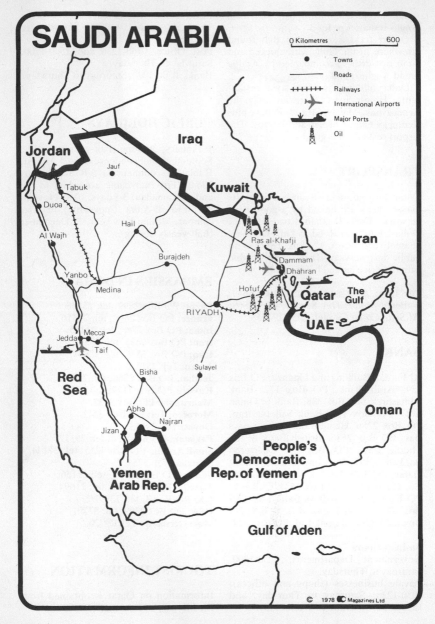

SAUDI ARABIA

0 Kilometres 600

- Towns
- Roads
- +++++ Railways
- International Airports
- Major Ports
- Oil

Iraq

Jordan

Jauf

Tabuk

Duoa

Al Wajh

Hail

Kuwait

Ras al-Khafji

Iran

Burajdeh

Yanbo

Dammam

Dhahran

Medina

Hofuf

Qatar

The Gulf

RIYADH

UAE

Jedda

Mecca

Taif

Bisha

Sulayel

Red Sea

Oman

Abha

Najran

Jizan

People's Democratic Rep. of Yemen

Yemen Arab Rep.

Gulf of Aden

© 1978 Magazines Ltd

SAUDI ARABIA

The traveller in Saudi Arabia is of necessity, a businessman, resident or pilgrim. Tourism as such does not exist for the western visitor.

For many people Saudi Arabia can be summed up in three words—desert, Islam and oil—but it is more than this. Certainly it has the largest sand desert in the world, the *Rub al-Khali* or Empty Quarter, but there are also the mountains of the Asir in the south west, where green, fertile valleys have supported agricultural communities for centuries, and the coastal plains of the Gulf with its coral reefs and traditions of pearl diving.

The Holy City of Mecca dominates one of the few passes from the Nejd in the centre of the country through the stark mountains of the Hejaz bordering the Red Sea coast. Millions of pilgrims descend on Mecca every year from all over the world and Saudi Arabia is proud of its continuing role as the focal point of Islam. Yet from the point of view of the tourist this can have its drawbacks, for the 18th century conservative fundamentalism of the Wahhabi sect still prevails, making it difficult, particularly for women, to move about the country freely.

The wealth from the oil, however, is resulting in rapid modernisation, and communication between the main towns is quite good. Development has in fact proceeded at such a pace in the commercial and diplomatic centres of Jeddah and Riyad, that much of the old character has been lost. Efforts are being made to preserve the traditional architecture of the holy centres of Mecca and Medina, and the Government has also begun a policy of wildlife conservation with respect to rare species.

In essence, Saudi Arabia is a land of contrasts where the past exists, sometimes uncomfortably, beside the present.

THE LAND AND THE PEOPLE

The Arabian peninsula is thought to have once been part of a much bigger continent which also included Africa, and certainly the wildlife and vegetation of the southern and western areas support this theory. It broke away after large rifts appeared which now form the Red Sea and the Gulf of Aden. The whole land mass then tilted and the western edge was lifted as the eastern side was lowered. The west was also the subject of further disturbances which produced the extensive lava fields which occur all along that side of the peninsula.

Thus, behind the very narrow coastal strip (Tihama) along the Red Sea, is a formidable mountain range with plateaux of up to 2,000m. The southern part of this range, the Asir region, has some peaks of over 3,000m. East of these mountains, in the north is the Nejd—a semi desert area with scattered oases. Farther south this gradually changes to sand desert eventu-

Moving sand dunes at Al Hofuf oasis

ally becoming the Empty Quarter which is completely uninhabitable. Along the Gulf coast is a low-lying and relatively fertile plain, giving way further inland to limestone ridges.

Saudi Arabia is one of the driest countries in the world with an average annual rainfall of only 20cm. Most of this falls in the southwestern Asir region—the only well watered area in the whole country—and often the *Rub al-Khali* (Empty Quarter) gets no rain at all. There are no permanent rivers with outlets to the sea.

Summer daytime temperatures are between 45° and 50°C and even higher in the desert areas, but they drop dramatically in winter and at night. Night time winter temperatures in the north can fall to -7°C.

In the semi-desert area the population is mainly nomadic, although there have long been small villages and towns in the central Nejd area. Most permanent settlement, however, has been in the coastal districts—in the Hejaz and Asir bordering the Red Sea and along the Gulf coast. But now the rapid expansion of the main towns bears witness to the development and modernisation which has resulted from the oil wealth. In the 1930s, for instance, the land could only support a

population of about two million, yet now this has increased fourfold with the advent of irrigation and the exploitation of underground water resources. Desalination is playing an increasingly important role in Saudi Arabia's water supply.

The heart of Saudi Arabia is the *Nejd* (highlands), or central province. It has always been somewhat isolated from the rest of the peninsula because of the mountains to the west and the desert on the other three sides. This and its poverty never made it worthwhile for the various civilisations which have held sway in the region through the centuries, to conquer it. For this reason it is considered by many to be the only remaining example of true Arab society. The Najdis have traditionally lived by camel and sheep herding. Tribal traditions and allegiance, which are still strong throughout Saudi Arabia, are perhaps best preserved in this area. The watchtowers which grace all the high points and the remnants of walls around the towns and villages are a reminder of a warfaring past.

To the west, the *Hejaz* (barrier), or western province, provides a contrast with its mountains and narrow coastal strip. It had long been a centre of trade and commerce and was conquered by successive civilisations from the Nabateans through the Babylonians, Jews and Christians to the Ottomans. Now, the Hejaz is most important because of the Islamic holy cities of Mecca and Medina which attract pilgrims from all over the world. The *Hajj* (pilgrimage) diversified the population even more as did the negro slaves brought in the past from East Africa. The Hejaz is also the commercial centre of Saudi Arabia and Jedda on the coast has become the diplomatic capital.

Perhaps the most picturesque area of Saudi Arabia is the *Asir* (difficult region), or southwest province. It was called the difficult region because the very high mountains made access almost impossible in the past, but now a modern highway links it to the rest of the country. Asir is the agricultural area of Saudi Arabia for it gets plenty of rain as a result of the monsoons. The hillsides are terraced to prevent soil erosion.

The population is mainly settled except in the Tihama lowlands to the west of the province where there are still some nomadic tribes. But tribal allegiance is also strong in the settled communities and there is a long history of feuds and fighting. The way of life, however, is altogether different from the other parts of Saudi Arabia, with brighter forms of dress and unique architecture.

The eastern province on the Gulf coast is different again, for only recently has it been effectively connected to the western side of the peninsula. The lowland plain is relatively fertile and there are some agricultural settlements. There is also a tradition of fishing and pearl diving along the coast. Farther inland the population is nomadic living mainly on the herds of goats whose milk is used to make yogurt and on the dates which grow in the scattered oases. Today, most activity in the province is centred on the growing towns of Dammam and Dhahran which are the focus of the oil industry.

HISTORY AND CULTURE

Saudi Arabia's history before the birth of the Prophet Muhammad is essentially a tribal one, although the peninsula was also influenced by the various civilisations which held sway in the Middle East from the Sumerians through the Assyrians and Persians to the Romans. The only really settled urban centres, however, were on the west coast where the towns of Medina, Mecca and Taif became fairly important trading centres.

Within a century of the birth of Muhammad in AD 571 Islam had spread as far as Spain to the north and India to the east, yet its effect on the Arabian peninsula itself was in some ways temporary.

The unification of tribes which it effected soon broke down while the Islamic unity of the whole Middle East lasted longer, reducing the importance of Arabia as a trading centre.

In the 16th century the peninsula came nominally under the control of the Ottoman empire but its influence was never strong, especially in the central Nejd area. Even before the First World War Britain had established a foothold along the Gulf coast of Arabia and the (British) government of India had good relations with the Nejd.

When Turkey entered the war in 1914, the British enlisted Arab help against the Ottomans, eventually persuading Sherif Hussain of Mecca to lead an Arab revolt, which was successfully launched in 1916. The following years saw the increasing power of Ibn-Saud, the ruler of the Nejd, and descendant of the puritanical and fundamentalist Wahhabis of the 18th century. It was Ibn-Saud who finally united the various provinces into the modern Kingdom of Saudi Arabia after displacing Sherif Hussain from the Hejaz in 1926.

The Saudis insist that their culture resides not in things but in their Islamic religion and the perfection of the Arabic language. When Islam replaced the animism of the Arab tribes in the seventh century, it incorporated many features from the old society. The Prophet Muhammad, who was born in Mecca in AD 571 of the Quraish tribe, sought to end tribal feuds by advocating unity in Islam, but the traditions were strong and tribal allegiance is still a powerful influence today.

The beauties of the Arabic language are best exhibited in its poetry. This was a powerful force in pre-Islamic days and played a fundamental role in inter-tribal relations. It extolled the virtues of heroic deeds arising out of tribal conflict and was also thought to have some mystical power which could be used either to benefit or destroy. This last aspect was frowned on by Islam, but in its form and to some extent in its content the poetry has survived, particularly in the nomadic communities.

Since Islam forbids the representation of the human form, decoration in Saudi Arabia, whether of houses, clothes or jewellery, is mainly performed with geometric patterns or illuminated Arabic writing. Often this is very beautifully done.

The Islam of Saudi Arabia is conservative and fundamentalist, based on the revivalist movement of Najd leader Shaikh Muhammad Ibn-Abdel-Wahhag which swept the area in the 18th century. This still has a profound effect on Saudi society, particularly on the position of women, who do not venture outside the house without covering themselves from head to foot in the traditional black robes (abaya) which also cover all of the face except the eyes.

Yet there are regional differences. In the Asir, the women wear gaily-coloured dresses and are not veiled at all. The architecture of the region is also notable for most of the houses are built with louvred walls as a means of weatherproofing. Inside they are decorated on the walls and ceiling with paintings, usually done by the women.

The way of life in the Najd, home of the Wahhabis, could not offer a greater contrast. Here all the traditional Arab and Islamic values predominate still. Poetry, much of it unwritten, is deep rooted and tribal loyalty is important. Marriages are arranged, as they are in many other parts of Saudi Arabia. The old sports of falconry, horse racing and camel racing are still followed.

For the tourist, the Hejaz has possibly the most to offer. In addition to Mecca, the site of the holy Kabaa which attracts over a million Muslim pilgrims each year, there is the other holy city of Medina and the beautiful mountain resort of Taif. Moreover, at Medina Saleh there are the well-preserved remains of a Nabatean city carved out of the mountainside like the famous rose city of Petra in Jordan.

Throughout the country many of the traditional handicrafts are still produced. There are fine bronze and brass ware, in particular incense burners and coffee mortars. Finely worked gold and silver jewellery is made and in the eastern provinces huge brass-bonded chests are to be found. Possibly the most typical metal work are the daggers and swords made in various sizes and designs—all richly decorated.

Saudi Arabia's traditional ways of life are being threatened by the very rapid modernisation and development of the country. This is particularly true in the big towns where much of the old architecture has disappeared to make room for the new office blocks and apartment buildings, while the markets are beginning to give way to new department stores.

Traditional dress, on the other hand, is well established for although Western clothing is often seen in the towns, it is usually being worn by visiting businessmen or expatriate workers. Saudi men wear the white robes and head-dresses (*ghotra*) universally associated with 'Arabs'.

ECONOMY

Saudi Arabia is the biggest oil producer in the Middle East and has one quarter of the world's known oil reserves. It is the wealth from oil which has transformed the country so dramatically in the past 40 years. Unlike some of the other oil states—Algeria and Iran for example—Saudi Arabia has made very little effort to industrialise. Some small factories have been built, but next to oil, petrochemicals and the construction industry are most important.

For transport, machinery, consumer goods and even food, Saudi Arabia relies heavily on imports. But still most of the income from the oil is invested in Western Banks. Saudi Arabia has lent money in the past to the World Bank and also gives aid to the less developed states, especially the poorer Arab countries. Other recipients of its aid are African and Islamic states.

Agriculture employs over half the Saudi population, although only 0.2% of the land is suitable for cultivation. However, an ambitious programme to combat water shortage and improve irrigation is under way. This includes surveys for underground water, the construction of dams and drainage networks and also the desalination of sea water.

WILDLIFE

Saudi Arabia is not generally thought of as important with respect to wildlife, yet it is the home of at least two fairly rare species of animal—the sand cat which closely resembles the domestic cat, and the oryx, a large antelope with straight antlers.

Although the oryx is probably now extinct in the Arabian Peninsula because of over hunting in the 1930s, the Government has now introduced a strict policy of conservation and hopes to reintroduce the species from some being bred in captivity in the USA.

The ibex (mountain goat) is still to be found in the northern Hejaz mountains and in the remote areas of the south the Dorcas gazelle and sand gazelle can sometimes be seen. The cheetah and caracal lynx also used to roam the country but these too are threatened with extinction because of hunting. As with the oryx, the Government hopes eventually to reintroduce these animals which are now protected.

GENERAL INFORMATION

Area: 2,149,690 sq. km.
Population: Unknown (estimates range from four to seven million).
Capital: Riyad.
Head of State: King Khaled Ibn Abdul Aziz.
Government: Absolute Monarchy.
Language: Arabic.
Religion: Islam.
Currency: Saudi Riyal (SR), divided into 100 Halaleh. $1=3.47SR. £1=6.64SR.
Time: GMT+3.

HOW TO GET THERE

By air: There are three international airports at Riyad, Jedda and Dhahran. Saudia (Saudi Arabian Airlines) has seven flights from London to Jedda weekly, continuing to Riyad and Dhahran. Jedda airport is served by the following international airlines: British Airways, MEA, KLM, Air France, Air India, Alia, Alitalia, EgyptAir, Iran Air, Iraqi Airways, Lufthansa, PIA, Sudan Airways. Dhahran airport is served by the following international scheduled airlines: Air France, Air India, Alia, Alitalia, British Airways, Gulf Air, Iran Air, Iraqi Airways, KLM, Kuwait Airways, Lufthansa, MEA, Olympic, PIA, Sabena, Swissair.

A vital tip to the traveller is that he must visit his airline office the day before departure to confirm his ticket and surrender his passport. This is purportedly in case of unpaid debts. Passports are returned at the airport on the day of departure when you are exhorted to report two hours before flying time.

By road: Links with Jordan, Kuwait and Qatar.

Visas and health regulations
All visitors must be in possession of a valid passport and a current visa, obtainable from Saudi embassies abroad. A certificate of religion is necessary for the granting of a visa. No tourist visas are granted, only business ones. Exit visas are also required.

Visitors must be in possession of an international certificate of vaccination against smallpox, also a certificate of vaccination against yellow fever and cholera if the visitor is coming from an infected region. Obtaining a visa is often a long and arduous process, involving finding a sponsor and justifying the purpose of the trip to the satisfaction of the embassy officials.

Currency and customs regulations
There is no restriction on the amount of currency that may be taken into or out of the country. Articles for personal use including any amount of cigarettes, cigars, or tobacco are allowed in duty free. The import of alcoholic beverages is strictly prohibited. Also the import of pig meat and pig meat products.

CLIMATE

Saudi Arabia has a desert climate. In Jedda it is warm and humid for most of the year. Riyad, much more inland is much hotter than Jedda in the summer and colder in winter, when occasional heavy rainstorms occur.

What to wear
Light-weight clothing is adequate in Jedda for most of the year. In Riyad and the Eastern provinces, tropical clothing is necessary from mid-April to mid-October. During December and January winter clothing and raincoats are necessary.

ACCOMMODATION AND FOOD

All hotels are air-conditioned and all rooms have private baths. Hotel tariffs fluctuate. A single room in one of the better hotels would cost approximately SR180-230 a night. All the large hotels have restaurants at which both western and oriental dishes are served. There are very few restaurants catering for visitors.

TRANSPORT

By air: All internal services are run by Saudia which operates services between Jedda, Riyad, and Dhahran. Air journeys from Jedda to Riyad and from Riyad to Dhahran take on average 75 and 45 minutes respectively.

By road: Good roads link the three main towns. Taxis are readily available in the main centres. Car hire facilities are limited. Taxi fares in the country are officially controlled. In Jedda, for instance, fares within the city are SR5 and rates are displayed both at the airport and in the downtown centre. It is, however, necessary to bargain with the driver as the official rates are not usually observed.

By rail: Riyad and Dammam are linked by a railway with a daily passenger service in each direction. The journey takes eight hours (compared with four and a half hours by road).

BANKS

Saudi Arabian Monetary Agency, P.O. Box 394, Airport Road, Jedda, tel: 31122-31130.
Arab Bank Ltd, P.O. Box 344, Jedda, tel: 22896.
The British Bank of the Middle East, P.O. Box 109, King Abdul Aziz Street, Jedda, tel: 23251.
First National City Bank, P.O. Box 490, King Abdul Aziz Street, Jedda, tel: 24155.
The Saudi Credit Bank, Riyad, tel: 29625.

Business hours
Banks: Saturday to Wednesday, 0830-1200 and 1700-1900. Thursday, 0830-1130.

Government Departments: Saturday to Wednesday, 0730-1430. Thursdays and Fridays are official holidays.
Business Houses and Shops: No standard hours. Roughly as follows: Jedda, 0900-1330; 1630-2000, (Ramadan, 2000-0100). Riyad, 0830-1200; 1630-1930 (Ramadan 1930-2330). Eastern Province, 0730-1200 1430-1800 (Ramadan 1900-2300). Aramco, Dhahran, 0700-1130; 1300-1630 (closed Thursdays and Fridays).

PUBLIC HOLIDAYS

Eid al Fitr 3-6 September. Eid al Adha 10-13 November. National Day 5 September.

EMBASSIES IN JEDDA

Algeria: Medina Road. tel: 53202
Austria: Medina Road, Kilometre 4. tel: 52548
Bahrain: Al Ruwais. tel: 51905
Belgium: Medina Road, Kilometre 2. tel: 53196
Canada: King Abdul Aziz Street. tel: 34598
Denmark: King Abdul Aziz Street.tel: 33044
Egypt: Airport Street. tel: 21011
Finland: Ministry of Defence Office Street. tel: 53192
France: Sheikh Mohamed Bin Abdul Wahab Street. tel: 21233
Germany: Medina Road. tel: 53545
Greece: Kandara Palace Hotel, Villa 13. tel: 34370
India: Medina Road. tel: 21602
Iran: Medina Road. tel: 52498
Italy: Sharafiyah. tel: 21451
Japan: Palestine Road. tel: 42402
Jordan: Palace Sea Port Road. tel: 23341
Kuwait: Ali Bin Abi Taleb Street. tel: 53163
Lebanon: Medina Road, Kilometre 3. tel: 52488
Libya: Medina Road, Kilometre 5. tel: 51273

Malaysia: Shuhada Street, Kilometre 3. tel: 52371
Morocco: Medina Road. tel: 52568
Netherlands: Medina Road, Kilometre 1. tel: 53611
Oman: Medina Road, Kilometre 2. tel: 53618
Pakistan: 92 Sea Port Road. tel: 27333
Qatar: Medina Road. tel: 52538
Spain: Mecca Road, Kilometre 4. tel: 23226
Sudan: Medina Road. tel: 20560
Sweden: Baghdadiah. tel: 21416
Switzerland: Off Medina Road, Kilometre 2. tel: 51387
Syria: Al Huda Street. tel: 51049
Tunisia: Mecca Road, Kilometre 3. tel: 32133
Turkey: Medina Road, Kilometre 7. tel: 54873
United Arab Emirates: Osman Bin Affan Street. No. 58. tel: 53770
UK: Ruwais. tel: 52544
USA: Palestine Road, Ruwais. tel: 52188
Yemen: Airport Street. tel: 24291

RIYAD

Riyad has been the capital of Saudi Arabia since the Kingdom was first set up in the 1920s. It has been the site of settlements in the Najd for centuries but has really expanded in the past 60 years. It is now the fastest growing city in the Middle East with over a million inhabitants. It is an essentially modern city well served by roads, a railway and airport and with plenty of hotels. Apart from the Royal Palace and an interesting museum, it boasts an elegant water tower which has become something of a landmark, and a massive race course and sports stadium.

Hotels
Al Yammamah (first class), Airport Road. tel: 28200
Intercontinental (luxury class), P.O. Box 3636. tel: 34500

Airport Hotel (first class), P.O. Box 1957. tel: 62193

Riyadh Hotel (first class). P.O. Box 1957. tel: 20006

Zahrat al Sharq Hotel, Airport Road. tel: 26031

Saudia Hotel, Nasriah Street. P.O. Box 244. tel: 24051

Al Khereiji Hotel, Batah Street. tel: 39913/19

Sahari Palace Hotel, As-Sulaimaniah. P.O. Box 16. tel: 61500

Al Hamra Hotel, Khazzan Street. tel: 28234

Middle East Hotel, King Faisal Street. tel: 29011

Al Asima Hotel, Abdubaku Siddiqe Road. tel: 24120

Samiramees Hotel, Batha Street. P.O. Box 166. tel: 27757

Restaurants
Green Valley, Saudia and the **Intercontinental Hotels** have good restaurants.

JEDDA

Jedda, Saudi Arabia's commercial and diplomatic capital, has been a port for more than 1,200 years. Now it is the biggest port on the Red Sea with a population of about 500,000. Like Riyad, it has expanded so fast that it has lost much of its character, although there is something of the old quarter left. Some 50 embassies are located in Jedda. It is well served by roads and has adequate hotel accommodation.

The visitor should visit the *souk*. There are fruiterers with giant fresh dates, hookah smokers, coppersmiths, incense sellers, jewellers and the like.

At prayer time recordings blare out from the mosques and devout shopkeepers rush off, leaving their wares untended. (Theft, as a result of the law of the Koran is minimal.) Those who don't are occasionally rapped by the religious police who wander around with their

canes. The *souk* is a melting pot of old and new, women balancing baskets on their heads walk beside 20th century luxury stores.

The only thing to do at the weekend—Thursday afternoon or Friday—is to follow the mobs to the beach. Jedda has its much frequented Creek which now boasts two hotels. But a drive out of town on a flat sandy road will lead you to various spots on the Red Sea where foreigners of all varieties repair. You can collect white coral, sport a bikini, or watch the Pakistanis and Arabs fishing as they immerse themselves fully clothed. You may prefer the swimming pool at your hotel, or the men-only health club.

Traffic in Jedda is a hazard. It is as much as a driver's life is worth, you are told, to knock you down. Nevertheless it takes an insane kind of courage to walk into that seething mass of dodgem cars and gesture to them with your bare hand to stop. But this is the only way to reach the other side. Being in a car is not much more secure, but again you quickly learn to relax.

Having put your life into your driver's hands, a further problem arises in that street names, by and large, are non-existent. Destinations can only be reached if you have detailed directions via a major landmark. But without these, it is best to get your quarry to meet you at your hotel or to send his own driver.

Hotels

Kandara Palace, (two star) P.O. Box 473. tel: 23155

Jedda Palace, (two star) P.O. Box 473. tel: 32387

Red Sea Palace, P.O. Box 824. tel: 28950 (two star)

Al Atlas, (two star) P.O. Box 1299. tel: 20609

Al Attas Oasis, (two star) P.O. Box 1789. tel: 20211

International Hotel, (two star) P.O. Box 1700. tel: 29412

Al Rehab Hotel, New Street. tel: 32302.

Asia Hotel, Bab Mecca. tel: 25111

Airport Hotel, P.O. Box 2012. tel: 33155

Quraish Hotel, Near Bakhashab Building. tel: 29499

Medina Hotel, P.O. Box 1026. tel: 33950

Riyadh Hotel, P.O. Box 4211. tel: 33944

Restaurants

Wimpy Bar, Medina Road.

Kilo 10, Mecca Road.

Kaymak, Baghdadiyah.

Black Tent, Medina Road.

Topkapi, Khalid Ibn Walid Street.

Al Hanva Casino, Corniche.

Koreana, Airport Sharahia Road.

MECCA

Mecca is built some 700m up in the mountains of the west where it dominates a pass through to the Najd from the coast. Because of its strategic siting, it was settled long before Islam made it the focus of world attention. As Muhammad's birth place it has the Sacred Mosque which houses the *Ka'baa* (House of God) which brings in over a million pilgrims each year. Although the city has expanded fast and is now easily accessible by road, an effort has been made to preserve the traditional architecture. Mecca has a new and impressive Islamic conference hall.

Hotels

Mecca Intercontinental, Ummal-Joud, P.O. Box 1496. tel: 31580

Hotel al-Fath , Shar'a al-Malik. tel: 31242

Mecca Hotel, Bab al-Umra. tel: 24987

Hotel Shubra, Jiyad. tel: 28240

Al-Haram Hotel, Shar'a al-Hijla. tel: 27720

MEDINA

The second holy city of Islam, Medina is also in the mountains but somewhat to the north of Mecca. It is the only settlement in that area and is able to support a permanent population because underground water gushes out from beneath the lava bed at that point. It is the centre of Islamic learning with the three colleges of the Islamic University and also has the Great Mosque with its magnificent green dome.

Hotels

Al-Haram Hotel, Shar'a as-Saha al-Jadid. tel: 23200

Al-Taisir Hotel, Shar'a as-Sumbulia. tel: 21425

Hotel Bahauddin, Bab al-Majidi. tel: 21340

Dar al-Hijah Hotel, Shar'a Malik Abdulaziz. tel: 22667

Hotel al-Rihab, Shar'a as-Sha al-Jadid. tel: 22000

Hotel Qasr al-Medina, Bab al-Majidi. tel: 21020

Hotel al-Hijaz, Shar'a as-Sumbulia. tel: 21110

TAIF

Taif, a little inland from Mecca is Saudi

Arabia's summer resort. Because of its altitude of some 1,600m, it is cool in the blistering summer and it is in Taif that the Royal family has its summer residence. This beautiful city is famous throughout the Middle East for its fruit groves and rose gardens.

Hotels
Al-Aziziah Palace Hotel, P.O. Box 17. tel: 21666
Orient Hotel, Shar'a al Malik. tel: 23651
Hotel al-Amal, Shar'a al Malik. tel: 22403
Hotel al-Masif, beside Riyad Taxi Station. tel: 24662
Shubra Hotel, beside bin Abbas mosque. tel: 21189

DHAHRAN, DAMMAM etc.

Dhahran is the main centre in a group of towns where Saudi Arabia's major oil wells exist. The other towns are Dammam, Khubar, Qatif, Rahima and Abqiq. Dammam is an important commercial centre, being the main port in the east of the country.

Hotels
Dhahran Hotel, Dhahran, tel: 3177
Al Gosaibi Hotel, Khubar, P.O. Box 51, Dhahran Airport. tel: 42160
Motel Rezayat, P.O. Box 90, Khubar. tel: 702156
Al Khajah Hotel, P.O. Box 45. Khubar. tel: 43122
Al Jabr Hotel, Shar'a Malik Khalid, Khubar. tel: 41348
Gulf Flower Hotel, Street No. 9. Khubar Road, Dammam. tel: 22170
Al Dossary Hotel, P.O. Box 5, Dammam. tel: 22740
Al Manara Hotel, P.O. Box 6, Dammam. tel: 24066
Al Haramain Hotel, Shar'a al Malik, Dammam. tel: 26421

The Ka'bah—the physical axis of the Muslims' faith, Mecca

CAMERAPIX

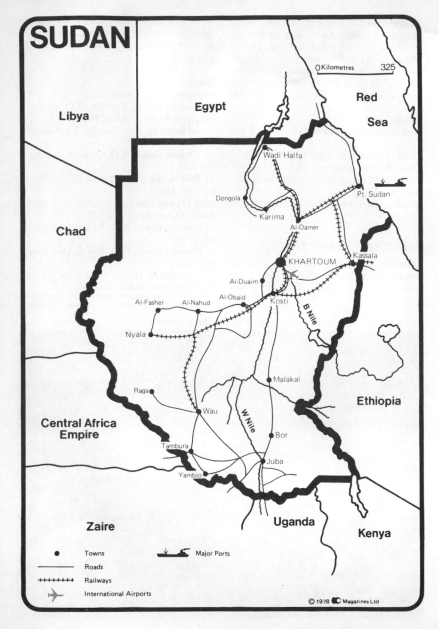

SUDAN

Until now tourism to Sudan has been virtually limited to a small number of keen explorers. The reason for this is twofold: the very limited hotel accommodation has been fully booked for months ahead and room rates have as a result risen to high levels, and in addition the Sudanese pound has been consistently very strong (mainly thanks to support from Arab oil-producing states) and this has turned the country into a relatively high cost destination.

The situation has not yet changed substantially, but the change has begun. A massive hotel development programme is being carried out and this will have transformed the accommodation position by 1980. At the same time, currencies in travel-generating countries (including the UK) are generally becoming stronger and so Sudan is tending to become relatively cheaper. To hasten this, the government is even considering a special favourable rate of exchange for bona fide tourists.

Most visitors will consider a visit to Sudan in two parts: a few days looking around Khartoum and examining it as a possible base from which to explore the interior, and a few days relaxation at the Red Sea. There are many interesting places to visit, particularly in and around Khartoum. But most travellers agree that the big attraction is the exceptionally cheerful and colourful combination of

African and Arab which is the Sudanese people.

THE LAND AND THE PEOPLE

Sudan is the largest country in Africa, covering an area of 2,505,813 sq. km. Although it is almost as large as Western Europe its population is only 16.5 million.

The country has great variety geographically and ethnologically. Much of the land is fairly flat, but lovers of scenic hills, hunting and camping will find these at Imatong in East Equatoria, Jebel Marrah (3,430 m.) and the summer resort of Erkowit (1,000 m.) in the Red Sea Hills. For the visitor interested in history there are the ancient monuments along the Nile.

Sudan's desert region, covered by the Libyan and Nubian deserts, lies in the north and extends south to Khartoum. The Nile runs through the middle of this area, making agriculture possible, and there is also some vegetation at scattered oases. The steppe region from Khartoum to El-Obeid in central Sudan is covered by short, coarse grass and small bushes; the Kurdufan plateau lies 500 m. above most of the area. South of the steppe are the savannah and equatorial regions consisting mainly of a shallow basin traveresed by the Nile and its tributaries. In the centre lies the Sudd, an enormous marsh of over 120,000 sq. km. Mount Kinyeti rises 3,480 m. on the Sudan-Uganda border.

The White Nile, which rises in Uganda, enters Sudan near Nimule and flows northwards 3,420 km. until it leaves the country at Wadi Haifa. The Blue Nile, rising in Ethiopia, joins the White Nile at Khartoum. In 1966 the Roseires Dam, supplying water to two million acres of land, was completed across the Blue Nile at Damazin, 576 km. south of Khartoum.

In the eastern Sudan lies the Red Sea coast with its beautiful marine gardens. The clear blue water and the coral reefs are a major tourist attraction. The ancient city of Suakin, 56 km. from Port Sudan, was once the capital of the Beja Kingdoms. Near Suakin is Erkowit, Sudan's only developed summer resort, which lies on a high plateau surrounded by mountains.

The Sudanese are of Hamitic and Negro origin, though in the north there has been much intermingling with the Arabs and the people there are traditionally nomadic or semi-nomadic. In the south, the Nilotic peoples predominate. The highest population densities occur along the Nile and around Khartoum.

Sudan has now largely recovered from its main political problem; the rebellion in the three southern provinces—Upper Nile, Equatoria and Bahr al-Ghazal—which lasted from 1956 until 1972. Unlike the north, which is largely Muslim and Arab, these provinces are much more African in culture. British policy had not been one of promoting national unity and the conflict was long and bitter. The south's main problem, now that the struggle for autonomy has been resolved, is one of isolation, and this has not been helped by the troubles in Uganda.

Sudan's agricultural potential is being developed with massive food-crop and sugar schemes financed by Arab oil-money and often managed by large Western corporations.

CULTURE

The Sudanese like to think of their country as a meeting point for the Middle East and Africa and they often speak of it as being a bridge between Africa north and south.

African dances and music can be seen or heard more in the three southern provinces; the north has its own tradition of Islamic music, which can be heard especially on Fridays in Omdurman (the largest of the three towns that make up Khartoum).

About 160 km. north of Khartoum is the Shendi area, where there are monuments dating back to the ancient Meroe kingdom. They include the antiquities of Naga, Masawarat and Bajrawia as well as churches and monasteries from the period when Sudan was a Christian country (AD 343-734).

North of Shendi, and half way between the Egyptian border and Khartoum in the middle of the Nile loop, is the town of Kuraymah, near the Barkal Mountain, site of the ancient Napata kingdom, centre of the first Sudanese Empire which ruled the whole of ancient Sudan and Egypt during the 24th Egyptian dynasty. The temple of the god Amun is well preserved. A few kilometres from Kuraymah are the pyramids of the kings of Napata. Across the river are the pyramids of Nuri. All these areas can be reached by rail, air or road from Khartoum.

HISTORY

The history of Sudan, especially the region north of Khartoum, was bound from ancient times with that of Egypt. In 750 BC the first Sudanese kingdom of Nafata flourished near the Barkal Mountain and its Cushitic kings also ruled over

Egypt. Meroe, near present-day Shendi, was the second of these ancient kingdoms, famous for its iron works which exported iron to other parts of Africa. The medieval kingdoms of Nubia, Maqurra and Abodia—which flourished in northern Sudan—were converted to Christianity during the sixth century. The next important phase came with the penetration of the Arabs and Islam. The 16th century saw the rise of the kingdoms of the Fung, Darfur, Tagali and other minor dynasties. During this period, Arabisation and Islamisation of the northern parts was completed, but the south has been largely unaffected by these influences.

Although little is known about the history of the south during this period, it is certain that the kingdoms similar to those elsewhere in Africa at the time also existed there. In 1820 the country was conquered by Egypt and the Turko-Egyptian regime was established.

In 1881 Muhammad Ahmad al-Mahdi led his successful revolt against the Turko-Egyptian rulers. General Gordon, who was employed by the Egyptian Government, failed to arrest the Mahdi's revolt; Khartoum was captured by the Mahdi and Gordon was killed in 1885. The Mahdi was succeeded by Khalifa Abd Ullahi. For 15 years the Khalifa attempted to resist the invasion from Egypt and to establsih a strong government, but he failed. In 1898 the armies of the Khalifa were defeated by British-Egyptian forces in the battle of Omdurman, and a year later the Khalifa himself was killed.

From then until 1956 Sudan was ruled by the Condominium Administration—a suposedly joint Egyptian and British Administration but in reality British. The achievements of the colonial administration included the establishment of railways, a modern system of education, the important Gezira peasant cotton scheme and a modern system of government.

Sudan became independent in 1956 and a parliamentary system of government was established. But in 1958 the parliamentary regime was overthrown by a military government, which was in its turn overthrown in 1964. In May 1969 the army came back to power, this time led by younger radical officers under Major-General Numeiry, who was elected President in September 1971. Agreement with the southern Sudanese rebels was reached in March 1972, at Addis Ababa, which gave the south regional autonomy and brought to an end the war which had sapped the strength of the country for 17 years.

There have been some violent rebellions against General Numeiry's rule, but his staying-power has made him the country's longest-serving President. Since 1969 he has steered the country through both left-wing and right-wing rule. By 1978 his Government was considered one of the more conservative in the Arab world, being ideologically close to both Egypt and Saudi Arabia.

Shilluk tribesman, Sudan

WILDLIFE

In the south the visitor can travel into the bush where elephants wander in herds of up to 400 and buffalo are estimated to exceed a total of 20,000. Giraffe and zebra are also plentiful. Hippo and crocodile are to be found in the reeds and swamps.

Darfur is another area rich in game. There are more addax and oryx here than in any other part of Africa. The ibex which is rare almost everywhere else, can still be hunted in the Red Sea Hills area.

The Dinder National Park is the best developed of the tourist areas and can be reached by road from Khartoum.

GENERAL INFORMATION

Area: 2,505,815 sq. km.
Population: About 16.5 million.
Altitude: Sea level-3,000 m.; mainly about 300 m.
Capital: Khartoum, taking in Omdurman and Khartoum North.
Head of State: Major-General Gaafar Muhammad Numeiry.
Government: Military, controlled by the political bureau of the Sudan Socialist Union, the only legal political party.
Date of independence; 1 January 1956.
Languages: Arabic (official) and many local dialects. English is widely spoken and is the language of the government in the south.
Religions: Islam in the north, traditional African in the south, with Christian communities.
Currency: Sudanese Pound (£S), divided into 100 piastres (PT) and 1,000 milliemes. £S0.667 = £1 sterling; £S0.348 = US$1.00
Time: GMT + 2

HOW TO GET THERE

By air: Khartoum Airport is served inter-nationally by Aeroflot, Alitalia, British Airways, EgyptAir, Ethiopian Airlines, Interflug, Lufthansa, MEA, SAS, Saudi Arabian Airlines, Sudan Airways and TWA. The national carrier, Sudan Airways, connects Khartoum with Bahrain, Egypt, Ethiopia, Germany, Greece, Kenya, Italy, Iraq, Lebanon, Libya, Saudi Arabia and the UK.

All passengers embarking on international flights from Khartoum must pay an airport charge of £S1. Taxis are available at the airport, which is about 10 minutes by car from the centre of Khartoum, on the eastern outskirts of the city. On request airlines sometimes arrange for passenger transport from hotels to the airport.

By sea: Ships from various parts of the world dock at Port Sudan on the Red Sea, the country's only seaport.

By road: Motorists must apply for permission to drive through Sudan well in advance of the journey. Applications should be made to the Under Secretary, Ministry of Interior, PO Box 770, Khartoum, or any Sudanese legation or embassy, and should list names and nationalities of travellers, number, make and horsepower of vehicles, reason for journey, proposed route and ultimate destination. Motorists must have a tryptique or carnet de passage from a recognised automobile club, or must pay a deposit or provide a guarantee signed by a known resident of Sudan, a bank or a business firm. Vehicles must be insured.

Permission to motor in, or through, Sudan may not be granted for less than two vehicles travelling together, and drivers should enquire about the state of roads before starting the journey. In main towns and their environs roads are surfaced but most outlying roads are rough tracks with sandy stretches, requiring strong vehicles.

Entry from Ethiopia has been impossible for some years because of the state of

Fishing in the Nile, Sudan

emergency in Eritrea.

By river and rail: From Egypt by train from Cairo to Aswan High Dam: by Aswan High Lake steamer, with rudimentary accommodation, from Aswan High Dam to Wadi Halfa: and from there by train to Khartoum. Accommodation on trains must be reserved in advance.

In normal circumstances travellers can take road transport from Ethiopia to Kassala, proceeding from there by train to Khartoum, and river transport operates from Uganda to Nimule (thence by road to Juba, steamer to Kosti and by train to Khartoum).

Visas and health regulations

Visas are needed by all visitors and should be obtained in advance from a Sudanese diplomatic mission abroad: they are not obtainable at Khartoum airport. Passports must be valid for at least two months beyond the period of intended stay.

Transit visas are available on arrival for visitors from countries with no Sudanese representation, provided they hold the required documents and have a confirmed reservation for a connecting flight within 24 hours. These visitors may not leave the airport. Admission to Sudan and transit rights are refused to holders of Israeli passports, or passports containing a valid or expired visa for Israel, Rhodesia or South Africa.

Visitors staying in Sudan longer than three days must report to the police. For travel to the southern regions—Bahr-al-Ghazal, Equatoria and Upper Nile, including Malakal, Wau and Juba airports—a special permit must be obtained from a Sudanese representative abroad, or from the Ministry of the Interior in Khartoum (which takes five days).

Inoculation against smallpox, yellow fever and cholera is compulsory.

Currency regulations

Foreign currencies in unlimited amounts

may be imported, provided these amounts are allowed by the country of origin. All foreign currency, including travellers' cheques and letters of credit, must be declared on entry and departure. Exchange should made be only at authorised exchange points—ie banks and certain hotels and travel agencies—and entered on the declaration form, which needs to be shown on departure. Export of foreign currency by visitors is limited to the amount imported. Import and export of local currency is prohibited.

CLIMATE

There is little rain in the extreme north. In the central region rainfall averages about 15 cm. a year, most of it confined to July and August. In the south the annual average is about 100 cm. and the rainy season lasts from May to October. Summers are hot throughout the country, with temperatures ranging from $27\,^\circ$C to $46\,^\circ$C. Winter temperatures are around $16\,^\circ$C in the north and $27\,^\circ$C in the south. Between April and October severe sandstorms (haboobs) sweep in from the Sahara desert, sometimes lasting three to four days. The best time to visit Sudan is in winter (November to March).

In Khartoum the coolest month is January and the hottest June.

What to wear
Lightweight clothing is essential for most of the year. Dress is almost always informal.

Health precautions
Precautions against malaria are advisable, although Khartoum itself is free of the disease. The water supplies of major towns are safe to drink. Swimming in slow-moving or static fresh water is not advisable as bilharzia is endemic.

ACCOMMODATION AND FOOD

There are a limited number of high-standard hotels in Khartoum and Port Sudan. Elsewhere there are rest houses, with variable standards and permission must be obtained in advance to use them. There are plenty of cheap hotels in the main towns, although proprietors may be unwilling to take foreigners unless they do not mind sharing a room. The only youth hostel is in Khartoum.

The restaurants in the Khartoum and Port Sudan hotels serve international cuisine. There are a few Greek and Middle Eastern restaurants.

Sudanese dishes served in small restaurants usually consist of *fool*—bean and bread and meat, and *dura*—cooked millet or maize. If you are invited into a Sudanese home you will be regaled with much more exotic fare.

Tipping
Hotels 10% of the bill; restaurants 10%.

TRANSPORT

Official permits are required for most journeys in the Sudan; they can be obtained from the Registry Office, Khartoum. You should also register with the police in each town you spend the night.

By air: Sudan Airways operates regular flights to Atbara, Dongola, Al-Fashir, Juba, Geneina, Kassala, Khashim al-Girba, Kosti, Malakal, Marawi, Annuhud, Nyala, El-Obeid, Port Sudan, Roseires, Wad Madani and Wau.

By rail: The trains are comfortable and clean (first class) and are a good way to see much of the country and its people. They are, however, extremely slow. There are trains to Port Sudan, Wadi Halfa, El-Obeid, Nyala, Wau, Roseires and Kassala. Sleeping cars and catering services are available on the main routes. Students' reductions are available on application to the Ministry of Youth.

By river: The main stretch of river transport is between Kosti and Juba. It is a long slow journey—although rewarding to wildlife lovers—taking up to 11 days. One needs to stock up with food in Kosti and Malakal.

By road: Motorists should make inquiries about road conditions and administrative restrictions in the places they intend to visit. Roads in the north are often closed during the rainy season (July-September). In the south a number of roads are open throughout the year, but surfaces are poor. Sudan has virtually no tarred roads. A complete spare-part kit should be taken on any long journey.

Cars can be hired in the main towns. Traffic drives on the right.

Khartoum's yellow taxis can be hailed in the street. They are not metered and fares should be arranged before the journey is undertaken, but the average rate for a short journey in town is only 30 piastres. It is not necessary to tip the driver. There are also collective taxis which can be found in Khartoum market place.

Buses run between the main towns, and leave from the central market place (there is one in each of Khartoum's 'Three Towns'). Trucks travelling long distances also take passengers. Hitch-hiking is not recommended.

BANKS

El Nilein Bank (PO Box 466, Khartoum); has branches in Omdurman, Port Sudan, Adueim, Kuraymah and Wad Madani. Other banks are Bank of Khartoum, PO Box 1008, Khartoum (formerly State Bank for Foreign Trade); Unity Bank, PO Box 408, Khartoum (formerly Juba Commerical Bank); People's Co-opera-

tive Bank, PO Box 922, Khartoum (formerly Msr Bank) and Sudan Commercial Bank, PO Box 1116, Khartoum.

Business hours
Weekly closing day: Friday.
Banks: 0830-1200.
Government offices: 0730-1430.
Post offices: 0830-1300 and 1730-1830.
Central Telegraph Offices: 24 hours daily, including holidays.
Shops: 0800-1300 and 1700-2000 (Friday 0800-1130) and some shops close on Sundays.

PUBLIC HOLIDAYS

Independence Day 1 January, National Unity Day 3 March, 1969 Revolution Day 25 May, Christmas Day, Easter Day (for Christians only).

The following Muslim holidays are also observed: Ramadan Bairam, Kurban Bairam, Islamic New Year's Day, birthday of the Prophet.

EMBASSIES IN KHARTOUM

Algeria: Junction Mek Nimr Street and 67th Street, PO Box 80;
Austria: Slavos Building, 29, 3rd Floor, PO Box 1860;
Belgium: Sharia Al Mek Nimr, House No 4, PO Box 969;
Egypt: Mogram Street;
France: 6H East Plot 2, 19th Street, PO Box 377;
West Germany: Baladiya Street, PO Box 970;
Greece: Block 74, 31st Street, PO Box 1182;
Iran: Baladia Street;
Italy: 39th Street, PO Box 793;
Jordan: 25, 7th Street, New Extension;
Kuwait: 9th Street, New Extension;
Libya: Africa Road 50, PO Box 2091;
Morocco: 32, 19th Street;

Netherlands: PO Box 391;
Qatar: Street 15, New Extension;
Saudi Arabia: Central Street, New Extension, PO Box 852;
Spain: Street 3, New Extension, PO Box 2621;
Syria: 3rd Street, New Extension;
Turkey: 71 Africa Road, PO Box 771;
United Arab Emirates: Street 3, New Extension;
UK: New Abulela Building, PO Box 801;
USA: Gumhouria Avenue;
Yemen Arab Republic: Street 35, New Extension;
Yemen Peoples Democratic Republic: Street 51, New Extension.

TOURIST INFORMATION

Sudan Tourist Corporation, PO Box 2424, tel: 70230, cable: Hababkum, Khartoum. There are regional offices in Port Sudan and Nyala. Travel Agent: Sudan Travels and Tourism Agency, PO Box 769, tel: 72119.

KHARTOUM

Khartoum is generally known as the 'Three Towns' capital, i.e. Khartoum, Omdurman and Khartoum North. Omdurman is considered to be the national capital, Khartoum the commercial and administrative capital and Khartoum North the industrial capital. The three towns lie at the junction of the Blue Nile and the White Nile. Omdurman is joined to Khartoum by the White Nile bridge; the Shambat bridge joins Omdurman to Khartoum North and the Burri bridge joins the eastern extension of Khartoum to Khartoum North across the Blue Nile.

After its destruction in 1885 Khartoum was rebuilt on modern and spacious lines with huge colonial buildings, but old houses with shuttered windows, narrow streets and colourful market-places can still be found.

Not far from the excellent museum is the zoo—a place to view animals or merely stroll on the lawns. A tree-lined embankment leads to the People's Palace

An aerial view of Khartoum

where there is a marvellous collection of antique field guns, swords and cutlasses, used by General Gordon before he was stabbed at the foot of the now-famous staircase by a soldier of the Mahdi's National Army. A few years later Lord Kitchener perpetuated Gordon's name when he gave Sudan the Gordon Memorial College. This is now the University of Khartoum.

OMDURMAN

Omdurman is rich in traditional Sudanese architecture: flat-roofed, baked mud or clay houses, city walls, narrow streets of dark little shops where some of the finest Sudanese handcrafts can be found. Omdurman was built by the Mahdi when he began his siege against Gordon in Khartoum, and it became the capital of the Mahdi's empire. It was captured in 1898 when Kitchener led the British and Egyptians against the forces for the Khalifa. You can see the Mahdi's tomb and the Khalifa's museum next door to it.

Omdurman has long been the meeting place of all the peoples of Sudan; the Jaaleen, Shaigiyya, Danagla, Rubatab and Mahas of the north live side by side with the Baggara and Fur of the west and the Shilluk and Dinka of the south.

In the bustling *souk*, the smell of incense fills the air as Arab and African traders conduct their business. Here you can buy carpets from Persia, ivory goods, silverware, beads and handcrafts of the Middle East, Central and Eastern Africa.

Hotels
Acropole, PO Box 48, central location, tel: 72860, cable: Hotelacrop.
Excelsior, PO Box 272, central location, tel: 81181, cables: Excelhotel.
Grand, PO Box 316, tel.: 72782 (closed for rebuilding, but should be open by summer 1978).

Oasis, PO Box 272, tel: 81101.
De Paris, PO Box 1808, tel: 44154.
Sahara, PO Box 2208, tel: 75240, cable: Sarotel.
Sudan, PO Box 1845, tel: 80811, cable: Sudatel.
Khartoum Meridien, PO Box 1716, tel: 73107.
Khartoum Hilton, at the junction of the White and Blue Niles, PO Box 1910, tel: 74100, tlx: KM 250, cable: Hiltels.

Restaurants
The outstanding 'international' restaurants are at the **Grand Hotel** and the **Hilton**. Also popular with visitors is the roof restaurant, at the **Sahara**. Other recommended places are **St. James** in Gomhouria Street and the **Blue Nile Casino** in Khartoum North.

Entertainments
National Theatre, Nile Avenue, Omdurman, tel: 51549—the season is 1 October to 30 June. **Gordon Music Hall**, tel: 72045, for dinner, dance and cabaret nightly. The **Hilton** open-air night club is popular. There are several cabarets and cinemas.

There are a sailing club and a nine-hole golf club, and the Cultural Centre has a good library and facilities for tennis and swimming. Golf and tennis are also available at the Hilton.

There are also a number of interesting Nile cruises. Launches with capacity for 15 persons can be hired: 24 hours' notice is required.

Additional entertainments are **Hamad Floating Casino**, Nile Avenue, Khartoum; **Blue Nile Cafeteria**, Nile Avenue, Khartoum; **Ali Abdel Latif Stadium**, Omdurman, and **Youth Stadium**, Omdurman; **Khartoum Stadium**, Khartoum; **Jimmy's Night Club**, Khartoum.

THE RED SEA

Port Sudan has been the country's port

The deserted city of Suakin

since the beginning of the century, when it totally replaced the old-established city of Suakin, 56 km. down the coast. The new port is now a bustling commercial centre with plenty of entertainment and interest. The 'marine gardens' with their exquisite coral and tiny fish can be visited in glass-bottomed boats. There is sailing in the harbour, swimming in a choice of pools and tremendous scope for fishing (barracuda, grey cod, shark, etc.). The main hotel is the colonial-style **Red Sea**. An hour's drive north of Port Sudan is the **Arousa** holiday village, isolated but good for sub-aqua enthusiasts.

A visit to the Red Sea is not complete unless it includes the deserted city of *Suakin*, with its crumbling but beautiful houses, many of them masterpieces of Islamic architecture. This is also a good spot for swimming, fishing and sailing.

Erkowit is a summer resort in the Red Sea Hills, inland from Suakin and Port Sudan, offering relaxation among beautiful mountains which rise to 1,200 m. above sea level. It has a good hotel with easy access from the railway station.

Shopping and markets
The best place for books is Khartoum Bookshop (PO Box 968). For ivory and skins go to Sudan Folklore House (67 New Abou Lela Building, tel.: 71729); it also has a picture gallery. Souvenirs can be obtained at Sudan Crafts (3/9 New Abou Ela Building in El-Kasr Avenue, PO Box 2207, tel: 77367). For hides and skins and excellent Sudanese chamois go to the Khartoum Tannery (PO Box 134, Khartoum South). A recommended boutique is Salwa Boutique, with branches in Khartoum and Khartoum North.

The bazaar in Omdurman has hand-beaten silver and copper; gold and silver filigree jewellery, ivory and ebony carvings, handbags, slippers, belts and wallets of lion, leopard and lizard skin, ostrich eggs, beaked coffee pots, etc.

OTHER PLACES OF INTEREST

Kassala is in the mountains near the border with Ethiopia. South of Khartoum by tarred road is **Wad Madani**, an important town with three hotels: **Continental**, **El Gezira** and **El Khawad**.

West and south of Khartoum lie the Nuba mountains, an area rich in folklore. The main town is **El-Obeid**, the largest market for gum arabic in the world. Further west is **Jebel Marrah**, a huge mountain rich in vegetation and natural beauty. There are water falls, volcanic lakes and springs (some cool, some warm, some hot). The rest houses in the region include that at **Suni**, near the summit.

The main town of the south is **Juba**, a centre for safaris and Nile crusies. It has the comfortable and pleasant **Juba Hotel**.

NATIONAL PARKS

There are three game parks and 17 game reserves and sanctuaries.

Dinder National Park (6,100 sq. km.) is open to visitors from Christmas to the end of April. It is 512 km. south-east of Khartoum and closer to Europe than any of the other more popular African big-game reserves. Visitors can stay in a specially built village with an attractive restaurant and bar area under spreading trees.

The visitor can expect to see many different types of animals and birds and a spectacular range of rolling savannah grasslands, sandy palm groves and tropical forest.

The most abundant animal species are the many types of antelope—the magnificent roan antelope, quite rare in most African game parks, the spiral-horned greater kudu, waterbuck, reedbuck, signa gazelle, oribi and bushbuck. There are also lion, giraffe, buffalo, warthog, several types of monkey, mongoose, fox and wild cat. The bird species include ostrich, eagle, vulture, guinea-fowl, pelican, bustard, crowned crane and large numbers of colourful smaller birds.

In the south are Numule National Park (192 km. south of Juba with its own holiday village in Gumeiza) and the Southern National Park (Bahr al-Ghazal Province—18,400 sq. km.). In these two parks and in other parts of southern Sudan, amid gigantic trees and high waving grass, elephants roam in herds which occasionally number as many as 400. Among the swamp reeds hippo, crocodile and buffalo are plentiful, as well as giraffe, rhino, zebra, leopard, lion and various types of cat. There are many types of antelope as well as countless birds, butterflies and beetles.

SAFARIS

The vast area of Southen Sudan is a paradise for the game hunter. Animals include the giant eland, bongo, nile lechwe (three of the rarest beasts in the world), white-eared cob, roan antelope, greater kudu and yellow-backed duiker. The white rhino is completly protected, but forms an excellent subject for photography.

Permits are required for making films and for hunting. Film permits are obtainable from the Sudan Tourist Corporation, PO Box 2424, Khartoum.

Safari formalities may be arranged through the Sudan Tourist Corporation (PO Box 2424, Khartoum). They specialise in Red Sea Coast Safaris, which combine ibex hunting, deep-sea fishing and aquasports, from December to May.

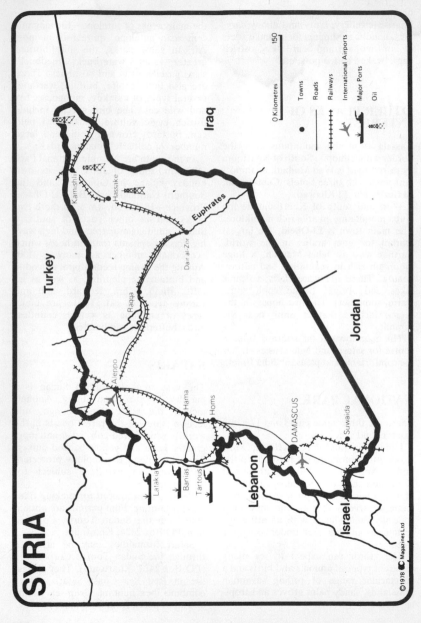

SYRIA

Turkey

Iraq

Jordan

Lebanon

Israel

Euphrates

Kamishli

Hassake

Dar al Zor

Raqqa

Aleppo

Hama

Homs

DAMASCUS

Suwaida

Latakia

Banias

Tartous

0 Kilometres 150

Towns
Roads
Railways
International Airports
Major Ports
Oil

© 1978 Magazines Ltd

SYRIA

Naomi Sakr

Syria is a country of both climatic and cultural contrasts. Archaeologically so rich that important discoveries are still being made (the remains of the ancient state of Ebla are still being uncovered and analysed) Syria has watched countless civilisations rise and fall on its soil in the course of the past 6,000 years, each of which has bequeathed its own particular monuments.

Not all Syria's attractions are remnants of the past, however. Lake Asad, the vast reservoir which forms part of the brand new Euphrates Dam has also become a potential resort in its own right. Leisure facilities are likewise in the course of development on Syria's 173km of Mediterranean coast, particularly at Ras al-Bassit near Lattakia where pine-covered hills slope straight down to a sheltered beach.

For most of its period of independence Syria has been too preoccupied with politics to prepare for any tourist boom, with the result that the recent surge in the number of visitors was not preceded by a corresponding increase in hotel rooms and other amenities. But this is now being rectified in a drive that should, before long, further enhance Syria's many centres of historic and scenic interest.

THE LAND AND THE PEOPLE

The country that is known as Syria today was carved by politicians from the much larger territory of 'greater' Syria at the end of the First World War. Before it came to be applied exclusively to the present republic, the term Syria referred to a geographical entity which included Lebanon, Palestine and Trans-Jordan. This area lay within the natural boundaries formed by the Taurus mountains to the north, the Syrian and Sinai deserts to the east and south and the Mediterranean to the west—a factor which enabled free movement between coast and hinterland and largely accounted for geographical Syria's prosperity and long-standing trading tradition.

Modern Syria is less advantageously placed. With the loss of the seaports of Beirut and Tripoli to Lebanon in the post-war carve-up and later on the loss of Iskenderun to Turkey, the Syrian centres of Damascus, Homs and Aleppo were no longer within such easy reach of their natural maritime outlets and Syria itself has been left to develop alternative facilities at Lattakia, Tartous and Banias, along a truncated stretch of coast.

If, historically, movement has always been possible across Syria from east to west through the various breaks in the country's coastal mountain ranges, the same cannot be said of passage from north to south. For although, topographically, Syria consists of five distinct zones all running roughly parallel with the shoreline along a north-south axis, no single strip is so homogeneous as to offer a continuous north-south route.

The fertile but narrow coastal plain, for example, varies from around 30km. in width in some places to no more than a few metres in others and the road that runs along the shore has to branch inland when it reaches Lattakia.

These idiosyncrasies also have their effect on climate and the distribution of Syria's population, which is made up of a mosaic of different religious groupings. Immediately next to the coastal strip in the north are the Nusairiya mountains, which, though relatively low, have very steep slopes—the 1,000m. drop down to the newly-developed agricultural area of the Ghab on the eastern flank is particularly sudden. As a result these mountains have traditionally afforded a number of vantage points. The Crusaders chose one to build their Krak des Chevaliers, a castle which can be seen from 30km. away or more. And they have provided places of refuge, particularly for the long-established indigenous community of Nusairis, or Alawis, a sect that combines elements of Shia' Islam with other non-Islamic beliefs and observances. Altogether, Syria's Alawis number something over half a million.

To the south of the Nusairiya mountain range, but separated from it by the valleys of the Orontes (or Asi) river and the Nahr al-Kabir and lying much further inland behind the border with Lebanon, stand the mountains of the Anti-Lebanon, extending southwards to Mount Hermon and the Golan Heights, occupied by Israel in the June 1967 war.

Further south still is the Jabal (mountain) al-Duruz, named after another, very secretive sect, the Druzes, who have inhabited this area from the early 18th century. The Druzes, of whom there are about 175,000 in Syria, consider themselves Muslims, but in terms of religious activity they keep themselves so much apart that outsiders tend to know little about their customs. As a community,

with other members living in southern Lebanon and northern Israel, they are an offshoot of the Ismaili sect, itself a movement which broke away from the main body of Shia' Muslims in the eighth century.

The Anti-Lebanon in general is much less readily penetrated by the climatic influence of the Mediterranean than are the Nusairiya mountains to the north, with the result that the area to the east of them is less well watered than are the northern steppes of Aleppo and the Jezira. The northern areas also benefit from the Orontes and Euphrates rivers. The Orontes flows some of the way along the great Red Sea rift valley which traverses Syria alongside the Nusairiya mountains, crosses through the Beqaa valley in Lebanon and continues southwards all the way to East Africa. The Euphrates flows from Turkey, through Syria and on to Iraq and is called upon to provide water for major hydro-electric and irrigation projects in all three countries—a demand which has proved a source of friction, actual and potential, amongst the three riparian states.

The southern part of Syria, in contrast, is much less fortunate in rain and rivers, which explains the huge diversity of Syria's weather and vegetation and the rapid degradation from fertility to desert as one moves east from the Damascus region. Mount Hermon, for example, (also called Jabal al-Shaikh) stands over 3,000m. high and is snow-capped for most of the year. On its southern side lies the productive soil of the Hawran plateau, which provides wheat and pasture and was once the granary of 'greater' Syria. That was before dry farming developments in the Jezira in the past 20 to 30 years proved that this latter spacious, relatively flat, triangular plain in Syria's north-eastern corner was better equipped to furnish the bulk of the country's cotton and grain.

The Hawran nevertheless remains,

along with the Damascus oasis, one of the most densely populated areas of the country and presents a striking contrast with the vast wasteland of the Syrian desert to the east. Stretching at its widest point for some 1,200km., this desert separates Syria from the populated river valleys of Iraq and is itself punctuated only by the sites of such ancient settlements as Palmyra, which then and now provides a resting place on the well-worn trade route between the Mediterranean and the Gulf. In the olden days it was the wells of the Kalamoun hills which branch out north-eastwards from Damascus to Palmyra that dictated the desert route, and modern roadways have followed the same path.

Syria's varied topography is reflected in the sharp distinctions between its urban, rural and nomadic populations. The country's principal cities, Damascus, Homs, Hama and Aleppo, are situated in valleys and plains where movement has been easier and there has been a greater intermingling of cultural and racial influences. These were the areas where Greek and Roman colonisers and Arab conquerors had their greatest cultural impact but where the physical traits of the incursors were also soon assimilated and obscured.

The inhabitants of these cities have traditionally formed something of an urban elite, which has coincidentally tended to follow the mainstream of religious thought, namely Sunni Islam, orthodox versions of Christianity or Judaism. A small Jewish community, in fact, remains in Damascus—its fortunes at the hands of the Syrian Government having attracted considerable publicity since they serve as a barometer of the Government's sensitivity to Western opinion.

Outside these urban centres, however, the lifestyle changes radically and more minority sects are found. The hundreds of tiny, ragged children standing in the village doorways are a testimony, both to Syria's exceptionally high birth rate and the persisting poverty of many of its rural inhabitants.

It is not that farming in Syria is unprofitable—the Euphrates project alone promises vast returns—but the agricultural sector has perhaps been the most vulnerable to the internal political upheavals that took place from independence right up until the onset of the 1970s, with the exodus or inertia of investors and the inevitably disruptive effects of land reform. The tradition of large land-holdings worked by poorly-rewarded sharecroppers is clearly illustrated by the fact that 95% of land around Aleppo was farmed in this fashion up until the late 1950s. Re-organisation of land tenure on such a scale is not without its ups and downs.

As for Syria's nomads, they, like nomads everywhere, have lost many of their customary tracks and haunts in the face of new roads, railways and irrigation schemes. Nevertheless, their contribution to the economy, particularly in providing wool for export, is recognised and their existence further exemplifies the diversity of Syria's ethnic and religious groupings.

And, in terms of language, there is not only Arabic—although Arabic is spoken by about 90% of the population—but also Kurdish, Circassian, Armenian and Assyrian. The Kurds in Syria are few, an overflow from the territory of Kurdistan which, with its own language, culture and national dress but sharing the Muslim religion, straddles Iraq, Iran and Turkey and spreads into northern Syria as well. Like the Kurds, the Circassians too are mountain folk who moved into Syria in large numbers from Turkey during the present century, when the Syrian-Turkish frontier was drawn. Many Armenians and Assyrians, have likewise come to Syria from Turkey and Iraq. Other immigrants to Syria have been the Palestinian refugees, many of whom live in camps around Damascus. The Palestinian community in Syria at present numbers around 175,000.

CULTURE AND HISTORY

Greater Syria was too rich and too important strategically to be left to its own devices for long by political and military forces outside. The site of human habitation for over 150,000 years—displaying signs of very early human advances in the domestication of animals, the cultivation of wheat and the use of copper—the area is also thought to have provided the world with its first consonantal alphabet. Its trading tradition, promoted first and foremost by the Phoenicians of the greater Syrian littoral, whose sturdy merchant ships were built from the renowned cedars of Lebanon, gave its people the opportunity to benefit from and promulgate the cultural and intellectual achievements of the ancient civilisations in nearby Egypt and Mesopotamia and beyond. But, as these exchanges grew, they soon attracted foreign powers and by 1600 BC an area stretching up as far as Damascus had come under the administrative grip of the Egyptian empire.

At about the same time the north was being overrun by Hittites, moving in from Anatolia. But, gradually, both Egyptian and Hittite domination receded, giving way to Assyrian and later Chaldean influence from what is now Iraq. Of all these incursions, however, with their inevitable cultural impact, the only group to leave any lasting ethnic imprint were the Arameans. For, despite the lack of any literary or other Aramean cultural heritage to speak of, the Arameans can be described as the forerunners of modern Syrians in much the same way as the Phoenicians are the acknowledged ancestors of the modern Lebanese. Originally they were nomads who had migrated from Arabia to the Euphrates, eventually settling around Damascus by around 1200 BC. They too were merchants whose travels enabled them to spread the innovatory Phoenician alphabet, which they adopted, together with their own language, Aramaic—the language of Christ which has survived in one small group of villages north of Damascus to the present day. Syriac, which evolved from Aramaic, is also still used as the liturgical language of Syrian Christians.

A new influence, that of the Greeks, had started to reach Syria before the arrival of Alexander the Great, but it was Alexander's conquest in 331 BC which launched a completely new phase in Syrian history—a phase marked by the spread of Greek learning and the deliberate mingling of Greek and oriental cultures. The Roman conquest of the area took place two and a half centuries later and the centre of the Syrian 'province' was at that point moved to Antioch.

Nevertheless, it is Damascus, the capital of the Aramean kingdom, which has served as the most consistent pivot for developments in Syria for as long as 4,000 years. So far as is known it is probably the oldest continuously inhabited capital in the world. Indeed, nowhere is the succession of outside influences more clearly illustrated than in the capital, where the same ancient sites have been adapted and venerated by Greeks, Romans, early Christians and Muslim Arabs in turn.

The best example is perhaps the famous Ummayyad mosque, where once there stood a temple devoted to the god of thunder and lightning, Haddad, the chief deity of the Arameans. The original building was enlarged and converted by the Romans into a temple of Jupiter but was then destroyed by the Byzantines who erected the Cathedral of John the Baptist in its place. But, when in 636 AD the first conquering Arab army entered Damascus bringing with it the teachings of Islam, the Christians relinquished their rights to the Cathedral, allowing it to be transformed into a mosque, which bears the name of the Ummayyad dynasty, the first caliphs of the Muslim world to succeed the four specially-revered caliphs who had followed immediately after the Prophet Muhammad. Damascus, as the seat of the Ummayyads, thus became imbued simultaneously with an Arab and Islamic identity, while both were in their prime.

Syria's special propensity for assimilating diverse cultures enabled it to play a unique role in transmitting elements of one body of learning into another. Just as it had acted as middleman between the Pharaonic and Mesopotamian civilisations, so it managed to translate and promote Graeco-Roman scholarship within the framework of Islam. And so, also, in the 10th and 11th centuries the Crusaders were able to leave their mark, penetrating easily among the many local principalities that had grown up. These invaders in their turn were overtaken by the Mamluks who, from their base in Egypt, defended Syrian territory against damaging Mongol attacks and ruled the area until the early 16th century when their place was taken by the Ottoman Turks. This early Ottoman imprint is still to be seen today in the Tikiyeh mosque in Damascus—its great dome, two slender minarets and series of separate domed alcoves designed by the Turkish architect Sinan Pasha and built in the 1550s on the orders of Sultan Sulaiman the Magnificent.

From the early 1800s, however, Syria's fortunes took yet another turn with similarly crucial cultural implications, when Ibrahim Pasha, the son of Mohammad Ali of Egypt, snatched Syria from the Ottoman Sultan and, imposing a strong centralised administration, allowed Western missionaries and educationists to establish themselves in the area.

This process, combined with other factors, led indirectly to an Arab cultural renaissance in the late 19th century, which in turn paved the way for the Arab nationalist movement that was to follow, fanned and inflamed by the three decades of French administration that came into force after the Sykes-Picot agreement of 1916. Syria has customarily seen itself as the pulsating heart of Arab nationalism and it was in modern Syria that the founder of the Baath party, which stands for an Arab renaissance, was born.

Baathism is not only a political doctrine. It embodies an integral attitude to that special Arab 'genius' which has played such an important historical and cultural role. But such intellectual reminders of Syria's cultural heritage are to a great extent rendered superfluous by the mere sight and sound of Syria's cities today, especially Damascus and Aleppo with their architecture, bustling markets, veiled women and amalgam of western and oriental dress. This and the wares on display—rolls of brocade with gold and silver threads, intricately-embroidered and brightly-coloured tablecloths, wooden tables and boxes inlaid with geometric shapes of ivory and mother-of-pearl—are all testimony to Syria's rich past and the days when luxury goods of low weight and high price were carried from east to west across the Syrian trade routes.

ECONOMY

Despite its relatively recent dismemberment (the memory of which goes a long way to explaining modern Syria's acute interest in events in neighbouring Lebanon and Jordan) Syria still has much to gain economically from its geographical position. The vast hinterland is made up of the Arab oil-exporting states and Iran, whose demand for Western goods has surged since 1973 and who rely heavily on Lebanese and Syrian ports. The oil states also require to export their oil westwards, which means that, potentially, Syria can still benefit from its position as a transit state, even though oil market forces in recent years have been such that the two oil pipelines already running through Syrian territory have lain idle for most of the time.

From the point of view of tourism and its own foreign trade, Syria is conveniently close to Europe and indeed the bulk of Syrian trade exchanges now take place with the countries of the EEC. In terms of exports alone, there is also a promising future for Syrian-manufactured foodstuffs, textiles and durable consumer goods on the Arab market next door. For the time being, however, and until the necessary industrialisation takes place, Syria's chief exports are raw materials—crude oil and raw cotton.

Cotton was for many years the leading source of foreign exchange, taking over from cereals as the country's most valuable crop shortly after the Second World War when high cotton prices on world markets stimulated large-scale cotton production on largely virgin soil in the Jezira. Cotton itself was then superseded by oil in 1974, when oil prices were quadrupled, and oil now accounts for some 60% of export income, which reached over £Syr4,000 million in 1976. There is still considerable scope for the relative importance of oil to increase yet further, since the Syrian oil industry is still in its infancy, oil production having started on a commercial basis only in 1968. Output currently stands at around 10 million tonnes a year, but much exploration remains to be carried out, encouraged by some recent finds onshore.

In addition to the finance it receives from other Arab states to help defray the heavy burden of defence expenditure, Syria is badly in need of capital to exploit its abundant economic resources. This general need, intensified by the enormous amount of damage caused to the country's infrastructure by Israeli bombardment in the October 1973 war, has led in the last few years to a relaxation of Syria's former hostility to foreign involvement in its economy and the gradual institution of an 'open-door' policy, along with the development of a number of industrial free zones.

GENERAL INFORMATION

Area: 185,180 sq. km.
Population: 7,120,000 (1974 estimate).
Capital: Damascus.
Head of State: President Hafez Al Assad.
Government: Republic. Power is in the hands of a faction of the Arab Socialist Renaissance (Baath) party.
Language: Arabic.
Religion: The majority are Sunni Moslems. There are small Druze, Alawite and Shiite minorities. In addition there is a small Christian minority and small Jewish communities in Damascus and Aleppo.
Currency: The Syrian pound (Lira) is divided into 100 piastres. £1=7.826£Syr; 1$=3.925£Syr.
Time: GMT + 2. From May to October GMT + 3.

HOW TO GET THERE

By air: The national airline, Syrian Arab Airlines has extended its network to Paris, London, Berlin, Moscow, Delhi, Dubai, Beirut and Cairo. The following international airlines operate through Damascus: Aeroflot, Air France, Alia, Alitalia, Austrian Airline, British Airways, EgyptAir, Iraqi Airways, KLM, Lufthansa, PanAm. There is an airport departure tax of 10.000£Syr.

By road: An international highway reaches Syria via Ankara, Adana and Iskanderun in Turkey. The country is also linked by good roads to Beirut in Lebanon and Amman in Jordan. There are regular cheap daily bus and shared taxi services to both destinations.

By rail and sea: Syria's ports handle only commercial vessels and there are no passenger lines linking them with European ports. By rail, Syria can be reached via the Orient Express by changing at Ankara in Turkey and taking the Taurus Express to Aleppo.

Visa and health regulations

A visa is necessary to enter Syria and this can be obtained from Syrian consular offices abroad.

An international smallpox vaccination certificate is required, and it is advisable to have a vaccination against cholera and typhoid.

Currency and Customs Regulations.

Only a limited amount of Syrian Currency (100£Syr) is allowed to be carried by the visitor in or out of the country. There is however no restriction on the import or export of foreign currency.

Articles for personal use are admitted free of duty but it is advisable to fill out a customs declaration.

CLIMATE

Syria's climate is characterised by hot dry summers and fairly cold winters. Nights are often cool throughout the year.

What to wear

Lightweight clothing is essential in the summer, and heavy winter clothing is advisable from November to March. Sunglasses and protective headgear are a necessity in the summer.

ACCOMMODATION AND FOOD

There are approximately 526 hotels in the country and new hotels are being built all the time. It is however advisable to book in advance as there is a shortage of hotel accommodation.

There are numerous restaurants in Damascus serving a variety of oriental and European dishes.

TRANSPORT

By air: Syrian Airlines operates services between Damascus, Aleppo, Palmyra, and Latakya.

By road: There are good asphalted roads linking all the major towns. Regular bus services and shared taxis are available to all parts of the country. In Damascus, taxis are readily available but fares should be negotiated with the driver before the journey.

BUSINESS HOURS

All government offices, banks and Muslim firms close on Friday. Government offices and banks: 0800-1400 Saturday to Thursday. Business houses and offices: May to October, 0830-1300 and 1700-2000 Saturday to Thursday, October to May, 0900-1400 and 1600-1900 Saturday to Thursday.

PUBLIC HOLIDAYS

New Year, 1 January; Muslim New Year, 2 December 1978; Prophet's Birthday, 20 February 1978; Revolution Day, 8 March; Evacuation Day, 17 April; Egypt's Revolution Day, 23 July; Union of Syria-Egypt-Libya, 1 September; Eid-al-Fitr (3 to 4 days), 3-6 September 1978; Eid-al-Adha (4 to 5 days), 10-13 November 1978; Christmas Day, 25 December.

EMBASSIES IN DAMASCUS

Algeria: Raouda.
Austria: Shawkat al-Aidid Street.
Belgium: Ata Ayoubi Street.
Egypt: Misr Street.
France: Ata Ayoubi Street.
German Federal Republic: 53 Ibrahim Hanano Street.

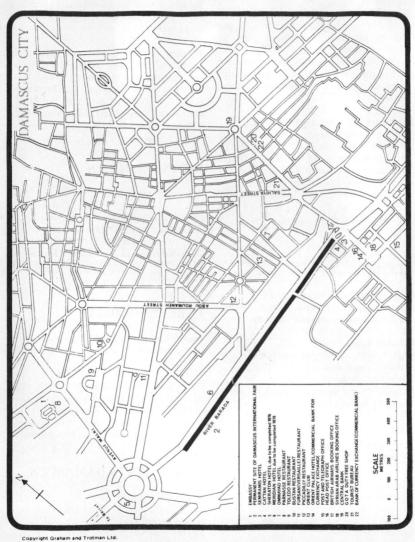

DAMASCUS CITY

SALHIYA STREET

ABOU ROUMANEH STREET

RIVER BARADA

AVENUE MAIN

1 EMBASSY
2 PERMANENT SITE OF DAMASCUS INTERNATIONAL FAIR
3 SEMIRAMIS HOTEL
4 CATTAN HOTEL
5 SHERATON HOTEL, due to be completed 1976
6 MERIDIAN HOTEL due to be completed 1975
7 OMMAYAD HOTEL
8 TOLEDO RESTAURANT
9 PARNASSE RESTAURANT
10 BUSTAN RESTAURANT
11 FURSAN (VERSAILLE) RESTAURANT
12 PICCADILLY RESTAURANT
13 ORIENT CLUB
14 ORIENT PALACE HOTEL/COMMERCIAL BANK FOR
   CURRENCY EXCHANGE
15 POST AND TELEGRAPH OFFICE
16 HEAD POST OFFICE
17 BRITISH AIRWAYS BOOKING OFFICE
18 SYRIAN ARAB AIRLINES BOOKING OFFICE
19 CENTRAL BANK
20 GOT A DUTY FREE SHOP
21 TOURIST BUREAU
22 BANK OF CURRENCY EXCHANGE (COMMERCIAL BANK)

SCALE
METRES
100   0   100   200   300   400   500

Copyright Graham and Trotman Ltd.

Greece: 57 Ata Ayoubi Street.
India: 40/46 Al Malki Avenue.
Iran: Kawakbi Street.
Iraq: Il Mansour Avenue.
Italy: 82 Al Mansour Avenue.
Japan: Kurd Ali Street.
Jordan: Abou Roumaneh Street.
Kuwait: Ibrahim Hanano Street.
Libya: 10 Mansour Avenue.
Morocco: Abdel Malik Ben Mrwan Street.
Netherlands: Abou Ala'a Al-Maarri Place.
Qatar: 8 Abu-Roumaneh.
Saudi Arabia: Al Jala'a Avenue.
Spain: 81 Al Jala'a Avenue.
Sudan: Hanano Street.
Sweden: Abdul Malik ben Marwan Street.
Switzerland: 31 M. Kurd Ali Street.
Tunisia: Rashid Street.
Turkey: 58 Ziad Bin Abou Soufian Avenue.
United Arab Emirates: Raouda Street.
UK: Muhammad Kurd Ali Street.
USA: 2 Al Mansour Street.
USSR: Aleppo Street.
Yemen Arab Republic: 43 Al Jala'a Street.

such as Prague, London or Baghdad, however, for where the Barada runs through the heart of Damascus it is very narrow and shrinks in summertime to a trickle. Nor can the city any longer be said to be 'nestling' against the Jabal Kassioun, since housing and other developments have started to creep further up the dusty hillside, where rows of what are now rather thirsty-looking saplings will eventually enhance the view.

The clamour and crush of the city centre—which gradually abates as one moves out into the tree-lined residential areas—is a constant reminder of the fact that the population of the capital and its immediate suburbs has swollen rapidly in recent years, trebling to a million and a half between 1960 and the present day.

The central feature of Damascus is the Ummayad mosque (see History), which is also the site of St. John the Baptist's tomb. The mosque, with its rich interior and spacious courtyard is approached through the covered al-Hamidiyah bazaar. Another relic of the city's Christian past is to be found at the House of

Damascus

TOURIST INFORMATION

Boulevard du 29 Mai, P.O. Box 201, Damascus.

DAMASCUS

Damascus is also often referred at as Al-Sham, the same name as is given to the Syrian region as a whole. Sited to the east of the Anti-Lebanon mountains, which form the rugged, dun-coloured backdrop to the city scene, 4,000-year-old Damascus owes its existence originally to the Barada river and its many tributaries. This does not mean there is any visual comparison with other river-bank capitals

Hanania in old Damascus, the refuge of St. Paul the Apostle. Hanania's House, with its underground chapel, is located off the famous Via Recta, the Street called Straight. Also of historical interest are the Sulaimaniya mosque (see History) and the 18th century Al-Azm palace which now houses a museum of Syrian folklore. The remains of the Country's ancient civilisations can be found at the National Museum, which also holds a splended collection of Islamic art—including many historic copies of the Koran with elaborate calligraphy and illuminations.

Hotels
International Airport Hotel (luxury). tel: 225401.
New Omayad Hotel (first class). Tajhiz Street. tel: 17700.
Cattan's Hotel (first class). Joumhourieh Street. tel: 112513.
Semiramis Hotel (first class). Sadallah Jabri Street. tel: 113813.
Meridien (luxury). Choukry Kouatly Avenue. tel: 222856.
Sheraton (luxury). Omayyades Square.
Damascus International (luxury). Bahsa Street. tel: 112400.
Samir (first class). Shuhada Square. Tel: 119502.
Venezia (second class). Bahsa Street. tel: 117031.
L'Orient Palace (second class). Mousalam al Baroudy Square. tel: 111510.
Atlas (second class). Sanjakdar-Nasri. tel: 228547.
Grand (second class). Shuhada Square. tel: 111666.
Ramsis(second class). Shuhada Square. tel: 116702.

Restaurants
Toledo. Khalil Mardam Bey Street. tel: 333810.
Al Chark. tel: 116397.
Caves du Roi. Ahmed Moureywed Street. tel: 330093.
Blue Up. Zahra Street. tel: 112111.

Abu Kamel. 29 Ayyar Street. tel: 115216.
Cafeteria Etoile. Mayssaloun Street. tel: 332286.
Ali Baba. Fardoss Street. tel: 119881.

ALEPPO

Aleppo is possibly even older than Damascus, being referred to in an ancient manuscript dating back to the third millennium BC. Its population, at around 650,000, is below that of the capital but in terms of their historical remains and their *souks*, the two cities are clearly rivals. Aleppo's citadel, a fine example of Arab military architecture with a particularly remarkable carved ceiling, stands on the old site of a Hittite acropolis and represents one of the city's principal attractions. The city has had its present Arabic name 'Halab' in one form or another since at least the time of the Hittites and possibly before. Early on it was the centre of a prosperous kingdom but its evolution has been interrupted both by the pillaging of invading armies and the destruction wrought by the last earthquake in 1822. Aleppo has retained its importance today mainly because the cession of the Sanjak of Alexandretta to Turkey in 1939 consolidated its position as northern Syria's major town. But key projects now in progress in the Euphrates basin should further reinforce this role. The visitor to Aleppo will be quickly impressed by the number of mosques—only Cairo is thought to match it in this respect. The city is also known for its old-style houses with their characteristic courtyards and fountains.

Hotels
Meridien (luxury). Near University.
Tourisme (luxury). Saad alah Al-Djabri Street. tel: 10156.
Baron (first class). Baron Street. tel: 10880.
Ambassador (second class). Baron Street. tel: 10231.

Granada (second class). Baron Street. tel: 24959.

HOMS and HAMA

Homs, situated on the main Damascus-Aleppo highway, is Syria's third largest city. Though, like other centres throughout the country it can boast a rich past, Homs is now best-known as the site of Syria's first and (until the Banias project is complete) only oil refinery and is destined to house a number of big industrial plants.

Hama, at 45km from Homs on the Orontes, retains a rather more colourful image with its famous, rhythmically-groaning wooden water wheels and its orchards. Of neolithic origins, Hama became the northern capital of the Arameans and is also notable for its Al Azm Palace and museum of ethnography.

Hotels
Basman (second class). Choukri al Kouatli Street. tel: 12838.
Cairo (third class). Choukri al Kouatli Street. tel: 12096.
Qasr Raghdan (second class). Kuwatli Street. tel: 25211.
Basman al Jadid (second class). Al Sham Street. tel: 26977.

LATTAKIA

Lattakia was first built by the Phoenicians and although, in centuries gone by, it has come under Assyrian, Babylonian, Greek and Roman rule, it is chiefly characterised by its Roman remains, its Temple of Bacchus and Triumphal Arch. The population of Lattakia, itself Syria's principal port, is comparable in size with that of Hama. As regards climate, the Lattakia region, with its thick forests, is spared the rigours of a continental climate by its sea breezes which raise the temperature in winter and moderate the summer heat.

Hotels
Tourist Hotel and Casino (second class). tel: 13400.
Gondole (second class). Andalous Street. tel: 13889.
Venice (second class). Al Azm Street. tel: 11672.

PALMYRA

Mention of Palmyra (or Tadmur) dates back to the 19th century BC. Located at 155km. from Homs in the Syrian desert, it was the capital of the famous queen Zenobia, whose ambitions provoked the Romans into achieving what other armies had for so long failed to do and crush the Palmyran kingdom. The ruins of its ancient buildings—best known of which is the Temple of Bel—are to be found over a wide radius from the city centre and are so stunning and well-preserved as to be considered among the finest not only in Syria but in the whole Middle East.

Hotels
Zanoubia (second class). Facing the ruins. tel: 107.
Tadmor (second class). In the village. tel: 156.

Damascus

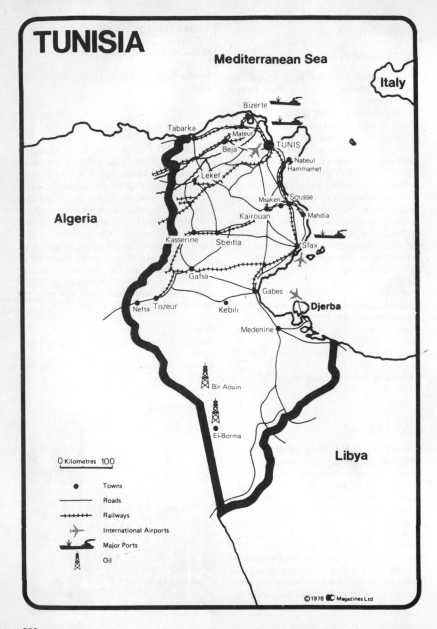

TUNISIA

Mediterranean Sea

Italy

Bizerte

Tabarka

Mateur

Beja

TUNIS

Nabeul
Hammamet

Lekef

Algeria

Msaken
Scusse

Kairouan

Mahdia

Kasserine
Sbeitla

Sfax

Gafsa

Gabes

Djerba

Nefta
Tozeur

Kebili

Medenine

Bir Aouin

El-Borma

Libya

0 Kilometres 100

	Towns
	Roads
	Railways
	International Airports
	Major Ports
	Oil

©1978 Magazines Ltd

TUNISIA

Modern Tunisia offers visitors constant blue skies and sunny beaches, historic fortresses, colourful markets full of beautiful craftwork, and a rich and varied culture. Even when the northern waters grow chilly, southern resorts like Jerba Island are still warm, and this indeed is the best time to visit the remarkable desert oases of the south. On the inland plateau are the magnificent Roman ruins of Dougga. Above all no visitor should miss the glory of Islam in Africa: the ancient mosques of the holy city of Kairouan.

THE LAND AND THE PEOPLE

About the size of England, Tunisia has a varied landscape, from the rocky north coast, the cork forests, the huge bowls of arable land and the orchards to mountains, salt-pans and desert in the south. The north is typically Mediterranean in climate, vegetation and geology; south of Gafsa and Gabes is the Sahara.

The Atlas mountain range flattens out into the fertile alluvial east coast from Bizerta to Sfax—an area constantly fought over by Middle Eastern and European civilizations; it now holds the majority of Tunisia's five million people. Here, too, a number of large towns—Tunis, Sfax, Sousse, Bizerta and Kairouan—have grown up around their *medinas* (old walled towns) and *souks* (markets).

The Cap Bon peninsula east of Tunis was probably once joined to Sicily, only 140 km away. Its delightful climate makes it the market garden of Tunisia and turns it into a riot of orange and lemon groves, vineyards, jasmine and roses. Farther south along the coast lie the orchards of Sousseu and the vast olive groves around Sfax. All along the coast are small islands, many of them uninhabited, but some are popular resorts like the island of Jerba in the hot south.

The land becomes increasingly harsh south of the Tell plateau: the steppe rises to the Dorsale—'backbone'—mountains around Kasserine, of which the highest is Jebel Chambi at 1,544 m, before dropping in the pre-desert belt down to the *chott* country. The *chotts* are glistening white salt-pans, lower than sea-level, which are interspersed with yellow-ochre sand. After the rains the *chotts* are quagmires but their cracked dry surfaces in summer produce curious mirage effects. Around the major Chott Jerid are a series of fruit-laden oases, now provided with luxury hotels which make desert-exploration relatively comfortable.

Although the Berber, as in Morocco and Algeria, were probably the country's original inhabitants, they were absorbed by successive invaders; their language is now rarely heard. The Arab invaders of the seventh century imprinted their culture and language throughout on the region's inhabitants who are a mixture of Arab, Roman, Greek, Spanish, Sicilian, French, Berber and Negro. The nomadic Bedouin still follow their traditional ways in the southern desert. A large Jewish community, established since the dispersion in AD 70, lives in harmony around Tunis and Jerba.

CULTURE

Tunisia's varied origins are exemplified in its architecture. Little still remains of the Punic period apart from numerous mausoleums built for the cremated, the ports at Carthage, and traces of houses at Kerkouane on Cap Bon. The Romans, at their height in the second century AD, are much better represented. Dougga is the best-preserved Roman site in Africa; El Jem colosseum stands out starkly from the surrounding scrubland; farther inland are the three great temples of Sbeitla, and scattered all over the hills are Roman baths, amphitheatres and forums, notably at Maktar, Thuburbo Maius, Bulla Regia and Utica.

The Muslim Arab invasion ushered in a new era in architecture. There are beautiful examples of the simple early Islamic style (ninth—11th centuries) at Kairouan where the Great Mosque is the oldest in Africa. The mosques of Tunis and the ancient *ribats* (fortified monasteries) of Sousse and Monastir are other important architectural survivals.

The Tunisian government has attempted to preserve many of the country's traditional crafts through the Office National de l'Artisanat (ONA), which helps craftsmen to train in the old skills and has encouraged the development of modern crafts as well. It runs excellent shops in most towns and sponsors local craft projects.

Carpets and rugs are widely produced. The introduction of the Asia Minor type of carpet to Kairouan is attributed to Kemla, daughter of a governor of the city in the early 19th century. These carpets, called *zarbia*, are woven on a high-warp loom and the stitches are knotted. The quality of Kairouan carpets has achieved some renown. A pile-less rug known as

mergoum, which is highly decorated, is also woven in Kairouan and the south. Another weaving industry is mat-making in Nabeul, and also in Houmt *Souk*. These are worked mostly with bulrushes on ancient looms and have colourful geometric designs. Attractive blankets are also made, especially on Jerba.

The centre of the pottery industry is in Nabeul. Decoration is typically geometric and often employs a fish motif. Traditional Berber earthenware is produced by the women of Sijnane. Modern and more ostentatious china and pottery is also on sale at ONA shops.

Other crafts include copper work, wood carving and stone carving and leather work (bags, shoes, slippers etc). The *souks* in all the main towns of Tunisia display the full variety of local work, and usually not far away are the workshops themselves. Jewellers use silver, gold, amber and coral for their elaborate ornaments. The history of Tunisian jewelry is best illustrated at the Bardo Museum which has collections of Punic, Roman, Berber and Arab jewelry.

A particularly Tunisian artifact is the ornamented bird-cage.

Traditional music is still popular. The *malouf*, played around Tunis, is Andalusian in form and was introduced by Moors driven out of Spain in the 15th century. Folk dances are local to their region. Troupes of travelling dancers often perform at the hotels.

Tunisia has developed an international reputation as an intellectual and cultural centre. The International Film Festival of Carthage is held every two years in October and was the first of its kind. It awards prizes for the best African and Arab films. Also in Carthage, at the Roman theatre, is an international festival of drama, dance and music every July and August. At the same time a similar festival is held in Hammamet at the International Cultural Centre.

Folk art festivals are held every two years in July in Carthage or Monastir.

Details of local festivals should be obtained from the National Tourist Office since every area has its own celebrations, including exhibitions of horsemanship and falconry, or religious festivals. Films and entertainments in Tunis are listed in the weekly *Semaine de Tunis*.

HISTORY

The ancient inhabitants of Tunisia, the Berber, are similar to those still living in Morocco and Algeria. They were called by this name from the Roman 'barbari'—hence the Barbary coast by which the Maghreb was known to Europeans. In early days they were also called Numidians or Libyans.

The Punic period (13th—second century BC): Seafaring Phoenicians, a Semitic people from Tyre and Sidon began establishing trading posts from c. 1200 BC, bartering with local Berber at Sousse (Roman Hadrumetum), Utica and Bizerta (Hippo Diarrhytus). In 814 BC, Elissa—nicknamed Dido, 'the wanderer', the sister of King Pygmalion of Tyre—fled from her country with many followers when the king killed her husband, a high priest. They founded the 'New City'—Carthage. According to legend, Dido burned herself on a funeral pyre rather than marry the local prince. Virgil, 700 years later, paired her rather with Aeneas, sailing back from his siege of Troy. According to Virgil, Dido killed herself when Aeneas left her; but historically the two were not contemporaneous.

Tunisia again enters Europe's earlier classical myths in Homer, for some have identified Jerba as the land of the Lotus Eaters visited by Odysseus.

Carthage prospered after the fall of

Folklore dancing on the beach at Kerkennah

Tyre to the Assyrians. As well as commercial ships, it had a war fleet of huge quinqueremes, propelled by five tiers of oars pulled by slaves, and an army of Berber horsemen recruited from Sicily and Spain.

After losing their control of the eastern Mediterranean trade in the sixth century BC, the Carthaginians branched out westward, making voyages to the British Isles in one direction, and down the Moroccan coast to West Africa in the other. Meanwhile, a formidable enemy arose: Rome, seeking naval power and control of Sicily. This led to the hard-fought Punic Wars (264-146 BC). The first war was mainly naval, and Carthage ended with control of Spain. In the second war the Punic general Hannibal led his famous elephants from Gaul (France) over the Alps to wage successful battles in Italy, but the Roman Scipio's attacks on Carthage itself brought him home to meet the decisive defeat at Zama in 202 BC. The city of Carthage was still a thorn in Rome's flesh and the Senate determined: 'Carthage must be destroyed.' After a three-year siege (149-146 BC), those who had not starved to death were burned and slaughtered; all the buildings were razed to the ground and the land ploughed up.

The Roman and Byzantine period (145 BC-AD 436): The Romans colonized the country thoroughly as far south as Gafsa, building magnificent towns (such as Dougga, Sbeitla and Maktar) all over the fertile Tell plateau, joined by straight roads which still form the country's basic network. Settlers worked estates with the aid of Berber slaves to make the area, with Egypt, the granary of Rome, as well as producing wine and olives.

The elite city dwellers could become Roman citizens while the despised local Numidians (Berber) in the countryside were—after a fierce rebellion led by Jugurtha, which was defeated in 105 BC—allowed some autonomy.

Early Christians here, as in Rome, sought shelter from persecution in the catacombs of Sousse, or were thrown to the lions in the amphitheatre at Carthage. But by the third century, when El Jem's colosseum was built, the Emperors themselves were becoming converted. The most famous Tunisian Christian was St Augustine of Hippo, Bishop of Carthage, converted after a wild youthful period in the city.

Schisms in the church, the decline of Rome itself, and increasing attacks by the Berber from the south—using camels in addition to horses—weakened the country until its final conquest by Vandals from Spain, led by Genseric, in AD 436. Their short rule left little trace. In AD 534 Christian Byzantium briefly reunited Tunisia to the Eastern Roman empire but their traces are mostly thick defensive walls and fortresses, designed to resist Berber onslaughts.

The early Muslim period (seventh-11th century): The invading Arabs, spreading Islam by the sword, took 30 years from the establishment of a new capital at El Kairouan in 670, through the second total destruction of Carthage (698) to the final defeat of Berber resistance under Queen Kahina at El Jem in 702. Many Berbers then joined the armies going to conquer Spain, but some, converted by then to the strict Kharijite sect, took over El Kairouan themselves.

Arab rule and unity were restored in 800 by the Aghlabid dynasty (800-909), loyal to the Baghdad caliphate under which many of Tunisia's finest early buildings were constructed. A religious schism in the east brought the Fatimids fleeing to Tunisia. From their base at Mahdia they spread their power from Morocco to Egypt, and moved capital to Cairo in 973, leaving the Zirid dynasty (973—1057) to rule for them in Tunisia. A Zirid effort to make Tunisia an independent Berber state (1048) caused the Fatimid ruler of Egypt to send some troublesome Arab nomads—the Beni-Hilal—from Upper Egypt to pillage Tuni-

Amphitheatre at Djem

sia, which they did most thoroughly (1053-1057). At the same time they made the population even more Arab than before.

The middle Muslim period (12th-16th century): After a brief conquest by Moroccan Almoravids, the Hafsid dynasty established themselves and in 1236 changed their capital to Tunis. This was a time when European Christians were becoming a greater threat to Islam. Normans were established just across the water in Sicily and in 1270 St Louis of France led a crusade on Carthage, where he died of the plague. The Christian defeat of the Moors in Spain brought immigrants to Tunisia: skilled Andalusian craftsmen and seafarers called corsairs, who proceeded to wage a constant battle as pirates against Christian ships from the rocky north coast. By the 16th century Tunisia was a bone of contention between Barbarossa pirates, working for the Ottoman Turks, and the Hapsburg kings of Spain. This resulted in the country becoming first a Spanish protectorate (1535-1574), and finally a Turkish province.

The Turkish period (1574-1881): Sinan Pasha conquered the country and made it a province governed by military officers: Deys until 1630, then Mouradit Beys who

tried to make the country independent of Turkey. A massacre and officers' plot in 1708 brought the Husseinid dynasty of Beys to power. This lasted until the 80-year-old last Bey was quietly deposed in 1958.

The cut-throat war of pirates continued throughout the 18th century and was a major souce of wealth for a languishing economy. Large harems led to succession problems, coups and assassinations. In the 19th century, though politically more stable, the Beys in their palaces at Mohammedia gained an international reputation for bisexual lascivious effeteness. Their misdeeds and bankruptcy (when finally forced to abolish piracy), became the pretext for France's invasion from Algeria. They set up a protectorate in 1881.

French period and after (since 1881): French mining firms poured in; settlers expropriated a fifth of the cultivated land; western techniques, Christianity and French education affected the new Tunisian elite. During World War Two many Tunisians, including Habib Bourguiba, supported the Free French and Allies, even setting up a provisional Government at Le Kef against Vichy occupation. The Germans fell back on Tunisia from El Alamein, to be finally defeated by Montgomery's troops in May 1943.

The post-war bid for independence, led by Bourguiba, met repression at first, and resorted to guerrilla tactics until the French, already hard-pressed in Algeria, allowed Bourguiba back from exile and granted the country its independence in 1957. Bourguiba steered a careful course, avoiding dependence on de Gaulle and continuing to support the FLN in Algeria, while at the same time avoiding the orbit of Egypt's President Nasser. He has driven through his own internal reforms such as nationalization and the emancipation of women. He is a believer in Maghreb Federation but has resisted all pan-Arabist union plans, believing that the Palestinians should manage their war with only moral support from other Arab countries.

There have been internal crises, reaching a peak in early 1978, with a general strike and widespread demonstrations against the policies of the Prime Minister, Hedi Nouira.

ECONOMY

Tunisia has recently undergone very rapid economic growth and is one of the richest countries in Africa in terms of GDP per capita. Recently, however, the prospects have been less encouraging. Tunisia relies for its export earnings on oil production—but this is only very limited in quantity—and on olive oil and phosphates, and these two products have suffered a decline in demand. There is acute unemployment in the country, and the earlier stability of the Bourguiba government has been undermined by student and labour unrest in a context of speculation about the nature of the next administration.

Agriculture provides more than half of the country's total employment but the system of land-use and tenure continues to produce a high rate of migration to the towns. The planning emphasis has now shifted to industry, with incentives for foreign and domestic export-oriented industries. Growth of the tourist industry has also been promoted very actively and the annual average number of visitors now exceeds one million. New tourist complexes are planned near Sousse and Tunis-Carthage.

GENERAL INFORMATION

Area: 167,000 sq km.
Population: 5.6 million (1975).
Altitude: Sea level to 1,544 m (Jebel Chambi).
Capital: Tunis.
Head of State: President Habib Bourguiba.
Government: Republican, based on single party, the Destourian Socialist Party.
Date of independence: 20 March 1956.
Languages: Arabic (official). French is spoken in all towns.
Religion: Islam. There are Christian and Jewish minorities.
Currency: Tunisian Dinar, divided into 1,000 millimes. £1 sterling=0.771 dinars. $1=0.413 dinars.
Weights and measures: Metric.
Time: GMT+1.

HOW TO GET THERE

By air: The airport of Tunis-Carthage is served by major international airlines, including Aeroflot, Air France, Alitalia, British Airways, British Caledonian, KLM, Lufthansa, SAS and Swissair. Tunis Air also flies from French and other European cities (including London) as well as centres in the Middle East.

The airport is about 13 km outside Tunis; buses and taxis provide a regular service into the city. There are also international airports at Monastir and Jerba. An airport tax of 1 dinar is payable on departure from Tunisia.

By sea: There are regular sailings between European ports and Tunis. Those from Marseille, Genoa, Naples and Palermo carry cars as well as passengers. The main shipping lines serving Tunisia are the Tirrenia Line, DFDS Seaways and Compagnie Generale Transmediterraneene.

By rail: There is a railway link from Algeria (from Annaba and Constantine) through Souk Ahras to Tunis.

By road: Well-surfaced roads enter Tunisia from Algeria (El Kala—ain Draham—Tabarka, Souk Ahras—Ghardimaou, Tebessa—Feriana—Gafsa. El Oued—Nefta—Tozeur) and from Libya (via the main coast road, Tripoli—Medenine). There are buses and taxis (*louages*) from both countries.

Motorists need an international driving licence, log book and insurance (international green card).

Visas and health regulations

All visitors must have passports, but no visas are necessary for visits up to three months, for citizens of the following countries: Austria, Barbados, Belgium, Canada, Chile, Denmark, Finland, France, Ghana, Gambia, Guinea, Iceland, Ireland, Italy, Ivory Coast, Japan, Liberia, Luxembourg, Malaysia, Mali, Mauritania, Mauritius, Netherlands, Niger, Norway, Pakistan, Rumania, Senegal, Spain, Sweden, Turkey, UK, Yugoslavia. The visa-free limit is four months for citizens of West Germany and the US, two months for Bulgaria and one month for Greece, Korea and Hongkong.

Holiday village on Djerba

CHRISTINE OSBORNE

No visa is necessary for Algerians and Moroccans.

For all other nationalities visas are compulsory. They can be obtained from Tunisian diplomatic missions abroad.

Visitors arriving direct from Europe are not asked for any vaccination certificates, although one for smallpox is recommended. Certificates of vaccination against smallpox, cholera and yellow fever are required for those travelling from an infected area.

Currency regulations

Any amount of foreign currency may be taken into Tunisia, but the import or export of Tunisian currency is strictly forbidden. It is advisable to change your currency or travellers' cheques in small amounts according to your needs, as it is difficult to rechange your dinars.

Keep all receipts when you exchange your foreign currency for dinars, and also keep receipts for any goods you buy for more than 30 dinars.

CLIMATE

Tunisia is famous for its almost constant clear blue skies. The climate is ideal for travelling all the year round but the best times for a visit are spring and autumn. The summer is hot, though the sea breeze can reduce the temperatures on the coast. Inland temperatures may range from 35°-42°C in summer.

The winter is mild but there is more chance of rain in November and December. The south of the country gets less rain. At the coolest time of year, November to February, it is warm in the middle of the day but can get cold at night.

On average there are only about 50 wet days a year. In recent years there have been some sudden and disastrous floods, though not in the most popular places for visitors. In the south there is very little rain.

What to wear
From June to September very lightweight clothes should be taken, though for the desert one needs something warm at night. Warm clothes are needed in winter.

Health precautions
There is no risk to health from the food and water in the main towns. In the far south the visitor is advised to avoid untreated water.

ACCOMMODATION AND FOOD

The national tourist office publishes its own comprehensive list of hotels. All hotels are classified from 'de luxe' to 'one star'. For the latest classifications and prices write to the Tunisian Tourist Office (see list below).

There are youth hostels in the main tourist centres. There are no organised camping sites, but much of the coast is good camping country. No charge is made but permission should be obtained from the local police or administrative authorities. Camping on private property obviously requires the owner's consent as well.

Tunisian food is memorable, particularly the authentic lamb or *dorado* (bream) *cous-cous*, the *mechoui* (barbecued lamb), the fish dishes, *tajine* and *brik*. Tunisian dishes can be cooked with olive oil, spiced with aniseed, coriander, cumin, caraway, cinnamon or saffron, flavoured with mint or orange blossom, rose or wild water.

Restaurants catering for tourists tend to serve rather bland dishes, and 'international cuisine'. Visitors who want to become acquainted with the local tastes, should try the small restaurants frequented by the Tunisians.

Prices in restaurants vary enormously, you will not necessarily get better meals by paying higher prices. Tunis and the main cities also have French, Italian and other international restaurants.

Tunisian wines are of excellent quality and inexpensive, there is a powerful national spirit called Boukha, distilled from figs.

Tipping
Taxi drivers do not expect to be tipped, but hotel and restaurant staff normally receive about 10% of the bill.

TRANSPORT

By air: The internal air services of Tunis air link Tunis to Monastir, Sfax, Gabes, Gafsa and Jerba.

By rail: The rail system links most of the main towns, though the farthest point south is Gabes. There are only two classes and the trains are small and uncomfortable so on special holidays and during the tourist season it may be advisable to go first class (which is cheap by European standards) if you want to be sure of a seat. A reduction is given on return fares, valid for up to eight days when the distance between travelling points is at least 300 km.

By road: Well-surfaced roads run to all parts of Tunisia. A number of good road maps are available from bookstalls and newsagents. Driving is on the right and Tunisian motorists are generally unhurried and courteous. Petrol stations are well distributed throughout the country.

There are regular and cheap bus services throughout the country. The central bus station in Tunis is at Blvd. Farhat Hached. But services in Tunis itself are very efficient. Ask at your hotel for the nearest bus stops for the destination you want. Also in the main towns there are *bebe taxis*, whose rates are extremely low.

Between main towns an efficient and fast means of transport is by *louage*. These are large taxis with seats for five passengers. They depart from key points in each town for each destination and only leave when full. The fares are fixed by law, and are only slightly more than those of trains and buses.

Car hire: *Avis*, 90 Ave. de la Liberte, Tunis. *Carop*, 14 Ave. de Paris, Tunis. *Europcars*, 39 Ave. Khereddine Pacha, Tunis *Hertz*, 29 Ave. Habib Bourguiba, Tunis. *Garage Ben Djemaa*, 15 Rue de Cologne, Tunis. *Tilden*, 46 Ave. de la Liberte, Tunis. These and other companies have offices in the main towns.

BANKS

There are several banks operating in Tunisia, with branches throughout the country. Main ones are *Société Tunisienne de Banque*, *Banque du Sud*, *l'Union Internationale de Banques* and *Banque de Tunisie*.

Business hours
The weekly holiday is Sunday. Banks: Monday to Friday at the following hours: Winter: 0800 to 1100 and 1400 to 1600; Summer: 0800 to 1200 only. Government offices: Winter: Monday to Thursday 0830 to 1300 and 1500 to 1745 and Friday and Saturday 0830 to 1330; Summer: Monday to Saturday 0700 to 1300.

Businesses: usually open Monday to Friday at the following hours; Winter: 0830 to 1200 and 1500 to 1800; Summer: 0730 to 1200 and 1600 to 1830.

PUBLIC HOLIDAYS

The following are the fixed holidays: New year's Day; Anniversary of the Revolution, 18 January; Independence Day, 20 March; Labour Day; Victory Day, 1 June; Republic Day, 25 July; President Bourguiba's Birthday, 3 August; Women's Day, 13 August; Evacuation of Bizerta, 15 October; Christmas Day; Boxing Day. The variable Muslim holidays are: Eid El Kebir, Ras El Am El Hejir (Muslim New Year), Mouled (Prophet's Birthday) and Eid Es Seghair (End of Ramadan).

EMBASSIES IN TUNIS

Algeria: 18, rue de Niger.
Belgium: 47, rue du Ier Juin.
Canada: 3, rue Didon, Notre Dame de Tunis, Cité al Mahdi.
Egypt: 1, rue Es-Soyouti, El Menzah.
France: pl. de l'Indépendance.
Germany, Federal Republic: 18, rue Felicien Challaye.
Greece: 4, rue El Jahedh, El Menzah.
Iran: 10, rue Dr. Burnet, Belvedere.
Iraq: 128, ave. de la Liberté.
Italy: 37, rue Abdennasser.
Jordan: 16, rue El Moutanabi, El Menzah.
Kuwait: rue Jacques Cartier, Belvedere.
Lebanon: 4 Impasse Ibn Chabbat, rue El Moezz, El Menzah.
Libya: 48 bis, rue du Ier Juin
Morocco: 5, rue Didon, Notre Dame.
Oman: 129, ave. De Lesseps.
Saudi Arabia: 16, rue de l'Autriche.
Switzerland: 17, ave. de France.
Syria: 128, ave. De Lesseps.
Turkey: 47, ave. Mohamed V.
UK: 5, pl. de la Victoire.
USA: 144, ave. de la Liberté
USSR: 31, rue du Ier Juin.

TOURIST OFFICES

In Tunisia
Office National du Tourisme Tunisien 1, Avenue Mohamed V, Tunis.

Abroad
Austria: Kruegestrasse 15 A, 1010 Wien.
Belgium: 18, Rue Ravenstein 1050 Bruxelles.

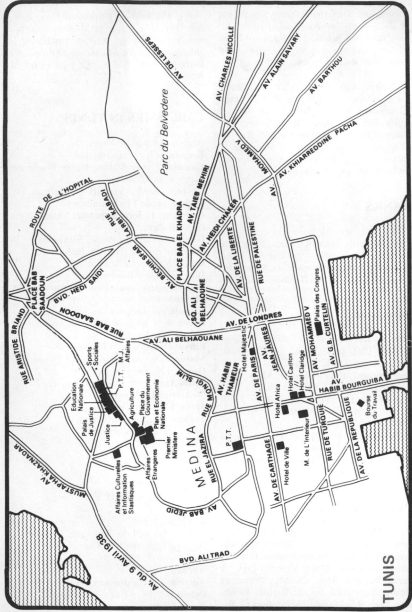

Copyright Graham and Trotman Ltd.

Canada: 18, Frontenac—case postale 1233. place Bonaventure, Montréal (Quebec h 5 A 1 G 1).
France: 32, Avenue de l'Opera, Paris 75002.
Holland: 61, Leidesestraat, Amsterdam.
Italy: 10, via Baracchini, 20 122 Milano.
Kuwait: c/o Ambassade de Tunisie, El Istiklal Street, Kuwait City.
West Germany: 6, Frankfurt/M. Wiesenhuttenplatz 28.
Sweden: Smalendsgaten 11, 11146 Stockholm.
Switzerland: Bahnhofplatz 7—8001 Zurich.
UK: 7a, Stafford Street, London W1.
USA: 630 Fifth Avenue, Room 863, New York, NY. 10020.

TUNIS

Tunis is a bustling modern capital. The main artery is the Avenue Habib Bourguiba. An easy one-mile stroll leads from the edge of Lake Tunis to the gate known as Bab el-Bahar, marking the entrance to the traditional *medina*—the capital since 1236—with its winding alleys, fine *souks* and lovely mosques. The *medina* and *souks* are best for leisurely exploring with or without a guide, peeking at the vaulted and ceramic tiled courtyards known as *zawias* and seeking out the streets specialising in various crafts.

Around every other corner in the *medina* are architectural delights—former religious schools known as *medrassa*, now converted into apartment houses; the Museum of Islamic Art open daily except Monday; the 18th century Palace of dar Hussein housing the National Institute of Archaeology and Arts; the Great Mosque of Zitouna mainly built in the ninth century opposite the National Library; the Lapidary Museum of Sidi Bou Krissan in the garden of the 11th century el-Ksar mosque with a collection of Arabic tombstone inscriptions.

Carthage, the famous Punic capital, whose name means 'New city', was founded in 815 BC. It may at one time have held 700,000 inhabitants. It was twice razed to the ground—by the Romans in 145 BC, whose own city there was destroyed by Arabs in AD 698—so that all that remains now in a pleasant suburb of Tunis is the Roman Baths of Antonius, Punic ports and some rubble.

The Bardo Museum, about 5 km to the north of Tunis, houses one of the finest collections of Roman as well as Punic and Islamic art in the world, including exceptional mosaics: open 0900—1200 and 1400-1730.

The port La Goulette has a massive medieval *kasbah* and a main street full of inexpensive seafood restaurants such as the Lucullus and the Venus.

Sidi Bou Said, alongside Carthage, is one of the loveliest villages anywhere on the Mediterranean—a dazzling blue and white hillside haven with magnificent views of the Gulf of Tunis and an attractive beach. It is a summer resort and a

The Grand Mosque, Kairouan

colony of artists who gather round the Cafe des Nattes.

Gammarth runs along a cliff road with fine beaches and good seafood restaurants such as the Pecheur, Sinbad and Tour Blance.

Hotels in Tunis (and suburbs)

Four Star
Africa, (Tunis) 320 beds. tel: 247.477.
Hilton, (Tunis) 474 beds. tel: 282.000.
Baie des Singes, (Gammarth) 274 beds. tel: 270.544.
Ezzahra, (Ezzahra) 252 beds. tel: 290.788.

Three Star
Du Lac, (Tunis) 400 beds. tel: 258.322.
Majestic, (Tunis) 198 beds. tel: 242.848.
Abou Nawas, (Gammarth) 174 beds. tel: 270.522.

Two Star
Claridge, (Tunis) 223 beds. tel: 258.688.
Maison Doree, (Tunis) 110 beds. tel: 240.632.
Carlton, (Tunis) 80 beds. tel: 258.167.

Others
Transatlantique, (Tunis) 62 beds. tel: 240.680.
Agriculteurs, (Tunis) 41 beds. tel: 246.394.
Bristol, (Tunis) 43 beds. tel: 244.836.
Métropole, (Tunis) 60 beds. tel: 243.102.

Restaurants

All the hotels have restaurants and there are also the **Chez Slah, Oriental, La Petite Hutte, Chez Nous, Hungaria** in Tunis as well as smaller ones: the **Strasbourg,** serving French food; **Le Malouf, M'Rabet** and **Palais** excellent for Tunisian food. Out of town are excellent seafood restaurants: the **Pecheur** at Gammarth, **Le Pirate** at Sidi Bou Said, **La Reine Didon** and the **Neptune** at Carthage and many others.

Entertainments and tours

There are nightclubs in most of the beach hotels as well as the Hilton and Africa in the city. A very popular open air nightclub is in Sidi Bou Said near the **Cafe des Nattes** where lively local bands play traditional music. Belly-dancing is a common cabaret feature, best seen at the **Palais, Malouf** and **M'Rabet** restaurants. Cinemas show mostly French films with Arabic subtitles and the National Theatre from November to May gives performances by local and visiting companies.

Sports

Opportunities for sport are excellent. Water sports include deep-sea fishing, waterskiing, skin-diving, available through hotels, sailing at La Goulette and Sidi Bou Said. Horse racing takes place from October to May and many stables offer beautiful Arab steeds for hire. There is camel-riding at the beach resorts and golf at La Soukra (11 km from Tunis).

Travel agents

Should you wish a guided tour these are available from several agencies, including Transtours, 14 Ave. de Carthage; Tourafic, 52 Ave. Habib Bourguiba, Siti Tour, 20 Ave. Habib Bourguiba, STET Voyages, 42 Ave. Habib Bourguiba.

THE NORTH COAST

Bizerta, one of the earliest Phoenician bases is now a city of 50,000 and until 1963, a French naval base. It has a splendid corniche, comfortable hotels, fine sand beach, an old port area, the massive Fort of Spain, a modern Congress Hall, and a 17th century Great Mosque. The *Office National de l'Artisanat* features local carpets, mats and embroidery.

Inland towards Tunis are the ruins of **Utica,** one of the most ancient of the Punic ports but now 10 km inland with its

Roman baths, sixth century BC necropolis and Antiquarian Museum showing lovely mosaic floors. On the point east of Bizerta is **Porto Farina** with its hillside fortress above a white sandy beach, near the wine-centre of Rafraf.

Hotels in Bizerta

Four Star
Corniche Palace. tel: 02.31.844.

Two Star
Jalta. tel: 02.32.249.
Nadhour. tel: 02.31.846.
Rimel. tel: 02.32.574.
There is a cheap **Maison des Jeunes** as well as several other hotels.

Tabarka is a newly developing beach resort in a small fishing port with coral-work crafts. It has fine hotels and the beach restaurants of Barberousse and Pescadou, noted for king prawns and lobsters. The coral formations are a paradise for the underwater fisherman. A fascinating drive inland behind Tabarka leads to the mountain village of **Ain Draham**, noted for its excellent wild boar hunting in winter in the nearby cork and oak forests of the Kroumirie range (Hotel: **Les Chenes**, two star, tel: 27) and beyond (66 km from Tabarka) the Roman and early Christian ruins of **Bulla Regia** where the people dug out their houses underground, apparently for coolness in the summer. (Hotel at **Jendouba** nearby: **Atlas**, two star, tel: 164). From here one can continue to Dougga.

Hotels in Tabarka

Three Star
Morjane. tel: 104.
Mimosas. tel: 50.

CAP BON AND HAMMAMET

This peninsula, which protrudes to shelter Tunis harbour, has some of the best known beaches in Tunisia, particularly **Hammamet.**

It is the fruit and flower garden of the country, fragrant with orange blossom and jasmine. Do not miss the best preserved Punic site in **Kerkouane**, 8 km from Kelibia, or the lighthouse at the end of the cape.

Hammamet is a bay, a white sand beach with a small medina and *souk* for brassware and carpets, turkish baths with personal scrubbing and the Great Mosque. It is the site of an international cultural centre; originally built by a rich Rumanian and which housed General Rommel.

Nabeul lying just north of Hammamet, Nabeul has a fine beach and gardens and good hotels. The Friday market is a good time to see its earthenware pottery, carpets, chipped stone, *haiks* (cloaks) sheepskins and other wares. There is also a livestock market.

Kelibia near the Punic site of **Kerkouane**, is a fishing port with a Roman castle. Farther along is the Cap Bon lighthouse the nearest point to Sicily.

Sidi Daoud is a centre for tuna fishing. Huge nets are spread from May to July to catch the fish during their migration. Offshore is **Zembra Island**, an international nautical centre with facilities for sailing, skin-diving and waterskiing.

Some hotels in Cap Bon

The Cap Bon hotels specialise in full-board for European tourists, offering their own night life, and bus tours to Tunis and elsewhere.

Four Star
Phenicia, (Hammamet) 720 beds. tel: 02 80 331.

Three Star
Continental, (Hammamet) 356 beds. tel: 02 80 11.
Sheraton, (Hammamet) 208 beds. tel: 02 80 555.
Miramar, (Hammamet) 308 beds. tel: 02 80 344.

Les Narcisses, (Nabeul) 400 beds. tel: 02 85 400.

Neapolis, (Nabeul) 208 beds. tel: 02 85 104.

Les Pyramides, (Nabeul) 576 beds. tel: 02 85 444.

Two Star

Neapolis, (Nabeul) 546 beds. tel: 02 85 296.

Dar Hotel, (Bordj Cedria) 400 beds. tel: 290 188.

In addition to the numerous luxury hotels there is a *Tourisme Jeune*, and villas may be hired through various real estate agents in Tunis.

DOUGGA

Anyone interested in Tunisia's past should visit the Roman ruins at Dougga, the country's finest site. (110 km from Tunis). The whole northern plateau of Tunisia is in fact dotted with Roman ruins, and if this is your primary interest you may like to stay in the central little hillside town of **Le Kef.**

The route to Dougga from Hammamet passes through the Zaghouan valley (whose reservoir once fed the city of Carthage by aqueducts), then to the ruins of Thuburbo Maius near Pont du Fars, 58 km from Tunis, with their Capitol, temples and baths.

Dougga flourished as a small Roman town in the second century AD. Most of the theatre is intact. The Capitol is one of the best-preserved Roman ruins in Africa.

SOUSSE AND THE SAHEL

South of Hammamet are a series of five resorts on the coast known as the **Sahel** from Sousse to the Kerkenna islands, while inland are the fascinating holy Muslim city of Kairouan (the third in the world) and the Roman temples of Sbeitla.

Sousse has lovely beaches, the Ribat fortress built in the ninth century, from whose watch-towers, there is a fine view of the *medina*, an excellent museum in the *Kasbah*, open every day except Monday, with Roman, Byzantine and early Christian mosaics. A Friday afternoon camel market, the July festival of Aous-(Neptune) along the esplanade and just off the Tunis road before entering Sousse, an extensive series of second, third and fourth century AD Christian catacombs (hunt for the guide, offer him a small tip, and make sure that he has plenty of candles). A massive new tourist complex is springing up near Sousse at **Port el-Kantaoui.**

The small town of Monastir along the coast just south of Sousse, is the birthplace of President Bourguiba.

The fortress, or *Ribat*, of Marthema, first built in the eighth century is an imposing site with summer *son et lumiére* to illuminate its walls. Visit the Islamic museum, the ninth and 11th century great mosque, and the highly modernistic mosque of Habib Bourguiba. Monastir has its own beach, esplanade and tourist boom. Nearby is the small resort of Skanes.

Mahdia is a charming fishing port shadowed by a fortress, renowned for its rich and varied crafts, beautiful extensive beaches and the attractive small streets of its *medina*. Inland is the colosseum of El Djem.

Sfax is Tunisia's second city, a major port, with several industries. It has a huge old *medina* with *souks* featuring metal and woodwork, painted and carved wood, and embroideries. The city is relatively prosperous and rather westernized, with a small Jewish community and two synagogues.

A 40 minute motor-boat ride from Sfax (a few vehicles are carried) lies the little archipelago of **Kerkenna** with palm-fringed beaches and fishing villages.

El Djem (63 km from Sousse, 66 km from Sfax) is a spectacular Roman Colosseum (third century AD) rising stark out of the plain. The third largest in the world, once holding 30,000 people, it is better preserved than that in Rome itself:

Kairouan 57 km from west of Sousse is the holiest Muslim city in Africa. For true believers, several pilgrimages here are equivalent to a visit to Mecca. It is also famous for its very fine rugs, carpets and leatherwear. The Great Mosque, built in the ninth century, is the oldest in Africa and is of impressive and noble proportions.

Sbeitla has the remains of the Roman town of Sufetula. There is a beautiful triumphal arch and forum, but its glory are the three magnificently preserved temples built in red sandstone which glow in the setting sun. They are believed to have been dedicated to Jupiter, Juno, and Minerva.

Maktar (100 km from Kairouan and 157 km from Tunis) is a Roman site which was built over an ancient Berber fortress and continued into Byzantine days with an amphitheatre, Trajan's arch and forum whose paving is well preserved, baths, a neo-Punic Temple and a Punic Mausoleum.

Some hotels in the Sahel

Four Star
El Hana (Sousse) 262 beds. tel: 03 21 846.
Sidi Mansour (Monastir) 254 beds. tel: 03 61 311.
Skanes Palace (Skanes) 300 beds. tel: 03 61 360.

Three Star
Hill Diar (Sousse) 388 beds. tel: 03 21 206.
El Ksar (Sousse) 520 beds. tel: 03 21 822.
Les Aghlabites (Kairouan) 124 beds. tel: 07 20 855.
Ruspina (Monastir) 346 beds. tel: 03 61 360.

Two Star
Salem (Sousse) 400 beds. tel: 03 21 966.

Alyssa (Sousse) 700 beds. tel: 03 20 713.
Mabrouk (Sfax) 82 beds. tel: 04 21 544.
Residence Chems (Monastir) 600 beds. tel: 03 61 138.

Others
Marhala (Kairouan) 68 beds. tel: 07 20 736.

In addition to hotels of all categories there is a **Maison des Jeunes.**

THE ISLAND OF JERBA

The mythical land where Ulysses found the Lotus Eaters has become an international resort of luxurious hotels because of its restful atmosphere, fine beaches and superb climate, which is especially pleasant in the European winter. There is an average of 344 days of sunshine each year.

A relaxing pastime is to walk or ride along the beaches or through the peaceful countryside with its farmhouses and ancient whitewashed mosques, olive and palm groves. The villages have interesting *souks*. The main town on the island is *Houmt Souk.*

An unfailing attraction on Jerba is the ancient Jewish synagogue, the symbol of a Jewish community that dates back 2,500 years and which still thrives. Tours of the island also take in the traditional pottery workshops and other handicraft centres. Tours are also available to the mainland and the Deep South. A long causeway links the island to the rapidly developing mainland beach town of **Zarzis.**

Jerba is served by an international airport and there is also a ferry to the mainland at Jorf. Most of the island's hotels are sited on the extensive coastline. Some, like the exclusive **Club Mediterrannée,** should be booked abroad well in advance.

Hotels on Jerba

Dar Jerba, tel: 05 57 191, telex: 40830, a huge complex providing 2,400 beds in individual domed cottages with its own bay and boating facilities, several restaurants, pools, shops, nightclubs and craft stalls. Accommodation available at different grades from 2-star to 4-star.

Four Star
El Menzel, tel: 05 57 070, telex: 40827.
Ulysse Palace, tel: 05 50 122, telex: 40832.

Three Star
Les Sirènes, tel: 05 50 190, telex: 40888.

Two Star
Calypso Beach, tel: 05 57 161, telex: 40839.
Meninx, tel: 05 57 051, telex: 40870.

One Star
El Arischa, situated in Houmt Souk, tel: 05 50 384.

Others
Touring Club, in Houmt Souk, tel: 05 50 146.
There are hostels for students and young people.

Hotels in Zarzis

Three Star
Zarzis, tel: 05 80 160, telex: 40848.

Two Star
Sidi Saad, tel: 05 80 377, telex: 40886.
Zita, tel: 05 80 246, telex: 40854.

GABES AND THE SAHARA

The beach-side oasis town of Gabes is the gateway to southern Tunisia and the Sahara. Although the town itself is rather ordinary its local crafts include carpets, wickerwork, wood, amber, leather and silver. A horse-and-carriage takes you to the delightful Chenini oasis nearby, past old women with vibrant henna-dyed hair, to a huge forest of date palms which shelter orange, peach, apricot and pome-

granate—the only oasis in the world so near the sea.

A fine excursion runs south over the 600 m **Mountains of Matmata** to the village in the valley of the same name. Here the local people are cave and pit-dwellers, digging into the soft soil to build 10 m deep homes, cool and refreshing in the Saharan heat. Two underground pit-homes have been converted into inexpensive and attractive hotels.

Galsa was a Roman site and Berber stronghold. Its walls are washed a rosy pink, its oasis of date palms and fruit thrives and its shops and craftsmen specialise in carpets, rugs and blankets. Its simple solid brick buildings are decorated in bold geometric patterns.

Tozeur (245 km from Gabes) is a striking oasis town, with its brick Sidi Abid Mosque, two minarets, and Great Mosque; a track climbs to a flower and fruit tree garden known as Paradise.

Nefta 24 km on, is an artificial date-palm oasis made by digging underground wells—unlike the *wadis* (dry river beds) that catch the run-off of flash floods, and underground streams that usually feed the oases. It has the site of the original

Souk at Sfax

Roman and Berber natural oasis with another garden named Paradise, a rug-weaving centre, and several mosques and shrines of the Islamic mystical Sufi sect. A hillside road climbs to the **Corbeille Cafe** with a panoramic view of the desert and the palm-groves. From either Tozeur or Nefta, the hotels organise Land-Rover excursions around the salt-pans—specially across the great Chott Jerid to **Kebili** and **Douz.**

Kebili may also be visited by a better road from Gabes, 115 km, which passes along mountain ranges and barren plains to the once fortified little oasis town. The town of **Douz,** 30 km south of **Kebili,** has a Thursday market to which *Tuareg* traders and their camels come from the Sahara interior.

The road south from Gabes leads to the remote towns of **Medenine** and **Tatouine.** Tracks from there take the traveller into the Ksour Mountains and to the fascinating and rugged ancient Berber villages south of Tataouine, the road becomes a Saharan trail suitable only for four-wheel drive vehicles. Tunisian military permission is needed to travel beyond their Saharan base at Remada. Those who make this trip can travel another 300 km to the French-built Borjel Hattapa where the Tunisian, Algerian, and Libyan borders intersect; if their papers are in order and visa obtained, they may cross to the Libyan oasis of Ghadames, where there is an hotel.

Hotels in the south

Four Star
Sahara Palace, (Nefta). tel: 46, telex: 47862.

Three Star
Chems, (Gabes). tel: 05 20 547, telex: 40868.
Oasis, (Gabes). tel: 05 20 381.
Jugurtha, (Gafsa). tel: Gafsa 216.
Continental, (Tozeur). tel: Tozeur 107, telex: 40849.

Tunisian-style dinner

Oasis, (Tozeur). tel: Tozeur 13.

Others
Atlantic, (Gabes). tel: 05 20 034.
De la Poste, (Gabes). tel: 05 20 718.
Marhala, (Matmata). tel: Matmata 15.
Sidi Driss, (Matmata). tel:Matmata 5.
Oasis, (Gafsa). tel: Gafsa 97.
Maamoun, (Gafsa). tel: Gafsa 584.
De Tunis, (Gafsa). tel: Gafsa 420.
El Jerid, (Tozeur). tel: Tozeur 81.
Les Palmiers, (Tozeur). tel: Tozeur 55.
Mirage, (Nefta). tel: Nefta 41.
Les Nomades, (Nefta). tel: Nefta 52.
Borj des Autruches, (Kebili). tel: Kebili 42.
Marhala, (Douz). tel: Douz 15.
Saharien, (Douz). tel: Douz 37.
Agip, (Medenine). tel: 05 40 151.
La Gazelle, (Tataouine). tel: Tataouine 10.

There is also modern accommodation at the ancient Berber fortresses at Ksar Ouled Dabbab, near Tataouine, and at Ksar Ouled Haddada, near Ghomrassen. There are youth hostels at Gabes and Gafsa.

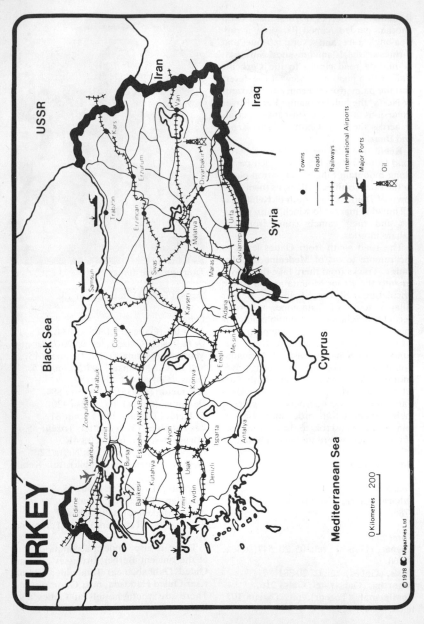

TURKEY

Metin Munir

If you want a quiet restful holiday don't come to Turkey. Turkey is for the adventurous . . . and this becomes more true as you go eastwards. You can find quiet and repose, but if you do, you will be missing the best of the country.

Vast by European standards, Anatolia presents staggering contrasts of terrain; enormous primeval forests, Asian steppeland, deserts, and Mediterranean coastal scenery. Its history is the history of man himself. Hittites, Greeks, Romans, Persians, Arabs, Crusaders, and Turks have all left their mark. Away from the big cities, however, Turkey is still virgin territory.

THE LAND AND THE PEOPLE

By European standards, Turkey covers a large area, but has a relatively small population. Its total area is greater than any European state, excluding the Soviet Union.

With an estimated 42 million, Turkey is the most populous country in the Middle East—but the population density is far below the level of Western European countries. Like its largest city, Istanbul, Turkey straddles two continents.

Asia Minor, or Anatolia, accounts for 97% of the country. It forms a long peninsula (1,650 km. from east to west, 800 km. from north to south) bordered to the north by the Black Sea and the Marmara, to the west by the Aegean, to the south by the Mediterranean. Two east-west mountain ranges, the Pontic in the north, the Taurus in the south, enclose the central Anatolian plateau, but join up in a vast mountainous region in the far east of the country. Here the two great rivers of antiquity the Tigris and the Euphrates, rise. The central plateau is surrounded by a fertile coastal region.

The undulating country of Thrace (European Turkey) is divided from Anatolia by the Sea of Marmara and the Bosphorus and Dardanelles straits. Turkey has land frontiers with Bulgaria, Greece, the Soviet Union, Iran, Iraq and Syria.

HISTORY AND CULTURE

The country's history is complex. At Catal Höyük, in central southern Turkey, remains of a neolithic settlement dating to 6000 BC have been found. The first settlement at Troy has been dated around 3000 BC. In the second millenium BC the Hittites established a great empire in Anatolia. They were followed by the Phrygians, the Lydians and the Persians. Alexander the Great conquered the entire Anatolian peninsula after defeating the Persians in 334 BC. Then came Roman hegemony, and in AD 324, Constantine selected Byzantium to be the New

Rome: for 16 centuries it was the capital of an empire.

The Selojuk Turks, migrating from their homelands in central Asia, arrived on the scene in the 11th century, eventually establishing a Sultanate in Konya with control of most of Asia Minor. Another Turkish group, the Ottomans, established their first principality in 1301, and went on to capture Byzantium in 1453. In the 16th century, Sultan Suleyman the Magnificent was Europe's most powerful monarch, his empire extending as far as Hungary and Saudi Arabia and including most of North Africa.

The Ottoman Empire survived until the first world war when it collapsed. Renouncing all claims to the Arab parts of the empire, Kemal Ataturk drove a Greek invasion force out of Asia Minor in 1922, and the following year proclaimed the Turkish Republic. Two brief periods of military rule aside, Turkey has been a multi-party democracy since 1950. Admiral Fahri Koruturk became President in 1973. The ruling party at the beginning of 1978 was Bulent Ecevit's left-of-centre Republican People's Party.

The Turks' cultural traditions are almost entirely Asiatic and Islamic, superimposed on the classical and Christian cultures they found in Anatolia. The modern Turkish Republic is committed to a policy of westernisation, initiated by Ataturk. Yet the mass of the people are small townsfolk or peasants, their way of life essentially Middle Eastern, they are pious Muslims (99% of the population are Muslims, even though the state is secular), they adhere to traditional values, and are fiercely nationalistic. The more sophisticated Turks of the cities consider themselves more European than Middle Eastern.

A huge social and economic gap yawns between the rural masses and the westernised city dwellers. More than half the population cannot read. The past ten years has seen mass migration into the big cities—Istanbul, Ankara and Izmir—which are surrounded by extensive shanty towns.

The four million or so Kurds who live in the mountains of the east are the largest ethnic minority. Arabic-speaking Muslims and Christians are to be found in the province of Hatay (Alexandretta), which joined the Republic in 1939. Armenian, Greek and Jewish minorities live in Istanbul, and are largely engaged in business.

Although Turkey has recently been seeking closer ties with the Islamic world (eg Iran) she has kept out of the Middle East conflict, maintaining diplomatic ties with both Israel and the Arab states.

ECONOMY

The Turkish economy has grown substantially since the early 1960s. In the 1970-1975 period Turkey was the fourth fastest growing economy in the democratic world and second among these without the benefit of oil revenues. But despite its impressive growth, the country is plagued with serious social and economic problems. The population increase, 2.4% per annum, is extremely high. About three million people, (20% of the work force) are unemployed. Inflation has been averaging over 20% since 1971 and shows no signs of slackening. The foreign trade deficit is large and growing, constituting the main concern for the economy. The growth in the GNP in 1976 was 8.1%. Gross national income per capita is still below $1,000.

The country remains predominantly agricultural although over the past decade or so Governments have followed a vigorous policy of industrial development. About 60% of the population is engaged in agriculture and agriculture's contribution to the GNP is about 30%. Agricultural exports, mainly tobacco, cotton, hazelnuts and raisins, account for nearly 70% of exports.

Agriculture, however, has been steadily declining in importance and the country's planners hope that it will be replaced by industry as the dominant sector in the early 1980s. Turkey's industrial base is the strongest of all the Middle East countries.

Nearly half of Turkey's trade is with the European Economic Community of which Turkey is an associate member scheduled to attain full membership in 1995. In the past few years or so, however, trade with the Middle East countries has been increasing. Exports in 1976 were $1,960 million and imports $5,129 million (leaving a trade deficit of $3,169 million).

In 1976, the drop in reserves coupled with low exports led to an economic crisis, forcing the government to adopt a programme of economic austerity measures. The Turkish lira was devalued by 10% and the prices of basic goods and services were steeply raised negotiations were opened with the IMF for stand-by credits.

GENERAL INFORMATION

Area: 780,600 sq. km.
Population: 40,197,669 (1975 census).
Capital: Ankara.
Head of State: Admiral Fahri Koruturk.
Government: Multi-party democratic republic
Language: Turkish.
Religion: Islam. Small Christian and Jewish minorities.
Currency: The Turkish Lira (TL) is divided into 100 Kurus. £1=34.70TL $1=19.25TL.
Time: GMT+2 (winter) GMT + 3 (summer).

HOW TO GET THERE

By air: There are airports for scheduled international flights at Istanbul, Ankara and Adana. There are daily flights between London and Istanbul or Ankara by Turkish Airlines, British Airways, and PanAm. Turkish Airlines travel to Amsterdam, Athens, Beirut, Brussels, Copenhagen, Frankfurt, Geneva, Milan, Munich, Nicosia, Paris, Rome, Tripoli, Vienna and Zurich. Other scheduled airlines which fly to Turkey include: Air France, Alia, Alitalia, KLM, SAS, Sabena, Saudia, Lufthansa, MEA, Olympic, PIA, Swissair, Iraqi Airways, Iran National.

By road: Turkey is connected with Greece, Bulgaria, Iran and Iraq.

By rail: There are scheduled services to Istanbul from Paris and Munich.

By sea: Turkish Maritime Lines have a regular passenger service to Istanbul from Barcelona, Marseilles, Genoa, Naples and Piraeus, and a car ferry from Venice and Brindisi to Izmir. There is also a regular service all the year round to Istanbul and Izmir by the Italian Adriatica line from French and Italian ports.

Visas and health regulations
A valid passport with a current visa, which can be obtained from Turkish

Ancient ruins, Didima, western Turkey

consular offices abroad, is necessary. British citizens do not require a visa.

Visitors are not required to produce international vaccination certificates. It is however advisable to get vaccinations against cholera as there have been recent outbreaks of the disease.

Currency and customs regulations

There are no restrictions on the import of foreign currency or its export. Only a small amount of Turkish currency may be taken in or out of the country.

Articles for personal use are allowed in free of duty. This includes 200 cigarettes or 50 grammes of tobacco or 20 cigars; one litre of alcoholic liquor and 200 grammes of tea. The export of antiques without a licence is prohibited.

CLIMATE

Winters tend to be very cold whereas the summer months are usually hot. The southern coastal districts, sheltered by the Taurus mountains, have a milder winter but are hotter and more humid in the summer.

What to wear

In winter warm clothing is essential throughout the country. In the summer tropical clothing is recommended in the southern areas, and lightweight clothing in the northern areas.

ACCOMMODATION AND FOOD

Hotels of all classes are plentiful throughout Turkey. A single room with a private bathroom in a luxury class hotel costs approximately 370TL in Ankara, and 430-530TL in Istanbul. There is an official Hotel Guide to Turkey issued by the Ministry of Tourism and Information.

Most hotels have their own restaurants, in addition there are a large number of eating places available, and Turkish food is world famous. Charges in Istanbul are higher than those in Ankara but in Izmir they are lower. A meal for one in a restaurant in Ankara costs approximately 100-120TL.

TRANSPORT

By air: Turkish airlines operate regular services between Istanbul, Izmir and Ankara.

By sea: There are regular steamship services between Istanbul and all the large coastal towns.

By rail: Istanbul is linked by rail with a number of coastal towns including Izmir Mersin and Iskenderun. There is a daily express service between Istanbul and Ankara (12 hours).

By road: Taxis are available in all the main cities; the most economical way is travel by shared taxis which operate between fixed points. The same system also operates between Istanbul and Ankara and other nearby towns. Self drive cars are readily available.

Bus services link most of the major towns.

BANKS

Ottoman Bank, Bankalar Caddesi, Karakoy, Istanbul.
Banco di Roma, Hayri Effendi Caddesi, Bahcekapi, Istanbul.
Banka Komerciyale Italyana, Bakalar Cad. 53. Karakoy, Istanbul.
International Industry and Commerce Bank, Bankalar Cad. 69. Karakoy, Istanbul.

Business hours

Offices and shops: 0830 to 1200 and 1300 to 1730 Monday to Friday.

Banks: 0900 to 1200 and 1400 to 1730
Monday to Friday.
0900 to 1300 Saturday.

PUBLIC HOLIDAYS

New Years Day, 1 January
Independence Day, 23 April
Spring Holiday, 1 May
Sports Festival, 19 May
Freedom and Constitution Day, 27 May
Victory Day, 30 August
Seker Bayram (end of Ramadan), 3
September
Republic Day, 29 October
Kurban Bayram, 9 November

EMBASSIES IN THE CAPITAL

Algeria: Cankaya, Cinnah Cad. 90/9-10.
Austria: Ataturk Bulvari 197.
Belgium: Sehit Ersan Caddesi 42/1-2-4.
France: Paris Cad. 70, Kavaklidere.
German Federal Republic: Ataturk Bulvari 114.
Greece: Fatma Aliye Sokak 1, Kavaklidere.
Iran: Tahran Cad. 10.
Iraq: Turan Emeksiz Sokak 11, Gaziosmanpasa.
Italy: Ataturk Bulvari 118.
Jordan: Dede Korkut Sokak 18, Cankaya.
Kuwait: Cinnah Caddesi 88/3-4, Cankaya.
Lebanon: Cinnah Caddesi 11/3, Cankaya.
Libya: Ebuzziya Tevfik Sokak 5, Cankaya.
Morocco: Ataturk Bulvari No. 223/9.
Netherlands: Sehit Ersan Cad. 4, Cankaya.
Portugal: Cinnah Caddesi 28/3.
Saudi Arabia: Abdullah Cevdet Sok, 18, Cankaya.
Spain: Abdullah Cevdet Sokak No. 8, Cankaya.
Switzerland: Ataturk Bulvari 263.
Syria: Cankaya, Abdullah Cevdet Sok, 7.

Bones of St. Nicholas, Antalya Museum, Ankara

UK: Cankaya, Sehit Ersan Cad. 46/A.
USA: Ataturk Bulvari 110.
USSR: Karyagdi Sokak 5, Cankaya.

TOURIST INFORMATION

Adana, Ataturk Caddessi No. 13 tel: 11323.
Ankara, Gazi Mustafa Kemal Bulvari 33 tel: 173012.
Bursa, Ataturk Cad. 82 tel: 12359.
Edirine, Hurriyet Meydani, 2 tel: 1518.
Istanbul, Mesrutiyet Cad. 57, Galatasaray tel: 456875.
Hilton Hotel entrance tel: 406300.
Izmir, Gazi Osman Pasa Bulvari 10/A tel: 142147.

ANKARA

Turkey's grim utilitarian capital has little to attract the visitor, and should be avoided in winter, when the pollution has no rival in the world.

Ankara's most interesting feature is undoubtedly the Musuem of Anatolian

Civilisations, housed in an Ottoman bazaar and *Han or caravanserai* (inn). It contains unique collections of Hittite, Phrygian and Urartaean work. Ruins of Roman baths, a Roman column and the Temple of Augustus and Rome can be seen in the city.

Hotels
Buyuk Ankara (luxury) Ataturk Bulv 183 tel: 1771106
Marmara (luxury) Ataturk Orman Ciftligi (outside the town) tel: 231361
Dedeman (first class) Buklum Sok 1 tel: 171100
Kent (first class) Mithat Pasa Cad. 4 tel: 177268
Bulvar Palas (second class) Ataturk Bulv 141 tel: 175020
Yuksel Palas (third class) Ataturk Bulv 51 tel: 250540

Restaurants
Altin Nal Lokantasi, Cinnah Cad. 47.
Kristal Restoran, Bayindir Sok 28/A.

Restoran R.V., Turan Emeksiz Sok 8.
Liman, Izmir Cad. 11 (fish speciality).

Night clubs
Gar Gazinosu, Istasyon Meydani.
Kosk Gazinosu, Gazi Mustafa Kemal Bul 71 Maltepe.
Yeni Sureyya Gazinosu, Bestekar Sok 14, Kuckesat.

ISTANBUL

The largest city, and capital of the Byzantine and Ottoman Empires, Istanbul is at once superlatively beautiful and staggeringly squalid. The old city is divided from the modern business centre where the principal hotels are situated by a heavily polluted inlet, the Golden Horn, crossed by the picturesque, archaic Galata Bridge. A third part of the city, largely residential, lies across the Bosphorus in Asia.

Justinian's sixth century cathedral of the Holy Wisdom *Aya Sofya*, became a

The Galata Bridge with the Suleymainye Mosque in the background, Istanbul

BENTE FASMER

mosque after the Turkish conquest, but is now a museum. The mosaics in the gallery should not be missed. The 14th century mosaics and frescoes in the *Kariye Camii* (near Edirnekapi) are a must, mosaics from the same period are to be seen in the *Fethiye Camii* (near Edirnekapi).

The old city abounds in Ottoman mosques, the finest, the 16th century *Suleymaniye*, includes a library and museum of Islamic art. The *Sultan Ahmet* or Blue Mosque dates from the following century, and has fine tile work. The tiles in the *Rustempasa* mosque are also excellent.

The palace of the Ottoman Sultans, the *Topkapi Saray*, lies at the tip of the headland on which the old city stands. The various kiosks stand in delightful gardens, with a view across the Bosphorus to the massive *Selimiye Barracks*, where Florence Nightingale nursed soldiers wounded in the Crimean War. In the beauty of this setting, it is hard to conjure up the dark plots hatched within the palace walls.

A fascination for western visitors is the extensive covered bazaar *Kapali Carsi*, where expensive jewellers, antique dealers and carpet merchants bargain endlessly.

Visitors tired of the noise and bustle of the city can take a boat from the Galata Bridge either up the Bosphorus, with its Ottoman villas on either side, or to the peaceful Princes' Islands—where bathing is reasonable. Bathing at the Black Sea village of Kilyos is not recommended, due to the dangerous currents.

Hotels
Buyuk Tarabya, (luxury) on the Bosphorus, out of the city tel: 621000.
Cinar, (luxury) at the airport tel: 732910.
Divan, (luxury) Cumhuriyet Cad. tel: 464020.
Hilton, (luxury) Cumhuriyet Cad. tel: 465050.
Intercontinental, (luxury) Taksim tel: 488850.
Sheraton, (luxury) Taksim tel: 489000.
Park, (first class) Taksim tel: 450760.
Pera Palas, (first class) Mesrutiyet Cad. tel: 452230.
Reasonably priced hotels near **Taksim,** cheaper ones near **Sultan Ahmet** in the old city and at **Aksaray.**

Restaurants
Liman: Rihtim Cad., Karakoy.
Galata Tower: In the Byzantine tower that stands opposite the old city.
Bogazici: Arnavutkoy.
Canli Balik: Mesa Burnu Cad. 4, Sariyer (Fish).
Dort Mevsim: Istiklal Cad. 509.
Haci Baba: Istiklal Cad. 49.
Fish restaurants are to be found in the Bosphorus villages, and on the Galata Bridge.

Nights clubs
Bebek Maksim Gazinousu, Cevdet Pasa Cad. 350, Bebek.
Bebek Park Gazinosu, Bebek.
Lunapark Gazinosu, Vatan Cad. 79, Aksaray.
Taslik Sark Gazinosu, Macka Besiktas.
Kervansaray Gazinosu, Cumhurikyet Cad 30, Harbiye.

IZMIR

Turkey's third city and main export port, Izmir was founded by Alexander the Great. The citadel, on the top of Mount Pagus, affords a view of the beautiful Gulf of Izmir. The *agora* of Hellenistic and Roman Smyrna is worth a visit, so is the Archaeological Museum, which houses finds from old Smyrna and other cities of ancient Ionia. In late August and September, an international trade fair is held in the Kultur Park, and finding hotels can be near impossible then.

Hotels
Buyuk Efes, (luxury) tel: 144300.
Kismet, (first class) 1377 Sok 9 tel: 144385.

Alanya, a small town on the Mediterranian in the province of Antalya

Izmir Palas, (second class) Ataturk Bulv.
tel: 132100.
Kilim, (second class) Ataturk Bulv. tel:
145340.

Restaurants
Cafe Plaza, Mustafa Bey Cad. 3.
Bergama Restoran, Ataturk Cad. 190.
There are fish restaurants along the quay.

Night clubs
Kubana Gazinosu, Kulturpark.
Mehemet Ali Gazinosu, Guzelyali.
Mogambo Gazinosu, Kulturpark.

BURSA

Lying at the foot of Bithynian Olympus
(Uludag), Bursa is one of the most attractive cities in Turkey: a cluster of Ottoman
houses, mosque and mausolea, set among
cypresses and cool springs. Throughout
the period of Ottoman greatness, Bursa
acquired a wealth of architectural monuments. Most notable are the *Yesil Cami*
(Green Mosque) built by Sultan Mehmet
I in 1424. Opposite is Mehmet's mausoleum, the *Yesil Turbe*. The *Yildirim Beyazit* mosque (circa 1400) and *Ulu* (great)
mosque (roughly contemporary) are also
not to be missed.

Uludag is Istanbul's principal ski resort, and is equipped with a cable car,
well worth a visit even in summer. Easily
accessible from Bursa is the attractive
lakeside walled town of Iznik—ancient
Nicaea.

Hotels
Celik Palas, (second class) tel: 196000.

318

TURKISH EMBASSY

Acar, (third class) tel: 20005.
There are also hotels by the ski slopes.
Bursa is well provided with inexpensive restaurants, but many do not serve any alcohol, other than beer.

EDIRNE

The 16th century architect Sinan built here what is seen as his finest mosque, the *Selimiye Camii*. The old mosque (*Eski Cami*), dating from the early 15th century, and the mosque of *Beyazit II* (late 15th century) should also be seen.

Hotels
Demir, (second class) tel: 2315.
Kervan, (second class) Talat Pashe Cad. 134 tel: 1355.
Sultan, (fourth class) Talat Pashe Cad. 134 tel: 1372.
Motels are to be found in the vicinity of the frontier posts with Greece and Bulgaria.

ANTALYA

The only ancient city of Pamphylia to retain importance today, Antalya is a delightfully shaded city with abundant water, and an attractive old harbour. The extensive old Ottoman town with its narrow streets and timber houses is one of the best preserved of its kind. Well kept public gardens on the cliff tops afford a superlative view across the gulf to the rugged mountains of ancient Lycia. An ethnographic museum now occupies what was once a church, and subsequently a mosque, with a distinctively grooved minaret, *Yivli Minare Camii*. The new archaeological museum, to the west of the town, houses finds from the ancient cities of the region. Avoid Antalya, in high summer.

Hotels
Antalya, (first class) tel: 5600.

Perge, (third class) tel: 1432.
Buyuk, (fourth class) tel: 1499.

Night clubs
Hisar Turistik Tesisleri, Restoran ve Kahvehane Kaleici Tophane MevkII.

ANTAKYA

The capital of the Roman province of Syria, Antioch on the Orontes, where the disciples were first called Christians, has a mild climate, even in high summer, and the surrounding country, particularly to the south, near ancient Daphne (*Harbiye*), is of considerable beauty.

The museum boasts a collection of late antique mosaics unrivalled anywhere, and no visitor should leave Turkey without seeing them. Outside the city, there is an ancient rock church, known as *St. Peter's cave*. Also worth seeing are the attractive old section of the town, and the view from the citadel.

Hotels
Atahan, (second class) tel: 1036.
Divan, (third class) tel: 1518.

ERZURUM

Most notable monuments in this high Eastern city are the 12th century *Ulu Cami* mosque, and the famous Selcuk double-minareted religious school, the *Cifte Minare Medressi*.

Hotel
San, (fourth class) tel: 2158.

KARS

Visit the 10th century Church of the Holy Apostles (now a museum) at the foot of the citadel. Thirty miles away, on the Soviet frontier, lies the old Armenian capital of *Ani*, founded in the 10th century, and now deserted. Permission must be first obtained from the military authorities in Kars.

A remarkable collection of frescoed Armenian churches is to be found in staggeringly beautiful natural surroundings.

Hotel
Temel Palas, (fourth class) tel: 1376.

KAYSERI

At the foot of an extinct volcano, *Erciyes Dagi* (Mt Argaeus), Caesarea was the capital of Roman Cappadocia, and a prominent city in both Selcuk and Ottoman times. Notable Selcuk monuments are the mosques, *Ulu Cami* and *Honat Hatun Camii*, and the religious school *Huand Medressi*, now the Archaeological museum. A Selcuk mausoleum, the *Doner Kumbet*, should also be seen.

Hotels
Turan: (second class). tel: 19 68.
Hattat: (fourth classs). tel: 93 31.

KONYA

Iconium fell to the Selcuk Turks in the late 11th century. It then served as capital of their Sultanate until the middle of the 13th century, when the Selcuks where defeated by the Mongol hordes. Konya finally was annexed to the Ottoman empire in 1466/7.

From the Selcuk period date the *Alaeddin* mosque, and three religious schools, the *Buyuk, Karatay, Ince Minare* and *Sircall.*

Konya's most famous monument is the monastery of the *Mevlana,* or whirling dervishes. Founded here by a 13th century mystic, this strange sect (disbanded in the early years of the republic) found its most direct route to God through ecstatic whirling, accompanied by music.

This is annually re-enacted at a December festival, when Konya is flooded by tourists.

Hotels
Basak Palas, (third class) tel: 11784.
Saray, (third class) tel: 11080.
Sahin, (third class) tel: 13350.
Selcuk, (fourth class) tel: 11259.

Restaurants
Konya is well served for reasonably priced restaurants, but alcohol can be hard to find.

DIYARBAKIR

Near the banks of the Tigris, Diyarbakir is distinguished by its massive basalt mediaeval walls. The *Ulu Cami* mosque is either an Arab structure or earlier.

Hotels
Demir, (third class) tel: 2315.
Sarac, (fourth class) tel: 2365.

The ancient temple at Avcilar, Cappadoncia, a result of volcanic rock erosion

CAMERA PRESS

MARDIN

Worth a visit for the striking view it affords over Iraq. See the Selcuk *Sultan Isa Medresesi*. In the region of the nearby town of Midyat, the palaeochristian monasteries of *Tur Abdin* should be visited.

Hotel
Turistik, (fourth class) tel: 338645.

URFA

There is little to be seen of the ancient Edessa. At the foot of the ruined crusader citadel is a large pool of sacred carp. Abraham is said to have stopped here. He also halted for several years at Charan, now Harran, a small village south of Urfa with distinctive Syrian 'beehive' houses.

VAN

Apart from the archaeological museum, there is little of great interest in the city, but the lake it is situated on, is both enormous by European standards (nearly 3,750 sq. km.), and of considerable beauty. Along the shores lies the dead city of Eski Ahlat, and on the opposite side of the lake there is the small island of Ahtamar, where a strikingly beautiful 10th century Armenian basilica stands.

Hotels
Bayram, (fourth class) tel: 1136.
Bes Kardesler, (fourth class) tel: 1116.

TRABZON

A pleasant Black Sea port and small town beautifully sited, Trebizond was the romantic last outpost of the Byzantine world. Do not miss the late 13th century frescoes in the church of *Aya Sofya*. East of Trabzon, the road to Rize and Hopa, near the Soviet frontier is spectacular. Visit the beautifully sited tea research institute *Cay Arastirma Enstitusu* in the otherwise uninteresting town of Rize. Inland from Trabzon, do not miss the deserted Byzantine monastery of *Sumela*, at the head of a spectacular gorge. This region of Turkey is unique, and should be given priority by the visitor, even though it frequently rains.

Hotels
Usta, (third class) tel: 2843.
Horon, (fourth class) tel: 1199.

Restaurants
Belediye Sahil Lekantasi, Sahil Yolu.

CENTRAL ANATOLIA

The Konya-Kayseri road is fairly free of traffic, and is marked by a succession of spectacular Selçuk caravanserais (inns), with remarkable carving in a very beautiful warm stone; most notable is *Sultanhani*.

Perhaps the most extraordinary phenomenon in all Anatolia, however, is the bizarre rock formation in Cappadocia, a result of erosion of volcanic rock thrown up by Erciyes Dagi. The resulting 'lunar' landscape became a refuge for ascetics from the fourth century, and churches have been carved out of the rock; in several cases they are frescoed. Most notable examples are in the Göreme and Peristrema (Ihlara) valleys. Equally bizarre are two entire underground cities six miles apart, connected by a tunnel, Kaymakli and Derinkuyu. There is no clue from above that these even exist. As one observer put it, they are a colossal monument to fear. While in this area, visit the Dervish monastery at Hacibektas.

Central Anatolia also boasts numerous Hittite cites. The most notable are Hattuşaş (Boğazköy) and Alacahöyük, near Ankara. These sites are not spectacular,

Pize, Black sea coast

the principal finds are in the museum in Ankara. Farther south, the most ancient city ever unearthed can be seen at Çatalhöyük.

Nevşehir hotels
Orsan Cappadocia, (second class) tel: 35.
Göreme, (second class) tel: 706.

Urgup hotel
Büyük (third class) tel: 60.

AEGEAN

Crossing over the Dardanelles from the Gallipoli peninsula, the graves and memorials to those who died during the Gallipoli campaign in the First World War can be seen. Gallipoli itself, now Gelibolu, is an attractive fishing village, and a good place to stay.

South of the straits, lie the remains of the ancient city of Troy, now Truva. Nine levels have been discovered, the city described in Homer's Iliad is the sixth.

Pergamum, now Bergama, is less old, and its period of glory was the second and third centuries BC, when it was the capital of a Western Anatolian Empire.

Its library rivaled Alexandria's, and a cut-off in papyrus supplies led to the use of pergamina (parchment) instead. Principal sights are the *Asclepion* (temple of the god of medicine), a second century AD basilica temple, the Kizil Avlu, and the *Acropolis.*

The most important city of the Roman province of Asia, however, was Ephesus—founded originally in the 13th century BC. The temple of Artemis was famous throughout the ancient world. To be seen today on either side of the ancient street are a theatre, odeon, baths and gymnasium. Notable finds from the site are in the museum in the nearby township of Selçuk.

Smaller sites of Ionian cities on the west coast are Foca, Priene, Assos, Miletus and Didyma.

Pleasant resorts are Ayvalik, Çeşme, Kuşadasi, Bodrum and Marmaris. The last three are over-crowded in high summer.

Inland, spectacular and unique water falls at Pamukkale should not be missed.

MEDITERRANEAN

In the inaccessible mountains of Lycia,

west of Antalya, the rock churches at ancient Myra (see of St. Nicholas, now Demre) are well worth the trouble. Twenty miles from Antalya is the spectacular site of Termerssos, theatre and necropolis.

In the Pamphylian plain, the remains of three ancient cities should be seen, Perge, Aspendos and Side. These sites are all in remarkable condition. The theatre of Aspendos is almost undamaged, and is regularly used today. The theatre of Side is recommended on a moonlit evening. Side is a rapidly expanding resort centre, and has numerous guest houses and motels.

Driving along the startlingly beautiful coast road (non-stop beaches), one passes the resort town of Alamya. At the bottom of the 'bump', at Anamur, there is a remarkable crusader fortress.

Inland from Silifke are the remains of Olba Diocaesarea (Uzuncaborc), with a notable temple of Zeus. But the most spectacular site is undoubtedly that of ancient Korykos. Twin castles (one called *Kiz Kalesi*) dwarf the theatre, palace and necropolis. North of *Kiz Kalesi*, yawn the

two pits of heaven and hell, *Cennet ve Cehennem Obruğu*; a ruined Armenian chapel lies by a grotto, and a narrow hole nearby, where condemned sinners were consigned.

ISHAK, PASA, SARAYI AND ARARAT

Near Dobgubeyazit, visit the striking late 17th century palace of a Kurdish chieftain, *Ishak Pasa*, strikingly set below Mount Ararat (*Buyuk Agri Dagi*), a volcano 5,165 metres high. Noah's Ark landed on the summit after the flood.

NEMRUT DAGI

In the region of Adiyaman, visit the bizarre funeral monument of Antiochus Commagenes, dating to the first century BC. It consists of an artificial mound on the summit of a mountain, surrounded by colossal stone statues, the heads of which can still be seen.

Manangat Falls at Antalya

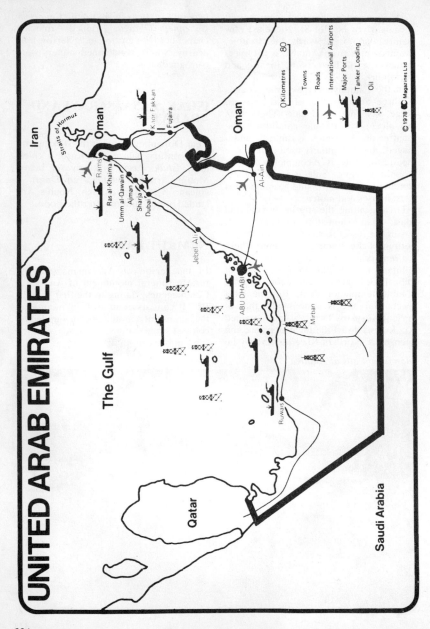

UNITED ARAB EMIRATES

Rosalind Mazzawi

At present tourist visas are not granted by the United Arab Emirates, although there are long-term plans for developing resort areas in the federation. Travellers must have business reasons for visiting, or have close relatives living and working there.

The UAE are a federation of seven small sheikhdoms on the former Pirate Coast, at the lower end of the Gulf. For a long time they were known as the Trucial States, on account of the truce and treaty imposed upon them in 1835 by the British Navy to refrain from plundering foreign ships that sailed up the Gulf. In December 1971 they were united in a Federation, whose President is Sheikh Zayed of Abu Dhabi, and Vice-President Sheikh Rashid of Dubai. The other five sheikhdoms are, Sharjah, Ajman, Umm el Quwain, Ras el Khaimah, and Fu-

Abu Dhabi

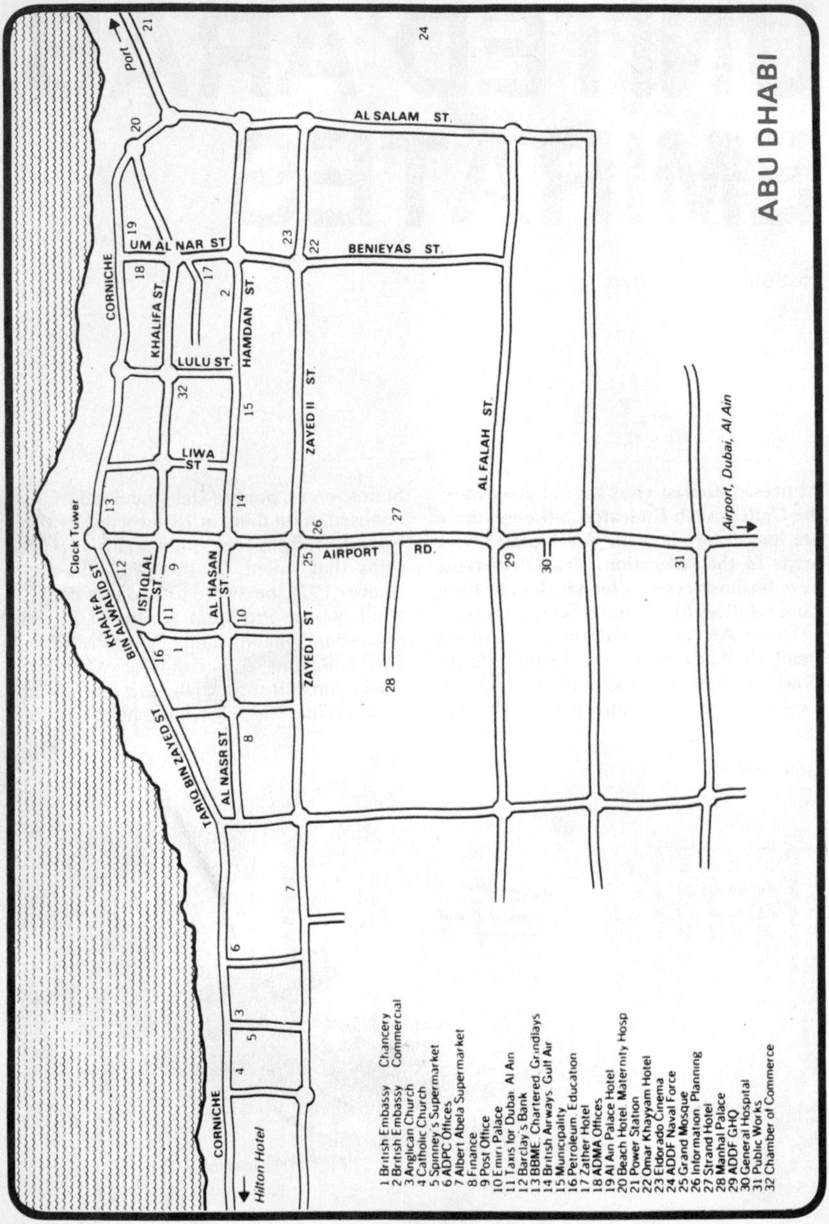

ABU DHABI

Map labels:
port, 21, 20, 24, AL SALAM ST., CORNICHE, 19, UM AL NAR ST., 18, KHALIFA ST., 17, 23, 22, BENIEYAS ST., HAMDAN ST., LULU ST., 32, 15, ZAYED II ST., LIWA ST., 13, 14, AL FALAH ST., Clock Tower, 12, ISTIQLAL ST., 26, 27, 25, AIRPORT RD., 29, 30, KHALIFA BIN ALWALID ST., 11, AL HASAN ST., 9, 10, 16, 1, ZAYED I ST., 28, 31, TARIQ BIN ZAYED ST., AL NASR ST., 8, Airport, Dubai, Al Ain, 7, 6, 3, 5, 4, CORNICHE, Hilton Hotel

Legend:

1 British Embassy   Chancery
2 British Embassy   Commercial
3 Anglican Church
4 Catholic Church
5 Spinney's Supermarket
6 ADPC Offices
7 Albert Abela Supermarket
8 Finance
9 Post Office
10 Emir Palace
11 Taxis for Dubai, Al Ain
12 Barclay's Bank
13 BBME Chartered Grindlays
14 British Airways, Gulf Air
15 Municipality
16 Petroleum, Education
17 Zather Hotel
18 ADMA Offices
19 Al Ain Palace Hotel
20 Beach Hotel Maternity Hosp
21 Power Station
22 Omar Khayyam Hotel
23 Eldorado Cinema
24 ADDF Naval Force
25 Grand Mosque
26 Information Planning
27 Strand Hotel
28 Manhal Palace
29 ADDF GHQ
30 General Hospital
31 Public Works
32 Chamber of Commerce

Copyright Graham and Trotman Ltd.

Nomadic dancing, Abu Dhabi

jairah. However, on the eastward-facing Batinah coast, each state has little enclaves which are very difficult to distinguish from each other (see map). Visitors there may well be unsure in which Emirate they find themselves.

Abu Dhabi is flat and sandy, with huge buildings springing up rapidly as the oil wealth increases. Sheikh Zayed has a philosophic attitude to the riches he controls. He is reputed to have said in 1973 to a foreign diplomat 'King or beggar, everything is brief, and changing.' Today, Sheikh Zayed has a personal income of roughly a billion dollars a year. He travels the world—preferring Pakistan next to his own country as good hunting territory. Abu Dhabi gives about $50 million a year—which both the state and the Sheikh can afford—to the Arab Development Fund. The town itself has grown so fast that roads tend to peter out in the desert, and herds of goats act as scaven-

gers, although the Beduin owners no longer need to consider them as a source of income.

Abu Dhabi is the largest of the Emirates; within its boundaries is the desert town of Al Ain, formerly part of the Buraimi oasis, where there is underground water, date plantations and an experimental farm where vegetables and fruit, especially cucumbers, tomatoes, melons and beans are grown in artificially cooled greenhouses on a hydroponics system. Al Ain has a museum of ancient archaeological discoveries, in an old fort converted for the purpose. Other museums exist in Dubai and Fujeirah. Al Ain is 100 km. from Abu Dhabi Town, linked to it by a four lane highway, bordered with oleander bushes.

Dubai is first of all remarkable for its deep-water creek, 16 km. long, which causes it to be called the Venice of the Gulf. The creek now has a bridge, which is most elegant at sunset, and a tunnel to cope with the ever-increasing traffic. On either side are tall concrete buildings, just finished or just begun, and crowds of people who seem to be eternally crossing the creek in small flat-bottomed ferry boats, propelled by one oar. The liner *Bon Vivant* is moored in the creek to serve as a hotel.

It is no secret that the fortunes of Dubai were founded on the gold trade with India. Perfectly legal until the fast boats carrying bars of bullion came within Indian territorial waters. Nowadays Dubai bids fair to become the Hong Kong of the Gulf: it is rapidly constructing vast port installations, has industrial ambitions, and an international airport. Cargo ships queue to unload, and the Japanese are omnipresent.

Sharjah is the former headquarters of the Trucial Oman Scouts, who used before independence to impose British order in the region. Now there is a federal force, and the airport which before 1939 used to be a staging-post for Imperial Airways on the route to India, has been replaced by vast runways for jumbo jets. It now specialises in freight. Sheikh Sultan has begun vigorous development of his mini-state since 1974, when oil was produced from Abu Musa island, just off the coast. A huge deep-water port is being constructed at Khor Fakkan, which has the advantage of being on the Batinah coast, facing the Indian Ocean. Ships do not, therefore, have to pass through the already over-crowded and hazardous Straits of Hormuz into the Gulf.

Ras el Khaimah is the fourth Emirate, in size, population and prosperity. It is rapidly developing its hotels, commerce, and housing. Sheikh Saqr el Qasimi, is the youngest of the UAE rulers. The largest agricultural research station in the UAE is at Digdagga, where students come from all over the Gulf. Improve-

Ras-al-Khaimah

BENTE FASMER

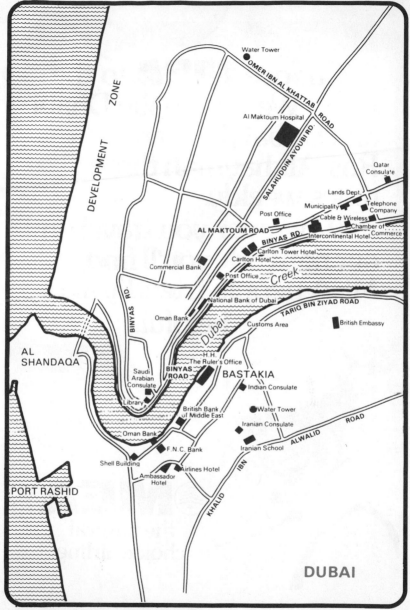

DUBAI

Copyright Graham and Trotman Ltd.

Choose **MEA** to the UAE. We serve Abu Dhabi and Dubai daily and Ras Alkhaymah three times weekly.

Wherever you travel on our network you'll find MEA people friendly and helpful.

MEA
the natural
choice airline

ment of crops and livestock, as well as their adaptation to the difficult climatic conditions, is carried out, and although the Emirates will never be totally green, they may well become self-sufficient in fruit and vegetables.

Fujairah, Ajman and **Umm el Quwain** are the smallest of the sheikhdoms comprising the UAE. Fujeirah is situated on the Batinah coast and has local tourist and agricultural potential. The old fort has become a museum of the local way of life; artifacts, rifles, jewellery, and coffee services are among the exhibits. The other two Emirates, next to each other to the north of Sharjah, were small fishing villages that are now beginning to be caught into the prosperity of the region.

Modern roads now link the Emirates, and one has just been built across the Hajar mountains to link Fujeirah and Khor Fakkan to the rest of the UAE. The 460 km. of road from Abu Dhabi which joins the Trans-Arabian Highway at al-Sila on the frontier with Qatar is nearing completion.

GENERAL INFORMATION

Area: 85,470 sq km. divided into seven Emirates.

Population:

Abu Dhabi	235,662
Dubai	206,861
Sharjah	88,188
Ras el Khaimah	57,282
Ajman	21,566
Fujeirah	26,498
Umm el Quwain	16,879
Other	3,000
Total (1975 census)	655,937

Federation: President: Sheikh Zayed bin Sultan (Abu Dhabi). Vice-President: Sheikh Rashid bin Said Al-Maktum (Dubai).

A Federal Council administers Defence, the Foreign Service, and certain

other joint projects. The population figures are somewhat misleading, for although they are correct, at least 200,000 of those listed above are foreigners living in the Emirates, some of them illegal immigrants. Once they are established and employed they can only be expelled if they break the law. In any event they are much needed for their technical expertise or their labour. Most of the civil servants below the heads of departments are of Palestinian origin, in the UAE as well as in the other Gulf countries: Bahrain, Kuwait and Qatar. Their loyalties account for the firm financial and vocal support given from these countries to the Palestinian cause.

Because there are so few citizens, the per capita income of the UAE is one of the highest in the world.

Languages: Arabic is the language of the country. English is widely spoken and understood.

Religion: Islam is the State religion. Christian, Hindu, and Parsee minorities exist and have their own places of worship.

Currency: The Dirham (DH) is divided into 100 fils. £1=7.47 DH, $1=3.90 DH.

Time: GMT + 4.

HOW TO GET THERE

By air: To Abu Dhabi, Dubai, Sharjah or Ras el Khaimah airports, on Gulf Air, Middle East Airlines, Air India, Alia, British Airways, EgyptAir, Iran Air, Iraqi Airways, KLM, Kuwait Airways, Lufthansa, PIA, Sabena, Saudi Airlines, Singapore Airlines, Swissair and Syrian Arab Airlines.

By sea: A regular passenger ship service is operated from Dubai to Bombay and Basra, and there are passenger-cargo sailings to the US, Far East, Australia and Europe. Dubai's Port Rashid and Abu Dhabi's Port Zayed are new and have deep water berths, warehouses, and cold storage facilities. Ras al Khaimah has also an artificial harbour, rapidly being extended. See also the chapter on Bahrain for land travel.

Visas and health regulations
Citizens of Bahrain, Kuwait, Oman, Qatar, and Saudi Arabia require only valid passports, not visas. Citizens of all other countries require visas, to be obtained from the nearest UAE embassy. Sponsors within the country are required. Business visitors without visas may be admitted for up to a week if they are met at the airport by a sponsor bearing proof of identity which should be a passport if the sponsor is not a UAE citizen. The visitor must then surrender his own passport, and leave from the place of entry. Flights beween the different UAE airports are regared as international and therefore travellers must possess multientry visas. Regulations are liable to change at short notice, and intending travellers should therefore keep up to date with them.

Vaccination against smallpox is required, as well as cholera inoculation for travellers coming from Bangladesh, India, Oman or the Yemen Arab Republic. Those from countries in which yellow fever is endemic require inoculation. TAB is recommended but not required.

Currency and customs regulations
There are no restrictions on the import or export of currency. Visitors personal effects are allowed in duty free.

CLIMATE

Hot and humid in the summer and mild in the winter. From December to the end of March the climate is pleasant while from May to October it is very hot and damp. The annual average rainfall is negligible.

What to wear
For most of the year lightweight or light clothing is adequate. From the end of November to the end of March medium weight clothing is suitable.

ACCOMMODATION AND FOOD

The hotel situation changes from month to month, as new hotels open, and construction begins on others. Visitors who are not staying with friends should be certain to reserve well in advance, and reconfirm their reservations shortly before arrival. Hotel charges are amongst the highest in the world, though the scarcity which prompted these is beginning to ease off.

Local fruit and vegetables are beginning to be available; there is excellent local fish at an ever-increasing price, and dates are a staple of the diet. The hotels serve both Arabic and European food, and there are Chinese and Indian restaurants. The various supermarkets supply frozen fare from all over the world.

TRANSPORT

Regular Gulf Air services link Abu Dhabi, Dubai, Sharjah, and Ras el Khaimah. Small aircraft and helicopters may be chartered.

The roads are good; taxis or private and rented cars may be used. Taxis are available throughout the U.A.E.; they may be hailed in the street or obtained from ranks at the major hotels. A fare within Abu Dhabi, Dubai, Sharjah, Ras al-Khaimah or Ajman should cost DH2; for longer rides and waiting, extra charges are applicable and should be settled beforehand with the driver. From Abu Dhabi to Al Ain the fare should be about DH60, return DH100; from Abu Dhabi to Dubai Dh130, return DH200; from Dubai to Sharjah DH5; from Ras al-Khaimah to Abu Dhabi Dh200. The fare from the airport to Abu Dhabi or vice versa is DH15-20; from the airport to

Dubai or vice versa DH10-15. Alternatively taxis may be hired for about DH20 per hour; *it is advisable to agree upon the fare in advance.* Airconditioned taxis cost considerably more. Long distance trips may be arranged through the leading hotels.

Car hire: Modern air conditioned cars can be hired for use in the Emirates from the following firms: UAE Rent-a-Car (Avis), Abu Dhabi, tel: 23760/1/2. Abu Dhabi Car Sales & Rental Company, Abu Dhabi, tel: 44351, 41185. Al Nabeel Quick Service, Abu Dhabi, tel: 43370. Mahommed Abdulla Al Sheibani & Sons National Company, Abu Dhabi, tel: 41610. National Rent-a-Car, Dubai, tel: 24647. Gulf Rent-a-Car, Dubai, tel: 25545. Dubai Rent-a-Car, Dubai, tel: 28886. Worldwide Rent-a-Car, Sharjah, tel: 075-25547. Business men wishing to drive hired cars must obtain a temporary driving licence from the Traffic Police. Passport (or passport receipt if on 96-hour visit), two passport photographs and UK licence must be produced.

HEALTH

There is a modern, British-administered hospital in Dubai (Al-Maktoum) and Government hospitals in Abu Dhabi, Al Ain, Sharjah, Ajman, Umm al Quwain Ras-al-Khaimah, and Fujairah. All offer a high standard of medical care for common diseases or accidents. European doctors practise in the Emirates, as well as Palestinians and Lebanese who have qualified in Europe or the USA. The water for Dubai and Sharjah is sweet well water piped from inland; it is perfectly drinkable. The Abu Dhabi town supply is provided by distillation plants.

BANKS

Abu Dhabi
United Arab Emirates Currency Board,
P.O. Box 854, Abu Dhabi, tel: 43728.
National Bank of Abu Dhabi, P.O. Box 4, Shaikh Khalifa Street, Abu Dhabi, tel: 43262.
U.A.E. Development Bank, P.O. Box 2449, Abu Dhabi, tel: 44982.
Barclays Bank International Limited, Shaikh Saif Bin Mohamed Building, P.O. Box 2734, Abu Dhabi, tel: 45313.
British Bank of the Middle East, P.O. Box 242, Abu Dhabi, tel: 43080.
The Chartered Bank, P.O. Box 240, Abu Dhabi, tel: 43077.
First National Bank of Chicago, P.O. Box 2747, Abu Dhabi.
First National City Bank, P.O. Box 999, Abdul Jalil Building, Shaikh Hamdan Street, Abu Dhabi, tel: 41410.

Dubai
Commercial Bank of Dubai Ltd., P.O. Box 1709, Abdul Nasser Square, Dubai, tel: 22101-9.
Dubai Bank Ltd., P.O. Box 2545, Deira, Dubai, tel: 21201.
National Bank of Dubai Ltd., P.O. Box 777, Dubai, tel: 22241/45.
Barclays Bank International Ltd., P.O. Box 1891, Riga, Dubai, tel: 26158.
The British Bank of the Middle East, P.O. Box 66, Dubai, tel: 32000.
Chartered Bank, P.O. Box 999, Deira, Dubai, tel: 31515.
First National Bank of Chicago, P.O. Box 1655, Dubai, tel: 26161.
First National City Bank, P.O. Box 749, Dubai, tel: 32100.
Grindlays Bank Ltd., P.O. Box 4166, Gamal Abdul Nasser Sq., Deira, Dubai, tel: Deira 26292-3.

Fujeirah
The British Bank of the Middle East, tel: 221.
United Bank Limited, tel: 231.
National Bank of Abu Dhabi, tel: 345.

Sharjah
Bank of Sharjah, P.O. Box 1394, tel: 23520.

Bank of Credit and Commerce International SA, P.O. Box 713, Al Arooba St., Sharjah, tel: 22983.
The British Bank of the Middle East, P.O. Box 25, Sharjah, tel: 22755.
The Chartered Bank, P.O. Box 5, Al-Khalij St., Sharjah, tel: 22247.
Commercial Bank of Dubai, P.O. Box 677, Sharjah, tel: 22520.
First National City Bank, P.O. Box 346, Abu Dhabi Bldg., Al Arooba St., Sharjah, tel: 22533.
Grindlays Bank Ltd., P.O. Box 357, Al Arooba Street, Sharjah, tel: 22472, 22371.

Ras al-Khaimah
British Bank of the Middle East, P.O. Box 9, Ras al-khaimah, tel: 8214.
Grindlays Bank Ltd., P.O. Box 225, Sabah St., Ras al-Khaimah, tel: 8452, 8453 (Man).

Business hours
Friday is the weekly holiday.
Government offices: Winter 0800-1400 Saturday to Wednesday and 0800-1200 Thursday; Summer 0700-1300 Saturday to Wednesday and 0700-1100 Thursday.
Oil Companies: *Abu Dhabi:* 0700 to 1400 Saturday to Wednesday and 0700 to 1300 Thursday; *Northern Emirates:* Summer: 0830 to 1300 Saturday to Thursday; Winter: 0830 to 1300 and 1600 to 1800 Saturday to Thursday.
Banks: *Abu Dhabi:* 0800 to 1200 Saturday to Wednesday and 0800 to 1100 Thursday; *Northern Emirates:* 0800 to 1200 Saturday to Thursday.
Private firms and shops: *Abu Dhabi:* Summer; 0800 to 1300 and 1600 to 1930 Saturday to Thursday; Winter: 0800 to 1300 and 1530 to 1900 Saturday to Thursday; *Northern Emirates:* Summer: 0900 to 1300 and 1630 to 2000 Saturday to Thursday; Winter: 0900 to 1300 and 1600 to 2000 Saturday to Thursday.

PUBLIC HOLIDAYS

New Years Day, 1 January.

The Prophet's Birthday, 20 February.
Ascension of the Prophet, 1 July.
Accession of the Ruler of Abu Dhabi, 6 August.
Eid al Fitr, 3-6 September.
Eid al Adha, 10-13 November.
National Day, 2 December.
Moslem New Year, 2 December.
Christmas Day 25 December.

EMBASSIES IN THE U.A.E.

Abu Dhabi:
Egypt, P.O. Box 4026, tel: 22950.
France, Commercial Section, P.O. Box 4036, tel: 44256.
Iraq, P.O. Box 4030, tel: 42326.
Jordan, P.O. Box 4024, tel: 42740.
Kuwait, P.O. Box 926, tel: 61340.
Lebanon, P.O. Box 4023, tel: 42792.
Libya, P.O. Box 2091, tel: 42750.
Morocco, tel: 45863.
Saudi Arabia, P.O. Box 45867.
Sudan, P.O. Box 2227, tel: 22750.
Syria, P.O. Box 4011, tel: 42786.
Tunisia, P.O. Box 2592, tel: 45260.
UK, P.O. Box 248, tel: 41305.
USA, P.O. Box 4009, tel: 61534.
Yemen Arab Republic, P.O. Box 2095, tel: 22800.

Dubai:
Iran, P.O. Box 2832, tel: 31157.
Kuwait, P.O. Box 806, tel: 21341.
Saudi Arabia, P.O. Box 806, tel: 22163.
UK, P.O. Box 65, tel: 31070.

TOURIST INFORMATION

Telephone numbers of Ministry of Information:
Abu Dhabi, tel: 41480.
Al Ain, tel: (03) 41595.
Dubai, tel: (178) 25433.
Sharjah, tel: (075) 22010.
Ras al Khaimah, tel: (077) 8138.
Fujairah, tel: 317.

WHAT TO SEE IN THE EMIRATES

The Emirates are a spectacular combination of sea, desert, and oases. This is not a tourist country, but one in which people live and do business. In summer the fierce heat prevents easy movement out-of-doors, at least during the day, but at other seasons the creek at Dubai, the sea corniches both in Dubai and Abu Dhabi, the beaches and fishing harbours along both coasts, and the Hajar mountains, are all worth exploring. Fishing boats are still built in the traditional fashion, the ancient forts survive as relics of a more turbulent past, and traditional sports have taken on a new lease of life. These include boat races for about thirty rowers in each craft, much resembling an elongated whaler, horse and camel racing and falconry. Traditional dances are performed on public holidays; in the last ten years football has become very popular, as has water skiing and speed boating.

There is an abundance of game fish in the Gulf, and people are beginning to show interest in fishing for sport rather than as a livelihood.

Inland, the Al Ain oasis is well worth visiting; the road there is a well engineered desert highway, and Sheikh Zayed has a fine stud of Arab horses, which are supervised by Sir Hugh Boustead, an Englishman with long service in the Gulf.

The new ports, at Khor Fakkan, Sharjah, and Dubai, are most impressive, and certainly worth visiting, whatever the traveller's business may be.

Falconry is the chief diversion of the Sheikhs, and of a good many other citizens. Indeed, hawks are everywhere, on gloved fists, perched on rails outside banks and offices, on the backs of car and aircraft seats, and being trained in open spaces to fly to lures. It is a spectacular sport, limited only by the paucity of prey. It is rumoured that pigeons may be imported for this purpose. There are cine-

World's first air-conditioning, wind towers in Dubai

CHRISTINE OSBORNE

Fisherman, Abu Dhabi

products if the customers demand them. Since customs duties are so low, 3% ad valorem, cars, record players, and all electrical goods are cheaper than in most countries, though transport costs make food and clothes more expensive. Housing is difficult to come by, but building continues apace, and the supply will begin to meet demand in a year or so.

Abu Dhabi hotels
Abu Dhabi Hilton, P.O. Box 877, tel: 61900, telex: AH 2122. 174 rooms, 16 suites, cabins, pearl restaurant, tariff coffee shop, pool snack bar, bars, falcon-entertainment and dancing nightly. *Facilities:* swimming pool, tennis, bowling alley, private beach. Five private dining rooms. Full conference facilities for 500.
Khalidia Palace, P.O. Box 4010, tel 62470, telex: AH 2506. Main restaurant and coffee shop, night club, dolphin bar. *Facilities:* swimming pool being built, private beach.
Al Ain Palace, P.O. Box 33, tel: 22377, telex: AH 227. 90 rooms, 14 suites, two restaurants, three bars. *Facilities:* swimming pool, tennis, croquet, two private

mas, discothèques in some of the hotels, but no casinos. Almost every kind of manufactured goods from all over the world can be bought in the shops and supermarkets of the UAE, and enterprising merchants will certainly seek out new

The Hilton, Abu Dhabi

dining rooms. Conference and party facilities.

Omar Khayam, P.O. Box 123, tel: 22101/22370, telex: 2520. 170 rooms, 15 suites. Restaurant and bar with group and dancing some nights. *Facilities:* two private dining rooms.

Beach Hotel, P.O. Box 244, tel: 22562, cable: Beachotel. 24 rooms and suites, 20 cabins. Restaurant and bar with orchestra nightly.

Zakher, P.O. Box 932, tel: 41940, telex: AH 2392. 70 rooms, six suites. Restaurant and bar. *Facilities:* two private dining rooms.

Strand, P.O. Box 821, tel: 41100, 42199. 68 rooms. Restaurant and bar.

Dubai hotels

Intercontinental, P.O. Box 476, tel: 27171, telex: DB 5779. 331 rooms. Rooftop restaurant, rooftop cocktail lounge, brasserie, snack bar. Mon's bar. *Facilities:* swimming pool, tennis. Eight private dining rooms, conference facilities for 550.

Carlton, P.O. Box 1955, tel: 22131, telex: DB 5447. 96 rooms 24 suites. Restaurant. Hotel and cocktail bars. *Facilities:* three private dining roms, conference facilities for 400.

Ambassador, P.O. Box 3226, tel: 31000, telex: DB 476. 74 rooms, seven suites. Venus restaurants, night club, four bars. *Facilities:* swimming pool, two private dining rooms. Conference facilities for 150.

Bustan, P.O. Box 1533, tel: 21261-3, telex: 5460 Bustan DB. 34 rooms. Two restaurants, two bars and night club. *Facilities:* swimming pool, tennis, cinema once weekly. One private dining room. Conference facilities for 300.

Oasis, P.O. Box 1556, tel: 25252-4, telex: 5494 Oasis DB. 34 rooms, three suites. Restaurant, bar, Mezzanine coffee lounge. *Facilities:* one private dining room. Conference facilities for 200.

Claridge, P.O. Box 1833, tel: 27141, telex: DB 5875.

Phoenicia, P.O. Box 4467, tel: 27191, telex: 5853.

Airlines, P.O. Box 736, tel: 31555, cable: Airhotel.

Bristol, P.O. Box 1471, tel: 24171, cable: Buraq Deira Dubai.

Hilton International Trade Centre, SS Bon Vivant, anchored in creek.

Sharjah hotels

Sharjah Carlton, P.O. Box 1198, tel: 23711/23811, telex: Carlton SH 5459. 170 air conditioned rooms, luxury suites, chalets. Restaurant with European and Lebanese food, dancing nightly. *Facilities:* Swimming pool, coffee shop, book shop and gift shop. Conference facilities.

Sheba Hotel, P.O. Box 486, tel: 22522/22554, telex: Sheba SH 80 53. 60 rooms. Restaurant, two bars, garden cafe, swimming pool.

Summerland Motel, P.O. Box 1081, tel: 23500, telex: Matta SH 8077.

Novotel.

Grand Hotel—Khalid Lagoon.

Royal Narnia.

Ras Al Khaimah hotels

Ras al-Khaimah Hotel, P.O. Box 56, tel: 8251, cable: Alabela. 39 air conditioned and centrally heated rooms. Restaurant, swimming pool, casino.

Fujairah hotels

Under construction: **Hilton Hotel**.

Resthouses

Ain Al Faidah, Al Ain.

Zoo Resthouse, Al Ain.

Hili Resthouse.

Sheikh Khalifa bin Zayed Resthouse, on the road between Abu Dhabi and Al Ain.

Resthouse, on the road between Abu Dhabi and Dubai.

Resthouse, on the road between Abu Dhabi and Qatar a Sila.

Sadiyat Resthouse.

Ajman Hotel

To be constructed—**Municipal Hotel**, 200 rooms.

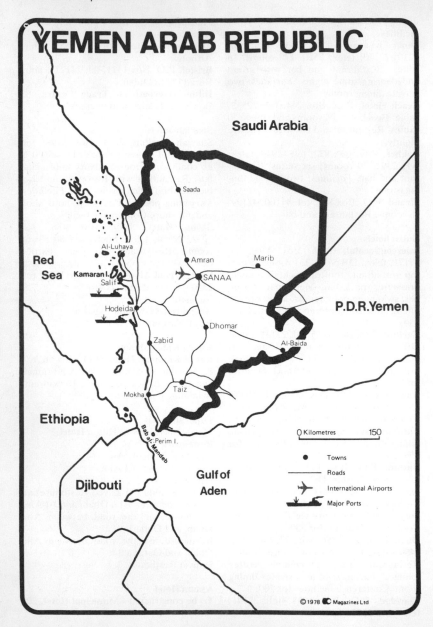

YEMEN ARAB REPUBLIC

Saudi Arabia

Red Sea

Saada

Al-Luhaya

Kamaran I.

Salif

Amran

Marib

SANAA

P.D.R.Yemen

Hodeida

Dhomar

Zabid

Al-Baida

Mokha

Taiz

Ethiopia

Bab al-Mandeb

Perim I.

Djibouti

Gulf of Aden

0 Kilometres 150

● Towns

—— Roads

✈ International Airports

⚓ Major Ports

©1978 Ⓒ Magazines Ltd

YEMEN ARAB REPUBLIC

Naomi Sakr

A traveller shown scenes from the Yemeni coutryside out of context would be hard put to guess that this is the Arabian peninsula. Shown scenes not too far inland from the Red Sea he or she might be more likely to opt for 'somewhere in East Africa'—'outside Nairobi' or 'northern Tanzania'. Indeed, Yemen—a country in which chilly mountain heights slope down to a hot and humid coast—forms the clearest living reminder of the fact that Arabia and Africa were once part of the same continent.

Helped by its rugged topography and peculiarly protective architecture to fend off outside influences until well into the present century, Yemen is also today the last refuge of those who would like to see the old Arabia before it is bulldozed into oblivion. Fortunately they still have time. For the risk that Yemen too will be razed to make way for the ubiquitous concrete and glass of modern building has been averted. The present authorities are well aware that the foreigner comes to Yemen in search not of beaches or night life but of beautiful scenery, extraordinary architecture and a strong sense of the past.

Anxious to promote tourism on this basis they are attempting to make the country more accessible and more comfortable (a Hilton features among the planned hotels) while retaining the characteristics that make a visit to the Yemen, or Arabia Felix as it was once known, so worthwhile.

THE LAND AND THE PEOPLE

The Arabia Felix of ancient times was probably more fertile than it is now, because of the presence of the great Maarib dam which, built in the seventh century BC, continued to function for well over a millennium until it was swept away, leaving irreparable damage, in the sixth century AD. The dam was considered one of the wonders of the world and is referred to in the Koran, together with the 'marvellous gardens' that grew 'to the right and to the left'. The luxuriant vegetation of the surrounding area was almost legendary—early travellers invariably remarking on the abundance and variety of fruit. This internally-generated prosperity combined with the quantity of spices and precious goods entering the country from across the Indian Ocean, help to explain how this part of Arabia earned the classical epithet 'felix'. Even now, however, the description is not entirely inappropriate. Admittedly the complete breakdown of the ancient irrigation system, the erosion of many mountainside farming areas and the departure of a large proportion of Yemen's farming population in search of more lucrative work in Saudi Arabia and elsewhere has meant an inevitable decline. Yemen, though potentially a source of food for the rest of the peninsula, now has to import cereals and other foodstuffs to feed itself. But the aerial view of the terraces, their contours rippling out across the basalt of the central plateau and their shades of green, brown and gold reflecting great fertility, comes as a tremendous relief after the interminable deserts of Saudi Arabia and pinpoints what is still Yemen's best but possibly most underrated asset—its good soil and farming skills.

Central Yemen, the home of this agricultural tradition and the site of most of the major towns, ranges in height from around 200m to the 4,000m peak of Jabal Nabi Shoueb, the highest mountain in the whole of the Middle East. This high part of the central plateau vies only with the coastal ranges of Lebanon as the wettest part of the whole Arabian massif. The diurnal temperature variations at these heights are extreme and in Sanaa, the capital, situated at over 2,000m above sea level, temperatures can fall below freezing at night.

To the west, in striking contrast, lies the Tihama, the flat coastal strip where rainfall is negligible and where the rain torrents and rivers flowing down from the moutains lose themselves in the sand. Some fertile patches are interspersed along the strip, flourishing in the alluvium left by the seasonal floods. In general, however, this narrow plain—which is

barely 80km across at its widest point—is intensely hot and humid and is sparsely populated, except for the ports of Mokha and Hodaida. The same is also true of the east, where the mountains suddenly drop away to the Rub al-Khali (Empty Quarter) and where, although the climate is more temperate, water is very scarce.

Perhaps because of its topography, the mountainous south-western corner of Arabia that today forms Yemen has generally been controlled as a unit in its own right, separate from the rest of the peninsula, throughout history. For the same reason, since the coming of Islam, the people of the region have represented an isolated outpost of Shi'a Islam on the edge of the Sunni stronghold of Saudi Arabia. Yet the Yemeni Shi'a, the Zaidis, are in many ways closer to their Sunni brethren than Shi'a in other parts of the Muslim world. They are not given to mysticism or saint worship or to the extravagant self-punishment with which other Shi'a sects usually mark the month of Muharram. Nor are they rigidly opposed to intermarriage with their compatriots, the Sunni Muslims, who themselves being of the Shafei school are not as strictly puritan as their Saudi neighbours farther north. Other than the small group of Ismailis far inland and the Yemeni Jews, almost all of whom have left for Israel, the Zaidis and Shafeis are the Yemen's only sects. And, in terms of numbers they are believed to be fairly evenly balanced, although, until the demise of the Imams, the Zaidis gained status from the fact that the secular ruler of the country was also their spiritual leader.

More important than any division of the population on sectarian lines, however, are the distinctions between the urban and rural ways of life and the highland and lowland peoples. The Shafei Muslims, who predominate along the coast, share that part of the country with small communities from the other side of the Red Sea—Somalis, Dankilis and Ethiopians—and their outlook might be said to reflect this more cosmopolitan experience. The Zaidi highlanders of the north are rather more inward-looking, operating a strongly tribal system with a measure of autonomy, led by the tribes of Hashid, Baqil and Zaraniq. As one moves north, into Saada for example, guns begin to become noticeable, slung over the shoulder and carried in addition to the traditional *jambia* or dagger, which every adult male throughout North Yemen wears in his belt. The daggers are essentially a sign of economic status and virility but the guns serve as a constant reminder of the unsettled history of the north—the power base of the deposed royal family during the civil war and republican Yemen's living political link with the conservative Arab regimes elsewhere in the Peninsula and the Gulf.

As for town and country differences, one clear example is the custom of veiling for women. Women in Sanaa, or even girls from the age of eight, either cover their faces completely with black or coloured cloth or swathe their heads tightly in black so that only their eyes are seen. In the villages, where women work in the fields, such customs are not observed.

CULTURE AND HISTORY

The two halves of Yemen—North and South—have been split since 1839 when the British occupied Aden (then Yemen's southern port) and set about concluding special pacts with each of the 30 or so Sultanates, Shaikhdoms and Emirates which then made up the southern hinterland. At about the same time the Ottoman authorities were once again attempting to tighten their grip on the northern part of the Yemen and reabsorb it into the Ottoman Empire having allowed it to drift into semi-autonomy after first defending it from rival international powers in the 16th and 17th centuries. Deserted Turkish forts dotted about the country are relics of this spasmodic Ottoman domination.

North Yemen has thus been a politically separate unit for nearly 140 years (even though its chief northern and southern boundaries remained vague until only some 30-40 years ago) but the Yemenis themselves have never grown wholly accustomed to this fact. Mobility between the North and South has remained a fact of life over the years. Refugees from the Imams' dictatorial rule and migrant labourers in search of work headed for Aden. And in more recent years, critics of the radical government in Aden attempted to bring about its downfall from the North. Since 1972 both halves of the country have begun officially to work towards reunification—a process that both sides seem to think completely logical no matter how tricky or long-term. It is within this context that Yemen's 3,000-year history should be surveyed.

Beyond its recent turbulent past, the most widely-known feature of Yemen's history dates back to the period from the tenth to second centuries BC, the time-span of the Kingdom of Sheba (or Saba). Balkis, the renowned Queen of Sheba, who was said to have visited King Solomon, is believed to have come to power around 997BC. The remains of her temple and the great dam at Maarib (the capital of Sheba, sited east of Sanaa) are still extant—a testimony to the genius of the Sabaean people and a promising archaeological site still in need of exploration. The dam, a colossal 650 metres long and 60 metres wide at the base, was still being relied on and renovated until 542AD and the markings on its stonework recount the details of the repair operations.

The theocrats of Sheba were replaced in 115BC by the Himyarite dynasty, from whom the modern Imams claimed descent. With the rise of the Himyarites, the capital of the country moved to the central city now known as Dhamar and it was in the fourth century, towards the end of their reign, that both Judaism and Christianity came to Yemen. An outburst of friction between the two religions provoked an invasion from Christian Ethiopia in 525, but Ethiopian domination lasted only 50 years, giving way to forces from Persia who absorbed Yemen into their Sassanid kingdom. This again only lasted until 628 when the governor of the 'province' was converted to Islam and the two main branches, Shafei and Zaidi, began to evolve and establish themselves side by side. The next major incursion was not until the arrival of the Turks in 1517, but by then the inhabitants of Yemen were sufficiently tightly-knit and independent-minded to prevent the invaders from having any more than nominal authority. When a second attempt was made to subjugate the centres of power in the mid-1800s, opposition was as fierce as ever and when the Zaidi leader, Imam Yahya, succeeded in driving the Turkish troops out of the country once and for all in the early 1900s he was able to capitalise on this achievement to assume the secular title of king and consolidate his position as ruler of the whole of north Yemen. Thus began half a century of tyranny with no obvious contemporary parallel in the Middle East. Maintaining themselves in power by purchasing tribal loyalties, holding hostages, murdering their relatives, barricading themselves in impregnable castles and subjecting the country to a policy of total isolation, Yahya and his son and successor Ahmad managed to keep Yemen in the Middle Ages until it was finally dragged away from them by the rising tide of local discontent. Yahya was assassinated in 1948 but his assassins, divided on the issue of a constitution, were unable to hold out against tribal forces who saw to it that Imam Ahmad was installed in his place. Ahmad in his turn miraculously survived numerous assassination attempts and finally died in 1962 from a combination of natural causes. But his departure marked the beginning of the

end for the monarchy. Ahmad's son Badr, a would-be reformer, floundered amid conflicting pressures from all sides and only eight days after his accession his Commander-in-Chief, Abdullah al-Sallal, shelled the palace and proclaimed the Yemen Arab Republic, with himself as President. As was the case in 1948, however, tribal forces rallied round the royal family and within a week a royalist government-in-exile was functioning from across the border with Saudi Arabia.

The country then sank deep into a state of civil war which can only be said to have come to a decisive end in 1970, when King Faisal of Saudi Arabia finally recognised the republican regime in Sanaa and that regime reciprocated by co-opting a former royalist to their number. In the years since then Yemen has leaned gradually further and further back towards its powerful northern neighbour and, consequently, towards the west. Major steps in this direction were taken by Colonel Ibrahim al-Hamdi who was president from the time of his bloodless coup d'etat in 1974 to his own assassination in October 1977 and his successor, Ahmad al-Ghashmi, promised to continue along the same lines.

The fact that Yemen was brought out of a state of the severest economic and political under-development only to be plunged back into the economic chaos wrought by war has left deep scars. In many ways, however, there are features of the Yemen's daily life that would be unlikely to change, whatever the prevailing economic or political climate. One such feature is the habit of chewing *gat*—a locally-grown shrub bearing shoots that have a narcotic effect. Every afternoon virtually every adult in the country indulges in this habit and all activity comes to a halt as cheeks stuffed with wads of masticated gat leaf begin to bulge and eyes glaze over in a gat-induced trance. The signs of gat are visible everywhere, in market places and cafes, but the place to chew in style is the guest room or *mafraj*

TREVOR MOSTYN

Sanaa, Yemen

which is found at the top of every typical multi-storeyed Yemeni house. There, sitting on brightly-coloured cushions arranged around the walls, and shielded from the sun by the stained glass of their arched and ornate alabaster-framed windows, the men of the household while away their time and their income with freshly-picked gat and the hookah. The general slowing-down effected by the drug is reflected in some of the traditional Yemeni dances, in which the performers link arms and sway slowly and rhythmically. When women dance among themselves they wear vivid colours, scarves woven with gold thread and valuable jewellery in which gold, silver coins and amber beads predominate. For the men too, the *jambia* and its sheath, sometimes made in intricately-worked silver, are a form of ornament, although nowadays modern gold watches are becoming

equally apparent as money floods into the country from Yemeni workers abroad and is spent by those at home on consumer goods. Although it is rarely used in anger, the dagger is occasionally drawn in dancing and either brandished or, in a show of virtuosity, made to slice the air within a hair's-width of the dancer's exposed forearm or thigh.

ECONOMY

The remittances sent back home every month by more than a million Yemeni workers abroad, particularly in Saudi Arabia, have become, since the oil boom, the country's primary source of revenue. The figures in this respect are staggering. For, while Yemen's annual exports of goods amount to around $18 million a year and income from foreign grants and loans accounts for about another $112 million a year, workers' remittances represent a flow of at least $50 million every month and possibly more. But there is a high price to be paid for this source of cash. While Yemenis abroad ease Saudi staffing problems they are creating massive labour shortage problems at home and this in turn exacerbates local inflation—making Yemen a very expensive place.

Inflation is further fuelled by the flood of cash, which, instead of being channelled into productive investment is spent (understandably for a population of seven million which found itself in 1962 with no more than three hospitals and a serious lack of schools) on washing machines, refrigerators, cassette recorders and Japanese-made motor bikes. Added to this is the fact that the neglect of the country's agricultural potential and the turning over of more and more land to gat (now that more people have the money to consume it in greater quantities) means that the bulk of Yemen's food needs have to be imported from abroad through a severely congested infrastructural network.

The possibilities for export crops, such as cotton and Yemen's famous Mokha coffee, are considerable, but both items have yet to show a steady increase on the levels attained in, for example, 1973/74. Salt is another area in which the Yemen has been singularly unlucky, having obtained Kuwaiti finance to expand its salt-mining operations only to find that its principal customer, Japan, had put a stop to purchases on grounds that there were impurities in the salt. Nevertheless, the country has embarked on an ambitious five-year Development Programme for the period from 1976/77 to 1980/81, in which it plans to spend four times as much again every year as it spent during the last year of the previous three-year plan. The transport sector forms the focus of the plan, which has been promised financial support from countries across a wide spectrum of political persuasions. Given Yemen's present prominence as a state bordering on the super-sensitive area of the Red Sea, these aid pledges, in particular those of the US and the Arab oil exporters, may be expected to be fulfilled.

GENERAL INFORMATION

Area: 195,000 sq. m.
Population: 6,741,893 (of these over one million live and work abroad).
Capital: Sanaa.
Head of State: Colonel Ahmad al-Ghashmi.
Government: Republic. Power is in the hands of the Military Command Council.
Language: Arabic.
Religion: The majority are Muslims of the Sha'i sect.
Currency: The Yemeni Riyal (YR) is divided into 100 Fiis. £1 = YR8.55. $1 = YR4.547.
Time: GMT + 3.

HOW TO GET THERE

By air: Direct flights from Sanaa to London are available twice a week, one by Syrian Arab Airlines and one by Ethiopian Airlines. Most direct flights to the Yemen are from neighbouring countries; from Jedda four times a week, Saudi Airlines; from Addis Ababa twice a week, Ethiopian Airlines; from Kuwait once a week, Kuwait Airways; from Djibouti once a week, Air Djibouti. An airport tax of YR6 is payable by all visitors leaving Yemeni airports.

There are no railways in the Yemen. Road access from Saudi Arabia or South Yemen could be dangerous and is not recommended. Cargo vessels call at Hodeida, the country's main port.

Visas and health regulations
It is necessary for all foreigners to obtain visas to enter the country. These can be

ASSOCIATED PRESS

The Palace of the Rock, Wadi Dahr, N. Yemen

obtained from Yemeni missions abroad. Two passport photos are required. Exit visas are also necessary.

Smallpox vaccination is compulsory, and all visitors should be inoculated against cholera. Travellers from Africa are required to have an international yellow fever vaccination certificate. Visitors are also advised to obtain TAB injections.

Currency and customs regulations
There is no limit on the amount of foreign or local currency imported or exported. Personal effects are admitted free of duty (but not alcohol).

CLIMATE

Climate varies with altitude. The coastal plain is hot, humid and dusty for most of the year. The highlands are more agreeable in summer and very cold in winter.

Most of the rain falls between July and September.

What to wear
Lightweight clothing is advisable in the coastal plain all the year round. Winter clothing is necessary November to April in the highlands.

ACCOMMODATION AND FOOD

There are a number of expensive hotels catering for visiting businessmen, and many other less expensive establishments. A single room with bath costs approximately YR100.

TRANSPORT

By air: There are occasional flights linking Sanaa, Taiz and Hodeida airports.

By road: Travel between three main cities is by taxi or shared taxi. There is also a regular inter-city bus service between the three main cities. It is advisable to fix the fare before the commencement of the journey. Self-drive hire facilities are available

BANKS

Central Bank, Liberation Square, Sanaa. Tel: 5216.
United Bank of Pakistan, Ali Abdul Mugni Street, Sanaa. Tel: 5012.
Arab Bank, Liberation Square, Sanaa. Tel: 5558.
First National City Bank, P.O. Box 2133, Sanaa. Tel:5796.
Bank of Credit and Commerce International SA, P.O. Box 160, Sanaa. Tel: 2168.
British Bank of the Middle East, 26 September Street, Hodeida. Tel: 2728.
British Bank of the Middle East, Gamal

Abdul Nasser Street, Taiz. Tel: 2671, 1937.

Business hours
Government offices: 0900-1330.
Business firms: 0800-1230, 1600-1900.
Shops: 0800-1300, 1600-2100.
Banks 0800-1200.

PUBLIC HOLIDAYS

Prophet's Birthday 20 February.
Corrective Movement 13 June.
Eid al Fitr 3-6 September.
Revolution Day 26 September.
Eid al Adha 10-13 November.
Moslem New Year 1 December.

EMBASSIES IN THE CAPITAL

Algeria: Ali Abdul Moghni Street.
Egypt: Gamal Abdul Nasser Street.
France: Gamal Abdul Nasser Street.
German Dem Republic: 26 September Street.
Germany, Federal Republic: Republican Palace Street.
India: Al-Amir Building, Gamal Abdul Nasser Street.
Iraq: Building Mohamed Zehrah, Zubairy Street.
Italy: Gamal Abdul Nasser Street.
Kuwait: 26 September Street.
Lebanon: Airport Road.
Libya: Airport Road.
Saudi Arabia: Arman Building.
UK: 11/13 Republican Palace Street.
USA: Beit Al-Halali.
USSR: 26 September Street.

SANAA

One of the most impressive things about Sanaa, the present capital of Yemen, is that virtually all its buildings—old and new—conform to the typical style of architecture. It is not just a few special houses which have white decorations on their exterior walls and decorative arched windows. It is the majority of houses and government office blocks. Each house, designed to be inhabited by one extended family, is usually seven to eight storeys high with its own central stairway and special plumbing system. The lower storeys are generally built in stone and those above in brick and the whole structure, with its solid door at ground level, is designed to keep intruders out. As for interior decor, one of the most accessible examples is the Dar al-Hamd—a former palace of a relative of the Imam which has been turned into a hotel without loss of low doorways, stone staircases, multiple windows or sculpted white walls. A similar building is the Rawdah Palace outside the city which is also an hotel but which is generally used for the benefit of Yemen Airline crews.

On a less secular note, Sanaa itself also boasts 45 mosques, some of them among the oldest in the Muslim world, the great mosque of Aroua dating back to the seventh century. These are not always freely accessible to non-Muslim visitors, however, and the same applies for all visitors to the Sanaa museum, which tends to be closed on Fridays. At such times, however, there is always the main *souk* of Sanaa, the Bab al-Yaman, situated around a gate in the ancient city walls. Here the shops are no more than tiny kiosks—wide enough to accommodate one salesman and barely more than one customer at a time. Daggers, jewellery and candlesticks are among the goods on display—occasionally piled in a dusty heap and sometimes coming not from Yemen but from Syria or India or other foreign parts. The best time to visit Bab al-Yaman on a weekday is the late afternoon. And this is also perhaps the ideal moment to leave Sanaa and drive 10 km. to the Wadi Dhahr so as to see it while the afternoon sun is casting dappled light and shade over the idyllic valley scenery. A favourite picnic spot is on the edge of the rocky precipice that overhangs the spread of cultivated greenery below, but the Dar al-Hajjar (the palace on the rock) in the valley itself should also be visited, even though a long climb is involved. Rather nearer Sanaa, at only 5 km. distance, are the gardens and orchards of Hadda, where special facilities for tourists have been built. Again near the capital stands the ghost town of Kawkaban with its white stone palace standing at nearly 3,000 m. above sea level.

Hotels
Hamd Palace, P.O. Box 2187 tel 5365.
Rawdah Palace (five miles out of town) tel: 9201.
Moha (very central), P.O. Box 533 tel: 2402.

TAIZ

The fact that Yemen's various rulers have opted for a series of different capitals at different times means that there are many different places of interest dotted around the country—Maarib, the small but picturesque town of Jibla, Dhamar, Zabid and so on. But the second capital of Yemen today has come to be Taiz, situated at four hours' drive south of Sanaa at a height of nearly 2,000 m., which makes for generally warmer weather than Sanaa. Taiz was a centre of commerce and scholarship in the period from the 13th to 15th centuries. Overlooked by Mount Sabr and the citadel of Al-Kahira, Taiz is encircled by a city wall and houses two important palaces (one now a museum) and the beautiful Sharafiya mosque.

Hotels
Plaza (central position), tel: 2687.
Ikhwa, P.O. Box 4413, tel: 2225.

Restaurants
Muntazah Restaurant.
Fiesta Restaurant (Lebanese food).

Taiz, North Yemen

ASSOCIATED PRESS

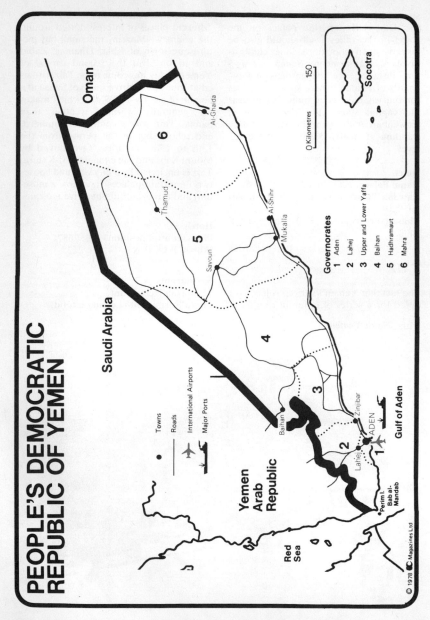

PEOPLE'S DEMOCRATIC REPUBLIC OF YEMEN

Oman

Saudi Arabia

Yemen Arab Republic

Red Sea

Gulf of Aden

Al-Ghaida

Thamud

Al-Shihr

Mukalla

Savoun

Baihan

Zinjibar

ADEN

Lahej

Perim I.
Bab al-Mandab

6

5

4

3

2

1

Governorates

1 Aden
2 Lahej
3 Upper and Lower Yaffa
4 Baihan
5 Hadhramaut
6 Mahra

Towns
Roads
International Airports
Major Ports

Socotra

0 Kilometres 150

© 1978 [C] Magazines Ltd

PEOPLE'S DEMOCRATIC REPUBLIC OF YEMEN

The People's Democratic Republic of Yemen, also known as South Yemen, and formerly as Aden or South Arabia, has an area of about 320,000 sq. km. and a population of around 1.6 million, with a further 300,000 believed to be working abroad.

It combines a wide variety of tourist attractions: unspoilt sandy beaches, spectacular mountain villages and scenery, and the historic architecture of the Wadi Hadramaut. Among Yemeni handicrafts are silver and gold jewellery, basket weaving, Yemeni textiles, and the fruits of the Indian Ocean—corals, sharks' teeth, turtle shells. Yemeni coffee, *mazqul*, made from the husks of coffee beans and spices, and the mincemeat and pepper dish known as *haradha*, are among local culinary specialities.

THE LAND AND THE PEOPLE

The mountains of Yemen have been the site of a settled agricultural population for over two and half millenia. The pre-Islamic settled civilisations Minaean, Sabaean and Himyarite have left behind a rich archaeological legacy, and today over 60% of the population of Democratic Yemen still work in agriculture. There are several thousand fishermen and women. Most of the rest work in towns; only a small percentage, along the edges of the northern desert, are nomads. The rural population rely on the infrequent rains for the water needed to produce their wheat and sorghum, and to feed the camels, goats and cows.

The area known as Democratic Yemen is that over which Britain extended control between 1839, when the port of Aden became part of the British Empire, and 1967, when the country gained independence. It is today divided into six Governorates, or provinces. The First Governorate consists of Aden the capital, plus the republic's islands. Much of the population of Aden has come in the past decades from the Yemeni hinterland and from the countryside of North Yemen. There are also substantial immigrant communities from Somalia and from India. The Second, Third and Fourth Governorates cover the southern part of the historic Yemeni heartlands, the rest of which is now included in the Yemeni Arab Republic to the north. Here the peasants live in compact villages and still wear the traditional clothes of the area, the Yemeni kilt or *futa* for men, and the coloured dresses for women. Whereas women in the towns often wear the black drape or *sheidor* this is much less common in the countryside.

The Fifth Governorate covers the area formerly known as the Hadramaut, a region which has relied for centuries on money sent by families who migrated abroad to East Africa, Singapore and Indonesia. The beautiful curved port of Mukalla, and the three architecturally rich towns of the Wadi Hadramaut in the interior (Tarim, Shibam, Seiyyun) are the products of this long relation to the outside world. Finally, in the sparsely populated Sixth Governorate, one can find many native speakers of the pre-Arabic language Mahri. This is a language with no accepted written form, and is closely related to Socotri (spoken in the island of Socotra) and to the languages in the neighbouring Dhofar province of the Sultanate of Oman.

CULTURE AND HISTORY

The religion of all Yemenis is Islam and small mosques and graves of holy men and women can be found in many parts of the country. At the same time there is a powerful literary tradition, which has taken the forms especially of short stories and of oral poetry. There is also a lively theatrical activity in the towns, and a revival of Yemeni literature, music and dancing has been part of the nationalist revival of the past few decades.

An important part of traditional Yemeni society has been the chewing of the narcotic green leaf *gat*, an activity normally carried out by men for several hours in the afternoon. Since 1976 chewing of gat has been limited to Thursday and Friday, but it is legal on those days. A bunch of gat leaves costs eight to ten shillings, and an afternoon's chewing is estimated to require four such bunches.

Prior to independence on 30 November 1967, Democratic Yemen was ruled by Britain. In the years just prior to independence, the country was the site of a bitter three-sided conflict between the colonial power, and the two nationalist groups, FLOSY and the NLF. In the end the NLF (National Liberation Front) was

victorious, and since 22 June 1969, when the radical wing of this organisation came to power, the country has been undergoing a process of radical change. Most land, property and businesses have been nationalised, and the NLF, with its associated mass organisations, has developed a single-party system, inspired by theories of 'scientific socialism'. Health and education in the towns and even more so in the rural areas have been improved drastically. A mass literacy campaign was launched in 1973, and the law relating to the family reformed to remove practices inimical to women. In 1971 a legislature, the Supreme People's Council, was created; it nominated the President, Salem Robea Ali (born 1934) and the Prime Minister, Ali Nasser Mohammad (born 1941). In 1976 and 1977 elections were held for Popular Councils, ie executive assemblies in each of the six Governorates.

Since independence Democratic Yemen has received economic aid from a variety of sources: from the Soviet Union, China, Cuba, the German Democratic Republic and other communist states, from the UN agencies and the World Bank, and from Kuwait, Qatar, Abu Dhabi and Saudi Arabia.

WILDLIFE

The sparse vegetation of the Republic supports a limited wildlife. In the shallow waters around Aden itself there are flocks of flamingoes, and in the interior there are hyenas, wild goats, and the *wabar* or coney, a rodent eaten by Beduin. By contrast, the coastal waters support a rich marine life and there is ample scope for diving and underwater observation.

ECONOMY

Prior to 1967 the economic life of the country was concentrated in Aden; but the closure of both the British base, and the Suez Canal in that year, plunged the country into a prolonged economic crisis. Only in 1971 did the economy begin to pick up again with the launching of a Three-Year Plan, totalling 40 million Dinars. This was followed by a Five-Year Plan in 1974-1978, the initial capital of which was 80 million Dinars, a sum that was increased later in the plan period. After 1971, GNP rose at about 5% per year, and a comprehensive expansion of industry, agriculture, communications and fishing took place. In 1977 Democratic Yemen had over 30 industrial plants, employing over 16,000 people, the largest being the refinery at Bureika (or 'Little Aden'), employing 1,600 people and opened in 1954, and the textile factory at Sheikh Othman, employing 1,400 people and opened in 1975. Agriculture was concentrated in under 90,000 hectares and was organised on the basis of produce co-operatives and state farms. The greatest hope for the South Yemeni economy is fishing, which has overtaken cotton as the main cash export, and where it is believed that output can be increased by 250%. Already prawns and lobsters are exported to the USA and Europe, and cuttle-fish to Japan. Despite comprehensive exploration efforts no oil has been found in Democratic Yemen by the end of 1977, but offshore drilling was continuing around Socotra Island, and land drilling in the Fifth Governorate. Some commercial quantities of metals have been found, and it is expected that in the Second Five-Year Plan (1979-1983) mineral production will, along with fishing, occupy a priority position.

GENERAL INFORMATION

Area: 320,000 sq. km.
Population: 1,600,000 (1976).
Capital: Aden.
Head of State: Salem Robea Ali.
Government: Republic, Single-party state. Main decision-making bodies: Presidential Council, Council of Ministers, Political Bureau and Central Committee of the National Liberation Front.
Language: Arabic is the main native language, with traces of pre-Arabic Mahri and Socotri in remote areas. Some Hindi and Somali spoken in Aden. Widespread and continuing use of English in state, business and education. Also some Russian and German.
Religion: Islam.
Currency: One Yemeni Dinar, is divided into 20 Dirhams or Shillings, and 1,000 Fils (ie one Shilling = 50 Fils). £1 = YD 0.654, $1 = YD 0.341.
Time: GMT + 3 hours.

HOW TO GET THERE

By air: Aden International Airport is served internationally by: Aeroflot, Middle East Airlines, Egyptair, Kuwait Airways, Air India, Pakistan International Airlines, East African Airways, Somali Airlines, Air Djibouti, Ethiopian Airlines, Yemen Airlines Corporation. Alyemda, the national airline, operates to Taiz, Jedda, Kuwait, Baghdad, Cairo, Beirut, Addis Abbaba, Djibouti, Mogadishu.

The airport, at Khormaksar, is about a 20 minute drive from the main tourist hotels in Tawahi.

By sea: Passenger ships on tourist cruises occasionally stop at Aden Port.

By road: The only land link used by visitors is the road between Aden and Taiz, in the Yemeni Arab Republic. Driving time is three to five hours, exclusive of customs stops.

Visas and health regulations
Citizens of Arab countries are exempted from visas provided reciprocal measures are in force.

Tourist visas, price YD 2.300, valid for

one month and can be renewed for a period not exceeding six months. These are available from PDRY embassies abroad. Transit visas, price YD 0.800, valid for 96 hours, are available on arrival in the PDRY. These are renewable, except for citizens of countries in which there is a PDRY Diplomatic Representative.

All visitors to the PDRY are requested to register with the Central Registration Office of the Ministry of the Interior within 48 hours of arrival. They must be in possession of return or onward tickets.

Photography of topics other than government buildings, the port, and military areas is officially permitted, but visitors are advised to use their cameras only after consultation with an official guide.

All movement by foreigners between Governorates is restricted. Prior permission must be obtained from the relevant authorities. Tourism outside the First Governorate is confined to groups.

A certificate of smallpox vaccination is necessary. Yellow fever and cholera certificates are required for those coming from infected areas. Precaution against malaria and polio is advisable.

Currency and customs regulations

Any amount of foreign currency may be brought into the Republic. It must be declared on a customs form when entering, and all exchanges should be registered with a relevant form. These are checked on departure against the original declaration.

Normal tourist baggage is exempt from tax. Visitors may bring in 200 cigarettes or 50 cigar units, or 250 grams of tobacco, two litres of alcoholic drinks, one litre of perfume and presents to a value of YD 20.

CLIMATE

Rainfall varies from 30 mm. on the coast to 350 mm. in the mountains. Temperatures in the summer rise to well over 35°C, and from October to March vary from 20° to 32°. The best time of the year to visit is between mid-October and mid-April. In the winter the nights can be cold in the mountains.

What to wear

Lightweight clothes are preferable at all times; dress is nearly always informal.

ACCOMMODATION

In Aden there are three hotels for foreign visitors: the **Crescent, Rock** and **Ambassador** Hotels. All are in Tawahi. In the Fifth Governorate there are hotels at Mukalla (al-Shaab), Seiyyun (al-Salaam), and Shihr (al-Sharq). There are two small hotels in the Third Governorate at Mukheiras, and Jaar. Two new international hotels in the First Governorate, each with 200 bedrooms, the Aden Hotel and the Goldmohur Hotel, are scheduled for opening in 1981. Hotels normally serve international cuisine.

Tipping is not conventional in Democratic Yemen.

TRANSPORT

Alyemda operates flights to all Governorates. The main internal airfields are in the Fifth Governorate, at Riyan near Mukalla, and at Ghuraf, near Seiyyun. There is a surfaced road from Aden to Mukalla (500 km.) and other roads are under improvement construction. There is no regular sea transport inside the Republic, and no rail transport at all.

There are taxis in Aden. Fares are fixed but should be confirmed in advance. Collective taxis and buses also link the different sectors of the city.

BANKS

The National Bank of Yemen is the sole bank operating. There is a branch in

Tawahi, near the three tourist hotels, and other branches throughout the Republic.

Business hours
Most government offices and businesses are open 0800-1300, 1400-1600, with half day on Thursday, and closure on Friday. It is advisable to concentrate visits in the period before 1300, and to arrange all visits in advance.

PUBLIC HOLIDAYS

Muslim New Year, 1 December.
Workers' Day, 1 May.
Prophet's Birthday, 20 February.
National Day, 14 October.
Independence Day, 30 November.
Eid al Fitr, 3-6 September.
Eid al Adha, 10-13 November.
Corrective Move Anniversary, 22 June.
Revolution Day, 26 September.
New Year, 1 January.

EMBASSIES IN ADEN

China: Khormaksar, tel: 23468.
Egypt: tel: 22652.
France: Khormaksar, tel: 22477.
German Dem. Rep.: Khormaksar, tel: 23411.
German Federal Republic: Khormaksar, tel: 24366.
Iraq: Khormaksar, tel: 22622.
Italy: Tawahi, tel: 23281.
Kuwait: Khormaksar, tel: 22622.
Libya: Khormaksar, tel: 22621.
UK: Khormaksar, tel: 24171.
USSR: Khormaksar, tel: 23792.

TOURIST INFORMATION

The sole body responsible for tourism is the Public Corporation for Tourism, which is part of the Ministry of Culture and Tourism. The Corporation's address is: PO Box 1167, Aden, People's Democratic Republic of Yemen. Tel: Aden 23603.

ADEN

With a population of over 250,000, Aden is the largest urban area in the Republic. It falls into several districts. **Tawahi**, or Steamer Point, includes the ship passenger landing area, free trade shops, and tourist hotels. It includes some ministries, the Presidential residence, the Port of Aden Authority building, and the Central Committee offices. **Maala**, dominated by the blocks of flats along Madram Street, includes the main docks, and a growing industrial establishment. **Crater**, the oldest part of Aden, is bounded on three sides by the barren rocks of the volcanic structure and can be approached only along the coast or through a pass from Maala. It contains old Adeni houses and the *souk*. **Khormaksar**, on the peninsula linking the volcanic area to the mainland, includes the main embassies, the airport, and residential villas. On the mainland are the districts of Sheikh Othman Mansura, and poorer residential areas with some industrial plants. Farther around Aden bay are two isolated areas: Madinat al-Shaab, site of Aden University and of the Ministries of Education and Foreign Affairs, and Bureika, comprising the refinery and a population of around 20,000.

There are a number of tourist sites to visit in Aden. In Crater there are the Tawila Tanks, ancient water storage units, surrounded by a pleasant garden; the Aidrus Mosque; the Minaret; and Sira Island. In Sheikh Othman the Kemisri Gardens, believed to have been laid out by a Persian merchant, are open to the public. There are three museums: the Archaeological Museum in Tawahi, the Military Museum of the Revolution in Crater, and the Ethnographical Museum, in the garden of the Tawila Tanks.

Tax-free shops can be found in Tawahi and Khormaksar. Shops in Tawahi sell

Yemeni handicrafts, at fixed prices. In Crater, around the main market square, can be found many interesting shops. Streets Two and Three in Section A, opposite the Military Museum, sell Yemeni gold and silver work. Elsewhere there are spice and perfume shops. Incense (*bukhur*) grown in Yemen for millenia is still sold in small round plastic boxes: but don't forget to buy the charcoal and pottery containers needed to burn it. Basketware, coloured mats and Yemeni textiles are also widely displayed.

Beaches for swimming are found about 5 km. along the coastal road beyond Tawahi. Entrance to the Gold Mohur Club requires a ticket, while that to the Yemeni Club next door costs 250 Fils per day. There is also a swimming club at Bureika which requires a card to enter.

Restaurants

Outside the tourist hotels there are virtually no restaurants, apart from those serving Yemeni popular food. The **Ching Sing Chinese Restaurant** (tel: 22261) in Maala, for Chinese food, the **Red Sea** in Crater, for North Yemeni food, are recommended.

A typical up-country town

CAN YOU HELP US?

If you have *first hand* experience of any of the countries included in this book, and have any suggestions or corrections which could assist in making our next edition more authoritative, please record your comments below and send to:

TRAVELLER'S GUIDE TO THE MIDDLE EAST
63 Long Acre, London WC2E 9JH

Name: ....
Address: ....

Name of Country? ....
Visitor or Resident? ....
Remarks: ....
....
....
....
....
....
....
....
....
....

Name of Country? ....
Visitor or Resident? ....
Remarks: ....
....
....
....
....
....
....
....
....
....

CAN YOU HELP US?

Name of Country? ....
Visitor or Resident? ....
Remarks: ....
....
....
....
....
....
....
....
....
....
....

Name of Country? ....
Visitor or Resident? ....
Remarks: ....
....
....
....
....
....
....
....
....
....
....

Name of Country? ....
Visitor or Resident? ....
Remarks: ....
....
....
....
....
....
....
....
....
....
....